Sir Francis Vere

SIR FRANCIS VERE

Sir Francis Vere
Elizabeth I's Greatest Soldier
and the Eighty Years War

Clements R. Markham

Sir Francis Vere
Elizabeth I's Greatest Soldier and the Eighty Years War

by Clements R. Markham

First published under the title
"The Fighting Veres"

Leonaur is an imprint
of Oakpast Ltd

Copyright in this form © 2016 Oakpast Ltd

ISBN: 978-1-78282-529-6 (hardcover)
ISBN: 978-1-78282-530-2 (softcover)

http://www.leonaur.com

Publisher's Notes

The views expressed in this book are not necessarily those of the publisher.

Contents

Preface	7
PART 1: SIR FRANCIS VERE	
The Veres	11
Boyhood of Francis Vere	12
The Theatre of War	19
The English Volunteers	30
Opening of the War	50
The First Campaign	62
Sluys	73
Bergen-Op-Zoom	88
Resignation of Lord Willoughby	103
Sir Francis Vere in Chief Command	110
Breda, and the Expedition into Westphalia	122
The Battle in the Betuwe	131
Sieges of Gertruydenburg and Groningen	142
Death of Robert Vere	151
Cadiz	166
The Island Voyage	181
Battle of Turnhout	194
The Bommel-Waart	202

The Eve of the Battle of Nieuport	215
The Battle of Nieuport	230
The Siege of Ostend	238
Death of the Queen, and Resignation of Sir Francis Vere	258
Marriage and Death of Sir Francis Vere	272
PART 2: SIR HORACE VERE.	
The Recovery of Sluys, and the Battle of Mulheim	283
Death of Barneveldt	294
The War in the Palatinate	305
Death of John Vere	325
The Sieges of Bois-le-Duc and Maestricht	334
Death of Lord Vere—Conclusion	350
Appendix	358

Preface

The War of Independence in the Netherlands, (1566-1609), had a lasting influence on the formation of opinion in England. It thus led to the civil war in defence of the liberties of the old country, and to the founding of colonies in America. Queen Elizabeth declared that the people of the Netherlands were justified in resisting the tyranny of rulers who infringed and attempted to subvert their rights and liberties. She made war on the tyrant, and espoused the cause of the oppressed people. Englishmen received the declaration of their queen with enthusiasm. During upwards of sixty years they continued to cross the sea and to fight for the cause of freedom. There was scarcely a man in England who had not either served himself, or known a relation or neighbour who had been in the wars.

During that period of sixty years the colonies were founded in America. There was cause and effect. The whole generation imbibed and imparted to their posterity a zeal for popular rights which tended to awaken that traditional love of freedom which is the inheritance of English-speaking people. We see the results in the resistance to monopolies during the last year of the queen's reign, in the rise of a parliamentary opposition to James I., in the foundation of the New England colonies, in the resistance to the tyranny of Charles I., in the overthrow of his attempt to establish a despotism on the plan conceived by Strafford, and in the final triumph of constitutional freedom.

It is these results, flowing from the struggle against Spain, which gives importance to the record of English military service in the Low Countries. Among those who became famous in the course of that memorable enterprise, the names of Sir Francis and Sir Horace Vere stand foremost. The story of their lives covers the whole period of the war of independence. While others came and went, the Veres remained steadfastly at their posts, devoted their lives to the cause, and saw their work completed. Placing the sense of duty above all other motives, they were examples of that type of conscientious public servants which is met with most frequently among English-speaking people.

Sir Francis Vere is the first great English general in modern history. He founded a school which was further developed by his brother Horace. In that school were formed those distinguished leaders who fought out the war between Charles I. and the Parliament of England. In the same school were formed those military advisers who accompanied the lovers of freedom to colonise America. The posterity of both the great branches of the English folk, of that in America as of that in the old country, ought therefore to know the story of the "fighting Veres."

I have attempted, in the following pages, to write a connected narrative of the life-work of the two brothers. But the work is mainly devoted to the biography of Sir Francis Vere, for his brother served with him for many years, so that the two lives are included in one story. The later chapters relate the events in the life of Sir Horace subsequent to his brother's death. It was during this period that the Pilgrim Fathers sailed from Delftshaven; and I have referred to that great event in the chapter which includes the twelve years' truce.

While condensing the portions referring to general history, my endeavour has been, with the materials I have succeeded in collecting, to convey a clear idea of the military events in which the Veres were concerned. Special attention has been given to descriptions of the localities. The story of the lives of the two generals includes diplomatic as well as military service and private or family history. The allusions to the general course of events are only intended to make the narrative clear and intelligible; my object being to present the lives of the men themselves, rather than to write a history of their times.

The materials for these biographies are to be found in the numerous reports and letters preserved in the British State Paper Office, in the British Museum, and at Hatfield. These materials include 227 letters from Sir Francis Vere, besides many from Sir Horace. Some of the military actions are described by Sir Francis himself in his published Commentaries, and these descriptions have been collated with the accounts of the same events in letters written long before, by himself and by other officers. The works of Strada, Meteren, and Grimeston, of Bentivoglio, Carnero, and Herrera, generally give full accounts of the events described in letters of the Veres and other English officers, frequently supplying additional information, and almost always yielding corroborative testimony. These histories, together with Prinsterer's letters of the House of Orange, have been consulted in the preparation of an account of each action in the Netherlands; while Camden, Stow, Wilson, Hexham, Monson's Tracts, and documents in Hakluyt, have been my authorities for other parts of the narrative. There are voluminous materials for a history of the Vere family. A more complete note on the sources of information will be found in an appendix.

PART 1: SIR FRANCIS VERE

CHAPTER 1
The Veres

The English people took an active part in the great war for freedom during the sixteenth and seventeenth centuries. Their rulers sometimes held aloof and sometimes assisted with money and troops; but the cause was one which moved the people, and their support was always given, warmly and heartily, to their neighbours in the glorious fight for liberty. Whether the government gave its countenance or whether it forbore, there were Englishmen fighting side by side with Dutch patriots from first to last. In that fight no two names are so conspicuous as those of Francis and Horace Vere. The brother warriors stand out prominently as the representatives of their race in the great fight for freedom. They never faltered, never grew weary, but faithfully and loyally devoted their lives to a cause which is dear to all English-speaking people.

The noblest and most ancient house in the baronage of England was falling from its greatness, and would soon be extinct. But, in the last two generations, it produced a company of able and gallant soldiers whose deeds alone entitle the family to veneration. No less than ten Veres crossed the seas to fight in the cause of freedom. Five were slain in battle. Two became great generals, whose lives should ever be had in remembrance, because their record is the record of deeds that form a part, and no unimportant part, of the history of their race.

It is quite true that the two brothers, Francis and Horace, "brought more glory to the name of Vere than they took blood from the family," (Sir Robert Naunton). Yet the characters of men are influenced by the race from which they spring, and by the traditions of the land where they are born.

CHAPTER 2

Boyhood of Francis Vere

The father of our heroes was one of the sons of the good Earl of Oxford, who was buried in Hedingham Church in 1539. That earl left four sons and four daughters. His heir was John de Vere, sixteenth Earl of Oxford, who was at the siege of Boulogne with Henry VIII. By his first wife, Lady Dorothy Neville, the sixteenth Earl had an only daughter, named Katherine, who was betrothed to the eldest son of the Protector Somerset, but who eventually married Edward, Lord Windsor. This earl had for his second wife Margaret Golding, the daughter of a neighbour in Essex. Her father was John Golding, of Belchamp St. Paul, near Hedingham,. one of the auditors of the Exchequer. Her brother, Arthur Golding, was in the service of the Protector Somerset, and afterwards lived at Sir William Cecil's house with his nephew, Earl Edward. He was the most voluminous translator of his age, and some of his metrical renderings have merit. (*Bariffe's Artillery Guide,* and the *Commentaries of Caesar*). By the Golding marriage, the sixteenth earl had a son and heir named Edward, born in 1550, and a daughter, Mary, married to Lord Willoughby.

There were three younger brothers—Aubrey, Robert, and Geoffrey. Aubrey married Margaret, daughter of John Spring, of Lavenham, where the church is full of Vere badges and shields of arms, in one place alternating with the Spring trademark. In the village street there is a quaintly carved Guild Hall. Side by side, in this busy little Suffolk town, dwelt the baronial Veres in their manor house and the commercial Springs in their shop. Now they intermarried, and Aubrey Vere had a son by Margaret Spring, whose son and grandson were the two last Earls of Oxford. He also had a daughter, Jane, who married a neighbour of rather doubtful repute named Henry Hunt, of Gosfield, and had a son, John Hunt. The third son, Robert, married, but his children did not live to grow up. He died on April 2, 1598, and was buried at Charlton in Kent. Geoffrey, the fourth son, was the father of our heroes. Of the four daughters of the good Earl of Oxford, Elizabeth was the wife of Lord Darcy of Chiche, who lived at St. Osyth in Tendring Hundred; Anne married Lord Sheffield; Frances married Henry, Earl of Surrey, and was mother of the beheaded Duke of Norfolk; while Ursula never married.

The intervention of Parliament was necessary to secure suitable provision for the younger sons, Aubrey, Robert, and Geoffrey Vere. It appears that, in the plenitude of his power, the Protector Somerset had betrothed his eldest son to Lady Katherine Vere, and had induced her father, the sixteenth earl, to levy a fine, the effect of which would have been to settle the whole inheritance on the marriage. The earl's brothers were left penniless. After the Protector's fall the betrothal with young Seymour was broken off, and an act of Parliament was passed in 1551 "frustrating the assurance to the Duke of Somerset made by the Earl of Oxford." The act declared the indentures concerning the proposed marriage to be void and of none effect. The fine previously levied was also declared to be utterly void.

It was then enacted that the earl's brother Aubrey should hold certain manors, which are named, for his life and for the life of his wife if he so ordains by will; remainder to the Earl and his heirs. On the same conditions the youngest brother, Geoffrey Vere, was to have the manors of Crepping Hall and Crustwick in the county of Essex. (In the Parish Register at Castle Hedingham, John Vere (burial 1624) is mentioned as the son of "Galfridus de Vere, of Crepping Hall." Then follow powers for the earl to assign other specified manors for his wife's jointure, and others for the portions of his daughter Katherine, and of any other children that might be born after the date of the act.

Geoffrey Vere thus became possessed of his two manors in 1551, and settled down as a country gentleman. Crepping Hall, in the parish of Wakes Colne, is on the top of a hill overlooking the Colne valley, surrounded by a moat. The original manor house was burnt down in 1810, and an ordinary farmhouse has taken its place. It is near the village of Fordham, and about a mile from the little Norman church of Wakes Colne. Crustwick (now Gutteridge) Hall is beyond Colchester, in the Tendring Hundred. It is in the parish of Weeley, adjoining St. Osyth, which was the home of Geoffrey's sister Elizabeth, Lady Darcy. Crustwick is now a farmhouse, with nothing of interest about it, except some possible indications of an old moat. At these two manors, in a country which was full of his relations, Geoffrey Vere lived, and he sought a wife from among the families of his neighbours.

In the village of Castle Hedingham there dwelt a family named Hardekyn, prosperous people, who had amassed some moderate share of wealth by trade at Colchester. We find that in 1486 Thomas Hardekyn, of Castle Hedingham, was enfeoffed of a capital messuage called Wottons, *alias* Hardekyns, in the parish of Gestingthorpe. He died in 1509, and was succeeded by his son Richard, who added to his inheritance by the purchase of Odwell and Ram-acre coppice. These places are all in the close neighbourhood of the Castle of Hedingham; and Richard Hardekyn possessed 570 acres of arable, pasture, and wood land. His residence, called Wotton House, with a moat round it, was on the side of the road leading from Hedingham to Sudbury.

Young Geoffrey Vere, living at Hedingham Castle, in the days of his father and brother, must have known the inmates of Wotton House from a boy. Richard Hardekyn had a son John and a daughter Elizabeth. (In some peerages Elizabeth is said to be daughter of *Sir* John Hardekyn, of Colchester. Her brother was John, her father Richard. Collins gives the names correctly). The great earl's fourth son became attached to his young neighbour. The friendship of early acquaintance ripened into love, and Geoffrey Vere was married to Elizabeth Hardekyn in the year 1556. Their married life was passed between Crepping Hall and Crustwick. Elizabeth's father died in 1558, and her brother, John Hardekyn of Colchester, who was born in 1537, sold Wotton and all his landed property to George Sayer, another Colchester merchant, in 1566.

John, the eldest son of Geoffrey and Elizabeth Vere, was born in 1558. Francis, the second son, was probably born in 1560, (see note following), either at Crepping or Crustwick. Then followed the death of the head of the family, the uncle of these two boys, John, sixteenth Earl of Oxford, leaving three children: Edward, the seventeenth Earl, born in 1550; Katherine, Lady Windsor; and Mary, afterwards married to Lord Willoughby. The sixteenth Earl of Oxford was a good landlord, generous, affectionate, very popular, and a keen sportsman. When Prince Eric of Sweden landed at Harwich in December, 1559, the earl showed him some sport in the valley of the Stour.

> After dinner my Lord of Oxforde had the prince forth a hawking, and showed him great sporte, killing in his sight both faisant and partridge.

★★★★★★

This is as near as we can get to the date of the birth of Sir Francis Vere. His elder brother, John, is known to have been sixty-six when he died in 1624. He was, therefore, born in 1558. We know, from the Earl of Oxford's will, that the next brother, Francis, was born before his uncle's death, in July, 1562. He must, therefore, have been born in 1559, 1560, or 1561. He is not likely to have been born in the year after his brother. Consequently 1560 is the most probable date. There is a gap in the entries of baptisms in the Wake's Colne Register, from 1559 to 1604. The earliest entry at Weeley is 1560, when the book was begun by the rector, Thomas Wynyngton. The jury, at the inquisition after the death of Sir Francis Vere, in 1609, declared him to be over forty. The age on the monument in Westminster Abbey is certainly a mistake, as it would make Sir Francis older than his elder brother.

★★★★★★

By his will, dated July 28, 1562, among numerous other legacies, the earl left 20 to each of his two little nephews, John and Francis Vere. After the earl's death, his brother Geoffrey had three more children: Robert, born in 1562, Horace in 1565, and Frances, afterwards Lady Harcourt, in 1567.

Geoffrey Vere died while his children were still young, and they were left to the care of a mother who brought them up with a loving solicitude which had its reward. She lived to a good old age. Her eldest son stayed with her, and made her a home at Kirby Hall, near Hedingham. The three others became valiant soldiers. Two rose to be great generals. The third found a glorious death on the battlefield. Her only daughter, Frances, was prosperously married to Sir Robert Harcourt, of Nuneham, the great navigator. There are full-length portraits of Sir Robert and his wife Frances, by Marc Gerard, in the dining-room at Nuneham.

We hear something of the boyhood and education of the cousin of these boys, Edward Vere, seventeenth Earl of Oxford, who was born in 1550, and was twelve years old when his father died. Although he was several years older than Geoffrey's sons, yet it is probable that they were often companions and associates, both as regards studies and sports of the field. The young earl was left to the guardianship of Sir William Cecil, the Lord Treasurer, and of his mother, the widowed Countess of Oxford. He passed his time between Cecil's house and his mother's home at Hedingham, and was much in the society of his learned uncle, Arthur Golding. The routine of studies for Earl Edward was as follows: He was to get up in time for his dancing lesson, from 7 o'clock to 7.30, and was to take breakfast from 7.30 to 8 o'clock. The next two hours were devoted half to French and half to Latin, and then there was half an hour for drawing. From half past ten to one there was play and dinner. Lessons began again at one, with an hour for cosmography, and two more hours for French and Latin, finishing with half an hour for writing. This made six hours of lessons altogether, and at five there were prayers and supper.

All the rest of the day was given up to riding, shooting, and walking. (Calendar of State Papers. Domestic. 1562, December. Vol. xxvi. "An order for my Lord's exercises.") The young earl's youth was distinguished by his wit and adroitness in his exercises, and he was sent to Cambridge, where Sir Thomas Smith was his tutor. But the treasurer was determined not to let so great a match slip from his family, and in 1571, when they were both very young, Edward, Earl of Oxford, was married to Anne, daughter of Sir William Cecil. Next we hear that:

> My Lord of Oxforth is lately growne in great credite, for the Queen's Majestie delitethe more in his personage and his daunsinge and valientness than any other. He presented her Majestie with a ryche jewell, which was well lyked.—Gilbert Talbot to the Earl of Shrewsbury, 1573.

He travelled in Italy, and was the first to bring embroidered gloves and perfumes into England. (Stowe). He also distinguished himself at jousts and wrote poems, some of which are preserved. (*The Paradise of Dainty Devices*). But he quarrelled with his wife and father-in-law, got into dissolute and extravagant habits, sold his estates one after the other, and ended by destroying the power and wealth of the great family of which he was the head.

The sons of Geoffrey Vere were no doubt associated with their cousin the earl when they were quite young; but he married while they were still boys, and they continued to study and enjoy field sports at the Essex manors, under the care of their mother. John Vere, the eldest, remained at home as a country gentleman, and soon after he came of age he entered upon possession of Kirby Hall by an arrangement with the Earl of Oxford, having resigned the manors of Crepping and Crustwick.

Kirby Hall, or Picard's as it was sometimes called, is only a mile from the Castle of Hedingham. It belonged to the Kirby family during the fourteenth century, and afterwards to the Picards, whence it passed to the Earls of Oxford. In about 1580 it became the property of John Vere, and here he made a home for his mother. Kirby Hall is pleasantly situated amidst pastures, in a well-timbered country. Two gables of the old hall still remain, with a wainscoted parlour, a huge kitchen fireplace, and clustered chimneys. There is also a kitchen garden, with old brick walls, and an ancient dove-cot, (there is an engraving of it in the *Vetusta Monumenta*). Here the widow of Geoffrey Vere was close to the home of her childhood at Wotton, in the next parish of Gestingthorpe.

While the eldest son remained quietly at home, the other three embraced the profession of arms. Francis and Robert were nearly the same age. They were initiated in the military art by old Sir William Browne, who served for many years in the Low Countries.

In their letters to Sir William they subscribed themselves "your loving sons," and addressed him as their "good father." Francis, when he was a mere lad, in about 1580 went with Captain Francis Allen to Poland, probably to serve in the Polish Army. But we know nothing beyond the fact.

******

Francis Allen, in a letter to Anthony Bacon, dated August 17, 1589, writes: "I must send you news of the which I pray rejoice with me. My brother Francis Vere is knighted. It is he that made the voyage with me into Polonia." (*Birch*, i.) The word "brother" must here be taken in the sense of "comrade."

There is a curious statement, under date August 27, 1584, in the certificate of search for the discovery of papists by Alderman Barnes, to the effect that Francis Vere and Thomas Baskerville were found in Bedlam. (*Calendar of State Papers. Domestic.* 1584.) The Bedlam of those days was in Bishopsgate Street without. It is true that several papists were arrested in 1584, but there must have been some mistake in the arrests of Vere and Baskerville.

******

When the Earl of Leicester prepared to embark for the Low Countries, as general of the auxiliary forces, Francis Vere had reached his twenty-fifth year, and was resolved to embrace the military profession. The portrait, which is engraved at the beginning of his Commentaries, gives us some idea of the personal appearance of Francis Vere at this time. It presents the profile of a young man with a high forehead and slightly aquiline nose, large eyes and well-marked eyebrows, full but firm lips, and the face clean-shaved, except a slight moustache and imperial. The face is oval, and a falling collar shows rather a long neck.

Francis Vere was the contemporary of great men. The queen and Leicester were his seniors by twenty-six years. Sir Walter Raleigh, Sir Philip Sidney, and Edmund Spenser were older by six or seven years. Sir Francis Bacon, Lord Thomas Howard, and Sir John Harington were the same age. Lord Mountjoy and William Shakespeare were four years, James I. and the Earl of Essex six years, younger. In such an age, and amidst such a generation, Francis Vere made his way to the front rank.

CHAPTER 3

The Theatre of War

While Francis Vere was still a boy at school, he must have heard stories of the cruelties of the Spanish governors to the people of the Netherlands. These stories were only too true, and they increased the indignation and sympathy of England year by year Margaret of Parma advised that all heretics should be killed, whether they were repentant or not, care only being taken that the provinces should not be entirely depopulated; and her successor, the Duke of Alva, actually slaughtered 18,600 persons in cold blood, by his own account.

★★★★★★

Margaret was the eldest child of the Emperor Charles V., but illegitimate. She was Governess of the Netherlands for her brother Philip II., from 1559 to 1567. She was married to Ottavio Farnese, nephew of Pope Paul III., who was created Duke of Parma. Her son was Alexander, Duke of Parma, the great general who became Spanish Governor of the Netherlands in 1578.

★★★★★★

William the Taciturn, the noble-hearted Prince of Orange, who had been *Stadtholder* of Holland and Zeeland, was in exile; and desperate men, known as the "sea *gueux*," had taken to piracy against the ships of their oppressors, as the only means of existence and of vengeance.

Several vessels, manned by two or three hundred of these outlaws, and commanded by William de la Marck, were ordered to leave the anchorage at Dover, where they had taken refuge. They set sail in the end of March, 1572, and on the 1st of April they anchored at the mouth of the Maas, seized the town of Brill, and repulsed an attempt of the Spanish Governor of Holland to retake it. A few days afterwards the town of Flushing rose, and expelled the foreigners; while English volunteers crossed the North Sea to range themselves by the side of the pioneers of liberty. The tidings of these events had an electric effect throughout the Netherlands. Nearly all the important cities of Holland and Zeeland, except Amsterdam, raised the standard of the Prince of Orange; and the government was formally offered to William by the States.

The Duke of Alva assembled his army of Spanish veterans, vowing vengeance. His son, Don Fadrique de Toledo, committed shocking massacres at Zutphen and Naarden, occupied Amsterdam, and began the siege of Haarlem in December, 1572. It took an army of 30,000 men to reduce that gallant city, and when at length the Spaniards entered it, after a siege of six months, they slaughtered 2,300 unarmed people. Alkmaar was successfully defended from August to October, 1573; and when the Duke of Alva was superseded, and relieved the Low Countries of his detested presence, on December 18, 1573, the people, led by the Prince of Orange, were still stubbornly resisting and unconquered.

Alva was succeeded by Don Luis de Requesens, and in the following February, 1574, Don Cristoval Mondragon, the ablest of the Spanish officers, was starved out, and forced to surrender Middelburg, the capital of Zeeland, to the patriots. A more striking reverse to the tyrant's arms was involved in the Spaniards being obliged to raise the siege of Leyden, on October 3, 1574, after its long and heroic defence. Requesens, aided by Mondragon, captured the island of Schouwen and its capital Zierikzee, by the remarkable military feat involved in wading across a long arm of the sea, in the following September; but Schouwen was retaken by Count Hohenlohe in November, 1576, and in the following year Requesens died. The year 1576 closed with the appalling massacre perpetrated by the Spaniards at Antwerp.

These great events inevitably aroused the sympathy of the people of England, who had long been knit together with the Netherlanders by numerous ties of commerce and friendship. Volunteers flocked across the North Sea, although the queen's government still hesitated to cast in its lot with the insurrection. Spain was in the height of her power. The Spanish infantry was unequalled by any other troops in the world, as was shown in the course of the year 1578. Don Juan of Austria, the victor of Lepanto and brother of King Philip II., had succeeded Requesens as Governor of the Netherlands, and in January, 1578, the mere presence of his army put the forces of the States to flight. Such was the Battle of Gemblours. Not a blow was struck, the Spaniards did not lose a man, yet it is said that 10,000 insurgents were slaughtered. On the 1st of August, Don Juan was repulsed by the raw levies of the States, behind entrenchments, at Rymenant. But as yet neither Netherlanders nor Englishmen could face the terrible *tercios* of Spain in the open field. Don Juan died on October 1, 1578, and was succeeded by Alexander Farnese, Duke of Parma, a nephew of Philip II., and one of the ablest generals of the age. He had to face a more organised resistance, for the Dutch patriots were no longer insurgents. They had founded a republic. On the 29th of January, 1579, the representatives of the States of Holland, Zeeland, Gelderland, Zutphen, Utrecht, and Friesland, under the presidency of Count John of Nassau, elder brother of William the Taciturn, signed the memorable Union of Utrecht; and on July 26, 1581, the States-General declared their independence at the Hague. The Prince of Orange became the successor of his former sovereign, Count of Holland and Zeeland, and Lord of Flushing and Veere. Then Philip invoked the aid of the assassin. In 1582 an attempt was made on the life of the great patriot; and another more successful crime was perpetrated eighteen months afterwards. William the Taciturn fell by the hand of an assassin on the 10th of July, 1584.

✶✶✶✶✶✶

William, Prince of Orange, by his first wife, Anne of Egmont, had a son, Philip William (who was taken prisoner by the Spaniards when a child, and remained a Catholic), and a daughter, Mary, married in 1595 to Philip, Count of Hohenlohe.

His second wife was Anne, daughter of Maurice, Elector of Saxony, whom he married in 1561. She was sent home for misconduct, and died in 1577. By her he had a son and successor, Maurice, born on November 14, 1567, and three daughters: Ann, married to William Louis, Count of Nassau Dillemburg; Amelia, wife of Emanuel, Prince of Portugal; and Louisa Juliana, wife of Frederick IV., Elector Palatine.

Charlotte de Bourbon, daughter of Louis, Duc de Montpensier, was his third wife, to whom he was married in 1577. She died in 1582. By her he had five daughters: Isabel, wife of Henri de la Tour, Duc de Bouillon; Catherine Belgica, of Philip Louis, Count of Hanau; Flandrina became a Catholic, and died a nun at Poitiers; Charlotte, wife of Claude, Duc de la Tremouille; Amelia, wife of Frederick Casimir, Palatine of Landsberg.

His fourth wife was Louisa Coligny, whom he married in 1583. She died in 1620. By her he had an only son, Frederick Henry, successor to his brother Maurice, who was born on February 24, 1584. He died on May 14, 1647, aged sixty-three.

★★★★★★

In August, 1585, after a long and memorable siege, the city of Antwerp was taken by the Duke of Parma. These irreparable calamities fell upon the cause of liberty in quick succession. They forced Queen Elizabeth into immediate action; and by the end of 1585 England had cast in her lot with the Netherlands, to fight shoulder to shoulder until the battle of freedom was fought out and the victory won. Francis Vere, who was destined to be a leading warrior in that mighty struggle, had just entered upon his twenty-fifth year.

The country which was the theatre of this memorable war is peculiar in many respects. At the first glance the network of land and water appears puzzling and without a clue. But a little study will dispel this first impression, and it is before all things needful that we should examine and understand the board, before we begin to arrange the pieces upon it.

Holland and Zeeland are the deltas of three rivers, the Rhine, the Meuse (Maas), and the Scheldt. But there is a peculiarity as regards these deltas. In very remote times a chain of sand-hills, called dunes, was raised along the sea face, which prevented the encroachment of the ocean, and caused the rivers to form a lake within the line of dunes. The width of the dunes averages from two hundred yards to a mile, and their height varies from fifty to sixty feet, but near Haarlem they attain a height of 196 feet, and, with the sun setting behind them, they present an outline like a range of mountains. Soon the lake began to be filled up by river deposits, and the rivers forced their way to the sea, forming several islands, the outer ones still with dunes along their sea face.

When the industrious inhabitants of this waterlogged region began to reclaim the land for cultivation, their most long-continued contests were with the rivers, rather than with the ocean, from which they were protected by the dunes. But a combination of flooded rivers, with a succession of westerly gales and a spring tide, often destroyed the labour of years and inundated vast tracts of country. Seven hundred years ago, in 1170, a noble district was swallowed up in Friesland, and the Zuyder Zee was formed, the havoc being completed two centuries later, in 1395. In the year 1421 the River Maas was in flood, and the waters were helped by a furious gale. They broke over the dikes, bored through during one night, and flooded the lowlands far and near. Altogether, seventy-two villages were swallowed up, with 100,000 souls. Next morning the tops of the church towers were just visible above the water. Where once there was a populous and fertile district, there is now a network of channels and reedy islands, called the *Bies-Bosch,* ("a wood of reeds."

The rivers are kept in their courses by dikes along either bank, and where there are no dunes, immense sea dikes are necessary, protected by stone slopes and piles. There are 1,550 miles of these dikes, and the dike of West-kappel, in the island of Walcheren, is over 4,000 yards long, twenty-three feet high, with a seaward slope, consisting of alternate rows of piles and blocks of basalt, 300 feet broad. Tracts of land at or below the sea-level, and surrounded by a dike, are called *polders.* These incessant encounters with and conquests over the elements could only have been fought out and won by a race endowed with very high qualities; not a race which would long submit to foreign tyranny, but one which would oppose such tyranny with the same stubborn and indomitable energy which kept back the ocean and the floods, and turned the saturated swamps into fertile fields.

The eastern part of the Netherlands consisted of more elevated, heathy country, with some forests, and in the Drenthe region there were extensive deposits of inferior peat called *hoog-veen.* Further west a line of hills of moderate elevation extends from south to north across the country. Near Maastricht the river Meuse flows past a ridge rising to a height of 650 feet, called the Pietersberg. The rock is a soft calcareous sandstone, perforated by subterraneous galleries. Further north the picturesque town of Cleves stands on a steep eminence overlooking the valley of the Rhine, with the woods of the Reichswald behind it; again at Nymegen, a range of high hills, covered with woods, rises abruptly from the flat pastures on the banks of the Waal. Crossing the Rhine, the high land behind Arnhem, with its charming forest scenery, extends northward over the Veluwe, and attains a height of 300 feet.

This range of elevated land influences the courses of the rivers, forcing the Maas to flow northward to the Waal, and the Rhine and Yssel to flow northward to the Zuyder Zee. From a military point of view, and looking upon the Netherlands as a fortress to be defended, the rivers become so many lines of defence, and the fortified towns along one line had to be reduced before an advance to the next line

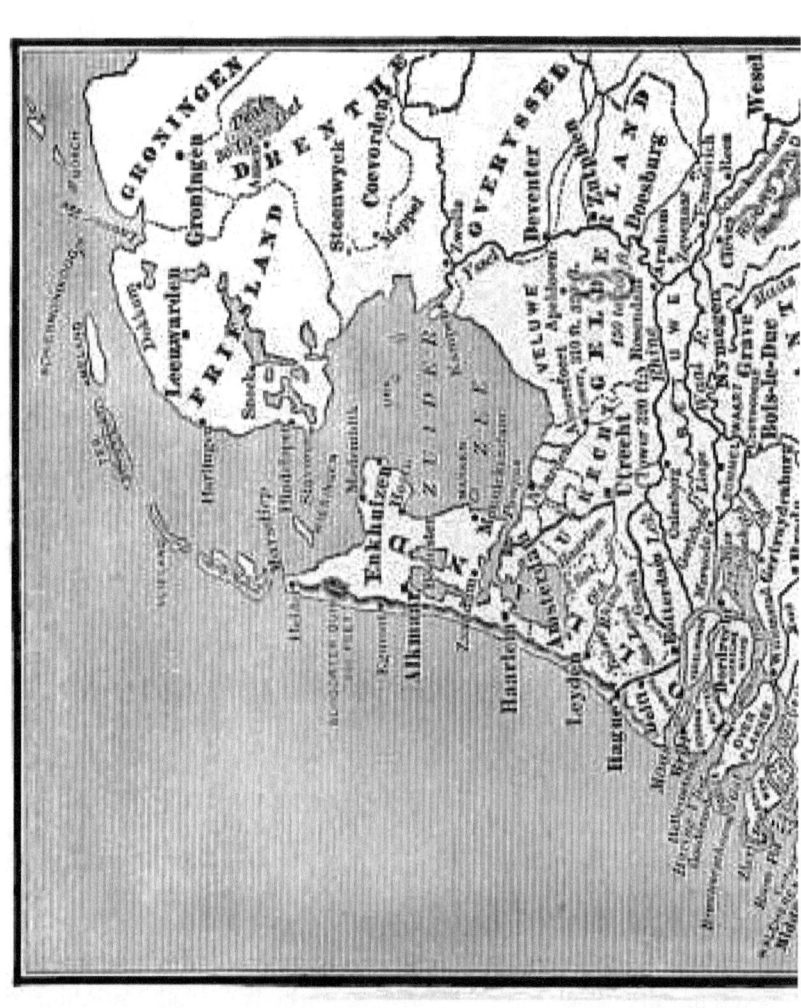

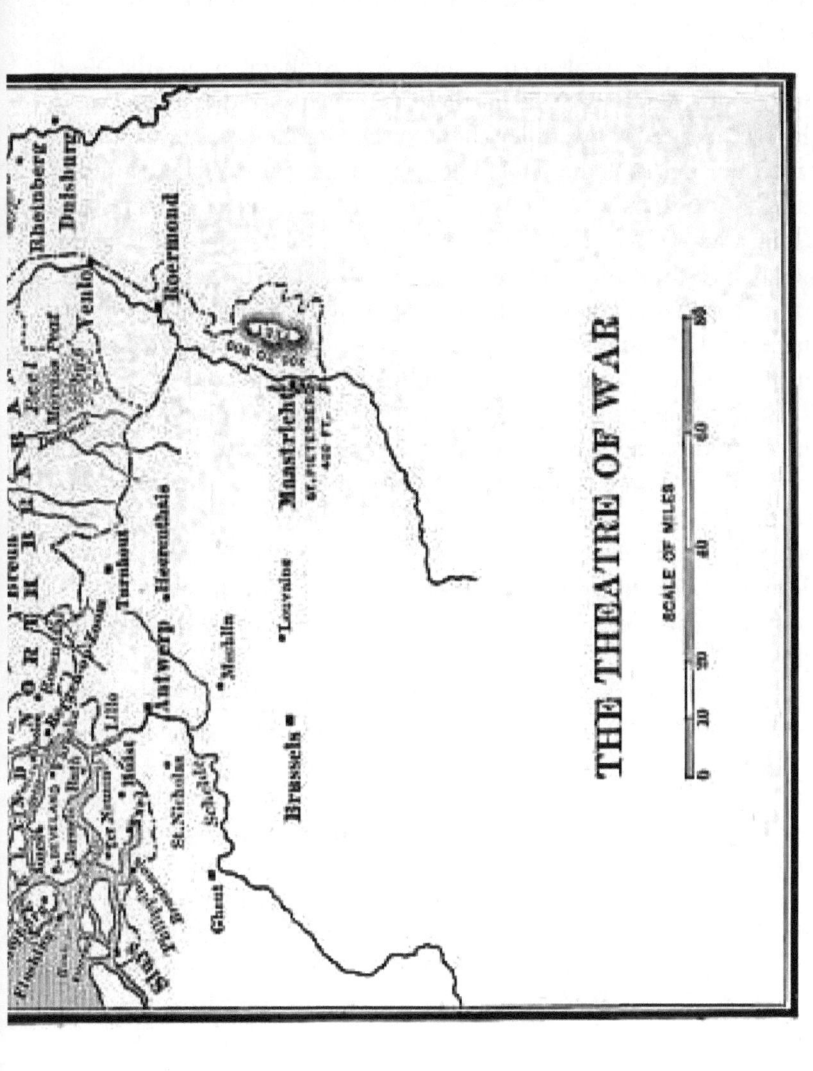

could prudently be made.

The outer and most eastern line was the Rhine and Yssel, skirting along the hills of Cleves and Arnhem, a broad stream from 600 to 400 yards across. The strategic points on this outer line were Neuss, Duisburg, Rheinberg (a town and fortress of the first importance), Wesel, Emmerich, Doesburg, Zutphen, Deventer, and Kampen by the Zuyder Zee.

Between the parallels of Cleves and Arnhem, while the Yssel branch flows onward in a northerly course, two other branches of the Rhine turn westward and flow to the German Ocean, which are called the Lek and the Waal. The Maas also turns westward until it mingles its waters with the Waal. The two Rhine branches thus form a long island called the Betuwe, with Arnhem on the right bank of the Lek branch, near the junction of the Yssel, and Nymegen on the left bank of the Waal. The second line is formed by the River Maas flowing northwards, and having on its banks the important fortified towns of Maastricht, Roermond, Venlo, and Grave.

In the country where the three streams turn westward there are three important towns, one on each river, nearly north and south of each other,—Grave on the Maas, Nymegen on the Waal, and Arnhem on the Rhine. Further to the westward, where the Maas and Waal unite, an island is formed called the Bommel-waart, with the town of Bommel on the Waal, and the larger city of Bois le Due about a mile from the Maas. As a strategic position, the Bommel-waart was often spoken of as the key to the Netherlands.

Below Bommel-waart the united Maas and Waal, called the Merwode, flows westward to Dordrecht on the south, while the Lek unites with them again by a channel above Rotterdam; and beyond this the northern stream resumes the name of the Maas to its mouth. Five islands form the delta of the united Rhine and Maas: Dordrecht Island, Hoeksche-waard, and Ysselmonde to the east, and Overflakkee and Goedereede, Putten and Voorn, with their western sides facing the North Sea. Flowing between the mainland of Holland on the right and the islands of Ysselmonde and Voorn on the left, the River Maas now becomes a great navigable channel. On its right bank are Rotterdam, Schiedam, and some busy fishing-ports nearer the sea, and on its left bank, at the mouth of the river, is the town of Brill on the island of Voorn.

South of Dordrecht is the network of channels and reedy islets called the Bies-Bosch, and on the southern side is the town of Gertruydenburg, with the great fortified city of Breda a few miles inland. Beyond Gertruydenburg the channel opens into a basin called the Hollandsche Diep, with Willemstad on its southern shore, and thence two channels lead to the North Sea: the Haring Vliet on the north side of Overflakkee Island, between it and Voorn; and the Brouwerschaven Gat between Overflakkee and the Zeeland island of Schouwen.

It was this treble line of rivers, ending in a network of islands, which separated the Catholic provinces under Spanish rule from the patriots fighting for freedom.

North of the line of the Rhine and the Lek were the flourishing Dutch towns, surrounded by their shady parks and rich meadows. Utrecht, the ancient see of an almost independent Prince Bishop, is nearly in the centre of the block which is bounded on the north by the Zuyder Zee and the Y, on the west by the sea, on the east by the Yssel, and on the south by the Rhine and Lek. This block includes part of Holland, all Utrecht, and part of Gelderland. To the east is the high land of the Veluwe, in the centre the great sandy plain extending south of the Zuyder Zee, and to the west the tracts of low land, below the level of the sea, bounded by the dunes.

Here were the richest towns of Holland,—Rotterdam, Delft and Gouda, Leyden, Haarlem, and Amsterdam; and here the counts of Holland had formed their park (Hague) and built their fortified residence, round which the charming village of the Hague had risen up. To the northward much of the land was still under water. The wide expanse of the Haarlem Sea spread out between Leyden, Haarlem, and Amsterdam. Another wide expanse, inland from Amsterdam, with Zandam on its banks, was formed by the Y; and there were large lakes, now reclaimed, in North Holland as far as Alkmaar.

The principal fishing villages were near the mouth of the Maas and in North Holland; while the ports on the Zuyder Zee, especially Amsterdam, Hoorn, Enkhuysen, and Medemblik, were beginning to develop an increasing shipping business.

On the other side of the Zuyder Zee the Frisians were comparatively clear of the strife, though further east the war was still to rage round Groningen, Steenwyck, and Coevorden. The Frisians, who are nearer to the English, both as regards language and appearance, than any other continental people, did good service to the cause of freedom, whether by the wisdom of the counsels of some, the learning and talent of others, or still more by their valour in the field.

Zeeland, the most southern of the provinces, and the nearest to

England, is the delta of the River Scheldt. That river, after passing Antwerp, separates into two branches, the Honte or Wester Scheldt to the south, and the Ooster Scheldt to the north, which enclose the three islands of North and South Beveland and Walcheren. On the south side of the Honte is the region now known as Dutch Flanders, which has been much altered. In those days it consisted of wide expanses of drowned land, with fortified places, such as Axel and Hulst, rising like islands above the flood. Further west were the islands of Breskens and Cadzand; and the town of Sluys on the Zwyn, still a seaport and important fortified place.

On the north side of the Honte were the coasts of South Beveland and Walcheren, with the seaport of Flushing. Middelburg, in Walcheren, was a flourishing city, the capital of all Zeeland; Veere, on the north side of that island, was a thriving port; and the city of Goes, in South Beveland, with a port opening by a canal on the north side of the island, was another important place. The Ooster Scheldt turns northwards from the Honte, separating South Beveland from Brabant; and here, on the Brabant side, was the strongly fortified town of Bergen-op-Zoom. A great calamity had befallen this eastern end of South Beveland in 1532, the sea having broken through the dikes and turned hundreds of fertile acres into swampy "*verdronken* land." Flowing seawards the Ooster Scheldt has the island of Tholen on the right, with the two smaller isles called St. Ana and St. Philip Land. As the channel opens out towards the sea it is called the Room Pot, (cream jug), having North Beveland and Walcheren on one side, Schouwen and Duiveland on the other. Schouwen contains the old towns of Zierikzee and Brouwershaven.

The industrious Hollanders and Zeelanders had thriven under their counts and margraves, in spite of family feuds and wars with the Frisians. The drowned lands had been reclaimed, industry and intelligent enterprise had brought wealth, and many cities had risen up at various centres, and had been fortified. Commerce and wealth had increased the wants of the people. Everywhere there were handsome brick houses, with ornamented gables, facing the canals, and with rows of shady trees in front of them. Large parks and woods were preserved, not only in the higher tracts of Gelderland, but also in Utrecht, Brabant, and parts of Holland. The face of the country, though flat, was pleasing and often picturesque.

During the rule of the Dukes of Burgundy the fine buildings became more numerous, and many churches, of cathedral dimensions, were built in the cities. At Middelburg there was a large abbey; lofty towers, overlooking the whole country, were erected, the highest being at Utrecht (320 feet) and Amersfoort; and beautiful stained glass filled the windows of many churches, and is still preserved at Gouda. The Netherlanders embraced the Calvinistic form of Protestantism, which was blindly iconoclastic, and hence there was much lamentable destruction of ecclesiastical decoration. But the vast churches, with their solid pillars and double-leafed capitals, were carefully preserved for the simpler worship.

In this rapid sketch of the topography of the theatre of war, all the names of important towns, rivers, and islands have been mentioned; for it is necessary that their positions should be clearly imprinted on the memory, if the reader desires to derive intelligent pleasure from a consideration of the heroic operations which finally secured the triumph of freedom.

CHAPTER 4

The English Volunteers

The English bands which flocked to the Netherlands to fight in the quarrel of their Dutch brethren had a continuous history and an inherited series of traditions for seventy years. They revived the military spirit in the British nation, and their deeds of arms and organisation form the first chapter of the modern military history of England. At first they were merely volunteers; then some were employed by the queen, and others by the States; after the queen's death all that continued to exist were under the States. But through all the changes there was a continuous tradition among officers and men from first to last. The history of the English regiments, fighting for the cause of freedom in the Netherlands, extends from 1572 to the Peace of Westphalia.

The first English volunteers formed raw levies, without discipline or experience. They could not stand against the soldiers of Philip, but fled before them, and in some instances behaved shamefully. But they and their successors persevered. In a severe school they acquired the military virtues. Gradually they gained confidence in themselves and in each other, and at length they saw the dreaded *tercios* of Spain retreating before them in the open field. The military art, the drills, the use of weapons, even the nomenclature, had to be learnt from the Spaniards, by the raw inexperienced English, before they could be a match for their foes in the field. But they had physical strength, indomitable pluck, and that proud endurance and patience which enabled them to bear up against reverses, and learn lessons from their defeats. It was a rough ordeal, and the islanders were the men to undergo it, and to profit by it. Only at first, and not for long, would the haughty Spaniards be allowed to see the backs of their enemies.

In April, 1572, there was a muster of 300 men before the Queen at

Greenwich. They were men ambitious of martial fame, they were led by bold Thomas Morgan, and their destination was Flushing. When the capture of Brill sent an electric shock through the Netherlands, the Duke of Alva hurriedly dispatched a garrison to Flushing. It was refused admittance. The troops retired to Bergen-op-Zoom, while most of the villages and fishing ports of Walcheren and South Beveland rose in revolt. The towns of Veere and Arnemuiden, in Walcheren, followed the example; and the insurgents besieged the city of Middelburg. When Pacheco, the chief engineer of the Spanish army, landed at Flushing, he was seized and hanged by the enraged populace. Alva then began to make serious preparations to crush the insurrection, while the Prince of Orange sent an officer named 't Zereets, or Sara, as the English called him, to organize defensive measures.

During the summer Captain Morgan, with his 300 volunteers, was received into Flushing. This was the first English band that served in the Netherlands. Its most distinguished member was the fire-eating Roger Williams, a man of furious quixotic valour, yet an accomplished soldier and student. A son of Thomas Williams of Penrose, in Monmouthshire, by Eleanor, daughter of Sir William Vaughan, Roger had received an education at Oxford, probably at Brazen Nose, before he commenced his adventurous career as a soldier of fortune. He was the guiding spirit in this undisciplined little Flushing garrison, which soon came to blows with the enemy. The Spaniards from Middelburg mounted some guns on an artificial hill, and opened fire on the walls of Flushing. Out came the garrison, with the fiery Welshmen in the van, and there was a hot encounter in the meadows, at push of pike. This was the very first action in which the English were engaged, and they came off with credit. At one moment the enemy had hold of Captain Morgan's ensign. It was gallantly rescued by George Browne and several other young gentlemen. About fifty English were slain, but the Spaniards were dislodged from their position.

These English sympathizers were very popular in Flushing. They asked no more than bare victuals and lodging, and they were eager to do their best in the way of fighting. Morgan was anxious for reinforcements; and it was arranged that Sir Humphrey Gilbert, Raleigh's half-brother, should come over as colonel of the English, and 1,500 men with him.

Gilbert arrived with these English bands, and, in concert with 't Zereets, a plan was matured for an invasion of Flanders, on the opposite side of the Scheldt. After making an incursion almost to the walls of Bruges, and routing a Spanish convoy, they embarked again and sailed across to the coast of South Beveland. Gilbert's plan was to besiege the city of Goes, which was occupied by a Spanish garrison, under a veteran officer named Don Isidro Pacheco. A vanguard was landed under Morgan's command, and began to march. But Pacheco was in ambush, and he suddenly opened a hot fire of shot upon them, then charging with a hundred pikes. The English wavered, turned round, and ran for their lives, most of them through muddy ditches. Roger Williams was with them, and he said, "I persuade myself most of them were afraid. I am to blame to judge their minds, but let me speak truth." (*The Actions of the Lowe Countries*). The abortive expedition returned to Flushing; but the people there refused to allow the fugitive troops to enter the town, until they had shown themselves worthy of being received. So they were obliged to encamp outside, in the unprotected little village of Souburg.

This disgrace aroused the courage of the young recruits. They were resolved to die rather than run away again, and their endurance was soon put to the proof. The Spanish Governor of Middelburg prepared a *camisado*, or night attack, upon them, but his disciplined troops were met most valiantly by the volunteers. Pikes were crossed, so that the ensign-bearers, Philip Watkins and Thomas Lovett, broke their ensign-staves at push of pike. The Spaniards were routed, prisoners were taken, and as it was found that they were provided with halters in the certainty of success, the English victors derived a grim amusement from the operation of hanging the intending executioners with their own halters. Captain Morgan was wounded with a musket-shot; and his men, with their reputations retrieved, were received once more by the Flushingers with open arms.

The great object of Sir Humphrey Gilbert was the taking of Middelburg, the capital of Walcheren, but it was clear that this must be preceded by the reduction of Goes, the chief town in the island of South Beveland, through which the Spaniards in Walcheren received supplies. Gilbert and his colleague 't Zereets, therefore, determined to make another attempt on Goes. The island of South Beveland, in the previous century, had been the most flourishing district in Zeeland. Goes is on the north side, with a port opening on the eastern Scheldt. The lofty spire of its great church is conspicuous for many miles, and the church itself, with its flamboyant windows and splendid organ, is one of the finest in the Netherlands. Goes is a charming old town, with many quaintly gabled houses, and there are vestiges of the palace where Jacoba, the ill-fated heiress of Holland, passed the last few years of her life in happiness, with her noble husband Francis van Borsselen. Here she died in 1436. The farms round Goes have orchards and willow garths near the homesteads, and elms and Lombardy poplars planted in rows along the roads and dikes.

The patriots of Flushing were well supplied with shipping, both from that port and from Veere. They had six pieces of artillery and other materials for a siege; and towards the end of August, 1572, they sailed up the western Scheldt to dislodge the veteran Pacheco from his stronghold at Goes. The adventurers landed near Biezelinge, a village on the south side of the island, and about four miles from Goes. At first there were some slight successes. Captain Morgan and Rowland Yorke captured the fort commanding the harbour, and the six pieces of artillery made a breach. Gilbert and 't Zereets then led their men to the assault. An attempt was made to take the place by escalade, but, after some desperate fighting, it was repulsed; and the inexperienced besiegers began to despond.

The Duke of Alva saw the importance of relieving Goes, and entrusted the duty to Sancho de Avila, the Governor of Antwerp, with that consummate old soldier, Cristoval de Mondragon, a Basque from the lovely valley of the Deva, as his lieutenant They concentrated a force of Spaniards and Walloons at the fortified city of Bergen-op-Zoom, on the eastern Scheldt; but here a difficulty arose. In former days a narrow channel, easily passable, separated Bergen-op-Zoom from the fertile *polders* of South Beveland. Now all was changed. A frightful storm, combined with a very high tide, blew during one winter's night of the year 1532, and at dawn the furious waves broke through the dikes and flooded the country. Villages were submerged, and hundreds of people perished miserably. A wide space of shallow water thus intervened between Bergen-op-Zoom and South Beveland, at least eight miles across, the area receiving the melancholy name of "*Verdronken* land." The problem for Avila and Mondragon to solve was how to transport their force across this submerged land, and they decided upon a course which could only have been attempted with brave and highly disciplined soldiers.

A native of Beveland, named Plumart, reported that there was a very narrow ridge, along which it was possible to wade from one shore to the other at low water, and he volunteered his services as guide. Mondragon resolved to make the attempt. He caused a canvas bag to be prepared for each soldier, containing biscuit and powder,

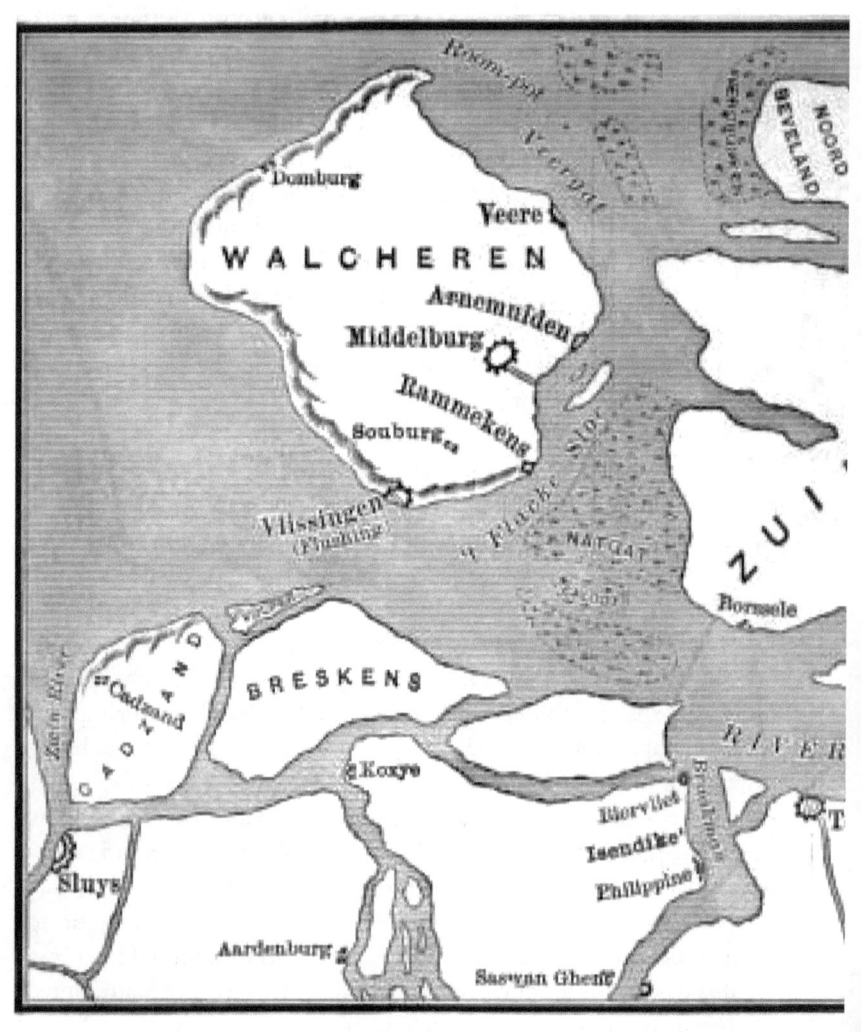

and selected a force of 3,000 picked men. It was a fine day towards the end of October, and the time chosen was when the tide was at half ebb. The aged veteran then led his men to the point where they were to enter the water, served out the bags, and delivered a stirring harangue, he exclaimed:

> I will plunge in first, and you will boldly follow me. Let the world judge if you have not proved yourselves to be worthy soldiers.

The Spaniards came first in double file, led by Mondragon, with Plumart the guide at his side. Each man was ready to support his comrade. The point to be reached on the Beveland shore was the village of Yerseken-dam. The whole thing was arranged so well that only nine men were lost, although they were frequently over their shoulders in water, and a false step would, in many places, have plunged them out of their depth. Mondragon landed his men safely at Yerseken-dam, which is five miles from Goes, and made beacon signals to Pacheco announcing his arrival. A short rest was necessary before advancing, (this account of Mondragon's exploit is from Bentivoglio).

When the besiegers heard of the arrival of Mondragon they did not wait to be attacked, but fled to their ships in complete rout. The Spaniards promptly followed them, and did much execution among the fugitives. Many were slain, and others were drowned in attempting to reach the ships. "Thus," says Roger Williams, "ended our ignorant poor siege." Gilbert, in despair, returned to England with his regiment, while Mondragon supplied the Spanish garrisons of Goes and Middelburg with provisions.

English volunteers continued to serve, both by sea and on land, but they still showed the consequences of inexperience and want of discipline. At Flushing they helped in the capture of Fort Rammekens in August, 1573, and in the great sea-fight, when the Zeeland ships attacked the Spanish fleet from Antwerp, with supplies for Middelburg. But in the following year the English serving under Chester and Gainsford were disgraced. They surrendered Valkenburg when they might have held out, and they were surprised and routed at Gouda, with a loss of 300 men and three colours taken.

Still they were learning in the school of adversity. There was no check in the enthusiasm which produced fresh volunteers. Still they came. In 1578, John North, the eldest son of Lord North, Henry Cavendish, and, above all, John Norris, arrived. John Norris was one of several warrior brothers in whom the queen took special interest. One of his grandfathers was that Henry Norris who suffered owing to the false accusations against Anne Boleyn. The other was that Lord Williams of Thame who had the custody of Elizabeth during her sister's persecution. His father had been created Lord Norris of Rycote, and his mother, Margery Williams, was one of the queen's earliest and dearest friends, a friend in the time of need and adversity. Queen Elizabeth called Lady Norris "her own crow," "being black in complexion," we are told, "a colour which no whit unbecame the faces of her martial issue." John had already served in France under Admiral Coligny, and in Ireland under Essex, when he placed his sword and his tried valour at the disposal of William of Orange.

Don Juan of Austria had just put the army of the States to flight at the Battle of Gemblours. He seemed to be carrying all before him. The Archduke Matthias, who had been invited into the Netherlands, had got together an army to oppose his cousin, consisting of Flemings and English and Scotch volunteers, under the command of Count Bossu and François de la Noue. The latter was a Breton, who had embraced the Protestant religion, and had borne arms from his infancy. He was in the Italian wars; he fought at St. Quentin, Jarnac, and Moncoutour, and lost his left arm at the siege of Fontenai-le-comte. He used one of iron, and was called "*Bras de Fer*." He now was forty-eight, a seasoned and weather-beaten veteran. (*Discours Politiques et Militaries*). The raw recruits were in need of such a man to command them. They numbered 14,000 men. Don Juan had a splendidly equipped force of 30,000 men, with his nephew, the Duke of Parma, as general of horse, Count Mansfelt as lord marshal, and Don Antonio Martinez de Leyva, among many other nobles, with a picked company, 200 strong, bearing colours with a crucifix on a sable ground. Leyva led the van.

La Noue selected a position very carefully, near the village of Rymenant, and not far from the city of Malines, in Brabant. His troops were drawn up between the village and the River Dyle, a tributary of the Scheldt. One flank was protected by a wood, and the other by trenches. The army of Don Juan advanced from Arschot, which is on the banks of the same river, and approached the enemy in good order. The object was to draw the inexperienced recruits out of their trenches, and overwhelm them in the open. There were skirmishes, but La Noue still held back his main body.

Colonel Norris and the English volunteers occupied a position apart from the Flemings, and Don Juan now resolved to dislodge them if possible, and to bring on a general engagement. He attacked the English with the flower of the Spanish infantry, the select company of Leyva being in the van. Scarcely a man in this company had not served as an officer, and was not of knightly rank. Leyva himself had equipped the company at his own expense. The assault was made with desperate valour, but it was not less bravely received by the English volunteers. The fight long remained doubtful. The Spaniards were assaulting an entrenched position, and they were repulsed again and again. At length they fell back, and Don Juan ordered a retreat, (Bentivoglio). This was on the 1st of August, 1578. The heat was intense, and the Englishmen fought in their shirt-sleeves. Norris, stoutly cheering on his men, had three horses killed under him. Young Bingham, serving as lieutenant to Cavendish, and William Markham, from Sedgebrook, in Lincolnshire, received special commendation; (Camden; Kennet), but all had done well.

It was an important engagement for the Englishmen, who were learning to be soldiers. They had now repulsed the formidable infantry of Spain on two occasions: first at Souburg, outside the town of Flushing, and again at Rymenant. They were learning their lesson.

Volunteers continued to come over during the following years, and to acquire a knowledge of the military art, the most distinguished being John and Edward Norris, Thomas Morgan, and Roger Williams, and later on came John Burrough, Edmund Uvedale, Thomas Wingfield, Robert Sidney, and Baskerville, all men with whom we shall soon become better acquainted. In 1580 we hear of John Norris with a company of 150 well-armed Englishmen, at Campen; and in 1582 he is still aiding the Netherlander to stem the torrent of invasion in Gelderland. In 1583 Norris was commanding the English in the Pay de Waas, opposite to Antwerp.

Meanwhile Roger Williams had been actually improving his military education in the enemy's camp. He had gone to Germany, owing to a report that the Prince of Condé was raising forces there to march into France, and he thought this would be a good opportunity of gratifying his desire to see strange wars. But he found that the report was untrue, and that he had spent his money for nothing; so he began his journey back to England. Entering Lier, in Brabant, he was brought before Julian Romero, the best infantry officer in the Spanish service. Among many other questions Romero asked the stranger what noblemen in England he knew best. He answered, the Earl of Pembroke, whom he served as a page. "What," exclaimed Romero, "the general of the English before St. Quentin? I never honoured any man more." So he earnestly requested Williams to remain in the Spanish army, assuring him that he might depart when it pleased him. Loath to return to England without seeing something, he promised to stay, and saw some service. (*Discourse of the Discipline of the Spaniards*).

But the time was now approaching for England to enter upon the quarrel as a nation. The Queen's government had long been negotiating with the States, and, besides allowing the volunteers to enter the service of the Prince of Orange, Queen Elizabeth had advanced at least ,284,000 in money between 1577 and 1581, which she had raised on her own credit, receiving the principal and paying interest to the Genoese bankers Pallavicino and Spinola, (State Papers (Holland).

The tentative efforts of the inexperienced volunteers were the forerunners of the more serious and extensive assistance which the freemen of England were to give to the patriots righting for freedom at their doors.

CHAPTER 5

The Art Military

The army which Queen Elizabeth was about to send to the Netherlands was the first that had been organised on the Spanish model. The various grades, the drill and evolutions, and even much of the military nomenclature, were borrowed from the system which had been founded by the Great Captain, and had produced the finest infantry the world had seen since the fall of the Roman Empire. The best regiments of Spain were in the Netherlands, under such colonels, or *maestros de campo*, as Romero and Mondragon. The "*Tercio Viejo*" under Mondragon, was so called because it included bands ("*vanderas*") of the time of the Great Captain Gonzalvo de Cordova and of Charles V. The military training and experience of the soldiers were unrivalled, their appearance superb, their bravery proved in scores of victories.

This *Tercio* was broken up by the Duke of Parma, and the men were distributed in other *tercios*, because their pride was considered excessive. Still that fault arose from a consciousness of having cause for pride, and it shows the sort of perfection to which the Spanish infantry had reached. They had no equal in Europe, and, in preparing to create such an equal, some English commanders strove to learn from the enemy, like Roger Williams, and all endeavoured to model their armies on this most approved pattern.

The general's staff of the English Army was organized almost exactly on the Spanish system. Under the general, and exercising supervision over the army, was the lord marshal, who selected sites for camps and arranged the stationing of pickets, sentries, and scouts. In the Spanish service he was called "campmaster general." The lord marshal gave orders to the provost marshal, the sergeant-major general, the quartermaster-general, and the scout-master, and arranged the marches and strategic movements of the army. He instructed the quartermasters as to the staking out the camp, appointed the limits of the market-place, divided the ground, and allotted spaces for each company.

The duty of the treasurer of war was to receive from the muster-master general, the victual-master, and provost marshal lists of all officers with their allowances. He was allowed a small staff of subtreasurers and clerks, and he had supervision over the work of the muster-masters. These officials were expected to have a knowledge and description of every man of every company, to be good accountants, and to take care that pay was not drawn for dead or absent men.

The lieutenant-general of horse commanded all the cavalry, and the colonel-general, sometimes also called lieutenant-general of foot, commanded the infantry. The sergeant-major general ranked next under the colonel-general.

Each regiment was commanded by an officer who, since the time of Henry VIII., had been called a colonel, equivalent to the *maestro de campo* of the Spanish service; and there was also a lieutenant-colonel. The sergeant-major of a regiment was selected from among the captains. It was his duty, with the aid of the captains, to keep the regiment in due form, and the sergeant-major general trusted to the skill and experience of the sergeant-majors of regiments to form an army in what line or figure was considered best by the general. The sergeant-major was allowed a horse, and when his regiment was on detached service he performed the duties of marshal. His chief duties were to insure good order in marching and in encamping, and perfect forms of embattling. He was expected to report himself daily to the sergeant-major general, to receive orders from him, to apply for necessary stores and provisions, and to visit the guards every night.

The captain of a company was usually a gentleman of some position, for the companies were much sought after, and before long a sort of purchase system was introduced. The number of men in a company varied very much, but 200 was considered a full complement. Besides his sword, the captain had a fair gilt partisan richly trimmed, and his colours carried by the ensign. His pay was eight guineas (eighty-four *gulden*) a month. The lieutenant of a company had his place in the rear advancing, and in the front retiring. His duties were to train and drill the men, and to see them properly dressed in their files, and he received £5. 16. a month. The ensign, or *alferez* of the Spaniards, had to guard the captain's colours; which consisted of a red cross on a white field, from which flew a streamer with the principal colours and charges of the captain's coat-armour. The ensign wore a burgonet and corselet, and was armed with sword and dagger. His pay was £4. 16. a month. In each company there were also a certain number of gentlemen volunteers and pages.

A company was divided into four squadrons, and there was a sergeant for every two. His duties were to fetch the watchword from the sergeant-major and deliver it to the corporals, to instruct in postures and the use of arms, and to draw up the files and see them in position according to the captain's orders. He was expected to be able to read and cipher, to keep a list of his men, and to assign duties. Like the ensigns, the sergeants wore a Milan corselet and burgonet, and carried a halberd of partisan. A sergeant's pay was £2. 8. a month.

The *cabo de escuadra* of the Spaniards was called a corporal by the English, and there was one for each squadron. His duties were to draw out the *corps du garde*, place sentries, receive the password, and draw victuals and stores from the clerk. He led the principal file of his squadron in attack, and received £1. 12. a month. The squadrons were divided into *camarados*, or fellowships, of ten to twelve men each, who were united together in their lodging and messing, and usually in their friendships. Each *camarado* was led by an assistant corporal, called a *cabo de camarado* or *lanspesado*. The Italian name was *lanze spezzate*. The *lanspesados* each received £1. 4. a month. Each company also had a clerk to keep the rolls and muster books, and receive stores and provisions; and a harbinger who received and distributed the billets, ascertained from the quartermaster-general the portion of ground on which his company was to encamp, and allotted the ground for building their cabins to the *camarados*. The harbinger was selected by the captain from among the corporals. His pay was £1. 8. a month. Each company also had a drummer and fifer, at £1. 4. each a month.

The soldiers of a company were divided into pikemen and shotmen. The Spaniards looked upon the pike as "*la señora y reyna de las armas*" the noblest of weapons. A pike had to be strong and straight, made of well-grown ash, and headed with a steel spike guarded with plates of iron. The length was eighteen feet, and about six feet from the head there was a patch of cloth or velvet to mark the place for carrying the pike in shouldering and sloping. It was trimmed with tassels, to turn off the water which, in rainy weather, would otherwise run down along the staff. (The use of the pike was abandoned in

France, by the advice of Vauban, in 1703, and in England at about the same time. A book of infantry exercise published in 1690 has the pike exercise; and the *Gentleman's Dictionary* (1705) describes the pike as "a weapon formerly in use, but now set aside.")

Pikemen were also armed with a sword having a basket hilt, blade a yard long, and a scabbard of strong leather. The sword used to be attached to a baldric, but afterwards a girdle was substituted, in which there was also a dagger; for the dagger, observes Robert Barret, "is a weapon of great advantage in pell-mell." Much attention was given to the defensive armour of pikemen. The Spanish *morion* was preferred to the old burgonet as a headpiece. It was well lined with quilted linen, and had ear-plates, also lined, with a string to fasten under the chin. Round the neck a gorget was worn, and over it a pair of cuirasses, breast and back pieces,—pike-proof, with clasps for fastening.

On the left of the back piece there was a hook for the morion. Fastened to the breastplate in front, there was a pair of taces, with several joints, defending the belly and upper half of the thigh. On the shoulders there was a pair of well-moulded pouldrons coming down to the elbows; but the vantbraces, from the elbow to the wrist, which were formerly in use, had been discontinued. Under the armour the men wore doublets of fustian or chamois leather, made high in the collar to protect their necks from cold and sun, and well stuffed at the shoulders. For hose they had large wide "greygescoes," lined with cotton and bound with strong canvas, to which the nether stockings were fastened, and gartered at the knees. A pikeman's pay was £1. 4. to £1. 16. a month. (Sir Edmund Uvedale, in 1590, gives a soldier's pay at £12. 3. 4. a year, or 8d. a day. *Cotton* MSS. Galba, D. vii.).

The shotmen of the company also wore a Spanish *morion*, and were armed with a sword, besides their muskets. Round the neck there was a piece of quilted leather, cut like a large gorget. Over the left shoulder and under the right arm they wore a bandoleer of leather, to which was fastened, by double strings at least nine inches long, one large priming charge and twelve other charges, all made of light wood or horn, covered with leather. At his girdle the shotman carried his bullet-bag, containing a mould, worm, screw, and priming-iron. The Duke of Alva brought muskets into use in 1567. Before that time the fire-arm, mounted on a stock, which was adopted in Europe, was the arquebus. It came in at about the end of the reign of Louis XII. The musket was much heavier than the arquebus, and necessitated the use of a staff, breast-high, as a rest.

The stock of the musket was of walnut wood, the barrel four and a half feet long. The wheel-lock had also been introduced by Alva. It was a small solid wheel of steel, fixed against the plate of the lock. An axis pierced its centre and went into the lock, a chain being fastened to the interior end, which twisted round it when the wheel was turned, and bent the spring by which it was held. A key was used to bend this spring, into which the exterior end of the axis was inserted. By turning the key from left to right the wheel was made to revolve, and by this movement a little slider of copper, which covered the pan containing the priming, retired from over it. By the same movement the cock, armed with a flint, was made ready to be discharged on pulling the trigger. The cock, falling on the wheel, produced fire, and communicated it to the priming. The wheel-lock was, however, generally used for pistols and carbines, and the match-lock for muskets.

******

In the time of Charles I. the *snaphaunce*, which was a flint-lock, took the place of the wheel-lock; and in 1670 the cartridge-box took the place of the dangling bandoleers. The noisy rattling of bandoleers betrayed the presence of an enemy, and even prevented men from hearing orders

******

The musket rest, which the soldier had to carry in his left hand, was of ash wood, with a half hoop of iron, to rest the musket on, at one end, and an iron pike at the other, to fix it in the ground. A shotman received £1. 16. a month.

The companies were formed in solid squares, the pikemen in the centre, and shotmen on the flanks; usually ten in rank and file. First a file of ten men, headed by the *cabo de camarado*, was marched up to the place where the square was to be formed, and halted. Then came the next file, marching shoulder to shoulder with the first, and so on to the tenth, the ensign marching in the middle file. A *maniple* was a detachment of so many ranks and files of a square of pikes, told off to march through any narrow place. The rule was that a file should never be more than ten deep.

The *corps du garde* was part of a squadron told off as a picket, or for sentry duty. It numbered twenty or thirty men, and was stationed where the enemy was most likely to make an attack.. The sergeant in command chose his sentries, and placed them at distances of thirty to forty paces from the *corps du garde*. These sentries were all shotmen, and had their rests fixed and muskets levelled. The Spaniards allowed the sentries to have the password, which enabled Roger Williams, at Venlo siege, to advance almost to the Duke of Parma's tent. But in the English service the sentry had orders. to allow no one to pass until he had called his officer, who alone had the word.

Rounders (*ronda* in Spanish) were select soldiers exempted from the duties of sentries, and chosen to be gentlemen of a company. They were called gentlemen rounders, or gentlemen of the round. Their duty was to visit the *corps du garde* and the sentries at certain hours of the night. They were entrusted with the password, and were leaders of the files in which they served.

Each company, on reaching camp, received a measured parallelogram from the quartermaster, for hutting. A soldier was expected to make one of a *camarado*, "to be as loving brethren." Having marched all day, and coming to the place where they were to encamp, one of them chose out the driest and warmest plot of ground he could find in the allotted quarters, and looked after all the clothes, arms, and baggage. Another went, with one of the pages, to get a supply of straw from some adjoining village, or of heath and ferns from the moorland, according to the country they were in. This was used both to roof their huts and to make their beds. The boys attached to the *camarado* carried a small hatchet, a leathern bottle for water, a small kettle to seethe meat in, and a bag of salt.

One soldier cut down forked boughs and long poles to make a framework for the hut, while another visited the *vivandiers* and victuallers to obtain bread and drink; if not otherwise provided, either by forage or pillaging. Another made the fire, stuck the forked stakes into the ground, and hung the kettle to seethe. Thus all the comrades were busily at work, and the men made themselves as comfortable as it was possible. But the life was a very hard one, and there was often much sickness. Sometimes they were sent on a night attack, or had to repel one. A night attack was called a *camisado*, because the soldiers often put shirts over their armour, the better to distinguish each other in the dark.

The queen allowed 120 rations for every 100 men, the surplus being divided amongst the officers. A ration consisted of one pottle of beer, one and a half pounds of bread, half a pound of butter, one pound of cheese, six herrings, two pounds of salt beef, and one pound of bacon. So that each man received six and a half pounds of solids a day and one pottle of beer, besides six herrings. The outfit of a soldier, apart from his arms and armour, consisted of a fustian doublet, a cassock or cloak for the winter, a pair of Venetian hose, two shirts and two bands, three pairs of woollen stockings, and four pairs of boots. The cost of this outfit was £2. 9. 2., defensive armour £1. 2., and the pike £0.4.6.; so that each recruit cost his country the sum of £3. 15. 8. In 1600 an infantry company was calculated to cost £270 a month for pay, or £3,240 a year.

A recruit was called a *bezonian*, from the Spanish word *bisoño*, which means raw, undisciplined, and is used for a recruit inexpert in the use of arms.

******

Modern writers seem to think that *bezonian* was a term of reproach. In Walker's dictionary, "a low fellow or scoundrel, a beggar," is the meaning given. But this is a mistake. When Pistol says to Slender, "Under which king, Bezonian?" (*2nd part of Henry IV*, Act 5, Sc. 3), he uses the word as we should say " greenhorn." Even in the mouth of Suffolk "Great men oft die by vile Bezonians" (*2nd part of Henry VI.*, Act 4, Sc. 1) the sense is merely that veterans or officers are often slain by recruits.

These are the two occasions on which the word is used by Shakespeare. It was in common use for a recruit, among the English in the Netherlands. Gervase Markham, in his *English Husbandman*, says, "The ordinary tillers of the earth, such as we call husband men, in Spain *besonyans!*"

******

During the war in the Netherlands the sieges were more frequent than battles in the open country, and no unimportant part of the duty of foot-soldiers was the expert use of the pick and spade. ("We are used to put the soldiers to the work of pioneers, who leave their tools and take their weapons when need requireth."—*F. Vere from the Hague, 24th April*, 1597. MSS. at Hatfield).

It was not uncommon for the men to have to dig and entrench themselves under a heavy fire. On such occasions they were protected by barrels filled with earth, in double rows. The officers had large bucklers or shields when they reconnoitred an enemy's fortifications.

The cavalry consisted of lancers, pistoliers, carbines, and light-horse. Lancers wore a buff coat with long skirts. They were provided with armour from the head to the knee, and bore a lance in the right hand, a sword on the left side, and a pair of pistols in holsters. The saddle was partly plated with steel. Their horses were strong and swift, generally fifteen hands. They charged the ranks of pikemen, and occasionally broke and routed them. The pistolier, instead of a lance, had a pair of French pistols, two feet long in the barrel, with wheel-locks. The carbines wore a morion, gorget, cuirass, and pouldrons. They were armed with swords, and petronels at their saddles, with flax, touch-box, and bulletbag. They charged on the flanks of the lancers and pistoliers, delivered their volleys at a greater distance, and when the enemy was routed they did great execution. Light-horse wore a morion, gorget, and light cuirass. They had a slender chasing staff and pair of pistols. Their duty was to gallop out as skirmishers, to charge loose wings of shotmen, to reconnoitre, and to pursue a broken enemy.

Dragoons were mounted musketeers for holding fords or bridges. There were eleven in a range, and when they came to the place to be held, ten dismounted, and the eleventh held the horses, threading the bridles one into another. They were formed in companies of no men. But this system of mounting infantry did not come into general use until near the close of the war.

A cornet or guidon of horse was equivalent to an ensign of foot. The colours were swallow-tailed and three feet long, and carried on a lance; unless the captain was created a banneret, when his guidon was made square.

The artillery was under the master of the ordnance and his lieutenant. Their staff consisted of master gunners, wagon-masters, trench-masters, and cannoniers. The heaviest battering-gun of those days was the double cannon, weighing 8,000 lbs., throwing a shot of sixty-six lbs., with a point-blank range of 800 paces, bore eight and a half inches. The cannon weighed 5,500 lbs., with a sixty pr. shot; and the demi-cannon weighed 4,000 lbs., with a twenty-four-pound shot, bore six inches, and point-blank range forty paces. These formed a siege train and were difficult to transport across country, but the network of rivers and canals in the Netherlands removed much of the obstacles caused in other countries by the labour of transport.

The largest fieldpiece was a quarter-cannon weighing 3,200 lbs., and throwing a 12 pr. ball. Its length was 8¾ feet, bore 4¾ inches, point-blank range 300 paces. This gun was between the culverin and demi-culverin, classes of ordnance which were not much used in the Netherlands. The small fieldpiece was called a drake or saker, and weighed 580 lbs. with a 6 pr. shot; length, 5 feet; bore, 3¾ inches; range point-blank, 100 paces. The falconet was a heavier piece, but throwing the same weight of shot.

The master of the ordnance directed the planning out and construction of bulwarks, curtains and cavaliers, casemates and trenches, as well as the mounting and working of the guns. Bulwarks were built at the angles of the enceinte of a city or fort, and were obtuse or rounded. They consisted of the traverses or flankers, the pome or shoulder, the front or curtain, the counter-front or spurs, and the parapets. The cavaliers were built within the curtain or walls of the bulwark, as places whence the curtain could be defended. The trench-master superintended this work. He was required to be a good geometrician, to have a quick eye and intelligent appreciation of any advantages offered by the nature of a country, and a clear intelligence.

While the quartermaster divided a camp into quarters for the different regiments, the trenchmaster drew up his plan for entrenching the camp according to the nature of the ground. Master gunners were required to have warlike stores at hand, and to see that guns were properly loaded and trained. He supplied sponges and worms, cotton, matches, priming-irons, quadrants and rules for pointing the guns, engines for mounting and dismounting, carriages, axle-trees, wheels, rammers, quoins, gabions, baskets, ropes, and entrenching tools. Sometimes the offices of master gunner and fire-master were separated, the latter making powder, and compounding all kinds of fire-works and charges for blasting.

The wagon-master and forage-master were under the orders of the lieutenant-general of horse. The former had charge of all the baggage of an army, and of all means of carriage. With the wagons marched the boys, such women as were allowed to accompany the army, and the victuallers. The victual-master was an important official, who had under him a staff of clerks, carriers, bakers, butchers, and coopers. He kept his accounts, for periodical submission to the treasurer.

The provost marshal took delinquents into custody, and had charge of all gyves, shackles, bolts, chains, bilboes, manacles, whips, gallows, scaffolds, pillories, stocks, and strapados,—a very formidable person. He watched over the cleanliness of the camp, kept the peace, and had the guard over all prisoners of war until they were ransomed or otherwise released. The judge marshal was the prosecutor at courts-martial, and the referee in all martial causes.

The scout-master was an accomplished and most valuable assistant to the general. He was expected to be a man of valour and judgment, a good cosmographer and describer of the nature of a country and the positions of places, and one who was quick to take in the whole aspect of a district at a glance. He was supplied with a guard of light-horse, and he rode in front of the army to gauge the depth of fords, to try the nature of bottoms of rivers, and to observe all hills, valleys, woods, and swamps, with the advantages or disadvantages they offered to his general's plans. He sent out *"vant-curriers"* (avant-couriers) in all directions to bring him reports.

Such was the system, mainly adopted from the Spaniards, which prevailed in the organisation of the forces raised to resist them. There were various modifications in practice from time to time; but the above details will furnish a fair general idea of the methods which guided our ancestors to eventual success in their efforts to assist the free people of the Netherlands, and of the materials whereby they achieved their grand object.

Chapter 6

Opening of the War

The sympathy for the people of the Netherlands increased in England as the struggle developed. But Spain was then the most powerful nation in the world. It was no light matter to defy such a power, and a war would place the very existence of England in jeopardy. It was right that long and careful deliberation should precede so momentous a decision. It was right that the government of Queen Elizabeth should hesitate. For years she continued to allow volunteers to cross the sea. For years she advanced money to the States. Both these measures were acts of war if the King of Spain saw fit to view them in that light His governors at Brussels sent embassies to remonstrate, the States sent envoys to entreat for intervention. The queen wisely continued to give evasive replies to both sides, while she watched the course of events.

At length the dreadful news arrived of the assassination of William of Orange. Elizabeth shared the horror of her subjects. She desired her agent at the Hague, in a letter in her own hand, dated July 3, 1584, to let the States know how greatly she grieved at the news of the death of the Prince of Orange. She grieved:

> Not only in respect of having lost so constant and good a friend, but chiefly in respect of the afflicted state of that country, being environed by the enemy as they are, to see them deprived of so good a Councillor and Director of their affairs in this their extreme necessity.

Her Highness's agent was instructed to let the States understand that, foreseeing the change in their affairs which must needs be caused by the loss of the Prince, and that they would require both advice and assistance, she had thought good to send him to consult with them. On

July 12, she wrote a letter of condolence to the Princess of Orange.

Prince Maurice, the son of William the Taciturn, was born on November 14, 1567, so that he was not quite seventeen; and though he afterwards proved a very able guardian of their liberties, he was as yet too young to lead the destinies of the Netherlanders unaided. He was accepted as his father's successor, and a council was formed to conduct the government, but all eyes were turned more anxiously than ever to the longed-for help from England. In the following year the successes of the Duke of Parma and his famous siege of Antwerp made the decision of Queen Elizabeth still more urgent. The time was now ripe for action. In June, 1585, the envoys for the States arrived in London. There were two from Brabant, one from Flanders, Olden Barneveldt and three others to represent Holland, one from Zeeland, Paul Buys from Utrecht, one from Dordrecht, and three from Friesland. They were lodged in Tower Street, and "had their diet very worshipfully appointed" at the Clothworkers' Hall in Mincing Lane. On June 29th they had audience of the Queen at Greenwich, when the Pensionary of Dordrecht delivered an oration in French, to which her Highness graciously replied.

The terms of a treaty were then agreed upon. The queen was to send an auxiliary force to Holland, consisting of 4,000 foot and 1,000 horse under a general, and to pay them during the war. The States were to repay this expenditure within five years after peace was made. The town of Flushing, with the castle of Rammekens, and the town of Brill, were to be delivered to the queen. Ostend was afterwards added. These cautionary towns were to be restored to the States when the accounts between the two countries were adjusted. The general, and two other Englishmen nominated by the queen, were to be members of the Council of the States. The States agreed to make no treaties without the advice and consent of the queen. Ships, for common defence, were to be provided, in equal numbers, by both contracting parties and at the common charges, and to be commanded by the admiral of England.

The queen then caused a declaration to be published, setting forth the reasons which had induced her to give aid to the afflicted and oppressed people of the Low Countries. It was dated at Richmond on October 1, 1585. It is one of the noblest state papers that was ever written, and it placed the English nation in a most honourable position before the world. It is not unworthy to take a place beside the Declaration of American Independence.

The queen wrote:

> We are moved to publish upon what just and reasonable grounds we are resolved to give aid to our next neighbours, the people of the Low Countries, being by long wars and persecutions of strong nations lamentably afflicted and in present danger to be brought into perpetual servitude.
>
> There has been a continual traffic and commerce between those Low Countries and our realm of England, in all ancient times, when the several provinces were ruled by several laws, and not united together, as of late years they have been by intermarriages, and at length reduced to be under the government of their lords that succeeded to the dukedom of Burgundy. There hath been, in former ages, many special alliances between the two people, for maintenance of commerce and intercourse of merchants, and also for special mutual amity, with provisions for mutual powers, affections, and all other friendly offices. By which mutual bonds there hath continued perpetual unions of the people's hearts together, and so by way of continual intercourses, from age to age, the same mutual love hath been inviolably kept.
>
> Of late years the King of Spain has appointed Spaniards, foreigners of strange blood, men more exercised in wars than in peaceable government, and some of them notably delighting in blood, as hath appeared by their actions, to be the chiefest governors of all the Low Countries, contrary to the ancient laws and customs thereof. The Spaniards have violently broken the ancient laws and liberties of all the country, and, in a tyrannous sort, have banished, killed, and destroyed, without order of law, within the space of a few months, many of the most ancient and principal persons of the natural nobility that were most worthy of government. Of the chiefest that were executed of the nobility, none was more affected to the Romish religion than the noble and valiant Count of Egmont, the very glory of that country. The Spaniards have also lamentably destroyed by sword, famine, and other cruel manners of death a great part of the natural people, and now the chief towns are held and kept chiefly with force by the Spaniards.
>
> We are sure that they could be pitied of none with more cause and grief generally than of our subjects of this our realm of

England, and those countries have by common language of long time resembled and called as man and wife.

For these urgent causes we have by many friendly messages and ambassadors to the King of Spain declared our compassion of this so evil and cruel usage of his people by sundry his martial governors, all strangers to these his countries. We have often and often most friendly warned him that if he did not otherwise by his wisdom and princely clemency restrain the tyranny and cruelty of his governors and men of war, we feared that the people of his country should be forced to seek the protection of some other lord. For they affirm that in such cases of general injustice, and upon such violent breaking of their privileges, they are free from their former homage; the proof whereof is to be read in the ancient histories of divers alterations.

Having regard to the continual and lamentable requests made to us by the States for our succours, and finding no hope of relief of these their miseries, but rather an increase thereof by daily conquests of their towns and slaughter of their people, and joining thereunto our own danger at hand by the overthrow and destruction of our neighbours; we, therefore, after long deliberation, determine to send certain companies of soldiers to aid the natural people of these countries to defend their towns from sacking and desolation, and to preserve their ancient liberties for them and their posterity, and so consequently to preserve and continue the lawful and ancient commerce between our people and those countries.

We mean not hereby to make particular profit to ourself and our people, only desiring to obtain, by God's favour, for the countries a deliverance of them from war by the Spaniards and foreigners, with a restitution of their ancient liberties and government.

The die was cast. The Netherlanders were transported with joy at having at length obtained the powerful aid of England. The King of Spain resolved to strike a blow at the islanders with his whole force; and meanwhile the queen ordered preparations to be pushed forward, in order to comply promptly with the terms of the treaty. Sir Fulk Greville said:

This she-David of ours ventured to undertake the great Goliath among the Philistines abroad, I mean Spain and the Pope, and takes (almost solitary) truth for her leading star.

The queen selected Robert Dudley, Earl of Leicester, her early friend and trusted councillor, to command the auxiliary force in chief. While military knowledge and experience were indispensable qualifications for his advisers, it was considered that the most important recommendation for the general, at that particular juncture, would be the confidence of his sovereign. Born in 1532, Leicester had now reached the age of fifty-three, a handsome, portly man with gray hair. But he had passed his life at court, and had no experience of martial affairs. Governors were also appointed for the cautionary towns. Sir Thomas Cecil, eldest son of the Lord Treasurer, became governor of Brill, and Sir Philip Sidney of Flushing and Rammekens.

Cecil was the eldest of the two English governors. Born in 1542, he had served in Scotland when aid was sent to the Regent Murray in 1574, and was knighted at Kenilworth in the following year. His government was a post of trust, for Brill, placed at the mouth of the Maas and commanding the main approach to Rotterdam, was a seaport of considerable importance. It was memorable as the spot where the standard of liberty was first raised by De la Marck and his "*sea gueux*," and it had since been in the hands of the patriots. Situated at the western end of the island of Voorn, the town of Brill even now retains several buildings which were familiar to the Elizabethan garrison.

The tower and roof of the old church at Brill are seen from a great distance, rising over a mass of foliage. In front of the church there is a small open space, with a fountain dating from 1590, and the streets leading from it contain several curious old houses, with dates 1577, 1588, and 1592 on their gables. Many have slabs between the windows, carved with a cow, or a galley, or a shield of arms, and the date beneath. The school has the date 1594, the prison 1623. A bronze statue of liberty, (erected in 1872), with the inscription "*Libertatis primitiae, 1 April, 1572*," stands on the site of the gate through which William de la Marck forced an entrance.

Brill is still, (1878), one of the most interesting and quaint old towns in Holland. It is quite hidden by the thick foliage of the trees round the ramparts, and when they are passed the picturesque canal appears, with old houses on either side, and the massive church-tower rising above them. Brill retains many of the features which presented themselves to Sir Thomas Cecil and his English garrison, when they entered the town in November, 1585, and were welcomed as deliverers by the inhabitants.

The first English governor of Flushing was a younger man than Thomas Cecil, having just reached his thirty-first birthday. Philip Sidney was entering upon the last year of a beautiful life which was to be closed by the death of a hero. He had formed friendships in many lands. He had served his queen in posts of high trust, and had done her that higher service of venturing upon frank and fearless expostulation. He had loved passionately and honourably, but unhappily. He had written poetry which will be read as long as the English language endures. He was beloved and admired by the leading intellects of a great period. On the whole, he was the most brilliant, the most chivalrous, of those bright spirits who formed the court of the great queen. He was now about to draw his sword in a just and noble cause.

His government of Flushing (Vlissingen), a town on the south side of the island of Walcheren, was even more important than Brill. It commanded the mouth of the Scheldt and the approaches to Antwerp. Walcheren itself was a place of considerable trade, being a well-cultivated island, including the city of Middelburg (the capital of Zeeland), only a few miles from Flushing; and the other seaport of Veere on the north side, also a thriving place. Flushing was originally a small fishing village; but William the Good, Count of Holland, raised it to the rank of a shipping-port, by digging a haven from the sea, in the year 1319. From that time there was a canal, with quays for loading and unloading, which cut the town in two. Philip the Good, Duke of Burgundy, built the walls in 1489, with five gates.

The Water Gates, where the canal entered from the sea, with a strong bastion, were completed in 1548. The "Gevangen," or Prisoners' Poort, faced the dunes. The Middelburgsche Poort was at the other end of the canal, facing the Water Gate. Through it the Spanish garrison was driven by the people in 1572. The Blaauw Poort was on the west side; and lastly the Altena Poort, on the sea face, was taken down in 1586, to make room for a new haven and dockyard. Just within the Blaauw Poort was the *Klein Markt*, where the people from the neighbouring village of Ritthem used to sell their farm and garden produce to the garrison and townspeople. This open space still remains, shaded by some tall elm-trees.

The old church, dedicated to St. Jacob, is large, and was once cruciform. It was founded in 1328. In it there are tombs of the Van de Putte family, which flourished in the time of Sir Philip Sidney, and produced one great traveller in after years. (See my introduction to *Missions to*

Tibet; Trübner). Here, too, rests Jan Lambrecht Coolen, who explored the Indies and New Guinea, and was a burgomaster of Flushing, dying there in 1619. A foot-bridge crossed the haven canal, dividing it into two parts, which were called the *Kaas Kaai* and the *Bier Kaai*.

On the eastern side was the Groot Markt, where once stood two monasteries of Carmelites and Friars Preachers, which were endowed by Adrian van Borsselen, the Count of Flushing, in 1466. But they were pulled down by the insurgents in 1573, and the stones were put on board ships and sunk off Fort Lillo, to stop the Spanish fleet. On the site of the monasteries rose the great town hall, on the model of that at Antwerp, which was commenced in 1596, during the English occupation. It contained the old bottle left by St. Willebrord, after which the town was named.; two great globes by Blaauw; and the helm and sword of the ill-fated Juan Pacheco, who was put to death by the insurgents in 1572. (The town hall of Flushing, with all its interesting relics, was burnt during the bombardment by the English fleet on August 14, 1809).

Flushing contained numerous houses of wealthy townsmen, besides the warehouses of the merchants of Middelburg, the city whose lofty towers formed a main feature of the landscape from the walls. Mr. Digges, the learned mathematician, submitted a very full report on the defences of Flushing, as soon as the English occupation began. The fort of Rammekens, which was included in the Flushing command, is about two miles from the town, at the entrance of the "Sloe" channel, separating Walcheren from South Beveland. It was an irregular parallelogram, without bastions, built of stone, with a wide moat, the main entrance being a doorway approached by a drawbridge on the landward side. Now the moat is full of long weeds, where a heron or two may usually be seen fishing, and the place has a dreary, abandoned appearance.

Sir Philip Sidney arrived with his English garrison on the 18th of November, 1585, the queen's accession day. He thus describes his landing, in a letter to his uncle:

> On Thursday we came into this haven, driven to land at Rammekens, because the wind began to rise in such sort that the master durst not anchor before the town, and from thence came, with as dirty a walk as ever poor governor entered his charge withal. I find the people very glad of me.—*Cotton MSS.*, Galba, c. viii.

He had a garrison of 750 men, with Edward Norris as his lieutenant.

Thus the two cautionary towns were duly occupied by English garrisons, and the general with his staff, and the rest of the expeditionary force, prepared to follow. Ostend had also been occupied by a garrison under Captain Errington.

The Earl of Leicester had many enemies, and he was attacked by anonymous writers. History has, to a great extent, indorsed the verdict of his contemporary assailants. But he could not have been without good qualities, seeing that he won the affection of such a man as his nephew, Philip Sidney, who answered his detractors with vehement warmth.

★★★★★★

One attack was printed abroad and anonymously, in 1584. Sidney answered it in the same year. The pamphleteer compared Leicester to Piers Gaveston, Oxford, and base Pole. Sidney, in his answer, says, "Their enemies did not stop with destroying them, but went on to kill their masters. The wolves that mean to destroy the flock hate most the truest and valiantest dogs. Who hates England and the queen must also withal hate the Earl of Leicester." The pamphleteer spoke of the blood of the Dudleys. Sidney replied that Dudley was an ancient baronial house, allied to Grey, Talbot, Beauchamp, and Berkeley, and that the Dudleys were lords of Dudley Castle long before the time of Richard I. Sir Philip concluded by telling the writer that he lied in his throat, which he was ready to justify upon him where he would.

★★★★★★

In spite of Leicester's alleged unpopularity many of all ranks flocked to his standard. On the 6th of December he came to Colchester with a great train, including the Earl of Essex, Lords North and Audley, Sir William Russell, Sir Thomas Shirley, Sir Arthur Bassett, Sir Gervase Clifton, and other volunteers to the number of 500 horse, all bravely appointed. The bailiffs of Colchester in scarlet gowns, with multitudes of people, met the earl on the Lexden road, and he entered the town with great solemnity, where he was most honourably entertained by Sir Thomas Lucas. At Colchester young Francis Vere joined the expeditionary force as a volunteer.

The fleet under the command of William Borough, Admiral of England, was waiting at Harwich.

※※※※※※

Correspondence of Robert Dudley, Earl of Leicester, 1585-86: edited by J. Bruce, F. S. A., for the Camden Society, in 1844. *Harl. MSS.*, 6845. Fol. 26 is Appendix I . "*Journal of my Lord of Leicester. Proceedings in the Lowe Countries*: By Mr. Stephen Borough, Admiral of the Fleet."

The Christian name *Stephen* is a mistake, for Stephen Borough died in 1584. Mr. Coote has clearly shown that the original docketing on the manuscript has been erased, and the word Stephen substituted for William by a later hand.

Stephen Borough was born at Borough, in the parish of Northam, near Bideford, in Devonshire, in 1525. He served under Chancellor in the first voyage to Russia, in 1553. In 1560 he led another fleet to the White Sea, and made one more voyage in 1561. Borough induced Richard Eden to translate the Spanish navigation book of Martin Cortes into English, in 1561; and in 1563 he was appointed chief pilot and one of the four masters of the Queen's ships in the Medway, including the duty of examining and instructing seamen in the art of navigation. He died in July, 1584, and was buried at Chatham.

William Borough, the younger brother of Stephen, was born at Borough in 1536, and served under his brother as an ordinary seaman in his first voyage to Russia, in 1553. He continued to serve the Muscovy Company in voyages to the White Sea, and in 1570 he commanded a fleet sent to Narva, in the Gulf of Finland, armed to resist attacks of pirates. In 1581 he published his *Discourse of the Variation of the Compass*, and in 1583 was comptroller of the navy. His next service was the command of the fleet to take the Earl of Leicester to Flushing, in 1585. In 1587 he was with Drake in the expedition to Cadiz, and he commanded a small ship in the Armada fight in 1588. William Borough constructed several valuable charts, and wrote instructions and sailing directions. He died in 1599.

The questions relating to the lives of these two eminent seamen Stephen and William Borough, have been ably discussed by Mr. R. C. Cotton, in a paper printed by the Devon Ass'n, 1880, and by Mr. Coote in the *Dictionary of National Biography*.

※※※※※※

The Earl of Leicester and his suite rode from Colchester to Manningtree, where boats were ready to take them down the River Stour to Harwich. Here the ships were ready for sea, and Leicester embarked on board the *Amity*. The fleet weighed anchor at three in the afternoon of Thursday, the 9th of December. At the same time another fleet of sixty ships sailed from the Thames. On Friday, the 10th, they were in the Scheldt, and Leicester landed at Flushing the same afternoon, under salutes from the ships, with bonfires and fireworks on shore. The fleet was then moored off Rammekens.

The Earl of Leicester was received with the greatest enthusiasm by the people of the Netherlands. Without aid from England their cause seemed hopeless, and the Duke of Parma was making great preparations for a mighty effort to subjugate the insurgent provinces in the coming year. At the sight of the English fleet the hearts of the people were filled with joy. On landing at Flushing, the earl was received by young Maurice of Orange and Sir Philip Sidney. He inspected the castle of Rammekens, which was garrisoned by fifty English pikemen, and then proceeded to Middelburg.

Over the gates of that city the red cross of England was painted beside the arms of the States. Leicester was lodged in the spacious apartments of the old abbey, and on Tuesday, the 14th of December, a grand dinner was given to him in the town hall, his hosts being the widowed Princess of Orange, young Maurice, and the principal nobles of Zeeland. The dinner lasted from noon to three o'clock; the crowd was so great that many guests could not find seats, and glasses were broken in the struggle for them. On the 17th, the Earl of Leicester and Prince Maurice left Middelburg for Dordrecht in a small *skute*, in company with fifty other boats, but there was some delay in the passage, owing to a dense fog. They were forced to heave to, between Middelburg and Dordrecht, for five days, "insomuch that a crown would have been given for a halfpenny loaf." (Letter from E. Burnham, 26th December).

At length they landed at Willemstad, a new town which had recently been fortified by the Prince of Orange, and reached Dordrecht on the 21st. Leicester kept his Christmas at Delft, and proceeded thence to the Hague.

On February 1, 1586, the Earl of Leicester was declared governor and captain-general of the seven States, a measure which was disapproved by the queen as giving her subject too much power; but the States explained their motive in all humility, and they were excused. Count Maurice was made governor of Holland and Zeeland, and Count Meurs of Gelderland and Utrecht. Early in the year the Earl of

Leicester held a grand review of his forces at the Hague.

Young Francis Vere had come thus far as a simple volunteer, without employment either from the Queen or the States. He hoped, however, to obtain a company through the influence of Peregrine Bertie, Lord Willoughby, who had married his cousin, the Lady Mary Vere, and who was expected to arrive at the Hague from his Denmark mission.

Peregrine Bertie was the son of Catharine, dowager Duchess of Suffolk, and Baroness Willoughby in her own right, and of Richard Bertie.

******

The Duchess of Suffolk was the fourth wife of that Charles Brandon, Duke of Suffolk, whose third wife was the Princess Mary, sister of Henry VIII. The Duke died in 1545, leaving two sons by his fourth wife, but they both died of the sweating sickness on July 14, 1551, when boys.

******

Mr. Bertie and his duchess were married in 1553, and went abroad to escape the Marian persecution. They took refuge at Wesel on the Rhine, where their son was born, on October 12, 1555, and named Peregrine. He succeeded as Lord Willoughby in 1580, married Lady Mary Vere, and in 1582 was sent on an embassy to Frederick II. of Denmark. He was engaged on a second mission to Denmark in 1585, to induce the king to give aid to Henry of Navarre. Having performed this service successfully, he proceeded to the Low Countries to obtain employment under the banner of the Earl of Leicester. Travelling by way of Emden, he reached the Hague on the 21st of February, 1586, where he found his young cousin anxiously awaiting his arrival. Francis Vere at once attached himself to the suite of Lord Willoughby with the certainty of seeing service, and the assurance of regular employment as soon as an opportunity offered itself.

The gallant English volunteers were full of enthusiasm and eager to be led against the enemy. The Hague presented a scene of bustle and activity during the winter of 1586, troops constantly arriving and departing, with reviews and stately ceremonials, and frequent musters of horse and foot. The feelings of the volunteers are well expressed in a letter from one of them, which has been preserved. Lord North thus wrote to the Lord Treasurer on the 28th of February:

The general and special love, both of the people and States, doth show such hope, giveth such courage to us all, as every man is willing to hazard his life and venture his all; assuring ourselves that the Lord God, who hath stirred up her Majesty's heart to seek his glory by assisting this action, will still continue and so increase the same, as will bring honour to her life, safety to her kingdom, peace to this people, and eternal fame of her virtue to all posterity.—*State Papers* (Holland), vol. xxxi.

Chapter 7

The First Campaign

The army of the Earl of Leicester was organised on the Spanish model. He selected as his lieutenant-general a German prince of high rank, who some years afterwards married a daughter of the Prince of Orange. This was Count Philip of Hohenlohe Langenburg, always called Count Hollock by the English. Leicester described him as:

> A wise, gallant gentleman, and a right soldier, and very well esteemed with many of the captains and soldiers. He hath one fault, which is drinking, but good hope that he will amend it.

In another letter he refers to him as:

> A right Almayn in manner and fashion, free of his purse and his drink, a very noble soldier.

This rollicking boon companion was scarcely a sufficient support to a general advanced in years and entirely without military experience. Leicester relied, therefore, on his veteran lord marshal, who did not arrive until July. This was William Pelham, third son of Sir William Pelham, of a Sussex family, by Mary, daughter of Lord Sandys of the Vine. Pelham commanded the pioneers sent to assist the Regent Murray against the French in 1560, and had the chief direction of the siege of Leith. In 1562 he joined the French Protestants, and was at the taking of Caen, and then went to Ireland, where he performed the duties of lord deputy until 1580. He had seen much service, and was well qualified for the important post of lord marshal.

The colonel-general was John Norris, who had already served in the Netherlands for many years as a volunteer. He had with him two brothers, Edward and Henry, gallant men and true soldiers of fortune, but hot-tempered, and without judgment or administrative ability.

Leicester wrote of John Norris as "a subtle, dangerous man, not having a true word in his mouth." Among the captains who had companies in this first campaign are the names of John Burrough, Edward and Henry Norris, Vavasour, Wingfield, Baskerville, Yorke, Morgan, and Uvedale.

The lieutenant-general of cavalry was Sir William Russell, fourth son of the second Earl of Bedford, who had been knighted for service in Ireland, and had already acquired the fame of a dashing and zealous officer. Lords Essex, Willoughby, North, Audley, Sir Robert Sidney, Sir Thomas Shirley, and Sir Nicholas Parker commanded troops of horse. Francis Vere was a volunteer in Willoughby's troop, with his cousin Hugh Vere, and Hugh's cousin Robert Spring, from Lavenham. Thomas Fairfax (afterwards the first Lord Fairfax), Michael Harcourt, and Jerome Markham, who was soon afterwards killed in a duel, were also serving in cavalry troops.

✶✶✶✶✶✶

Jerome Markham was a very young man, and was bullied into a duel by one George Nowell. After the meeting was settled, Nowell came into the house of Edward Stanhope and proclaimed that he was going into a field to fight Markham. Those present represented to him that Markham was a very young man and without experience in any affray, in answer to which Nowell swore that he would thrust at him, and if he looked not well about him, he would thrust him through. He then went out and attacked young Markham, wilfully murdering him after his sword was broken. Next day Nowell picked a quarrel with Thomas Molyneux, and he was reported to be a brawling bully, always seeking occasion to provoke a duel. *Domestic* (Eliz.), vol. 28.

✶✶✶✶✶✶

The sergeant-major general was Thomas Wilford; the master of ordnance, Sir Richard Bingham, and afterwards Sir John Conway; the treasurer, Richard Huddleston, and afterwards Sir Thomas Shirley of Wiston, (appointed February 1, 1587, he got into sad trouble with his accounts, his distinguished sons, Anthony and Thomas, were also serving in the army); the judge marshal, Dr. Sutcliff; the provost marshal, James Spencer. The mustermaster-general was Thomas Dishes, one of the most eminent mathematicians of his time, whose services were equally valuable in reporting upon the defences of fortified places. His father was Leonard Digges, who was also a renowned mathematician and surveyor; his mother was Bridget Wilford, sister of the sergeant-major general. Thomas Digges was educated at Oxford, and was author of several works on military engineering, (he was father of the more famous Sir Dudley Digges). The Earl also had Dethick, the Windsor herald, in attendance as a member of his staff.

In March, 1586, Lord Willoughby received the government of the important fortified town of Bergen-op-Zoom, in Brabant. He afterwards told Secretary Walsingham that "it was resigned to me by the singular love of your honourable son-in-law." (*State Papers*;Holland, vol. xli.) Sir Philip Sidney himself wrote:

> For Bergen-op-Zoom, I delighted in it, I confess, because it was near the enemy, but especially having a very fair house in it, and an excellent air, I destined it for my wife. But I have resigned it to my Lord Willoughby, my very friend, and indeed a valiant and frank gentleman, and fit for that place.—Letter to Walsingham from Utrecht.

Lord Willoughby was accompanied by his cousin, Francis Vere, when he proceeded to his new command, and in the following May the first brush with the enemy took place. Hearing of a great convoy of 450 wagons going to Antwerp, Lord Willoughby marched out of Bergen-op-Zoom to attack it with 200 horse and 400 foot. In the encounter 300 of the enemy were slain, eighty taken prisoners, and all their wagons were destroyed except twenty-seven, which were captured. This was the first piece of active service in which Vere was engaged, soon to be followed by a more important expedition under the lead of his cousin.

The people fighting for their freedom were now aided by the whole power of England. Hope revived in spite of the threatening army of the Duke of Parma. The Netherlanders had their own gallant forces, and in addition they had the auxiliary army of their allies, and hundreds of sympathizing English volunteers, whose numbers were augmented every week. The Earl of Leicester found himself in command of a respectable force, behind the encircling rivers. He held all Holland and Zeeland, Utrecht and part of Gelderland, with the fortified posts of Bergen-op-Zoom and Gertruydenburg in Brabant, Sluys and Ostend in Flanders. He necessarily acted on the defensive, and waited for the first move from the Duke of Parma. That able general already held Nymegen on the Waal, and Zutphen on the Yssel.

In March he opened the campaign with the intention of securing all the fortified towns along the lines of the Maas and the Rhine. He first laid siege to Grave, a very strong place on the Maas, and Leicester promptly took steps to relieve it. He trusted a good deal to the daring enterprise and bravery of a partisan warrior of Gelderland, named Martin Schenk, who supplied him with information and was ever ready for a desperate raid into the heart of the enemy's country. He also relied upon the same qualities in the veteran Roger Williams, who was a kindred spirit. Schenk and Williams were generally far in advance of the main body of Leicester's army. But the general organised an efficient force under Hohenlohe and John Norris for the relief of Grave, consisting of 3,000 picked men.

After a desperate encounter with the Spanish besiegers, Grave was successfully provisioned, and with an efficient commander the town would have been safe. But the governor basely surrendered at a time when Leicester believed the place to be out of all danger, and was preparing to besiege Nymegen as a diversion. The Duke of Parma then captured Venlo, and so secured the whole line of the Maas. This success enabled him to turn his attention to the line of the Rhine. Zutphen and Doesburg on the Yssel were already in his hands. Neuss was taken by storm, and Parma commenced the siege of Rheinberg, an important fortified town on the Rhine, above Wesel.

These great successes were secured by the Spanish general between March and July. But Leicester was not idle. He had provisioned Grave, had overrun the Betuwe between the Waal and Lek, and was threatening Nymegen. In the previous April he had conferred the honour of knighthood on John Norris and Martin Schenk, and he now employed the latter on a very important service. This was to erect a strong fort on an island at the point where the Rhine and Waal divide, at the foot of the hills of Cleves. Schenk's detachment consisted of one Dutch and two English companies, led by Edward and Henry Norris. He rapidly threw up the earthworks, with five bastions, and a ditch in rear connecting the two rivers. The fort has ever since been known as Schenken Schanz. He reported that in two weeks he had brought the fort to such perfection that he feared not the enemy with all his forces. On the 18th of May Leicester himself inspected Schenken Schanz, and fully appreciated its strategic importance.

The earthworks of this famous post may still be traced, a modern village nestling within them. To the south are the wooded heights of Cleves, crowned by the beautiful Swan Tower; to the north, the steep hill of Elten; away eastward, the steeples of Emmerich, and all around the green meadows of the Rhine valley. The natural features have changed in the lapse of time. The point where the Rhine and Waal divide is now four miles further west, and the old fort is left, as it were, high and dry, between the present river and the former course of the Rhine. But at the time when the fort was built by Schenk, and inspected by the Earl of Leicester, its importance could scarcely be exaggerated.

While these measures were being taken to check the advance of Parma, a diversion was projected by the young Count Maurice and Sir Philip Sidney from the side of Flushing. They proposed to cross the Scheldt and attack the town of Axel on the Flemish side. Leicester entered heartily into the plan, and went himself to Bergen-op-Zoom, where it was arranged that Lord Willoughby, with a small force, should take part in the expedition. This was the second action in which Francis Vere was engaged. The rendezvous was Flushing. Lord Willoughby, leaving Bergen-op-Zoom at midnight, proceeded to join Prince Maurice and Sir Philip Sidney with 500 men. The combined force, of about 3,000 men, landed at Terneuzen, on the left bank of the Scheldt. The country had been flooded for defence, and the approach from the coast to Axel was by three causeways, the distance about five miles.

It was a long, silent march in the dead of night, and the surprise was complete. Axel was surrounded by a moat, but the garrison was unprepared, and the walls were easily escaladed by volunteers, who swam across and opened the gates from within. The Dutch company entered first, followed rapidly by Willoughby and Sidney. Sir Philip made a speech to his soldiers before the attack was made, explaining to them for what cause they fought, and that the people of the country were their friends and neighbours. By two o'clock in the morning they were masters of the town. The garrison consisted almost entirely of Germans, there being only two Spaniards. (Leicester to Walsingham, July 8, 1586; and to the queen, same date. Also letter from Sir Thomas Cecil).

A wonderful change has come over this town of Axel and the surrounding country since those days. Axel is now a small open town, without a trace of defences, except some indications of a moat on the south side; and the whole country, which was then under water, is now carefully cultivated. There is, however, a long serpentine lagoon to the south, called the Axelsche Kreek. The pilgrim who follows in the footsteps of Sir Philip Sidney from Terneuzen to Axel, and thinks of his midnight march by starlight, with sheets of stagnant water on either side of the causeway, must needs draw upon his imagination;

for the changes in the outward surroundings are very great. He now walks between double rows of Lombardy poplars. There are prosperous farms on either side, with orchards and rich meadows, and occasionally rows of exquisitely clean cottages, each with its little vegetable garden. Outside Terneuzen, a farm, with thick walls and angle buttresses, marks the site of an old Spanish fort. The change in the face of the country is mainly due to the triumph of that cause for which Willoughby and Vere bled, and Sidney died.

The capture of Axel was only an episode. The very tough problem which the Earl of Leicester had to solve was the best way of resisting the advance of the Duke of Parma. (He had just succeeded to the title, both his father and mother died in 1586). That general was besieging Rheinberg, which was being gallantly defended by Martin Schenk. His object was to take all the strong places along the line of the Rhine and Yssel, as he had already done along the Maas.

Leicester assembled his forces at Arnhem on the Rhine. Pelham, as lord marshal, joined him from England with reinforcements. Sir Philip Sidney came from Flushing; Lord Willoughby from Bergen-op-Zoom, accompanied by young Francis Vere; and Count Hohenlohe from Gertruydenburg, of which he was the governor. There, too, were Lords Essex, North, and Audley, Sir William Russell, Sir Thomas Wilford, the Norrises, and Roger Williams. A council of war was held. It was decided that the allies were too weak to attack Parma before Rheinberg. It was, therefore, resolved to make a diversion by threatening Doesburg and Zutphen, the towns held by the Spaniards on the Yssel. On Sunday, the 28th of August, Leicester reviewed the army, which was afterwards formed in hollow squares outside the town of Arnhem, and the preachers delivered sermons.

Siege was then laid to the town of Doesburg on the Yssel, six miles below Arnhem. Artillery and provisions were conveyed by water, and nine siege-guns were brought to bear on the walls. At night, the general went with the lord marshal to see the pioneers at work in the trenches, and Pelham was struck in the belly by a spent caliver shot. A constant fire was kept up until the 2nd of September, when two breaches were made, which, however, were filled up by the garrison. Still an assault was resolved upon. There was a dispute about the leadership, and Leicester decided it by giving one breach to Hohenlohe and the other to Norris. The attacks were about to be delivered when, at two in the afternoon, the garrison surrendered at discretion. Pelham was only slightly hurt; but Roger Williams must needs run up and down the trench with a great plume of feathers in his gilt morion, and could hardly expect to escape. He was wounded in the arm. Only twelve men were killed.

Leaving a garrison in Doesburg, Leicester then prepared for the investment of Zutphen, fourteen miles below Arnhem. The Yssel is a broad, tranquil stream, where the ancient city of Zutphen stands on its right bank, and where the small river of Berkel, rising in the moors to the eastward, flows into it, and forms the moat round Zutphen walls. Huge barges, laden with little cubes of peat, float on the placid bosom of the Yssel. In those days a wall with round bastions rose from the brink of the river. An ancient brick water-gate still spans the Berkel, with machicolated turrets at each end; and the lofty brick tower of St. Walburga rises above the town as it did when Parma climbed to its summit to watch the army of Leicester. The Spanish garrison at Zutphen was commanded by Juan Baptista Taxis, who also held two detached forts, called the Zutphen Sconces, on the opposite side of the river. They had been constructed by the advice of Don Francisco Verdugo, the marshal of the Spanish Army.

Leicester encamped his army on both sides of the Yssel, a short distance above the town of Zutphen, and made a bridge of boats across the river, to keep his communications open.

These operations had the intended effect. Parma raised the siege of Rheinberg, and hastened to the relief of Zutphen. Collecting wheat and other supplies on his march, he advanced rapidly to Borquelo, a town to the eastward. He then entered the threatened city with a small escort, and reconnoitred Leicester's camp from the top of the church-tower. He would have remained in the town, but Verdugo dissuaded him, and he returned the same evening to Borquelo to organise a force which was to escort a long train of provision wagons into the besieged place (Herrera, *iii. lib. i.* cap. 4.).

He advanced with his whole force to the village of Lockem, within a league of Zutphen, in the evening of September 21, 1586, and dispatched the convoy very early next morning. The conduct of this important service was entrusted to an officer of the highest distinction. Alonzo Davalos y Aquino, Marquis of Pescara and Vasto, was grandson of the nobleman of the same name who was a commander at the battle of Pavia, Governor of Milan, and whose epitaph was written by Ariosto.

✶✶✶✶✶✶

He found the Chevalier Bayard mortally wounded, treated

the dying hero with kindness and generosity, and had a tent pitched over him. He died with the reputation of being one of the greatest generals and ablest politicians of that century, aged thirty-six.

※※※※※※

His father was Viceroy of Sicily. The marquis who served under the Duke of Parma was worthy of his ancestry. He was renowned alike for valour, conduct, and humanity. The force entrusted to him consisted of 5,000 horse and foot. The infantry numbered 1,500 of the best soldiers of Spain under Manuel de Vega, with companies led by Juan de Herrera, Viedma, and Artajona. The cavalry was mainly Italian, commanded by Annibal Gonzago, Giovanni Creçia, and Apio Conti. It was a perilous service, for the long train of wagons had to be convoyed over a plain, with their whole left flank exposed to attack by the neighbouring English army. Near Lockem there are some sandy hills, covered with fir-trees, on which the Duke of Parma was encamped. Thence the road passes over wild moorland covered with heather to within a mile of the village of Warnsfeld, where cultivation commences.

From the church to the east gate of Zutphen the road is perfectly straight, and to the south a flat plain extends to the Yssel. There was a thick fog, which cleared as the convoy approached Warnsfeld church.

The proximity of the relieving army was known to Leicester the night before. But he was taken by surprise when the fog rose a little, and the long moving column of the enemy was momentarily exposed to view, and then again hidden. In hot haste the English cavalry, under Sir William Russell, was called out to charge. Lord Willoughby was ready to lead his men in full armour, and Francis Vere was among his followers. Lord Essex, Lord North, Lord Audley, Sir William Pelham, Sir Philip Sidney, Captain Thomas M. Wingfield, rapidly came up with their troops. Norris and Stanley formed an advanced post near the road, and had given the first alarm. The chivalry of England was drawn up ready to charge. The leaders waited for the fog to clear, which was so thick that a man could scarcely be made out ten paces off. Suddenly it rose, and the enemy was seen in overwhelming superiority close to Warnsfeld church.

In a moment the English knights, numbering only 200, were upon them, led by Sir William Russell, who broke his lance at the first crash of the combatants. He then "so played his part with his curtle axe that the enemy reported him a devil, and not a man," (Stowe). Lord Willoughby, with lance in rest, unhorsed Giovanni Creçia, who rolled into a ditch and was made prisoner. Lord North, though bruised on the knee from a musket-shot, sprang from his bed at the first alarm, and with one boot on and the other off, "went into the matter very lustily," (Leicester). For two hours this heroic little band of cavalry fought with desperate valour. Annibal Gonzaga was mortally wounded by a great sword-cut on the head. The Marquis del Vasto was himself in considerable danger, for the English knights cut their way to the centre of his bodyguard, and a blow was aimed at his head.

The cavalry escort was defeated; it fell back and gave place to the Spanish pikemen, dauntless veterans, who stood like a wall. In the foremost rank were Juan de Ugarte from Tordesillas, and Pedro Venero, a Basque from Bilbao. They held their ground until a reinforcement of musketeers came up from Lockem and opened fire. Then at length the English assailants fell back, and the convoy was brought safely into Zutphen, (Carnero, *lib. viii. cap. vi.;* Bentivoglio, *pte ii. lib. iv.*). The English loss was 34 killed and wounded, while 250 of the enemy were slain. Three colours were taken, two being sent to the queen.

Leicester wrote:

This hath flesht our young noblemen and gentlemen, and surely theie have won her majestie at this day as much honour as ever so few men did their prince.— Leicester to Walsingham, September 28, 1586.

Sir Philip Sidney had given his cuisses to Sir William Pelham, and his only defensive armour was a breastplate. At the close of the action he was shot in the left thigh, but he was able to return to the camp on horseback.

Being thirsty with excess of bleeding, he called for drink, which was presently brought him. But as he was putting the bottle to his mouth he saw a poor soldier carried along, who had eaten his last at the same feast, ghastly casting up his eyes at the bottle, which Sir Philip perceiving took it from his lips before he drank, and delivered it to the poor man with these words: 'Thy necessity is greater than mine.'—Fulke Greville's *Life of Sidney*.

The wounded hero was put on board a boat and taken to Arnhem. Count Hohenlohe, who was wounded in the throat by a musket-ball, was also sent to Arnhem. This generous prince neglected his own safety to succour his comrade. His surgeon coming to dress the count's wound, he inquired after Sir Philip. The doctor replied that he was not well, on which Hohenlohe, caring more for his friend's wound than his own, exclaimed:

> Away! Never see my face again till thou bring better news of that man's recovery, for whose redemption many such as I were happily lost.—*Life of Sidney.*

The noble Sidney lingered until the 17th of October, when he expired in the arms of his dear friend William Temple. The body was embarked at. Flushing on November 1st, and was interred with great pomp in St. Paul's Cathedral on the 16th of February, 1587. The pallbearers were the Earls of Leicester, Pembroke, Essex, and Huntingdon, Lord Willoughby and Lord North. Three of them had charged with him at Warnsfeld.

The Earl of Essex and Lords Willoughby, Audley, and North were created Knights Bannerets on the field of Warnsfeld, and Leicester conferred knighthood on John Wingfield and Henry Norris, and on Goodyere, the captain of his guard. Sir William Russell succeeded Sidney as governor of Flushing.

Although Leicester failed before Zutphen, he captured the forts on the opposite side of the river, and he succeeded in his object of drawing Parma away from Rheinberg. Winter was now approaching. He made Sir William Stanley governor of the important town' of Deventer, on the Yssel, some miles below Zutphen, and gave Rowland Yorke charge of the Zutphen Sconces. He then proceeded to Utrecht and the Hague, returning to England on the 4th of December, while the troops went into winter-quarters. Lord Willoughby also went to England for the winter.

The Earl of Leicester had acquitted himself well. He had shown great activity, constantly visiting every part of his charge; he had fearlessly exposed his person under fire, and had made the best disposition of his forces that the circumstances rendered possible.

★★★★★★

His activity and disregard of danger surprised Lord North. "My Lord of Leicester did so notably advise and direct the making of the trenches, a thing I did not look for, I confess; and to view this place he did put himself in danger of musket shot too much." (Letter to Walsingham, May 23, 1586, *State Papers* (Holland), vol. xxxii.)

★★★★★★

He had successfully provisioned Grave; had occupied and fortified a most important strategic position at the junction of the Rhine and Waal; had captured Axell, Doesburg, and the Zutphen Sconces, and had forced Parma to raise the siege of Rheinberg. But he was unfortunate. The misconduct of the governor of Grave led to the loss of that place; and during the winter Sir William Stanley, governor of Deventer, and Rowland Yorke, who held the Zutphen Sconces, both papists, became traitors, and delivered up those places to the enemy. These men were nominees of Leicester, and their treason excited great exasperation against the Earl in the minds of Dutch statesmen. But Leicester undoubtedly displayed zeal and anxiety to perform to the best of his ability the excessively difficult service on which he was employed. He was ready to adopt the advice of military men, and to profit by their experience; and on the whole this first campaign furnished good grounds for hopeful anticipations in the future.

The young volunteers had acquired experience and had seen some service. An official list was framed of those who had been most distinguished, and who were competent to command companies.

******

The names of such gentlemen as I know to be serviceable, and well acquainted with the wars of the Low Countries: Mr. Norris, Mr. Morgan, Colonel Bingham, Rowland Yorke is very valiant, C. Carleille, Captain Salisbury, C. Norris, Captain Huntley, Captain Wilson. The following are all valiant young gentlemen, most sufficient to be lieutenants or cornets to any company, and some able to command any company, W. Powell, Francis Vere, Francis Allen, T. Baskerville, M. Morgan, G. Barton. (S. P. O., Holland, vol. xcv.)

******

In this list the name of Francis Vere appears. He had a zealous friend in Lord Willoughby, and in the autumn of 1586 he obtained a company in the Bergen-op-Zoom garrison. He is entered as captain of a company of 150 men, to receive pay from the 12th of November, 1586. The young captain settled down to garrison duty with several congenial companions, including Francis Allen, the comrade in his journey to Poland. It is here that, for the first time, we obtain a glimpse of his character and disposition; but this period in his history belongs to another chapter, and meanwhile we shall see him winning his first laurels during the memorable siege of Sluys.

CHAPTER 8

Sluys

The Duke of Parma resolved to open the campaign of 1587 with the siege of Sluys. He accordingly assembled his army at the city of Bruges on the 8th of June, consisting of the pick of the Spanish infantry and regiments from Italy, commanded by the Marquis del Vasto, Camillo Capizucca, and Carlo Spinelli. The Italians had been recruited chiefly in Urbino and the Romagna. In order to deceive the enemy, Parma sent the marquis with the Sieur de Hautepenne to make a diversion in the direction of Bois le Due. This drew off a large force under Count Hohenlohe, who fought a successful action, in which Hautepenne was slain and the fort of Crevecoeur, on the Maas near Bois le Duc, was captured. Still the duke gained his object by scattering the forces of the enemy. He then prepared for the investment of Sluys, having first garrisoned a fort at Blankenburg near the seacoast, to check any advance from Ostend.

Arnold de Groenvelt, the valiant old Dutch governor of Sluys, sent a pressing letter to Sir William Russell, at Flushing, for troops and provisions. Grain was rapidly collected, and a ship-load reached the threatened town in safety. Troops were assembled from Bergen-op-Zoom and Flushing, which also arrived before the approaches were closed, making up the garrison to 1,600 men. They entered Sluys on the 12th of June under the leadership of Roger Williams, the principal officers being Nicolas and Adolf Meetkerk and Charles de Heraugière, commanding the Dutch contingent, and Thomas Baskerville, Francis Vere, Francis Allen, Huntley, Hart, and others at the head of the English troops.

Sluys was once the seaport of the great commercial emporium of Bruges, and the changes which in the course of centuries have taken place in the surrounding region are most remarkable. Five hundred years ago there was a long arm of the sea, called the Old Zwin, which connected Bruges with the port of Sluys, and reached the mouth of the Scheldt between the islands of Cadzand and Breskens. Later, a new channel was formed to the west of Cadzand, called the New Zwin, or Sluische Gat. These islands, and others formed by branch channels, were originally small, but the land continually gained on the water, and by 1528 there were as many as a dozen polders won from the waters of the Zwin. Still, in the fourteenth century the width of the channel at Sluys was 465 yards.

Richly laden fleets discharged their cargoes, which were brought up to Bruges in barges, and in 1468 as many as 150 merchant ships came up to Sluys in one tide. These green islands at the mouth of the Scheldt, with their winding channels, have been the scenes of stirring events, both in peace and war. When, in 1337, the Count of Flanders garrisoned Cadzand with a number of knights and their retainers, with the object of harassing the allies of England, Edward III. sent a small force, in ships from the Thames, to dislodge them. The English vessels ranged up close to the land, and a volley of arrows was discharged at the Flemish troops before the English landed, under the lead of the Earl of Derby and Sir Walter Manny. There was then a desperate hand-to-hand combat, in which the English were victorious. They took and pillaged the town of Cadzand, and returned in triumph to the Thames. In midsummer of 1340 there was a more memorable battle before Sluys.

The French fleet of upwards of 120 large ships, under the command of Sir Hugh Quiriel, was cruising off the coast, between Sluys and Blankenburg, when Edward III. embarked for Flanders. When the king's fleet reached the opposite shore they saw so many masts in front of the town of Sluys that it looked like a wood. Edward was told that those were the ships whose crews had burnt his good town of Southampton, and had taken his large ship the *Christopher*. The king replied that he had long wished to meet with them, and that now, please God and St. George, he would fight them. The English sailed boldly up the Zwin, the archers and crossbow-men shot with all their might at each other, and the battle raged fiercely. The *Christopher*, which led the van, was recaptured, but the English were hard pressed, as the enemy's ships were far more numerous and were gallantly fought.

The English were at length completely victorious, and not a single French ship escaped. King Edward remained on board all night, and landed at Sluys, with his nobles, on midsummer day. He then went on foot to our Lady of Aardenburg, to return thanks for the victory, which shows that there was continuous land, unbroken by water-channels, between Sluys and Aardenburg at that time, (Froissart).

Sluys was also the scene of festive receptions in the days of the Dukes of Burgundy. Hither the Princess Isabella of Portugal had come, in 1429, on her way to those splendid nuptials in honour of which Philip instituted the order of the Golden Fleece. Again, in June, 1468, Margaret of York, the fair sister of Edward IV., with her ladies and attendants, was conveyed in a fleet of sixteen vessels to the port of Sluys. Here she had her first interview with Charles the Bold, and rested for a week before proceeding in her barge to Damme, where the marriage ceremony was performed. Those were the most prosperous days for Sluys; but in the following century it was still a place of some trade, and was fortified, though not very efficiently. A wall and wide moat surrounded the town, and at the north end there was a citadel connected with the town by a long bridge, which also had to be defended; making altogether a line of defences nearly two and a half miles round.

The castle, surrounded by a wide moat, was connected with the town by a bridge. Along the northwest side of the town several gates opened on a wharf, where ships were loaded and unloaded in the Zwin, and bridges led across an inner moat to the town gates. Nearest the castle was the St. George Gate, and the others were the St. Anne, St. John, St. Jacob, and St. Nicholas Gates, and the Gate of our Lady. Then came the haven, a channel leading from the Zwin into the town; and at the angle farthest from the castle there was a great round tower rising from the river. The West Gate opened on a bridge which crossed the moat at the extremity of the town farthest from the castle. In this part of the walls there were extensive cellars under the ramparts, for storing wines arriving for the merchants of Bruges, and a windmill stood on the bastion flanking the bridge. On the eastern face were the South and East Gates, and a postern by the *Verloren* sluice, (waste sluice), where the water of the haven found its way to the moat. A dike from the East to the West Gates divided the moat into two channels.

The walls of Sluys enclosed a considerable space, occupied by fields and gardens, besides the houses, and seven windmills stood on the ramparts. The town was then a busy place, with numerous large houses and public buildings, and three open spaces used for markets. Above the roofs rose the towers of the church of Our Lady and of St. John, that of the Gray Friars, and the handsome tower of the town hall, which still remains. There were guilds of merchants and artificers,

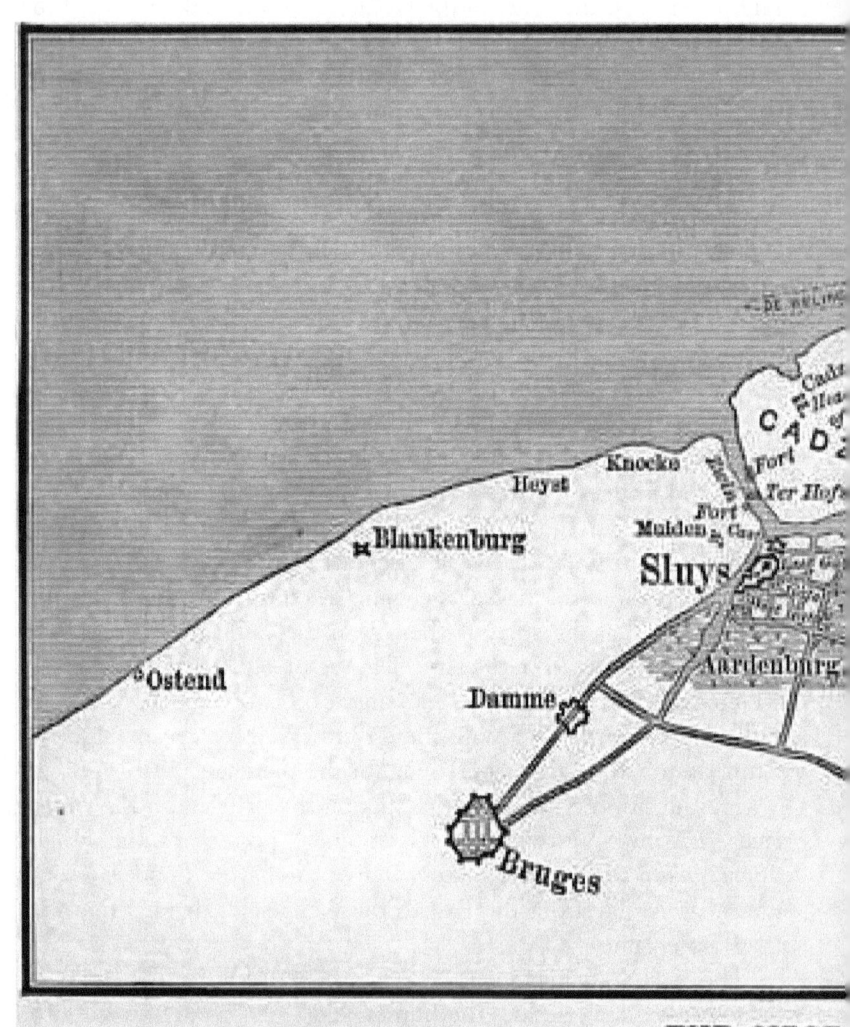

THE SIEGE

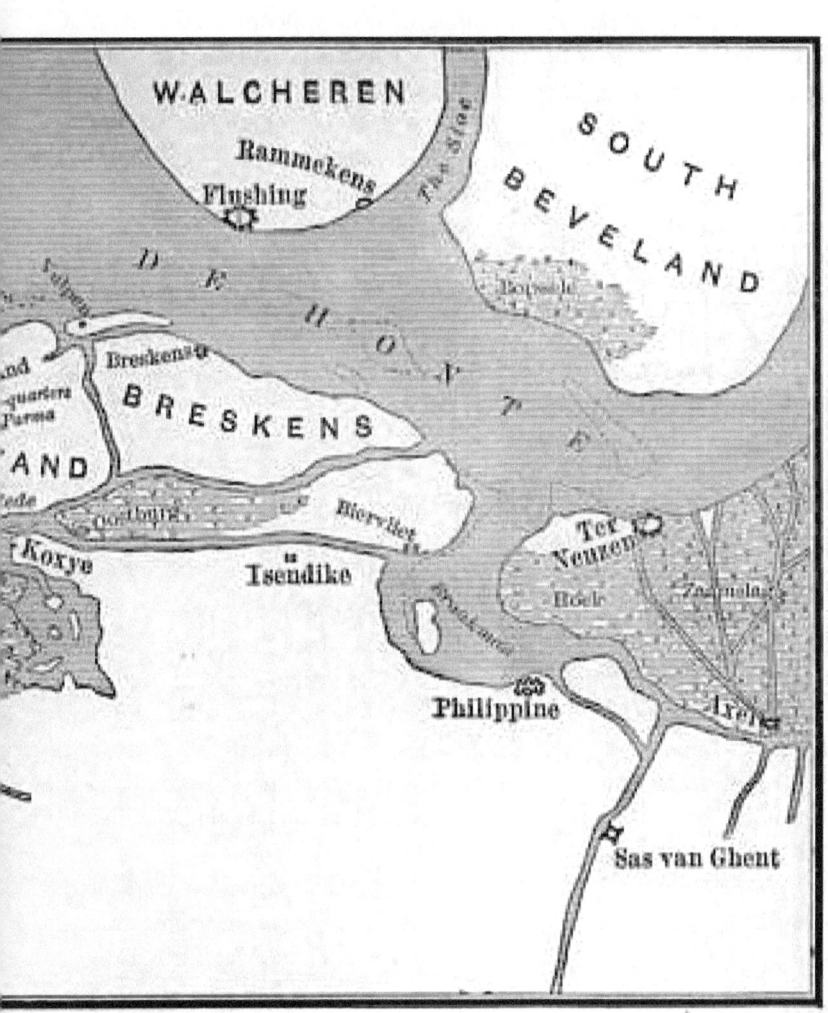

OF SLUYS.

houses and ranges for crossbow practice, and several inns for the entertainment of strangers. The people were Protestant, and had warmly embraced the cause of freedom.

If the brave Dutch governor had been left to himself, he could not possibly have held out against the army of the Duke of Parma. It was therefore with feelings of grateful joy that he welcomed the arrival of ships from Flushing with reinforcements and provisions. Good men and true landed at the haven, raising the garrison to 1,600 men. Roger Williams had already seen many years of campaigning, and his deeds of reckless bravery had won him renown far and wide.

******

He is worth his weight in gold, no more valiant than wise, and of judgment to govern his doings. (*Leicester Letters.*)

******

Cheerful and sanguine, Williams inspired others with his own confidence, while he drove away care and despondency by his animal spirits and jovial conversation.

******

I wish you sometimes to hear Sir Roger Williams in his satirical humour, which maugre your greatest pain would make you heartily to laugh. (*Letter to Anthony Bacon*, in Birch.)

******

Thomas Baskerville and Huntley had, like Williams, been engaged for several years in the wars. But Captain Francis Vere, and his companions Sir John Scott, Sir Edmund Uvedale, Allen, Hart, Shott, Merrick, St. Leger, Foulke, and Ferdinando Gorges, were about to win their first laurels in the defence of Sluys. Dutch and English were both fully resolved to make a desperate resistance, and they worked hard at the defences during the respite which the enemy gave them while he was preparing for the siege.

We have seen that the Duke of Parma had detached his Italian troops, with one Spanish *tercio* under Manuel de Vega, to make a diversion, under the command of Hautepenne and the Marquis del Vasto. This left him a force of 6,000, (Carnero and Herrera), men with which to commence the siege of Sluys. Among them were the two most renowned regiments in the Spanish service, the *tercio viejo*, commanded by Don Juan de Castilla, and a *tercio* under Juan de Aguila, (Herrera, *lib. iii. cap. i.*). The rest of the besieging force consisted of Walloons and Germans. Williams enumerates the enemy as composed of 52 companies of Spaniards, 4 regiments of Walloons, 24 cornets of horse, 1 regiment of Burgundians, a number of boats with munitions, and most of the mariners of Dunkirk. (Roger Williams to the Queen, 2 June, 1587).

Having masked Ostend by garrisoning the fort of Blankenburg, Parma occupied the island of Cadzand during the last week of May, 1587, where he established his headquarters. His object was to place himself between Sluys and the sea, and to secure a point of vantage whence to prevent any attempt at relief. His cavalry watched the coast whence the towers of Flushing were in sight, patrolling the Cadzand shore from the mouth of the Zwin to Breskens. The first operation of the besieging general was to block up the approach to Sluys from the sea. A battery of six guns was mounted at Hofstede, on the west side of Cadzand Island, and another on the opposite side of the Zwin, while boats were moored, head and stern, right across the stream. The preliminary measures were watched with great anxiety by the garrison, Captains Hart and Allen twice gallantly swimming out to communicate with friendly vessels in the Scheldt, before the channel was finally closed.

Having effectually blocked the only way by which succour could come from Flushing, the Duke of Parma began the regular siege works. The dikes had been cut and the open country inundated, so that it was difficult to occupy positions whence to approach the walls, or on which to form a camp. Houses were built of wood, strengthened with bags of earth brought from a distance; but, owing to the frequent and determined sorties of the garrison, there were heavy losses while the camp was being formed. Parma's first efforts were directed against the castle forming the northern extremity of the works, and connected with the town by a long bridge. After working hard at trenches for many days, and battering from the other side of the Zwin, the castle became untenable. Brave Arnold de Groenvelt saw that the enemy might easily destroy the bridge of boats, and so cut the defenders of the castle off from the town. He also reflected that he had to guard the town, which was a hundred times more important than the castle. So, after long and careful consultation with his officers, it was resolved to abandon the castle, after removing artillery and warlike stores, and to concentrate their efforts on the defence of the town.

Next day the enemy moved his siege-pieces, and opened fire on the walls. Parma determined to make his approaches by the west port, where there was more solid ground on which to plant batteries than on the eastern side. The garrison continued to make desperate sorties,

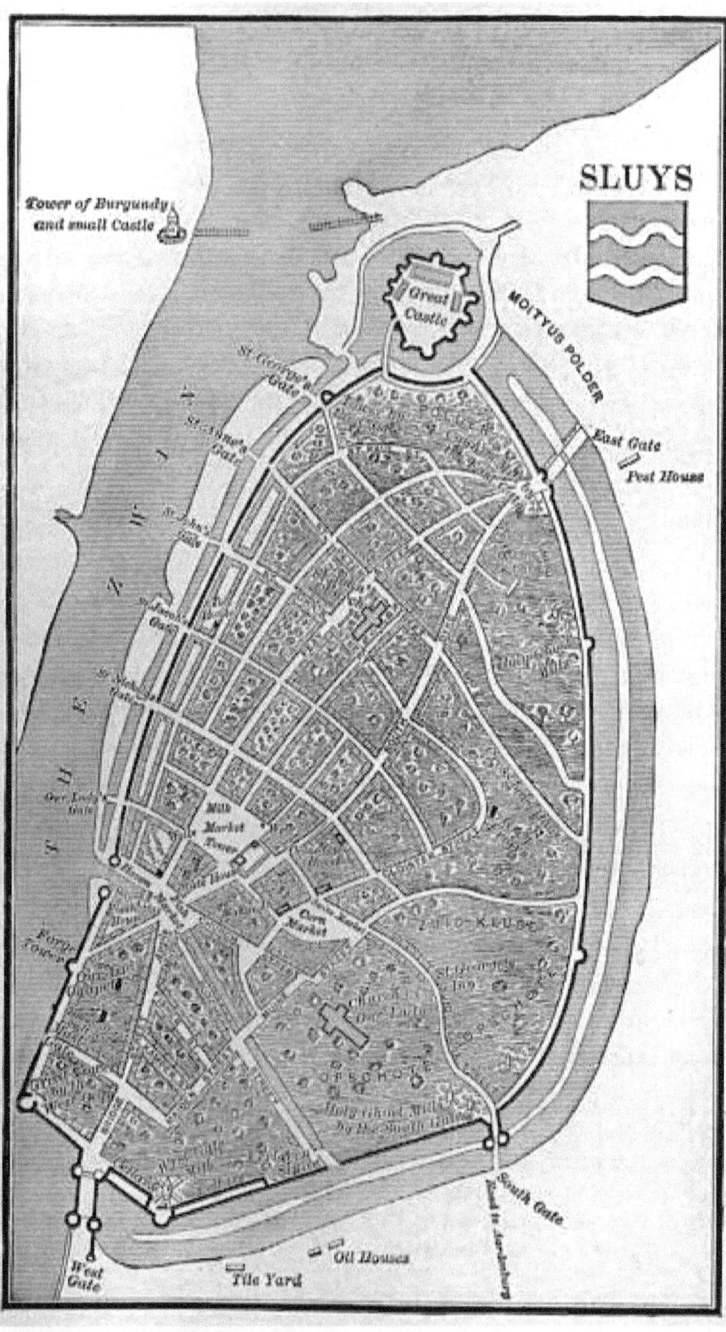

but eventually the Spanish infantry got possession of the dike which divided the moat into two channels, and were thus close under the ramparts. Groenvelt made an effort to dislodge the besiegers. Sallying out of the south gate, the gallant English and Dutch assaulted the west dike. But the Spaniards were already entrenched 500 strong, and were constantly reinforced by boats from the Zwin. After a desperate struggle with pike and arquebus, the garrison retreated at great risk, returning by the south gate.

A furious cannonade was then commenced, with thirty cannon and eight culverins. The great fusillade was on St. James's day, when 4,000 shots were fired between three in the morning and five in the afternoon. At length a breach 250 paces long was made in the wall, and a bridge of large boats was constructed from the west dike to the foot of the rampart. This service had already cost the duke hundreds of his soldiers, forty of his bravest sailors, and several valuable officers. The Marquis de Renty, a Flemish nobleman, had charge of the trenches until he was wounded; next a Spanish officer named Mota took command, but he was disabled by having an arm shot away.

Count Charles de Mansfelt succeeded, and was also badly wounded; and finally Don Bartolomè de Torralva, a Spanish veteran, came to the front. There was necessarily much danger, owing to the exposure, for there was great want of earth to make entrenchments, the surrounding country being flooded. The Duke of Parma at last caused wooden engines to be built of bullet-proof planks, on wheels, and about six feet high, behind each of which four men could work. The breach was made along the rampart from the west gate, and an assault was organised, which was to be delivered against the ravelin, under which were the wine-cellars.

The garrison had not been idle. They had worked day and night, making incessant sorties, and had constructed a half moon round a windmill, as a second defence in rear of the threatened ravelin. They now braced themselves to receive and hurl back the assault. The Spaniards were led by Domingo de Idiaquez, of the gallant San Sebastian family, Antonio Gomez, and Juan Bravo. They rushed up the breach with desperate energy, and were encountered by a line of pikes. Hurled back again and again, they still came on. Alternately, and day by day, there were cannonades and assaults, the whole being arranged with great care by Don Juan de Aguila, the *maestro de campo*, and his colleague, Juan de Castilla. They advanced slowly and step by step, until at last the ravelin and west gate were carried. But their work was only commencing.

Now it was that the valour and endurance of the defenders were to be tested to the uttermost They were face to face with the cream of the Spanish infantry, the renowned *tercio viejo*. There was scarcely anything between them,—an open breach and some hurriedly constructed earthworks on the rampart. There was no rest day or night, but incessant fighting. Meals were brought up to the ramparts, for there were no reliefs, and no one could be spared to go into the town. Furious assaults were as furiously repulsed with pike, sword, and curtle-axe. Ever foremost in the fray was Roger Williams, leader of the English, with Baskerville and Francis Vere. Day after day, and in fight after fight, the Spaniards saw the white plumes of Baskerville and the crimson mantle of Vere in the thickest of the battle; and time after time the enemy fell back before them. Twice was Francis Vere wounded, but he was not disabled. Roger Williams urged him to retire, but the gallant young soldier replied that "he would rather be killed ten times in a breach than once in a house." (Grimeston). The defenders were reduced from 1,600 to 700 men, and for eighteen days the survivors never left the breach.

The Duke of Parma despaired of forcing a way through the living wall which supplied the place of the rampart he had taken. He observed with admiration the valour of the heretics, and especially of the leaders with the white plumes and the red mantle. He saw that within the walls of Sluys there were soldiers who were even a match for the *tercios* of Spain. He resolved to proceed by sap, which, though a longer and more tedious, was a surer way of capturing the place. Mines were driven through the outer walls, and counter-mines were made by the garrison, led by Captain Uvedale. The miners and counter-miners found themselves in the great cellars, where there were fierce encounters while the battle was also raging overhead. The enemy could refresh and relieve their men daily, but the same defenders had to work continuously day and night.

Arnold de Groenvelt had exhausted his powder. His artillery was disabled. His garrison was so reduced that half the walls were left undefended. He beheld a fresh force of the enemy, embarked in forty large boats on the Zwin, and about to land on the wharf near St. John's Gate, which was unprotected. Endurance had reached its utmost limit; and at length the governor was obliged to open a parley with the enemy on the 2nd of August, the very day on which a fresh Spanish regiment marched into camp under Juan de Vega. The Duke of Parma, full of admiration at the extraordinary gallantry of the defence, granted most honourable terms. The garrison was to march out with all their baggage and arms, matches lighted, and colours displayed. They were to proceed to Breskens, whence they were to embark for Flushing. The Duke of Parma entered Sluys on the 4th of August. He asked Roger Williams to introduce him to Baskerville, whom he embraced, declaring that no prince in Christendom was served by a braver soldier.

★★★★★★

Sir Thomas Baskerville was the son of Henry Baskerville, of Hereford. In 1589 he went with Lord Willoughby to France, and afterwards commanded troops in Picardy. He died of fever at Picquigny on the Somme, on June 4, 1597, and was buried in St. Paul's Cathedral. The monument to his memory was destroyed in the great fire of 1666. By his wife Mary, daughter of Sir Thomas Throckmorton, he had a son Hannibal, born at St. Valery, in Picardy, on April 5, 1597, only two months before his father's death. He lived at Sunningwell, in Berkshire, where he led a charitable but very eccentric life, and died in 1668. He married his cousin Mary, daughter of Captain Nicholas Baskerville, by whom he had sixteen sons. One son, Thomas, was an antiquary, and died in 1720.

★★★★★★

Williams wrote a report, containing generous but well-deserved praise of his comrades. The Dutch, he said, were constant, resolute, and valiant, especially those brave captains Meetkerk and Heraugière. The English officers received warm commendation from their veteran chief. But their highest acknowledgment was from their noble enemy. Parma declared that he had lost more men before Sluys than he did during the previous campaign before Neuss, Venlo, Grave, and Rheinberg put together.

★★★★★★

The accounts of the siege of Sluys, from the Spanish side, are contained in the narratives of Strada, Bentivoglio, Herrera, and Carnero. On the English side are the letters and reports of Roger Williams in the *Cotton MSS.* (Galba, c. viii., ix., x., xi.), and in Grimeston's work. Meteren also gives a narrative of the siege; and the official report of Arnold de Groenvelt, governor of Sluys, with a rough sketch map of Parma's defences on the Zwin, is in the State Paper Office, (Holland, vol. xlv., dated

August 26, 1587.) There is an engraved plan of Sluys of the date 1588, "*Slusa teutonicae Flandriae opp. admodum elegans,*" and an engraved view of the town taken from the Zwin; also a plan of Sluys and the surrounding channels, made to illustrate the siege of 1604.

✶✶✶✶✶✶

Queen Elizabeth attached great importance to the retention of Sluys, and pressed forward measures for its relief. It was known that Philip II. was preparing a gigantic expedition for the conquest of England. Parma was to embark an invading army, and both Sluys and Ostend would be important points at which to collect his forces. Unfortunately the Earl of Leicester was on bad terms with the States, owing to the treason of Stanley and the loss of Deventer, and on other grounds. There was an absence of that cordial cooperation which alone could insure success. Leicester, however, left England in June, with supplies of money and reinforcements.

✶✶✶✶✶✶

All the young noblemen and courtiers longed to share the glory of defending Sluys. An example of this ardour is shown in Robert Cary's *Memoirs*. He says that the young Earl of Essex stole from court, after Sluys was besieged, with intent to get into the town if he could. The queen sent her cousin, Robert Cary, after him, with orders to use the best means he could to persuade him to return to court. Cary found him at Sandwich, and with much ado got him to return. As they were riding post back, Cary stayed a little behind the earl, and when Essex was out of sight he returned to Sandwich. The Earl of Cumberland was there, and had provided a small bark, in which he and Cary embarked to go to Sluys. When they came off Ostend they got into the ship's boat and pulled to the shore, only to receive news of the surrender of Sluys. Cary remained with his brother in the Ostend garrison for some time, and then went with him to Bergen-op-Zoom, where he passed the summer, returning to England at Michaelmas. He was created Earl of Monmouth by James I. His autobiography was published in 1759, from a manuscript belonging to the Earl of Cork.

✶✶✶✶✶✶

Sir William Pelham followed with more troops and numerous volunteers.

✶✶✶✶✶✶

Among them was Francis Markham (brother of Gervase, the writer on farming, farriery, and gardening), who was then twenty-one years of age. He served with Sir William Pelham until his death, and afterwards he continued his military studies under Sir Francis Vere. They resulted in the publication of a work which contains the best treatise on the duties of the various officers of an army in those days. (*Five Decades of Epistles of War*, by Francis Markham. London, folio, 1622.)

✶✶✶✶✶✶

After the siege had lasted seven weeks, Prince Maurice and his half-brother, Justin of Nassau, collected transports at Flushing, and Leicester embarked for Ostend with twenty-five companies of foot and six cornets of horse. He marched towards Sluys, and laid siege to the fort at Blankenburg. The duke advanced against him, and, despairing of success, Leicester withdrew to Ostend, and gave up the attempt. Another scheme for attacking the besiegers on the Flushing side was also abandoned. On the 29th of June Roger Williams sent out a note to Leicester, written on a narrow scrap of paper, which reached its destination. He wrote:

> Let Lord Willoughby and Sir William Russell land right against Cadzand with 4,000 men. Here are valiant captains and valiant soldiers that had rather be buried in the place than be disgraced in any point that belongs unto (rest illegible).

But the pilots of Flushing discouraged the project, and it was given up. Sluys was lost after one of the most gallant defences recorded in history.

The Earl of Leicester returned to England in November, and resigned his command on December 17, 1587. (He died at Cornbury Park, in Oxfordshire, on September 4, 1588). Sir William Pelham died at Flushing on November 24th. Lord Burgh succeeded Sir Thomas Cecil as governor of Brill on February 6, 1588. Sir Robert Sidney (Sir Philip's brother) became governor of Flushing, in succession to Sir William Russell, with Captain N. Errington in command of Rammekens, on June 27, 1589, and Sir John Conway was governor of Ostend. Few public men have been assailed with more indiscriminate abuse than the Earl of Leicester, especially by modern historians. He was not an estimable character, but the detraction has been overdone, and on some points his memory has been unjustly treated. On his resignation Prince Maurice was chosen Governor of the States and General of their forces, and Lord Willoughby succeeded as General of the English auxiliary army.

Sluys remained in the power of the Spaniards for twenty years, when it was retaken by Prince Maurice. From that time the water became shallower, and the town gradually lost its trade. In 1715 only very small craft could reach it, and in 1756 Bruges lost this fluvial highway to the sea. The very name of Zwin was forgotten. In 1812 Napoleon finished a canal from Bruges to Sluys, which was dug by Spanish prisoners of war. The old channels were filled up, and in 1872 a polder was formed right across the mouth of the Zwin. There was a marvellous change. The flourishing seaport, once the great *entrepôt* of Flemish trade, became a small agricultural town. Where there were once arms of the sea and swamps there are now rich pastures and waving cornfields. Yet the *enceinte* of the old walls can still be traced, and the landmarks of former greatness are clearly recognizable. The old town hall, with its picturesque tower, is still standing. Tall trees conceal its walls on the side facing the open square, but on the other side there is an ornamental façade with six windows. The interior contains an interesting collection of books and curiosities relating to Sluys.

★★★★★★

They were collected and arranged by J. H. van Dale, keeper of the Sluys archives, and author of *Een Blik op de vortning der Stad Sluts en op den aanleg haven vestingwerken van* 1382 door 1587 (Middelburg, 1871). Among the books in this collection are *Het Casteel van Sluis*, etc., by H. A. Callenfels (Zierikzee, 1844), a manuscript list of inscriptions on tombs in St. John's churchyard at Sluys, made in 1811, and an account of Sluys published by J. Bageleat, at Dordrecht, in 1749. There are also the arms of Sluys carved in stone, and painted on wood, remains of former grandeur; two iron balls and a Spanish sword, dug up at the West Gate in 1875; a fine stone boss, consisting of two angels with the pyx and vine leaves, probably from the old church; seals of the Church of Our Lady and of the smiths' guild at Sluys; a manuscript volume, curiously illustrated, containing the ordinances and statutes of the Sluys guilds; and a collection of coins and medals.

★★★★★★

The great Church of St. John has entirely disappeared. It was burnt down in 1811. The Church of Our Lady is also gone. But there is much remaining of the West Port and other works memorable for the scenes of the gallant defence. The vast mass of brick-work was too solid to remove without great labour and expense. There are the walls of the entrance with grooves for a portcullis, vaulted passages on either side, and a spiral staircase leading to the cellars. Tall rows of elm-trees mark the line of the walls; but the castle has disappeared, a mound indicating the site. It was dismantled by the French, after Moreau took the place in 1794, and the walls were removed in 1820.

The old haven remains, (1878), and communicates with the new canal to Bruges. But it is strange to reflect that those rich crops and pastures full of cattle and horses occupy the site of the Zwin with its crowded lines of shipping. The view from the grassy ramparts, along which there is a pleasant shady walk, extends over a bright green country, with the farms and villages of Cadzand, embosomed in trees, on the horizon. This happy change is due to the final triumph of the good old cause for which Francis Vere struggled so valorously on the ramparts of Sluys, just three hundred years ago, (1588).

******

There is a map of the fortifications of Damme and Sluys on the staircase of the town hall at Bruges, drawn by Jacques Lobbrecht in 1660. But these fortifications were, for the most part, constructed in the seventeenth century, so that the plan does not furnish a guide for the study of the siege of Sluys in 1587.

******

Chapter 9

Bergen-Op-Zoom

The siege of Sluys made Francis Vere famous. When he was mentioned it was as "young Vere who fought at Sluys," or as "Captain Vere, one of the defenders of Sluys." Robert Cecil, in speaking of the officers whose acquaintance he made at Ostend in 1588, says:

> There be many tall gentlemen, especially Captain Francis Vere that was in Sluys, who is a very proper man, and was as ready to have shown me any courtesy as I could have desired it.—R. Cecil to Lord Burleigh, March 10, 1588.

He served with Lord Willoughby in the field until the troops went into winter-quarters, and he was at Arnhem in September, 1587, whence his earliest letter that I have met with was sent to Lord Willoughby.

******

> Dated September 19, 1587. Vere encloses a letter which he had received from the traitor Stanley, saying that his attempts to corrupt officers or men by bribes or "persuasion of his traitorous religion must be carefully watched." The request which Stanley makes in this letter is that Vere will deliver up an outlying fort of which he was in charge. Vere adds: "I would have come to your Excellency myself, but that he, hearing of my sudden departure (as no doubt that he hath correspondence with some papists of the town), might doubt that, I had disclosed his wicked intent." (British Museum, *Cotton MSS.*, Galba, D, 11, 71.)

******

On the retirement of the Earl of Leicester in November, 1587, the queen selected Lord Willoughby to succeed him. Willoughby had shown that he was a good diplomatist and a valiant soldier, but he felt himself to be unequal to the difficult and thankless duty that was thrust upon him. The States were discontented with the English alliance, begrudged the supply of provisions, and were constantly at cross-purposes with their allies. It was Willoughby's belief that the numbers and condition of the army rendered it quite unequal to cope with the Duke of Parma, and he looked forward to nothing but disaster and disgrace for its commander. He at least felt himself to be unequal to the task of doing his country good service in the face of such perplexities and difficulties. He entreated Walsingham to get him excused, if possible. He recommended several officers as far better able to fill the post, mentioning Sir John Norris, Sir William Pelham, Sir Richard Bingham, or Lord North. But it was of no avail.

The queen would not excuse him, and his commission was signed on the 10th of November, 1587. He was styled "*Locum tenens Dux generalis totius exercitus et copiarum.*" He assumed command on the 4th of December, and the States, at the same time, made Prince Maurice Governor of Holland and Zeeland and General of their armies, who thus became the colleague of the English general, with superior rank. The Queen nominated a war council to advise Lord Willoughby, consisting of the veteran Sir William Read, Sir William Russell, the governor of Flushing, Captain Errington, the commandant of Rammekens, and Captain Wilford, who was in garrison at Bergen-op-Zoom, and had been Leicester's sergeant-major general.

Lord Willoughby received a supply of money equal to £10,000, which enabled him to pay the troops, leaving a small sum in hand. The pay of a company, including officers, was £220 a month. There were many abuses, and proper checks were often wanting. It was also very difficult for the queen's government to furnish the necessary supplies of money and stores as they were required. But the statements of modern historians on this subject are grossly exaggerated. They quote from the gossiping news-letters of diplomatists at the Hague, instead of relying upon the reports of responsible officials. The state of affairs at this time is very clearly explained by Mr. Digges, the muster-master general. He admits that the abuses were many, and most subtilely contrived. (*State Papers* (Holland), vol. liv.).

> Many bands of 150 were not able to muster sixty, and those in such poverty and misery as was lamentable to behold; and yet *Her Majesty during all that time paid full and complete without any check.*

He is speaking of the times before the arrival of the Earl of Leicester. Afterwards he says that discipline and order were established in the musters, and there were allowances for supporting commissaries in all the garrisons. In a short time the companies were brought up to their full complement, and well armed and equipped. He added that there had been a falling off since Lord Willoughby took command; but he attributed this to a reduction in the number of his deputies and clerks, anticipating that with a proper staff he could insure a restoration of efficiency. The difficulties were very great, and there were self-seekers among the officers; but there were many loyal men who worked for their country's service with single-minded zeal, and devoted all their energies to securing the efficiency of their companies, which included the wellbeing and comfort of their men.

Among these good men and true, none was more devoted to his profession and to his country's service than the general's cousin, Francis Vere. His company formed part of the garrison of Bergen-op-Zoom, where he was destined to pass the winter of 1587-88, and the greater part of the ensuing year. Among his most intimate comrades at this time there were several officers who gained distinction in the queen's wars. Thomas Baskerville, with whom he had fought side by side on the ramparts of Sluys, belonged to an old Herefordshire family. Edmund Uvedale, or Udall, came from Dorsetshire, of a family allied to the Sidneys. Captains Pooley and Wingfield were neighbours from Suffolk, the latter a cousin of the Veres. Scott had also served at Sluys. Bannaster was a veteran. Salisbury, Blount, Parker, Knowles, Audley, Danvers, and Powell were younger men.

******

> The Uvedales were of More Critchill, a place which in later years became the property of the Napiers and Sturts. Nicholas Udall, born in Hampshire in 1506, was of the same family. He became headmaster of Westminster in 1555, a very learned person mentioned by Strype, who translated the works of Erasmus.
>
> The Pooleys came from Boxted, near Lavenham, in Suffolk.
>
> Having spent many years in the wars, and growing old, Captain Bannaster retired, and went
>
> home in November, 1589.
>
> Salisbury was afterwards suspected of treasonable communication with the enemy. He was a Roman Catholic. *State Papers* (Holland), vol. xliii.

******

These, with the veteran Thomas Wilford, were the messmates and comrades of Francis Vere during many long months of garrison duty at Bergen, and afterwards they shared the glories of its defence. Mr. Bodley reported to Secretary Walsingham that:

> There is not any other garrison in the Low Countries where the captains and companies are more obedient to their governor, at better agreement among themselves, and more at quiet with the burghers of the town.

The fortified town of Bergen-op-Zoom, in Brabant, on the Oster Scheldt, is the key to Zeeland. It commands the channel separating the mainland from South Beveland and Walcheren; and it protects the town of Tholen to the north, which is the key to the islands of Tholen and Schouvven. Its possession was consequently a matter of great importance, and a strong English garrison was prepared to hold it to the last. The name of Bergen-op-Zoom is not derived from a river, as old authors inform us, (Meteren and Bentivoglio), but from a rising ground or hill (berg) called Zoom. It is "the hill at *Zoom*." There is no river, merely a drain passing through the town to the haven. The walls, surrounded by a moat supplied from the Scheldt, enclosed the town in the form of an irregular pentagon, with prolongations on the western side to protect the haven.

The walls were strong, and were provided at intervals with semi-circular towers, four of which were gate towers. On the northwestern side was the Steenberg Gate, leading to Tholen; on the east, the Wouw Gate led to the village and castle of that name on the road to Breda; and the Bosel Gate, on the south side, opened on the road to Antwerp. A fourth gate, called the Oude Poort, led from the town to the haven. It is still standing, and consists of two massive circular towers with pointed roofs, and a pointed archway with two chambers above it. The Oude Poort opens on the haven, which is a canal leading to the Wester Scheldt. The town wall and moat were continued along either side of the haven, and at its junction with the Scheldt there were two important forts, one on each side.

The northern one, called the *Noord Schans*, was small; but the *Zuyd Scha*ns was a larger work, with a moat and bastions, and it was connected with the haven by a small gate called St. Jacob's Poort, with an outlook. The whole tract on the north and south side of the haven was "*Verdroncken Landt*," swampy and overflowed at high tides, so that the water forts at the entrance of the haven could only be approached at low water, and then only by narrow causeways. The view from the site of the water forts takes in a wide expanse of water, with the green line of South Beveland in front, and Tholen, with its massive church-tower surrounded by trees, to the north. Now high dikes keep out the water, the country is pasture sprinkled over with black and white cows, and along the margin of the Scheldt there are extensive oyster-beds. The water forts have disappeared. All is changed.

Bergen-op-Zoom was made a marquisate by Charles V. in 1523, and the *Hof*, or palace, of the marquises is in the street leading from the great square to the Steenberg gate. It is a very large edifice, built round a courtyard, with a great archway, having a groined vaulted roof, leading from the street The court has a monastic appearance. In the gateway there are pillars with capitals carved with foliage, and an arcade gave a cloistral look to the walls. In the rear, there was an extensive fruit and flower garden. It was this "very fair house" and the excellent air of Bergen-op-Zoom which made Sir Philip Sidney wish for the governorship. But, with characteristic unselfishness, he resigned his claim to his friend Lord Willoughby.

In this spacious *Hof* it is probable that the principal English officers of the garrison had their lodgings, while others lived in a street which is still called the English Street; and the great monastery of the Minim Friars, on the north side of the town, had also been converted into an inn or *gasthuis*. In the centre of the town was the great market square, one side of which was formed by the fine old church dedicated to St. Lambert. It is of vast proportions, and its massive tower was a landmark for miles around. The town contained houses of nobles and wealthy merchants, and there were extensive gardens and orchards within the walls. Mr. Bodley reported that "the *burghers* in short time had grown to be very wealthy. Three years ago there were but a thousand souls, now three thousand at the least."

Lord Willoughby had to resign the governorship of Bergen-op-Zoom when he became general, and he appointed Sir William Drury to succeed him. He also begged that Wilford might be lieutenant-colonel of infantry, and Vere sergeant-major. Of Vere he reported:

> Though but young, he hath experience, art, discretion, and valour sufficient to exercise the office.—*State Papers* (Holland), vol. liii.

But his recommendations were not attended to. The queen thought that old Colonel Morgan, who led the very first band of volunteers,

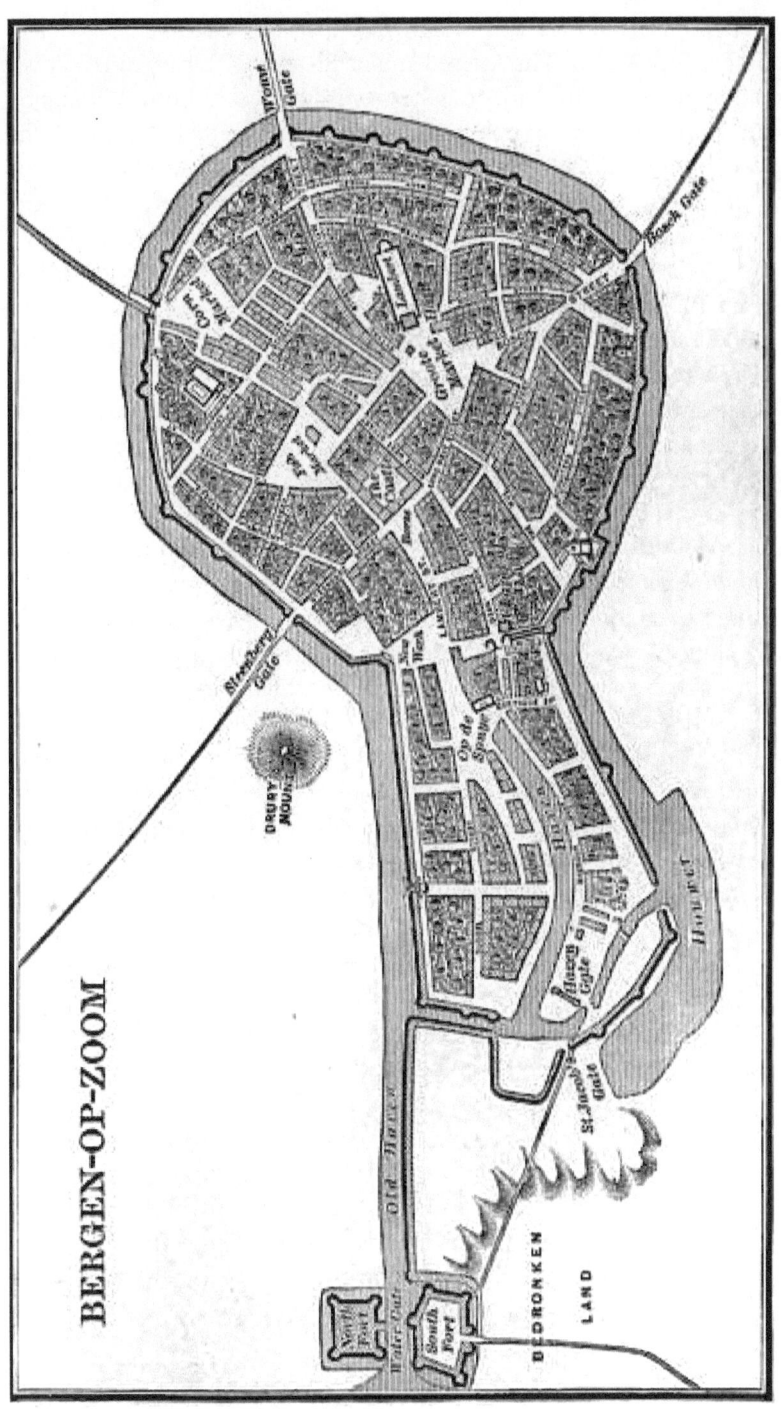

must be provided for, and she ordered that he should be governor of Bergen-op-Zoom. This caused much ill-feeling. Drury was known and respected by the officers, who were also loyal to Lord Willoughby, and Morgan was very unpopular. When he arrived, in May, 1588, he was not very cordially received, and he complained that all the officers were ill disposed towards him. But this was untrue. The officers did not allow their own feelings and wishes to interfere with their public duty. Secretary Walsingham wrote privately on the subject, both to Francis Vere and to Baskerville.

The former replied that he derived singular comfort from the care the Secretary had taken to reconcile him with Colonel Morgan; that what causes he had to dislike the new governor he would pass over in silence and forget; and that no man would obey him more willingly. Baskerville gave Walsingham the same assurance, both in his own name and in that of Captain Uvedale and his other brother officers. The officers of the Bergen garrison set an example of subordination and public spirit. None were on better terms with the townspeople, and none were more vigilant and eager to harass the enemy, which their proximity to Antwerp rendered easy, especially as the Dutch squadrons of cavalry under the brothers Bacx formed part of their force.

Lord Willoughby had spent large sums of his own in the public service, and had mortgaged his estates. He was harassed by demands for troops to be sent to England, and his wife had been obliged to come over to Holland because her straitened circumstances did not allow of her residence at home. In July, 1588, she was on board Lord Willoughby's yacht, off Gertruydenburg, where the garrison was in a state of mutiny, owing to the neglect of the Dutch authorities to pay the soldiers. The general, with much trouble, succeeded in pacifying them for a time.

All eyes were now turned to the mighty Spanish Armada, which was approaching the shores of England. Parma with his army was ready to embark at Dunkirk as soon as the fleet had cleared the Channel of English ships. Men and armour were hastily dispatched from Holland for the reinforcement of the army of defence which was gathering at Tilbury; and Francis Vere was sent to Flushing with 260 men, in readiness for any descent on the coast. The young captain was very anxious to be employed in the defence of his country against the threatened Spanish invasion. Writing to Walsingham, he suggested that:

If news of the Spanish fleet continue it will be very necessary to choose some companies from here, in which number I hope, by your honour's favour, to be one. I would set down a young soldier's opinion as one that sometimes thinketh of those matters, but I dare not presume so far. This much I assure your honour, no man can enter more willingly into that action than myself.

He was instrumental in the destruction of one great Spanish ship. In the end of July the mighty Armada appeared off the Lizard, and beacons flashed the news along the English coast. On the 31st the running action commenced in the Channel; on the 6th of August the Spanish admiral was off Calais, on the 8th his ships were defeated, and on the 10th a furious gale scattered his fleet and drove it into the North Sea. The *San Mateo* grounded between Ostend and Sluys, and Vere was sent out from Flushing to capture and destroy the huge ship.

The defeat of the Spanish Armada was a turning-point in the war. Before that momentous event the Queen had always hoped for peace. Now that hope was gone. There could be no peace without the complete independence of her allies, and from that time she entered heartily upon the war. The last fifteen years formed the most glorious period in her long reign.

Another result of this memorable defeat was that the allies in Holland were immediately placed on the defensive. When the Duke of Parma broke up his camp at Dunkirk, he felt bound to attempt something before he went into winter-quarters, and he determined to undertake the siege of Bergen-op-Zoom. He came to this decision against the advice of the veteran Mondragon and his council of war. Daily raids were made by the Dutch cavalry under Bacx, who captured rich booty and sometimes secured wealthy prisoners. The roads to Antwerp were rendered unsafe by the proximity of the Bergen-op-Zoom garrison, while the capture of the town would place the keys of Zeeland in the duke's hands. For these reasons he persisted in his design in opposition to the opinions of his most experienced advisers.

The Duke of Parma marched through Brabant, sending a regiment of Tyrolese under the Marquis of Burgau, with troops under Count Mansfelt, the Prince of Asculi, and the Duke of Pastrana, in advance. They were to attempt the capture of Tholen, an important town to the north of Bergen-op-Zoom, on the opposite side of the channel separating the island of Tholen from the mainland of Brabant. Lord Willoughby worked hard to put Bergen in a good posture

★★★★★★

Writing to Burleigh, on the 6th of September, he said: "I beseech your Lordship, in all humbleness and earnestness, let some better pylot than I, well acquainted how to face the difficulties of this place, be employed to guide the helme. For I assure your Lordship my skill cannot tell how to stere out of the frith I am left in, which I more willingly endure than the reproche after. It had been and were an enterprize for the greatest souldier to warre against such a power as assayles us, without men or means. But if it tell out well for Her Majesty I would not care. Pray God that I may be deceaved, and that Her Majesty lose not her people, her travayle, and her treasure."

★★★★★★

He constructed two blinds outside the Wouw Gate, to cover the drawbridges and protect sallying parties, and some other outworks, connected by covered ways. In these operations he had the benefit of advice from Count Everard Solms, who came over from Tholen, where he was commanding the Zeeland regiment.

★★★★★★

The muster at Bergen-op-Zoom in September, 1588, was as follows: present, 802; absent, 502; dead pays, 145. Reinforcements were sent from Flushing and Brill on Parma's approach.

★★★★★★

On the 7th of September, 1588, the Duke of Parma arrived in person, and ordered the Marquis of Renty to attempt the capture of Tholen. Count Solms lined the parapet of a dike with his regiment, and opened such a fire on the enemy that they retired with a loss of 400 men. This failure made it impossible for Parma to prevent supplies from coming by sea, unless he could capture the water forts; so he no longer delayed his main object, surrounding Bergen-op-Zoom by land with an army numbering 20,000 men. He had collected gabions, planks, artillery, and boats for the attack on these water forts, and had planted guns on the levee to batter them. On September 14th the garrison sallied from the Steenberg Gate to prevent the besiegers from occupying a position just outside, and, after a hot skirmish, drove them back to their camp.

On the 16th there was another sally, under cover of which powder and stores were brought in from Zeeland; and while the Duke of Parma was reconnoitring the town from the Antwerp side, two of his pages were killed by a shot from the walls. The cavalry, under the brothers Bacx, frequently made sudden charges out of the gates, sometimes extending their incursions as far as Wouw, and taking prisoners. In one of these sorties Francis Vere received a wound in the leg from a pike. (Letter from Bodley to Lord Burleigh, dated October 10, 1587. This letter is in the collection of the Marquis of Bute. Vere himself never mentioned the wound).

******

A castle and village about three miles to the eastward, the intervening country being a wild, sandy heath, now a good deal planted with firs. Wouw is a large village, with very neat, clean houses built round a green planted with rows of trees. The church (in the hands of the Catholics) is of great size, with a tall, square tower. The choir stalls are of elaborately carved oak, and above them are seven carved-oak figures on each side, with most delicately chiselled drapery, lace, and fringes.

******

Among the prisoners there were two commissaries of ordnance, named Pedro de Luco and Tomas Swegoe. They were committed to the safe-keeping of Master Redhead, the deputy provost, who dwelt in English Street. There was a good deal of conversation between the prisoners and the deputy's friends, who often dropped in for a chat. Among these was one William Grimeston, who saw reason to suspect that the pretended Italian, Swegoe, was really an English deserter, who had gone over with the traitor Stanley. In order to draw him out, Grimeston observed that he wished he were fighting on the King of Spain's side, under Sir William Stanley. Then the spy eagerly showed his cards. He told Grimeston and Redhead to be merry and of good cheer, for that he was born in Seething Lane, and he had a sister who attended on my Lady Lumley. He added that, if they would be guided by him, they would be rich men in no time; for that if they arranged to give up a certain fort to the duke, they would be bountifully rewarded.

The first object of the besieging general was to get possession of the water forts; for so long as they were in the hands of the besieged, the garrison could be regularly supplied with provisions. Parma, with the traitor Stanley, had concocted an elaborate scheme for surprising the north fort by treachery; but they were destined to be hoist with their own petard. Lord Willoughby, advised by Count Solms, was fully impressed with the importance of attending to the security of the water forts. He had entrusted the command to one of his most reliable officers, his cousin, Francis Vere. One day, Redhead and Grimes-

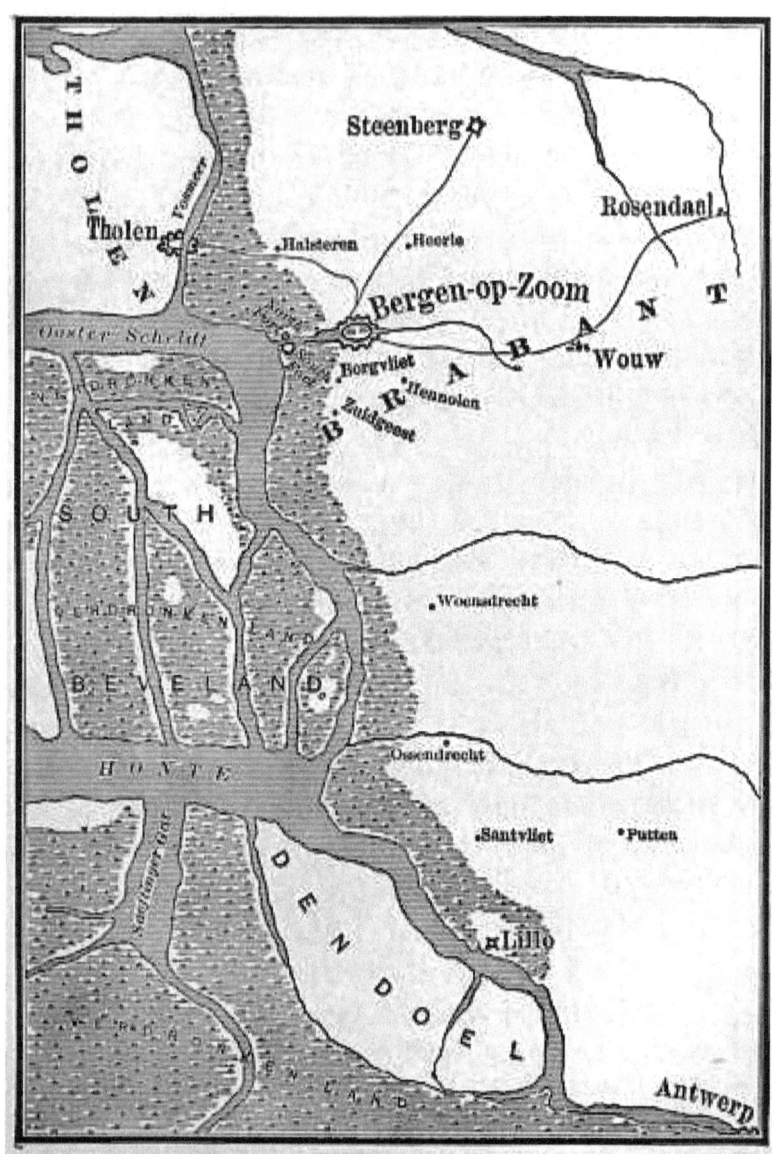

THE SIEGE OF BERGEN-OP-ZOOM.

ton came to Lord Willoughby, and repeated the conversations of the unsuspecting spy. The general approved a plan by which Grimeston should promise to deliver up the northern sconce to Parma, and so decoy the enemy's troops to their overthrow.

The spy wrote letters to the duke and to Stanley, and Redhead, after having first shown them to Lord Willoughby, took them to the enemy's camp. At midnight on Sunday, the 6th of October, both Redhead and Grimeston had an interview with Parma, and promised to deliver up the north fort on the next Wednesday night. Sir William Stanley then took them to his tent, where a banquet was prepared, and two gold chains were sent them from the Duke of Parma. An agreement was made that Robert Redhead should receive 1,200 crowns, and William Grimeston 700 crowns and a commission in Sir William Stanley's regiment of traitors. They then took their leave, returned to Bergen-op-Zoom, and related all that had taken place to Lord Willoughby. He sent them back to induce Parma to agree to a delay of three days, which he considered necessary for making all his preparations. Vere was in the secret, and had everything ready at the north fort.

On the appointed night, the 22nd of October, Grimeston reported himself. He found, to his great alarm, that the Spaniards had become suspicious. He was bound, and led by a captain named Ortiz, with a drawn dagger, ready to stab him if there was treachery. The attacking column consisted of 3,000 picked men, including Stanley's regiment. There were also many volunteer knights. The leader was the *maestro de campo*, Don Sancho de Leyva. With him were Don Juan de Mendoza, (afterwards Marquis of Hinajosa and governor of Milan), Don Alonzo de Idiaquez, (of a San Sebastian family, he was afterwards Viceroy of Navarre), and Sir William Stanley.

It was a dark, gloomy night; but, as they approached, the drawbridge of the north fort was seen to be down, and the portcullis up. It seemed as if Redhead had kept his word. In reality Vere was ready at the portcullis, calmly watching, and Lord Willoughby was there in person, with 2,000 men. It was a veritable mouse-trap. It was low water, for the drowned land over which the Spaniards advanced was flooded at high tide. On they marched, along the causeway, with Grimeston in front, guarded by Captain Ortiz. They crossed the drawbridge, and about fifty had entered, when Vere suddenly let fall the portcullis and the drawbridge was hauled up. At the same moment Grimeston tripped up the heels of Ortiz, and so escaped his avenging dagger. A furious discharge of musketry and artillery from the walls killed 150 of the attacking party, while those inside were quickly slain or taken prisoners.

******

Among the prisoners was Don Inigo de Guevara, afterwards Count of Oñate. He had come to the Low Countries in 1584, when he was very young, to serve under his uncle, Don Pedro de Tassis. His rank was not known to the English, and he got away with a common soldier's ransom.

******

The Spaniards made a gallant but vain assault on the palisades. Meanwhile the tide began to flow, and the soldiers who had easily waded across the moat were washed away and drowned by scores in attempting to return. Never was discomfiture more complete. It practically ended the siege. The Duke of Parma raised his camp on the 12th of November, and returned to Brussels, after a siege which had lasted six weeks.

******

Lord Willoughby had a short journal of the siege kept, which he sent home. *State Papers* (Holland), vol. lvii. There are also accounts of it in Grimeston, Meteren, Bentivoglio, Herrara, and Carnero, and several letters from the officers among the *State Papers* (Holland). See particularly Sir William Russell's account of the stratagem, in a letter to Walsingham. Vol. lviii.

******

Lord Willoughby had achieved an important success and had done the queen good service, in spite of his extreme diffidence. He had done so in the face of many harassing difficulties; and old Colonel Morgan had been a thorn in his side. But he was able to report in terms of the highest praise of all his officers. Writing to Lord Burleigh, he said:

> I could not omit to advertise your Lordship of the particular valour of Sir William Drury, who broke his lance valiantly in the face of the enemy, which, in my judgment, deserves the greater commendation, that with all humility he obeyed Her Highness's command, and yet served her more forwardly than those that received the sweet; (meaning old Morgan). My cousin Vere, Baskerville, and Parker did very valiantly, and, amongst others, I should speak of that noble gentleman, Mr. Wylford, who is lightly shot in the leg.—September 20, 1588. *State Pa-*

pers (Holland), vol. lvii.

The following officers were knighted by Lord Willoughby when the siege was raised: Sir Francis Vere, Sir Thomas Wilford, Sir John Pooley, Sir Nicholas Parker, Sir Thomas Knowles, Sir Edmund Uvedale, Sir John Scott, Sir Charles Danvers, Sir Christopher Blount, Sir John Poore, Paul Bacx, and Marcellus Bacx. Lord Willoughby also wrote in generous but qualified praise of Sir Thomas. Morgan. "A very sufficient, gallant gentleman, and in very truth a very old soldier. For action he is undoubtedly very able, if there were no more means to conquer than to give only blows."

During the time that he was stationed in Bergen-op-Zoom the character of Francis Vere was developed. Hitherto we have only seen him as a valiant soldier, fighting bravely and untiringly, and displaying devotion to duty and great powers of endurance. But at Bergen he appears as a prudent adviser of his general, a cautious commander, and a resourceful contriver of stratagems. His correspondence shows the interest he took in the affairs of his cousin, Lord Willoughby, the intelligence with which he watched the development of diplomatic negotiations, and the good fellowship that existed between himself and his brother officers. It also shows that he was prompt to express disapproval of any conduct that appeared to be unbecoming or selfish. We find him applying to Walsingham on behalf of a young brother of his comrade, Captain Audley, who died at Bergen, and writing strongly to Lord Willoughby respecting the grasping and unofficerlike proceedings of Captain Wingfield.

★★★★★★

Captain Thomas Maria Wingfield had captured a prisoner at the water fort, named Juan de Mendoza. But all the captains had agreed that Lord Willoughby should bestow the prisoners on Redhead and Grimeston, as their reward in managing the whole stratagem, at great risk. Wingfield refused to agree, and complained.

The matter was brought before a council of war, and Lord Willoughby's action was approved. Wingfield continued to address complaints to the Queen's Council, and at last the general deprived him of his company: most justly, in the opinion of Sir Francis Vere. This T. M. Wingfield was a brother of one of the first settlers of Virginia, who for a short time had charge of the colony,

★★★★★★

He also wrote very gratefully to Secretary Walsingham, especially thanking him for his good offices with her Majesty, who had lately spoken graciously of him, "a thing which, above all others, I have most desired and will most carefully seek to deserve." (Vere to Walsingham, 3 Aug. and 21 Aug., 1588. *State Papers* (Holland), vol. lvi.).

The time had now arrived for Sir Francis Vere to obtain leave of absence in England, after a continuous service of three years. He went home with a letter from Lord Willoughby to the Lord Treasurer, dated November 3, 1588:

> I have made choice of my cousin, Francis Vere, as my most sufficientest reporter. If it please your lordship to afford favour of credit, I would in few words say that your lordship with him may boldly trust his speech and easily find the worth of the man.—*State Papers* (Holland), vol. lix.

Thus introduced, Sir Francis made a favourable impression on Lord Burleigh, who introduced him to the queen. Walsingham was already his firm friend, and he had several relations at court. Queen Elizabeth was in the full majesty of her regal greatness. She had reached her fifty-fifth year, and had reigned for thirty years. The halo of success was around her; she was in the flood tide of prosperity, and the centre of devoted and romantic loyalty. As in many other gallant spirits, this feeling, which was practically identical with patriotism, became a passion in the breast of Francis Vere,—a passion the ardour of which continued unabated until the death of the queen.

Such feelings are unknown in these days, (1878). They are not understood, and are therefore ridiculed; but in the time of Elizabeth they were real, and there was neither exaggeration nor affectation in their expression. Having been graciously received by the queen, Sir Francis Vere joyfully turned his face towards his Essex home, and passed a few happy weeks with his mother and sister and his three brothers, at Kirby. When he returned to the theatre of war, in February, 1589, he took his brother Robert with him, intending to get him a cavalry appointment, and eventually a company. The two brothers enjoyed each other's society through the subsequent campaigns, until, six years afterwards, young Robert Vere found a soldier's death on the battlefield.

CHAPTER 10

Resignation of Lord Willoughby

When Sir Francis Vere returned to the Netherlands with his brother Robert, in January, 1589, he was appointed sergeant-major general of the forces by Lord Willoughby, with the full approval of the queen's government.

******

Since my coming over it hath pleased my Lord General to establish me in the office of sergeant-major, a place which divers months since his Honour intended to call me to, but performed no sooner, doubting, as I judge, thatt for my yonge yeares I should nott att home be heald capable of so great a charge. But after I had informed his Lordship of your Honour's favourable inclination to doe me good he presentlie possessed me of the same, wherefore I doe yeald your Honour a great portion of thanckes due for the benefit!, assuring your Honour that nobody shall readyer deserve a good turne than mysealf. (*Francis Vere to Walsingham*, from Middelburg, 24th Feb., 1589. S. P. O., Holland, vol. lxii.)

******

The general had always had a high opinion of Vere's abilities and of his qualifications for command. This view was now shared by the home authorities, and after three years of service, Vere took his place on the staff, in a position second only to the general.

Lord Willoughby continued his earnest solicitations to be relieved of the command, and his representations that his forces were quite unequal to a serious encounter with the army of the Duke of Parma. In 1588 troops had been called away on the approach of the Armada, and now, in 1589, Sir John Norris came over with a commission to arrange with Lord Willoughby for a supply of veterans to man the fleet which he and Sir Francis Drake were equipping for what was known as the "Portugal action." In January, 1589, there were, in the five English garrisons, 6,517 men out of a nominal force of 7,400. (See list following). The annual cost to the queen's government was £150,300.

******

Flushing garrison, 1,732 men, on the list, 2.000; Brill, 852 men, list 950; Ostend, 1,166 men, list 1,350; Bergen-op-Zoom, 1,732 men, list 1,950; Utrecht, 135 men, list 150; cavalry, 900 men, list 1,000: mustered, 6,517 men, list 7,400.

******

The fact was that the queen entertained a very high opinion of the ability, trustworthiness, and valour of Lord Willoughby, and, in spite of his diffidence, she had great confidence in his capacity for command when the moment of action arrived. After the siege of Bergen-op-Zoom was raised she wrote him a letter in her own hand:—

Good Peregrine: Suppose not that your travail and labours are not accepted, and shall be ever kept in good memory.

Such an approving note, in which the queen herself addressed her faithful subject by his Christian name, was a great honour. Men in those days loved their sovereign with romantic ardour. They loved her because she identified herself heart and soul with her people and her country. To love Queen Elizabeth was to love England. The "good Peregrine" of that short note was more than equivalent to a Grand Cross of the Bath in these days.

At length Lord Willoughby obtained permission to return home on leave. He departed in the end of February, and arrived in London on the 14th of March, 1589. His expenses, as general of the queen's forces in the Netherlands, had swallowed up his whole income. He had cut down his woods, pawned his plate and his wife's jewels, and mortgaged his lands in Norfolk. Yet he was still £4,000 in debt.

Sir Francis Vere, as sergeant-major general of the forces, had to take up the threads of Lord Willoughby's difficulties and perplexities, in his absence, and to deal with them as best he could. The greatest trouble was the mutinous conduct of the garrison at Gertruydenburg.

Gertruydenburg was a fortified town on the banks of the old Maas, and about fifteen miles north of the important city of Breda. It was near the channel leading from Zeeland to Dordrecht and Rotterdam, and derived its prosperity from the fishery of sturgeon and salmon. One wall, with water-gates, was, in those days, on the very bank of the river, and the other sides, facing inland, were well fortified; the River Donge sweeping round the southern and eastern faces and forming the moat. The town was built round a long market-place, shaded by trees, with short streets leading to the water-gates, and a tall, square church-tower at the eastern end.

★★★★★★

Gertruydenburg is now a decaying place, with the coehorn ramparts round it, all planted with trees. At present it is a mile from the old Maas, which once bathed its walls. The long market-place has rows of limes trained in front of the houses, with gables rising above them. In the church there is a curious picture of the town, with the date 1616. The broad waters of the old Maas are here shown, washing the town walls, and the great brick church-tower rises above the houses,

★★★★★★

For some years Count Hohenlohe had been governor. He was very unpopular, and the garrison complained bitterly that they received no pay. There had been an outbreak of discontent even before the siege of Bergen-op-Zoom, which had been partially appeased by Lord Willoughby, and he had induced the garrison to receive his brother-in-law, Sir John Wingfield, as their governor.

★★★★★★

Sir John Wingfield had married, as her second husband, Susan Bertie, Countess of Kent, the sister of Lord Willoughby, and he had a son named Peregrine Wingfield, born in Holland. His grandmother was Elizabeth Vere, sister of John, sixteenth Earl of Oxford, which made him a cousin both of Lady Willoughby and of Sir Francis Vere. His grandfather, Sir Anthony Wingfield of Letheringham, in Suffolk, was knighted by Henry VIII. for services at Terouenne and Tournay. He was a Knight of the Garter, and one of the executors of Henry's will.

★★★★★★

In the winter of 1589 the discontent broke out afresh: the soldiers of the garrison had been unjustly treated by the States, there were long arrears of pay, and at first Sir John Wingfield espoused the cause of his men. Sir Francis Vere passed a most anxious time, striving to arrange matters, and visiting Gertruydenburg more than once with this object. But the Dutch authorities were headstrong and unjust. At last the garrison became so exasperated that communications were opened with the enemy. Eduardo Lanzavecchia, the governor of Breda, offered the soldiers all their pay and much more if they would deliver up the place to the Duke of Parma. Prince Maurice was furious. He accused Wingfield of seeking his own profit rather than the public interest, and in March, 1589, he began the siege of Gertruydenburg.

✶✶✶✶✶✶

> Wingfield sent an indignant reply. He wrote, "I will maintain with my sword that it is not true, and that I am a gentleman in my country, and am here in the service of Her Majesty my mistress, and without her I will recognise no other.

✶✶✶✶✶✶

He made an attack on the water side, in flat-bottomed boats, and a furious assault was led by Count Solms and Count Philip of Nassau. But the garrison defended the walls with great resolution. The besiegers were forced to retire, having suffered serious loss, especially among the officers. (Letter from Bodley, March 31, 1589. S. P. O., Holland, vol. xliii.).

The States then applied to Bodley, the queen's agent at the Hague, and he wrote to Sir John Wingfield, requiring him, in Her Majesty's name, to take special care that the town should not fall into the hands of the enemy. A defiant reply came from the mutineers, which showed that the governor was no longer a free agent. Maurice then offered a pardon to all, and on the 5th of April he declared that any demands made by the malcontents would be conceded. It was too late. On the 9th Gertruydenburg was delivered up to the Duke of Parma, Wingfield and the officers being allowed to retire whither they pleased.

The States were naturally furious, but they carried their anger beyond all bounds, and published a slanderous *placcart*, (dated May 10, 1588), denouncing several English officers who were as innocent as they were themselves. The governor, captains, and garrison were all declared to be traitors, and they were to be hanged if at any time any of them were caught. The Dutch authorities even included Sir Francis Vere in their intemperate denunciations. Writing to Walsingham, on April 20, 1589, Vere said that he had been included in the list of alleged traitors.

> I so behaved myself in the first trouble of that town that I deserved rather recompense than blame. I would say these accusations arise from malice against our nation, and to excuse their own rash enterprise which caused the loss of the place. I pray God their malice extend not to prejudice Her Majesty.

On the 13th of May he reported to Walsingham that the States had withdrawn their charge against him. "For me they confess their error, and have razed me out of their list."

Lord Willoughby was very indignant at the libel published by the States against English officers, and especially at the false accusation of treason levelled at Sir John Wingfield, who was an officer of spotless honour and integrity. He was put under arrest by the garrison when they began to treat with the enemy. Lord Willoughby wrote from London:

> As to the proceedings of lewd persons of the States who offer money to kill Her Majesty's subjects as traitors, I hope Her Majesty will not tolerate more for her general and subjects that give their lives for her, than an honourable master would do for an honest private servant, when he is abused and slandered. If this may be suffered let me commend to your honourable wisdom that, amongst so many true English hearts, there mayhap be found such a one as, if these false accusers may not be lawfully punished, will make his revenge with his own hands. We are no subjects to these very traitors and accusers.

The intemperate and unjustifiable character of the proclamation in which the States denounced the English officers fully deserved the indignant protest of Lord Willoughby. But these misunderstandings increased the friction, and rendered the task of his lordship's successor still more difficult.

On May 28, 1589, Lord Willoughby once more sent in his resignation, and it was at length accepted. He submitted that:

> For a general to be without authority, credit, or men is but a dangerous charge to his Sovereign, and an unrecoverable disgrace to himself. For the present numbers that are to be drawn to the field, there is Sir Francis Vere, sergeant-major, able to take charge of twice as many. For them in the towns the governors are most sufficient. For the Council, Mr. Bodley and Mr. Gilpin. Wherefore I pray that I may be called upon to resign my office.

Lord Willoughby was relieved of the command of the queen's forces in the Netherlands, which he had long declared to be a heavier burden than he was able to bear. But his services were still required. He was almost immediately appointed to command a force of 4,000 men, which Queen Elizabeth had resolved to send to the assistance of Henry IV. of France. They landed at Dieppe in September, 1589, and

Lord Willoughby did good and acceptable service in France during several ensuing months. In December the queen honoured him with another letter of sympathy and friendship:—

> My Good Peregrine: I bless God that your old prosperous success followeth your valiant acts; and joy not a little that safety accompanieth your luck.
>
>   Your loving Sovereign,
>
>   Elizabeth R.

In 1597 Lord Willoughby was appointed Governor of Berwick and Warden of the Eastern Marches, and he died at Berwick in June, 1601, in his forty-sixth year.

******

Lord Willoughby has been fortunate in his biographer. His life was written by Lady Georgina Bertie, the wife of one of his descendants (*Five Generations of a Loyal House.* Part 1. *Lives of Richard Bertie, and his son Peregrine Lord Willoughby.* Rivingtons, 1845). This book is charmingly written, and at the same time it has the merit of accuracy. Its accomplished author spared no pains, and the work is based on much careful research.

Lord Willoughby's eldest son was created Earl of Lindsey in 1626, and was slain at the Battle of Edge Hill, fighting on the side of Charles I. His grandson, Montagu, second Earl of Lindsey, was wounded at Edge Hill and Naseby, and died in 1666. He left two sons. The eldest was third Earl of Lindsey, and his son was created Duke of Ancaster and Kesteven in 1715. The second son, James (by his second wife, Bridget, heiress of Lord Norris), became Lord Norris of Rycote, and was created Earl of Abingdon in 1682. He was the first English peer to join William III. on his landing.

******

When Lord Willoughby resigned, a number of veteran officers of distinction were withdrawn from the Netherlands to serve in France or Ireland. Among them were Sir John Norris, Sir Roger Williams, Sir Thomas Wilford, Sir William Drury, Sir Thomas Baskerville, and Sir John Burrough. Any one of these was qualified, as regards length of service, to succeed Lord Willoughby; and they had strong claims. Some of them, Sir John Norris especially, were high in the queen's favour. But the sovereign had watched them closely, and there can be little doubt that she and her ministers had formed definite conclusions with respect to their fitness. Some were deficient in temper, others in judgment and tact, others in grasp of mind and administrative skill. They were still in high favour, and would receive such commands as were suited to their respective capacities. But the command of the troops in the Netherlands was a post requiring rare gifts, not often found combined in one man. It was a position of extreme delicacy and difficulty.

The three previous campaigns had served to bring out the abilities of a young officer who had been fixed upon as the man that was wanted. The withdrawal of so many veterans left the field open to one who was possessed of the very qualifications that were required. There would be no general for some time to come. The governors would continue to command in the cautionary towns. But there would be an officer of approved valour and conduct, enjoying the confidence of his sovereign, who, in spite of his youth, would be the real leader of the English troops. From August, 1589, Sir Francis Vere, with the rank of sergeant-major general, was to be in command of all Her Majesty's soldiers in the field.

Chapter 11

Sir Francis Vere in Chief Command

Relief of Rheinberg

Sir Francis Vere received his appointment from the queen as:

Sergeant-Major, with authority to command as well those soldiers already in the field as those which Her Majesty is intentioned to send during the absence of the lord-general and his lieutenant.

His pay was two florins a day, or £73 a year. (In 1590 increased to "a noble a day for allowances." (S. P. O., Holland, vol. lxxi.) In theory there was still to be a general and a lieutenant-general over the sergeant-major, but those posts were never filled. Vere's official title was "Her Majesty's Sergeant-Major in the Field." The governors of towns with English garrisons had independent commands, and supplied troops for service in the field according to their discretion. But Sir Francis was on excellent terms with them, even with old Sir Thomas Morgan at Bergen-op-Zoom.

******

In September, 1589, complaints against Sir Thomas Morgan were referred to Sir Francis Vere and Sir Robert Sidney. Morgan then wrote that he was "well content: the gentlemen I know both honourable." In 1590 Vere writes: "I am going to Sir Thomas Morgan, to see what troops may be spared from Bergen."

******

His pay was most inadequate, but he received a very encouraging letter from Walsingham, to which he replied, (October 28, 1589):

I received your Honours letter containing the great contentment your Honour had at the hearing of our victories, as also Her Majesty's most gracious conceyte of me, with some hope of better maintenance.

Vere's official position brought him in contact with various elements of antagonism and possible discord, which called for the exercise of tact and caution. There were the queen and her government; there was the government of the States; the English agent at the Hague; Prince Maurice in command of the army; the governors of the cautionary towns; the officers and men of the force under his own command; and lastly the enemy.

Maurice was a young man of three-and-twenty, with experience and military knowledge yet to be gained. He was, however, devoted to martial pursuits and to the cause of his countrymen. He did not impress Robert Cecil favourably when he saw the young prince at Ostend in 1588. Cecil wrote:

> I met with Count Maurice today, in whom is neither outward appearance of any noble mind, nor inward virtue. In my life I never saw worse behaviour, except it were one lately come from school.—To Lord Burleigh, March 10, 1588. S. P. O.

Lord Willoughby had a more favourable impression. He wrote:

> Maurice is young and hot-headed; he hath wit and spirit.—S. P. O., Holland, vol. xlix.

Vere knew him more intimately than either Cecil or Willoughby, and was a better judge. He said:

> His Excellency is worthy to be esteemed, for I hold him to be as rare a young gentleman as is in Europe, and one that may prove a good and able servant to Her Majesty and the States. (*ibid lxx.*) ... He is very likely to grow great. He useth me well, and I am persuaded he desireth much to be well thought of in England.—S. P. O., Holland, vol. lxviii.

Maurice habitually consulted Vere, and relied upon his military skill and judgment; and besides commanding the English contingent, Sir Francis usually acted as marshal of the camp for the whole of Maurice's army.—Bodley. S. P. O., Holland, vol. lxxiii.

Among the Dutch statesmen, Barneveldt was always very friendly to Vere, and showed confidence in his generalship. But at first the commander of the troops looked to the queen's agent at the Hague for advice and guidance in his dealings with the States. This was Sir Thomas Bodley, who became the queen's envoy at the Hague, and was admitted as one of the States Council, in accordance with the treaty, in 1588.

******

Thomas Bodley was born at Exeter, March 2, 1544. His father was an enemy to Popery, and during the Marian persecution he fled with his family to Wesel, and afterwards to Geneva. Here Bodley learnt Hebrew under Chevalvius, Greek under Beroaldus, and divinity under Calvin and Beza. On the death of Mary the Bodleys returned to England, and settled in London. Thomas was sent to Oxford, and became a Fellow of Merton in 1564. In 1565 he undertook the public reading of a Greek lecture. But his desire was to devote himself to the public service. For four years, from 1576 to 1580, he was studying modern languages in France, Germany, and Italy. In 1585 the queen employed him on missions to Denmark and to several German princes to induce them to join with her in aiding Henry of Navarre; and he was next sent to Henry III. of France. Burleigh was always his steady friend. Sir Thomas Bodley was the queen's envoy at the Hague from 1588 to 1597, and Her Majesty left much to his discretion. From 1597 he lived in retirement, devoting himself to the care of the library at Oxford. He died in 1612, and was buried at Merton College.

******

Sir Francis Vere declared his intention of following Bodley's directions, being persuaded that he did nothing but on good grounds, he added:

Myself, though the States have done me wrong, will not forget my duty to this country, so long as I shall be in Her Majesty's service.

There were cordial relations between the envoy and the commander of the English forces. After Vere had been a short time in command, Bodley reported:

No man's advice is more respected and followed than Sir Francis Vere, who doth content the country exceedingly for his carefulness in all things, as well for direction as execution.

******

Bodley, Aug. 19, 1591. S. P. O., Holland, vol. lxxiii. Vere's eminence as a military leader was well known to the enemy. Bentivoglio spoke of "Sir Francis Vere, an Englishman who had already gained the opinion of a gallant officer, and whom the United Provinces made use of in their most weighty military occurrences." Carnero alludes to Vere as *"un muy prudente soldado."* Meteren says: *"Le Chevalier François Veer estoit homme fort habile, et agreable aux Provinces, plus qu'aucun autre estranger."* (Fol. 333.)

★★★★★★

The first operation under Sir Francis Vere's orders was the relief of Rheinberg by Sir Martin Schenk, for which service some English companies were dispatched, with Sir John Pooley as their leader. The enterprise was successfully carried out; but Vere strongly felt the necessity for reinforcements he reported.

The army of the Hollanders is very small, and much out of order by reason they have no great soldier to command except Schenk.(July 27, 1589, to Walsingham).

In August, Sir Martin Schenk was killed in an abortive attack on Nymegen; and thus fell the man whom Sir Francis Vere considered to be their only efficient general. Yet the turning-point of the war had arrived. From the date of Vere's appointment success followed success, until Spain had to treat on equal terms with the revolted provinces for a long truce.

In July, 1589, Sir Francis Vere advanced with a small force into the Bommel-waart, the island between the Maas and Lek, to watch the movements of Count Charles Mansfelt, who was threatening an invasion of the liberated provinces on that side. Vere only had 1,140 men, of whom 650 were English. (Vere to the Lords of the Council. S. P. O., Holland, vol. lxv.)

Mansfelt was collecting flat-bottomed boats, and preparing to cross the Maas with a large army, numbering 12,000. It was a critical position; and one day Sir Francis Vere was visited in his quarters by Prince Maurice and Count Hohenlohe, who wished to consult with him whether it would not be best to abandon the island. Vere dissuaded them from any retreat. He said that considering the importance of the position, and that this was the first occasion on which the prince had commanded in person as general-in-chief, it would not be advisable to yield any ground without the knowledge and order of the States. Sir Francis undertook to hold the position until orders should arrive, and his advice was taken. (Vere's *Commentaries*).

He worked hard at the entrenchments, planted artillery, and prepared to resist the overwhelming force which was about to attack him. Mansfelt had already embarked his Walloon and German troops to cross the river, when the Spaniards mutinied and refused to go into the boats. The invasion was abandoned, and on the 25th of August Mansfelt marched away. (Vere to the Lords of the Council. S. P. O., Holland, vol. lxvi.)

This danger having been averted, the States General turned their attention to the relief of Rheinberg, now closely besieged by the Marquis of Warrenbon, a Burgundian nobleman.

The Earl of Leicester had saved Rheinberg in 1586 by drawing Parma off to protect Zutphen, and the Spaniards had hitherto been unable to reduce it. Schenk had thrown supplies in during the summer, but now the garrison was again running short of food. The States, therefore, ordered Count Meurs, the governor of Gelderland, to undertake their relief, with English troops under Sir Francis Vere, and some companies commanded by Counts Overstein and Potlitz. Rheinberg was in the territory of the Archbishop of Cologne, whose romantic love for Agnes Mansfelt had induced him to forswear celibacy and espouse the cause of the Protestants. Another prelate had been appointed in his place, but the soldiers of Queen Elizabeth and of the States upheld the rights of the expelled Archbishop Truchses.

The town of Rheinberg was of no great extent, but it was important from its strength, and from its commanding position on the banks of the great fluvial highway. The walls were built of basaltic stones, brought down the Rhine on rafts, and strengthened with earthworks. There was a bastion at each angle, and a gate in the centre of each side. The walls on the eastern side rose from the river banks, and in the centre a channel was cut into the heart of the town, up to the foot of the church tower, which formed a harbour. In the north wall was the Rhine Gate, leading to Wesel; on the west side the Guelder Gate opened on a plain bounded by an eminence crowned by the little chapel of St. Anne; and on the south was the Ursoy Gate.

In the northeastern bastion the circular toll tower rose above the river, with high pointed roof; and near it was a long brick building, with stone-dressed gables in steps, which was used as the archbishop's brewery and wine-store, and also as a hospice. The church, dedicated to St. Peter, is fairly proportioned, with aisles and an apsidal ambulatory. Its tower faced the head of the harbour, and there was a monastery with another tower, and a town hall in the market-place. An island in the river, opposite the town, had a fort upon it, which was occupied by the garrison.

★★★★★★

The scene is now entirely changed. Rheinberg is a little market town, separated from the river by wide meadows and gardens. The Rhine has altered its course, and is a mile and a half from the town. The walls are gone, and the moat is yielding rich green pasture. On the line of the ramparts grow avenues of shady horse-chestnuts. The north east bastion is occupied by an apple-orchard, and in one corner are the crumbling ruins of the old toll tower. Near it the great brick building, formerly the brewery and hospice of the archbishop, is still standing. A pleasant walk leads to the bastion at the southeast angle, shaded by trees. The town hall, a building dating from the seventeenth century, stands in the centre of a square, and contains a small museum of antiquities. In 1880 Herr Pick, the judge of Rheinberg, was president of a small *verein* for the study of local antiquities, which met under a veranda covered with vines, opening on a charming garden shaded by the trees in the southeast bastion. Here the members smoke and drink beer, while they talk over the departed glories of Rheinberg.

In the town hall there is an interesting old picture of Rheinberg. It shows the river washing the base of the stone wall, with an opening for the harbour. On the right is the lofty toll tower, with the gable of the hospice rising above the walls. To the left is the tower of St. Peter, and a line of high roofs and gables peeping over the parapet.

★★★★★★

The defenders were hard pressed by the Marquis of Warrenbon, and Mansfelt was marching from the scene of his failure in the Bommel-waart, to swell the numbers of the besieging host.

Early in October, 1589, Sir Francis Vere joined Count Meurs at Arnhem with 900 men; but a day or two afterwards the count was so injured by an accidental explosion of gunpowder that he died in a few hours. The States of Gelderland then called the English commander before them, and their spokesman, the chancellor Ivry, requested him to proceed with the enterprise. He was accompanied by Count Overstein, a young kinsman of Meurs, at the head of twelve companies of horse. The troops crossed the Yssel and marched to Rees, where they were' ferried over the Rhine. The wagons, laden with provisions, waited for them at a fort which had been constructed by Schenk near the Rhine, and opposite the town of Rees. Vere then marched direct to Rheinberg, surprised the besiegers, who were scattered in isolated entrenchments, put the provisions into the town in full view of the enemy on the 3rd of October, and returned to the fort opposite to Rees. (Vere's *Commentaries*).

Meanwhile, the States received news that Count Mansfelt was assembling forces in Brabant, with a view to pressing the siege more closely. They therefore collected larger supplies, and requested Sir Francis to undertake the dangerous service of relieving Rheinberg a second time, in the face of these increasing forces of the enemy. This time Vere resolved to advance by a shorter route, nearer the banks of the Rhine, which would take him through a wood with dense undergrowth in one place. He therefore took four small fieldpieces with him, 900 English and 900 Dutch infantry, and 800 cavalry under Count Overstein; the force amounting in all to 2,600 men. (*Official Report*. Writing from memory afterwards, Vere gives the number of fieldpieces as two, in his *Commentaries*).

Marching through the town of Xanten, they came to a dense wood, with a castle or country house, called Loo, on its outskirts. They had to make their way along a very narrow path, with exceedingly thick underwood on either side, and swampy ground. On this spot there is still a wood, through which the road passes from Alpen to Wesel, crossed by the Rheinberg and Xanten road. There is also a country house, called Loo, standing on the verge of the wood. Vere calls this part of the road a "strait."

The enemy came out of the Loo enclosure to gall the men and horses while passing through the wood. Vere ordered the Dutch foot and the cavalry to pass through the strait as rapidly as possible, with ensigns displayed and drums beating, and to form on the other side, while he himself remained behind with the English reserve and about fifty horse. The enemy increased their numbers, and Vere attacked them vigorously, driving them back to the protection of the castle. He then led the rest of the troops through the strait, which is about a quarter of a mile long, with the cross-roads in the middle of it.

As soon as he was in the open, Vere marched his whole force rapidly for a short distance, and then formed his men in line of battle facing the wood, which appeared to be full of the enemy. Soon they began to deploy and form for a charge outside, before Vere's troops were all

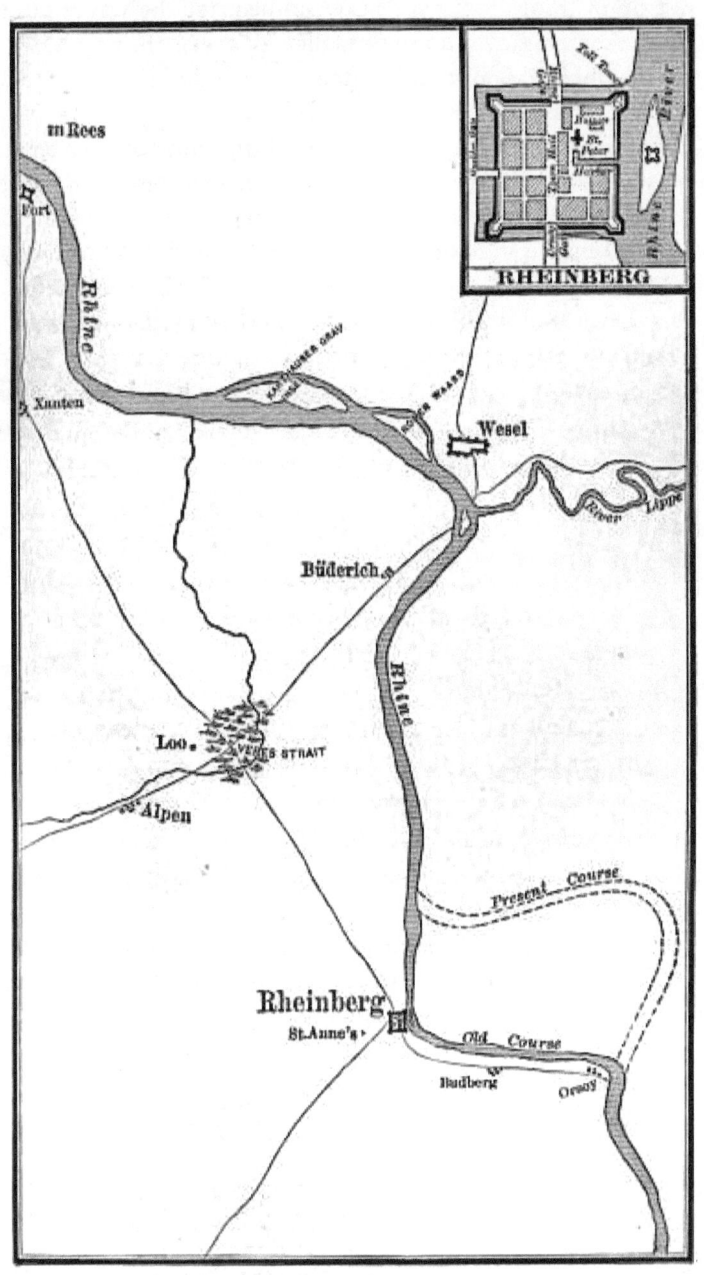

RHEINBERG AND ADJACENT COUNTRY.

in their places. He therefore took a detachment of pikes and shot, and marched rapidly against the enemy, with the object of giving time for the rest of his troops to form. Almost immediately he was at push of pike with them. His own horse was killed by a pike-thrust, and fell on him, so that he could not rise. (He does not mention this in his *Official Report*. The fact is recorded in his *Commentaries*).

Seeing his danger, the English pressed on with resolute tenacity, and he was rescued with no other harm than a contused leg and several pike-thrusts through his clothes. While the pikemen on both sides were maintaining a stubborn fight, the English shotmen spread along the skirts of the wood, and galled the flanks of the enemy so effectually that they began to fall back, closely followed by the English pikemen. Four times they rallied and turned upon their pursuers, but at last they broke and scattered among the brushwood. The English pikes remained in a serried, unbroken line, advancing upon the enemy's cavalry, who dismounted and fled through the thick undergrowth on foot. The Marquis of Warrenbon was there in person. His horse was captured, and Sir Francis sent it to England, as a present to Secretary Walsingham. (S. P. O., Holland, vol. lxvii. Vere to Walsingham, Dec. 17, 1589).

Marching onwards, Vere next encountered twenty-four companies of Neapolitan infantry, who were easily put to flight. The defeat was decisive. Vere resumed his march, and entered Rheinberg two hours after sunset. The battle was fought by one English division of 450 men. The other, under Sir Oliver Lambart, followed as a reserve.

★★★★★★

Oliver Lambart was the only son of Walter Lambart by his wife Rose, daughter of Sir Oliver Wallop. He was knighted by the Earl of Essex at Cadiz. In 1601 he became governor of Connaught, and was created Lord Lambart of Cavan in 1617. He died in 1618,. and was buried in Westminster Abbey. His son, Charles Lambart, was created Earl of Cavan in 1647.

★★★★★★

The cavalry and Dutch infantry remained on the open plain, under Count Overstein. The enemy consisted not only of the besieging force under Warrenbon, but also of the reinforcements with which Mansfelt had just arrived from Brabant. They were waiting for Vere on the road he had taken before, and on discovering their mistake they hurriedly marched across to the wood, and were routed in detail. (Vere's *Commentaries*. The official report, in Vere's own handwriting, is among the Cotton *MSS.*, Galba, D.V., f. 226).

The next morning was fortunately thick and foggy. At break of day Vere set out on his return, and reached the fort opposite to Rees late in the evening, a distance of sixteen miles, without again encountering the enemy. His gallant relief of Rheinberg enabled the town to hold out until the following January, when at length the garrison was obliged to surrender.

★★★★★★

Maurice retook Rheinberg in August, 1597. It was retaken by the Admiral of Aragon in 1598. In July, 1601, Maurice again took the place, and in August, 1606, it was again surrendered to Spinola.

★★★★★★

Sir Francis then made his headquarters at Utrecht, a good position, whence he could oppose any body of the enemy that might make an attempt to cross the rivers, before going into winter-quarters, (Gilpin to Lord Burleigh, Oct. 20, 1589. S. P. O., Holland, vol. lxvii.); and in November he proceeded to the Hague.

During the winter of 1589-90, which was long remembered for the length and severity of the frosts, Sir Francis Vere was very actively engaged in reforming the arrangements for the supply of arms and clothing, and for the more regular payment of the field force, in improving the discipline, and in making agreements with the governors of the cautionary towns as regards the employment of part of the garrisons. His commission gave him sole command of all troops in the field. Great inconvenience and expense were caused to the companies from having to send to Flushing for all supplies of arms, clothing, and accoutrements. Vere drew up a scheme for establishing a central depot at Utrecht, and he obtained sanction to receive tenders from the merchants of Amsterdam for the supply of powder and saltpetre. He also issued rates for apparel and rations. He caused ordinances and instructions for musters to be promulgated, to prevent frauds and secure an efficient system of checks; and he published orders for reforming abuses among the captains of companies.

His correspondence shows the interest he took in the welfare of comrades with whom he had served, and the persistency with which he advocated their claims. During this winter he was anxious to obtain suitable employment for his old friend Francis Allen, with whom he made the journey to Poland, and who had served with such gallantry in the defence of Sluys. He wrote three times to Walsingham on the subject of Captain Allen's claims, and twice to Lord Burleigh; and at length, in September, 1590, he obtained a company for him. He also proved a warm friend to young Throckmorton, against whom there appears to have been a prejudice on account of his family. Vere strongly represented that the young man, both as ensign and lieutenant, had lived like an honest soldier and a good subject, that he had been wounded while fighting valiantly at the relief of Rheinberg, and that he ought not to suffer for the fault of his relations.

Throckmorton took home Vere's despatches on two occasions, and, by dint of importunity, his patron obtained for him the company rendered vacant by the death of Captain Smyth. That officer, while riding from the Betuwe to Doesburg, was set upon by some of the enemy's scouts and mortally wounded. In November, 1589, Sir Francis Vere made a kindly appeal to Walsingham on behalf of an old comrade of the Bergen-op-Zoom days. Captain Bannaster had spent many years in the war with credit and reputation. He was growing old, and he undertook a journey to England in the hope of obtaining some means of living in his declining years. He relied a good deal on the help of Walsingham, and his appeal was warmly seconded by Sir Francis Vere, who wrote:

> I think the considerate recompensing of such an old soldier would very much encourage men to continue in the service.

We can only hope that poor old Captain Bannaster was granted some subsistence allowance.

Vere also appears as an intercessor for countenance to a young officer who had become engaged at Flushing. The fair Netherland maidens were attractive from their modesty and grace, and there were many love passages between them and the English officers, especially in the garrison towns. The burghers were hospitable, and the society of their families was very agreeable; but marriages were rather sternly discountenanced and frowned upon, as tending to unfit soldiers for general service. Among other enamoured youths was young Arthur Randolph. His love was returned, and, without asking permission, he was so rash as to enter into a contract of marriage with the beautiful daughter of Jacques Gelleet, an influential *burgomaster* of Flushing. He had to give bonds in consideration of her portion; but he had nothing to offer to her father save some warrants for arrears of pay.

When this proceeding became known, Secretary Walsingham, who was an old friend of Randolph's family, was very angry, and Sir Francis Vere kindly interceded in the young officer's behalf. These good offices saved him the loss of his company, of which he would otherwise have been deprived, and the marriage took place. So long as Randolph's company remained at Flushing the young couple were perfectly happy; but in 1592 it was ordered to Brittany. Then there was great tribulation. The *burgomaster* entreated that his son-in-law might be excused from this French journey. Both Sir Robert Sidney and Sir Francis Vere interceded for him, and he was allowed to remain.

These frequent kindly intercessions in favour alike of old comrades and of young officers, which continually occur in Vere's correspondence, give a very pleasant impression. He was a man of warm, sympathetic feelings, and a true friend. After the campaign of 1589 was over, Vere sent his brother Robert to England, to visit their mother and to bring out their youngest brother, Horace, who began his military career in 1590. Robert continued in command of a troop of cavalry, while young Horace commenced his service in the infantry company of Sir Francis. Thus the three brothers were happily united as comrades in the service of their queen and country, while John Vere, the eldest, remained at home to take care of their mother, at Kirby.

CHAPTER 12

Breda, and the Expedition into Westphalia

While Sir Francis Vere was actively engaged in his administrative improvements and in completing the complements of his depleted companies, the Dutch commanders were maturing an audacious scheme for surprising the important and strongly fortified city of Breda. Vere was kept fully informed from time to time of what was going on, and as early as December, 1589, he reported confidentially that all the details were arranged. (Vere to Walsingham, Dec. 17, 1589. S. P. O., Holland, vol. lxvii.)

He gives the credit of designing the plan to Prince Maurice himself. Having heard that several large boats laden with peat were received into the town during the winter, without search, Maurice conceived the hope of winning the place by that means. On further inquiry, he found that one of the captains of these boats had once been a servant of his father. (Vere to the Lords of the Council, Feb. 24, 1590. S. P. O., Holland, vol. lxvii.) His name was Adrien de Berghe. This man was approached very cautiously. Count Philip of Nassau, (son of Count John, who presided at the Union of Utrecht, John was the eldest brother of William the Taciturn), conferred with Charles de Heraugière, a captain from Cambray, who had distinguished himself in the defence of Sluys. Heraugière persuaded Adrien de Berghe to attempt the hazardous service. His boat was in a canal at the village of Lier, three miles from Breda, and here it was prepared with great secrecy. (Carnero says the boat was at Teteringen. Lib. ix. cap. ii. But Meteren is probably correct).

Upright props were secured amidships, to support a light deck of planks, leaving sufficient room below for about seventy men. Right aft there was a small cabin, as is usual with these barges, separated from the hold by a light bulkhead. The men to form this forlorn hope were selected by Heraugière with great care from the garrisons of Count Philip at Gorcum and Lowesteyn. They were all young men, few with beards, and were chosen for their strength and hardihood. On the 26th of February they were ready to embark. There was some delay, caused by the ice, but on Thursday, the 1st of March, they were all stowed in their cramped and comfortless quarters, each with two days' provisions. The peat was then piled on the deck, and made to look as if the barge was full from the keelson.

Breda was a fortified town of the first class. The River Marck flowed through it to join the old Maas, and supplied the moats with water. On the western side, where the river left the town walls, was the old castle, with a moat of its own and special fortified lines. Two semicircular bastions frowned over the river, and beyond them was a quay where vessels discharged their cargoes. It was called the fishmarket, and it led to an open space in front of the castle gates. High above the roofs of the houses rose the lofty spire of the great church. Edoardo Lanzavecchia, the governor of Breda, happened to be absent, superintending the fortification of Gertruydenburg, and the place was in charge of his son, Paulo Antonio Lanzavecchia. He had 600 infantry, in five companies, to garrison the town, 100 infantry in the castle, and 100 cavalry of the regiment of the Marquis del Vasto, under a young lieutenant named Tarlatini. There were very strict orders with regard to the examination of all vessels entering the harbour, and there was a guard-house on the quay, whence a close lookout was kept night and day.

From Friday to Saturday morning Adrien de Berghe waited in the River Marck for the tide to rise. He was moored off the *Heronnière*, just outside the castle. The boat began to leak, and the nearly frozen water came up to the men's knees in the hold. As soon as Adrien passed the castle wall and reached the harbour, the corporal of the guard came off in a small boat. He went down into the dark cabin, and pushed aside a plank which separated it from the hold. A whiff of cold air rushed in, and it was all the soldiers could do to prevent themselves from coughing. A lieutenant named Matthew Helt, feeling that he could not stop a sneeze, presented his dagger to his next neighbour, to cut his throat. But the corporal went up, and the immediate peril was over. The harbour was much encumbered by ice, and the soldiers of the guard helped to haul the vessel alongside the quay. "It was like the Trojans dragging in the Grecian horse," observes Meteren. Two soldiers were then ordered to unload the turf. They worked away, and Adrien felt that all was lost if they threw out much more and discovered the false deck. So he suggested to them that it was getting late, and that they could unload the rest the first thing in the morning. He added: "I have got an *escudo* to spend; so let us go on shore, and have drinks all round." ("*Si quereis vamos a beber, que tengo un escudo que gastar.*"—Carnero). So they all went to a public-house until it was dark, when the soldiers went away, and Adrien returned to the boat.

Meanwhile, the men in the hold were nearly dead with cold and hunger, besides being up to their knees in freezing water. They began to move, Adrien making as great a clatter as he could with the pumps, to drown the noise caused by the men coming up. It was nearly midnight. The chosen seventy Dutchmen rushed on shore, led by Heraugière, who divided them into two parties. Approaching the guard-house, a sentry challenged, and Heraugière ran him through without a word. They then overpowered the guard, and threw open one of the town gates.

Maurice, accompanied by Count Hohenlohe and Sir Francis Vere, was anxiously waiting with a sufficient force. Two hours before dawn Hohenlohe, at the head of 300 cavalry, thundered into the town, closely followed by Prince Maurice, Count Philip of Nassau, Sir Francis Vere with 600 English, and Count Solms; in all, 1,700. Paulo Antonio Lanzavecchia, the acting governor, was in the castle. Hearing the noise, he rushed out with some of his men, and came on the open space in front of the castle. Here Heraugière was engaged in a hand-to-hand fight with another *corps de garde*, and they were all driven back into the castle, Lanzavecchia being wounded in two places. He surrendered. But there were still several hundred soldiers in the town. The officers lost their heads, and hearing that the castle was taken, they counselled flight. A young ensign, Count Vicencio Capra, proposed to break down the bridge leading to the castle, and defend the town. He urged that succour would arrive from Antwerp, if they would hold out but for a short time. The other officers hesitated, and while they wavered, Hohenlohe dashed in upon them. They broke, and fled along the Antwerp road.

The news had reached the old veteran Mondragon, governor of Antwerp, with almost incredible celerity. He assembled 500 men and marched rapidly towards Breda, but, to his dismay and indignation, he met the flying garrison. He then knew that all was lost. ("*Siendo el acto*

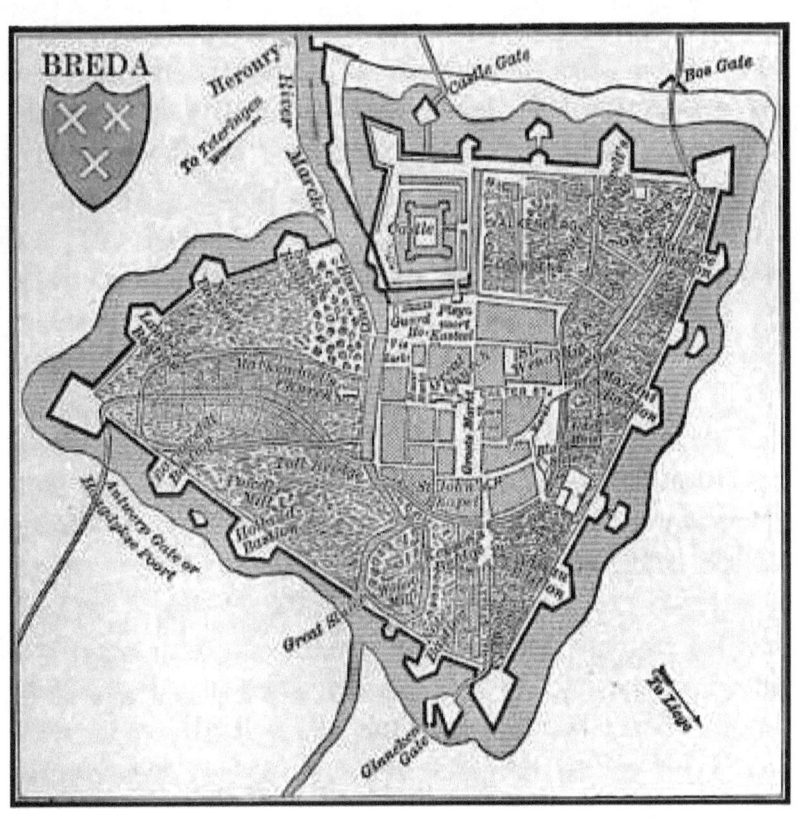

mas vil que ha hecho esta nation."—Carnero.)

On Sunday, the 4th of March, Breda was in the hands of the Dutch, and Heraugière was appointed governor. The Duke of Parma caused all the principal officers to be beheaded, except young Capra; and the corporal and two soldiers who unloaded the boat were hanged.

The capture of Breda more than made up for the loss of Gertruydenburg. Sir Francis Vere reported that Breda was a place of very great importance, very strong, and provided with all manner of munitions and stores, sufficient for 2,000 men for one year. (Vere to the Lords of the Council. S. P. O., Holland, lxviii.). Sir Francis added: "Count Maurice hath gotten great honour in this enterprise."

Standing by the quay at Breda on a moonlight night, one may recall the whole scene in imagination. There are the two semicircular bastions rising from the river; the barges lying along the quay; the open space before the castle; houses where the guardhouse stood; and the beautiful church-tower rising over the roofs, with its graceful spire shooting up into the starlit sky. Within the great church of Breda is the tomb of Engelbert of Nassau, the recumbent effigies beneath, and four mythical kneeling figures supporting a slab on their shoulders, on which are the helmet, sword, and armour of Engelbert. This famous tomb furnished the idea for the monument to Sir Francis Vere in Westminster Abbey.

Count Charles de Mansfelt advanced to the neighbourhood of Breda, devastating the country. Maurice took counsel with Hohenlohe and Vere, the result of which was that the army of the allies marched into the Betuwe, and began to throw up entrenchments on the banks of the Waal. The immediate object was to divert the attention of Mansfelt, but there was a serious ultimate intention of capturing the city of Nymegen. On the 6th of May 2,800 men were before Nymegen, on the opposite side of the Waal, of whom nine companies were English, under Sir Francis Vere. They were all employed on the construction of a strong fort exactly opposite Nymegen, and they worked at it steadily for several months. It was intended to threaten Nymegen, and also to check the incursions of the enemy into the Betuwe, the land between the Waal and the Rhine.

The people of Nymegen were Catholic, and partisans of the Spaniards; and they had raised a company of clubmen, called Knodsendragers; so the fort was named Knodsenburg, because it was built in spite of these clubmen. Vere was an officer who superintended every detail personally, and saw that each order was executed in the right way.

Francis Markham, who served under him, has the following remark on his qualifications as a trench-master:

"Sir Francis Vere, both by experience and observation, was wonderfully skilled in the work of entrenching. Though he had excellent skilled officers under him, he still, in these great and important affairs of fortifications, performed all things by his own proper commands and directions. In spite of many wounds, he ever performed these services in his own person."— Francis Markham's *Epistles of War* (1622).

By the end of July, 1590, the fort at Knodsenburg was finished. It was a strong and thoroughly well-planned work, constructed in spite of a heavy fire which Mansfelt opened on the camp from Nymegen. It was provisioned for six months, and furnished with a garrison of 600 men, under Gerart de Jonghe, a brave and able Dutch officer. Maurice then stationed his army along the line of the Waal, from Schenken Schanz to Bommel, to prevent the passage of the enemy, and the States caused a new dike to be constructed across the lower part of the Betuwe, below Nymegen, from the Rhine to the Waal, to protect the country from inundations.

In July, Sir Francis Vere was employed on detached service of an adventurous and rather hazardous character, as it entailed an advance into the enemy's country, far from all supports. Some troops of the States had got possession of the town of Recklinghausen, with its castle of Litkenhoven, in Westphalia, for Archbishop Truchses, and were closely besieged by troops of the Duke of Cleves and of the new Archbishop of Cologne. The relieving force was composed of 800 English infantry and 500 cavalry. Vere's brother Robert accompanied him. The distance of Recklinghausen from the Rhine near Wesel is twenty-five miles. Two rivers flow from east to west into the Rhine: the Lippe, rising in the hills of Lippe Detmold; and the Emscher, to the south, a small parallel stream with a shorter course, falling into the Rhine below Duisburg. The country between the two rivers is ten miles across, and the town of Recklinghausen is nearly on the water-parting, being just on the Emscher slope. The country is an expanse of sandy moor, with junipers scattered over it, and occasional woods of birch and stone pine.

Vere marched rapidly across the moors, in the hope of surprising the besiegers. At break of day, on a bright July morning, the town came in sight, at a distance of about a mile. Recklinghausen is a very picturesque old place, on a gentle slope descending eastward to a swampy stream, a tributary of the Emscher. It was a walled town with a moat, which is now full of little gardens and apple and cherry trees. The walls, with two towers, are still standing in the northwest angle, which is the highest part, and here stood the castle of Litkenhoven. The church has a square, solid tower and a richly decorated Romanesque doorway, and there was a small cloister near the western gate. Sir Francis Vere gazed on the beleaguered little town by the light of the early morning sun, and he saw that the enemy had built a fort, with bastions in the angles, in front of the west gate of the town, facing Litkenhoven Castle. This took him by surprise. He did not expect that they would have thrown up entrenchments, and he had brought neither artillery nor scaling-ladders. They had raised earth walls of good height, and had fixed gabions on them, which added six more feet, so that it would be scarcely feasible to climb over them. He had not brought sufficient provisions to enable him to lay siege to the fort.

Vere was a man of resource, and he never gave up an attempt until it was evidently impracticable. He resolved to take the fort. He divided his force into eight detachments, and disposed them, as secretly as possible, so that two detachments should be in position to assault each of the four bastions. At the first roll of the drum one detachment was to assault each bastion, and at the second roll the second detachments were to come up as supports. As soon as all was ready, Sir Francis summoned the fort. The answer was that they would like to see his artillery before they surrendered. He replied that if they made him wait until his artillery arrived, he would give them no conditions. They told him to do his worst, and his trumpeter returned.

Vere then gave the signal, and his men assaulted all four bastions, but were unable to force their way against the desperate resistance of the garrison. Their leader waited to send forward the second detachments until he thought that the defenders had exhausted all the charges in their bandoleers. Then he gave the second signal, and with a hearty cheer the reserves rushed to the support of their comrades. One soldier helped another, until at last they climbed over the parapet and drove the enemy back. More and more continued to pour over, and the place was taken. The besiegers then fled in all directions, and Recklinghausen was relieved, with a loss of about eighty killed and wounded in Vere's force.

After having given his men a few days' rest in the rescued town, the indefatigable sergeant-major marched back to the Rhine, and found that the small town of Buderich, with its fort, on the left bank, opposite Wesel, had in the mean time been taken by the troops of the

States. But the enemy held a stronger fort near the Rhine bank, and facing Wesel, which enabled them to pass their forces across the river without hindrance. Vere determined to take it. He remained quietly in Buderich for a day or two, busily making scaling-ladders with such rough materials as were at hand, while his brother Robert commanded a guard of cavalry to prevent the soldiers in the fort from receiving provisions and ammunition out of Wesel. The fort had neither moat nor palisades round it, but the walls were high. He therefore resolved to attempt to carry it by escalade.

It was a large work, capable of holding 1,500 men, and had four well-constructed bastions at the angles. Vere's plan was to have false alarms at three of the bastions, and to make a serious attack on the fourth. Eight men, four shot and four pike, were appointed to carry, plant, and mount each ladder. On a given signal one half the ladders were to be planted on one side of the bastion, and the other half on the other. This was done; the men ran up, and fought gallantly over the parapet, where the garrison was ready to receive them. But the ladders had been hastily put together; several broke with the weight and movement of the men, and Vere deemed it prudent to call them off. The false alarms had drawn most of the defenders to the other bastions, and the loss was trifling. But there were several broken heads, for the day being sultry, the soldiers had left their morions behind. Their commander used such diligence that headpieces were provided for the men, and the ladders were repaired by next morning.

The number of ladders was increased, for Sir Francis had persuaded the cavalry to take some also, as their pistols were efficient weapons for escalading. The attack began before daybreak, the men using the ladders as stands whence to fire over the parapet at the garrison, before entering. But when daylight broke the heavy guns were turned upon them from all sides, and once more they were forced to retreat. Vere was about to lead on a third assault, when he received a message from the governor to the effect that if he could have the honour of one piece of artillery being shown him, he would surrender. Anxious to gratify so moderate a petition, but having no artillery with him, Vere at last found an old gun at Büderich, which he planted in sight of the fort before morning, and sent a summons.

The garrison marched out at once, and four double cannons, with good store of ammunition and victuals, were found inside. (Vere's *Commentaries*. The present Fort Blucher must be nearly on the site of the fort taken by Vere). The surrender of this strong place was important, especially in the event of any future plan for the recapture of Rheinberg. In reporting these successes to the Lords of the Council, Sir Francis Vere observed that Büderich and the fort opposite Wesel "might be made singular accompt of, as it was their principal passage over the Rhine."—Vere to the Lords of the Council, Sept. 20, 1590. S. P. O., Holland, vol. lxxi.

This was a satisfactory termination of the campaign. In November Vere was at Flushing, receiving 400 recruits, which had been sent over, at his earnest request, to fill up gaps in the companies, (Vere to Lord Burleigh, Nov. 28, 1590. S. P. O., Holland, vol. lxxi); and during the winter the commissaries went through the musters, and great attention was given to all needful preparations for the labours of the coming year. Including the garrisons, there were 7,450 English infantry and 500 cavalry in the Netherlands, at the opening of the year 1591.

Chapter 13

The Battle in the Betuwe

Ever since Sir Francis Vere had taken command of the field force he had been eager to recover Deventer and the Zutphen Sconces, and thus wipe the stain off the British escutcheon, with which it had been smeared by the two traitors Stanley and Yorke. At last the time seemed to have arrived for this enterprise, but, in the first place, Prince Maurice was bent upon undertaking a project analogous to that of Breda. He wanted to make an attack on Dunkirk in the dead of winter, a plan which was disliked by the Lords of the English Council. The expedition sailed in January, 1591, and landed near Dunkirk, where "one who had long dealt in the town promised to take us where we might plant our ladders undiscovered." Such was the ground for hoping to surprise the place, as related by Sir Francis Vere. Maurice sent Colonel Meetkerk to reconnoitre, who confirmed the correctness of the information, and thought the enterprise easy. Then Vere and Count Solms went with Meetkerk to inspect the ground, and they were seen by a sentry. The troops opened fire. Vere was wounded in the leg, and the attempt was abandoned. The wound proved to be serious, and Sir Francis was conveyed to the Hague, where he remained during the rest of the winter months.

While he was on his sick-bed he received a visit from the veteran Sir John Norris, with a message from the Queen. Her Majesty offered him the choice of having a regiment in Brittany, or of remaining in his former command in the Netherlands. His wound made it impossible for him to move for some time, and he chose to retain the old command; but the thoughtful kindness of his sovereign excited warm feelings of gratitude. He wrote to Burleigh:

Her Majesty's care for me hath given me exceeding content,

and inflamed me with a most zealous desire to obtain the continuance of her gracious conceit towards me by all means possible.—Vere to Lord Burleigh, Feb. 3, 1591. S. P. O., Holland, vol. lxxii.

The absence of the Duke of Parma in France, with a large part of his forces, encouraged the States to attempt the conquest which was nearest to Vere's heart. Maurice got his army ready to take the field in May, 1591. The rendezvous was Arnhem, and the determination was to recover the places which had been betrayed by the English papists. Vere, with his contingent, was at Doesburg by the 14th of May.

Maurice wrote to Sir Francis Vere, requesting him to advance to Zutphen and cooperate with him in the siege. But Vere determined to recapture the Zutphen Sconces, on the opposite side of the river, before the garrison became aware of the intention to lay siege to the town. It was necessary that this should be done by means of a stratagem. Vere therefore selected a number of lusty young soldiers, and dressed most of them like the countrywomen of Gelderland, and the rest as *boers*, (Dutch name for peasants).

He gave them bundles and baskets of eggs and vegetables, such as the people usually took with them to market, and provided them with short swords, daggers, and pistols, to be hidden under their clothes. They were instructed to come, by twos and threes, to the Zutphen ferry, as if they were waiting to be taken across to the market in the town, and to sit about as near the gate of the fort as possible without exciting suspicion. At break of day they were assembled at the river bank. Then Vere showed some cavalry, as if approaching, and the pretended country people ran in feigned terror towards the fort. The gates were thrown open to receive them; they all streamed in, threw off their disguises, and were in possession in a few minutes. (Vere's *Commentaries*, Bodley to Lord Burleigh, May 21, 1591. S. P. O., Holland, vol. lxxiii.)

Vere being now in an advantageous position, prepared for the siege of Zutphen itself, sending to Maurice for assistance. The Prince arrived with eleven companies of infantry, boats, and other materials, on the 15th of May. Zutphen surrendered on the 20th, but the army of Prince Maurice suffered one serious loss. Count Overstein and Sir Francis Vere were reconnoitring too close to the walls on the day before the surrender, when the former received a wound, of which he died in a few days, and the latter had his horse killed under him.

The city of Deventer, the capital of Overyssel, had been betrayed by an Englishman, the infamous Stanley, and was now in the hands of the enemy, strongly garrisoned by a force commanded by Count Herman de Berghe. Its recovery was eagerly desired by Sir Francis Vere, for the treason of Stanley had cast a slur upon the English name. The very day after the surrender of Zutphen Prince Maurice complied with Vere's earnest wish, and encamped within a mile of the betrayed city. The siege-guns were brought down the Yssel in boats.

Deventer stands on the eastern bank of the River Yssel, which washes its walls. It is now a flourishing manufacturing town. The central market-place, of irregular shape, is shaded by horse-chestnut trees. The principal edifice is the great church, which stands in an open space near the wall along the banks of the Yssel. It is dedicated to St. Libuinus, the apostle of Overyssel and Drenthe, and the ancient crypt, with its Romanesque pillars, dates from 1020 $A.D.$ Over this interesting relic of a distant past rises a church of grand proportions, with a massive tower of great height. Near the church of St. Libuinus is the town hall, a quaint building of the sixteenth century; and there is another smaller church, with two towers, on high ground to the south. The town was surrounded by a strong wall and ditch; but Sir Francis Vere, who had given the subject very close attention, had reasons for doubting the boasted strength of the works round Deventer. The approaches were commenced at once, Prince Maurice having encamped his army round the walls.

It was debated in council whether to build a fort on the opposite side of the Yssel and blockade the town, or to carry it by assault. The latter course was chosen, and eight days were spent in entrenching and making approaches. Then they battered the walls facing the river, from four in the morning until two in the afternoon, with twenty-eight pieces of artillery. A breach was made, and the post of honour was given to Sir Francis Vere and his English companies. But the bridge of boats for crossing the river was too short, and he was obliged to retire, with some loss, intending to remedy the defect during the night and to assault next morning. Maurice was discouraged, and even meditated a withdrawal of his artillery, until he was persuaded by Vere, who undertook to guard the bridge during the night, to remain, and open another fire next day.

Sir Francis fully expected that if this course were taken the enemy would ask for terms, for the wall facing the Yssel, where the breach had been made, had no flanking bastions. It was built of brick, and had been razed to the foundation in the breach. Moreover, the town was close behind, and there was no space in rear to throw up new defences. He was right. Count Herman de Berghe, who had been wounded by a spent shot, capitulated next morning, June 2, 1591, and he was allowed to march out with his garrison. (Vere's *Commentaries*, Meteren. Vere to Lord Burleigh, June 2, and to the Lords of the Council, June 3, 1591).

Vere's loss was three officers and thirty soldiers killed, including the gallant Colonel Meetkerk, and eighty wounded. He begged that Meetkerk's brother, "a gentleman with very good deserts," might succeed to his company, and that the gallant conduct of his own lieutenant, young William Allen, might be borne in mind. The losses caused by the mistaken confidence which the Earl of Leicester had placed in the traitors Stanley and Yorke were now fully recovered. The country men of those miscreants could again look a Dutchman in the face without any shame or misgiving.

These successes, following one upon another without a check, were partly due to the absence of the Duke of Parma, with a portion of his army, in France. After the fall of Deventer the season was still before them, and the States thought the opportunity should be seized of making an attempt to complete the liberation of the northern provinces,—Drenthe, Groningen, and Friesland.

The people of Friesland had chosen Count John, of Nassau, as their *stadtholder*; but Groningen was still in the hands of the enemy, as well as the strongly fortified towns of Steenwyck and Coevorden, further south. Francisco Verdugo, who commanded in these northern parts, had risen from the ranks. He was one of the ablest officers in the Spanish Army. Maurice marched northwards with the intention of besieging Groningen, but he found that Verdugo was so well prepared to receive him that he turned aside, and surrounded Delfziel on the land side. This place is on the shores of the Dollart, a large inlet dividing the Dutch province of Groningen from the German district of Emden, whence the Spaniards obtained supplies. After four days, during which Vere had worked indefatigably at the trenches, and when the guns were all in position, the place surrendered. (Vere to the Lords of the Council, June 20, 1591).

> The place is strong, and we found it provisioned sufficiently of men, munitions, and artillery, if their hearts would have served. Count William, (son of Count John of Nassau), as belonging to his government, hath appointed garrison.

Alarming news from the States obliged Maurice to retrace his steps with all possible speed from Delfziel, and to leave the capture of Steenwyck, Coevorden, and Groningen for another year. By the beginning of July he had returned to Arnhem, and the crisis was so alarming that the States had also proceeded there, to consult with the leaders of the army and further their movements. The Duke of Parma had mustered all his forces, crossed the Waal into the Betuwe, and laid siege to the Knodsenburg fort, opposite Nymegen. This work had been prepared with great care by Maurice and Vere, and the States attached the utmost importance to its retention. It is true that the walls were of earth and could not be damaged by shot, that the ditch was broad and deep, and that the garrison had been well provisioned by Count Solms. Still the duke had arrived with a large army, had repulsed several sorties, had opened trenches, and seemed resolved to reduce the fort and relieve Nymegen from threatened danger.

The States, assembled at Arnhem, anxiously consulted with Maurice and Sir Francis Vere, insisting that an attempt must be made to raise the siege of Knodsenburg. The generals represented the great superiority in numbers, and the strength of the positions held by the Duke of Parma. The council eventually broke up, after receiving an assurance from the leaders of the army that every effort would be made to harass the enemy and save the place. The States might well be satisfied with this assurance.

Sir Francis Vere, after a careful examination of the position, and an attentive and thoughtful watch of the enemy's proceedings, worked out a plan which was accepted by Maurice. Vere observed that the enemy were acting with great vigour, and that large troops of their cavalry were daily told off to drive in the patriot scouts. This evident eagerness made him think that "they were likely to bite at any bait that were cunningly laid for them." Vere's plan required the employment of 1,200 foot and 500 horse, a force which was readily placed under his orders by Prince Maurice. The distance between the two armies in the Betuwe was four or five miles, along the two routes leading from Arnhem to Nymegen. One ran along a dike well raised above the low lands, and was most used in winter; the other was broader. Both were bordered by deep ditches, beyond which were trees and underwood.

About two thirds of the way from the patriot camp there was a bridge over the broader road. Vere marched to this bridge early one morning, and sent 200 light horse to beat in the enemy's outposts and then retreat. Meanwhile he placed his infantry in ambush, one body close to the bridge, the other about a quarter of a mile further back, and the rest of his cavalry in the rear.

The light horsemen were to retreat leisurely to draw the enemy's cavalry after them, which he intended to receive with his two bodies of infantry. But if they came in greater force, with horse and foot, he anticipated that they would march by the other road, and attempt to cut off his retreat. In the event of this contingency arising, Maurice arranged to be at the cross-road where the two routes met, with a choice body of horse and foot, to cover Vere's retreat.

The light horse gave the enemy the alarm at about noon, and retired according to orders, but were not followed. Vere then fell back to the cross-roads, where Maurice was waiting, and made a halt by the roadside at a short distance, where his men were concealed by the underwood. After about half an hour the scouts brought word that the enemy was at hand. Suddenly, without orders, about 800 of Maurice's cavalry galloped off in the direction of the foe. Vere whispered that they would come back quicker than they went, and in worse order. Sure enough, they passed by again at full gallop, with the enemy at their heels in great force.

This made it necessary for Sir Francis to enter upon the scene sooner than he intended. He led his men out, and so galled the enemy on his flanks, both with shot and pikes, that they not only abandoned the chase, but turned their backs. Instantly the reserve of Vere's cavalry charged them, and followed them up closely in furious running fight, until they were entirely routed. A great number of prisoners were taken, some of them officers of rank, and 500 horses. (Vere's *Commentaries.* Sir F. Vere to the Lords of the Council, July 27, 1591; Bentivoglio, Meteren.)

The Duke of Parma appears to have been disheartened by this reverse, added to the stubborn defence of Knodsenburg. He prepared to raise the siege on the very next day, and to retreat across the Waal, a little above Nymegen. This manoeuvre was ably conducted, Ranuccio Farnese, the Duke's eldest son, being present. Parma then went to drink the waters at Spa, leaving Verdugo in command in the field. Thus all obstacles to the reduction of Nymegen were removed, and the wisdom of having constructed the Knodsenburg fort, and of having obstinately retained it, was clearly demonstrated. On the 22nd of October Sir Francis Vere announced that, after the army had spent three days in making preparations to attack Nymegen, the city surrendered without a shot being fired. Yet the citizens were very warlike. Over the gate of the town was written:

Melior est bellicosa libertas quant servitus pacifica.
Beter is eene strijdbare vrijheid dan eene vreedzame slavernij.

Verdugo was then encamped at Grave, but he did not make any further attempt to save the place. (Vere to the Lords of the Council, October 22, 1591).

Sir Thomas Bodley, the queen's envoy, entered Nymegen on the 12th of October, 1591, with Prince Maurice and Sir Francis Vere. He reported that the fire from Knodsenburg had done some injury, but that otherwise Nymegen was a fair town, and greatly beautified with ancient buildings of the Romans.

★★★★★★

The palace of Charlemagne stood on the Valkhof, at the eastern end of Nymegen. Engravings of 1784 and 1785 show an extensive pile of buildings, with an oblong tower rising from the centre. Now there are groves of tall trees, shrubberies, and lovely views up and down the rich valley of the Waal and across the Betuwe, with the towers of Arnhem and a background of hills in the distance. There are two ruins among the trees of the Valkhof. One is the ancient baptistery of Charlemagne, rebuilt in the eleventh century, an octagon with a vaulted arcade and gallery above. The other is the apse of a very ancient Romanesque chapel. In remote times this chapel was the only place of worship for Nymegen. But a great church was built and dedicated to St. Stephen in 1272. It contains a fine tomb of Catherine de Bourbon, mother of the last Duke of Gelderland. It is in black marble, with an effigy of the duchess, and shields of arms in brass.

★★★★★★

He added:

The inhabitants are exceedingly devoted to the Pope and the Spaniards, howbeit with much ado they have taken an oath to join with these provinces in the general union. They have been very well entreated. When we entered the town we found their shops open, and the people as much busied about their daily traffic as if no innovation had happened to them.—Bodley to Lord Burleigh, October 16, 1591.

Nymegen rises from the south bank of the Waal, on the side of a hill, with the wooded height of the Valkhof to the east, whence a line of hills extends towards Cleves. Exactly opposite, on the north side of the river, is the pretty little village of Lent, with clumps of tall trees and pleasant walks round it. Here there are some slight traces of the Knodsenburg fort.

There was no rest for Sir Francis Vere during the winters which intervened between the active campaigns in the field. He was hurrying from one cautionary town to another, negotiating with the governors for the supply of troops; personally arranging for the transmission of arms and clothing; consulting with Maurice and the States, and with the queen's envoy; and shipping troops for France. In these years England was giving active assistance to Henry IV., and troops were constantly called away from the Low Countries. These periodical demands for companies, the loss of which decreased the efficiency of Vere's force, would have driven poor Lord Willoughby nearly mad. Vere simply obeyed orders, did all he could to comply with the wishes of the queen's government, and devoted the best energies of his mind to do the most useful service possible with the means left at his disposal. He had naturally entered heart and soul into the struggle for freedom in the Netherlands, and had formed many warm friendships there. He had no wish to be transferred either to France or to Ireland; and the opening of 1592 found him busily engaged in preparations to cooperate once more with the States, and to furnish forth an effective contingent to Prince Maurice's army.

At the opening of 1592 Sir Robert Sidney was governor of Flushing, with a nominal garrison of 1,250 men; Lord Burgh was governor of Brill, Sir Edward Norris of Ostend, and old Sir Thomas Morgan was still at Bergen-op-Zoom. Captain Errington had retired, and Sir Thomas Baskerville commanded the garrison at the Rammekens. Including 926 men dispersed under Vere's orders, there were 5,235 effective British troops in the Netherlands. Of this body Sir Francis Vere was able to assemble 1,344 men with Maurice's army, consisting of twelve companies of infantry under Horace Vere, Oliver Lambart, John Buck, John Audley, Roger Smyth, T. Williams, A. Meetkerk, and J. Christmas; and four troops of cavalry, under Sir Robert Sidney, who left Flushing to take the field, Sir Nicholas Parker, Sir John Pooley, and young Robert Vere. Maurice had, besides, a force of 6,000 foot and 2,000 horse. He was surrounded by a brilliant staff, including Counts Hohenlohe, William and Philip of Nassau, Solms, Floris de Brederode, and Groenvelt, the brave old defender of Sluys.

The States determined to prosecute the reduction of Spanish garrisons in the north with all possible energy, and relieve Friesland and

Groningen of the presence of foreign invaders. The Duke of Parma had again marched into France, leaving old Count Mansfelt as his deputy, while Verdugo was in command in Friesland. The States determined to open the campaign with the siege of Steenwyck, a strongly fortified town on the route from the Yssel at Deventer to Groningen. Steenwyck is in that northern corner of the province of Overyssel, bordering on the Zuyder Zee, called Vollenhove. The town is still surrounded by its moat, and there are walks through shrubberies along the ramparts. The Steenwyck Diep, a sluggish stream, flows round the northern side, and through the suburb of t'Verlaat to Blokzyl on the Zuyder Zee, eight miles to the westward. The flat plain round Steenwyck is now a checkboard of small holdings, belonging to the Overyssel peasant proprietors. The little village of Giethorn is rather under four miles to the S. S.W. At the northern end of the town is the fourteenth-century church of St. Clement, with a lofty brick tower visible for miles around; and on the south side, with a street leading to it from the shady market-place, is the smaller but more richly decorated church of Our Lady.

Maurice was enabled to bring his siege train of fifty pieces of artillery by water, and on the 7th of May, 1592, he encamped before Steenwyck. The place had been strengthened with earthworks and well provisioned, the governor being Antoine de Cocquille. From the 7th of May to the 10th of June the entrenchments were being prepared; the approaches being mainly on the south side, where the infantry was encamped. The cavalry was quartered at the village of Giethorn. A cavalier was raised, nineteen feet high, whence to batter the parapets, and fifty guns were got into position. Vere directed the works on his side, working unceasingly, in spite of a slight wound in the leg. His brother Horace was also wounded. By the beginning of June the counterscarp had been reached on all sides; on the 13th the guns began to batter the walls, and on the 23rd a ravelin was captured on the west side.

The besiegers then constructed a tower on wheels, made of masts, called a *lymstande*. It was an invention of Captain Cornput of Breda. This *lymstande* was built in nine stories, each twelve feet high, and on each there was a parapet and a wall of canvas as a cover. It was brought close to the ditch, and manned by musketeers, who not only shot soldiers on the ramparts, but also people walking in the streets. Although the garrison succeeded in battering down two storeys of the *lymstande*, the others remained effective. Meanwhile the battering continued, but the walls were so strong that no practicable breach could be made. Mining was then resorted to, and by the 19th two mines had been run under the defences, besides a way through the ditch, from the English approaches. Three days were then passed in perfecting the mines and placing the charges of powder.

On the night before the 23rd of June the whole army was secretly drawn into the trenches, and at dawn the mines were to be fired and a general assault delivered. As the sun rose over the heathy moors of Drenthe, three tremendous explosions announced the firing of the mines. One party, led by Count William of Nassau, dashed forward, and the men carried the ruined bastion. Sir Francis Vere rushed into the thick of the blinding cloud of dust and mortar, followed closely by his Englishmen. In a few minutes they were on the parapet. The third explosion also made a great breach, but here the assailants were so injured that they could not dash into the ruins with the necessary speed, and the enemy had more time to prepare for defence. The other assaults were decisive. A flag of truce was sent out, and the governor asked for terms. These were soon arranged, and the garrison marched out on the 5th of July.

Prince Maurice lost 600 men, and he was himself slightly wounded in the face. Sir Francis and Horace Vere, Sir Robert Sidney, Captains Lambart and Buck, were wounded, beside 152 of their men. (Meteren, Bentivoglio, Grimeston. Sir F. Vere to the Lords of the Council, March 31, May 29, June 12, June 25, 1592). Sidney returned to Flushing.

Maurice next proceeded to lay siege to another strong place to the eastward of Steenwyck, and near the Westphalian frontier, called Coevorden. This town was well fortified, and held by a garrison commanded by Count Frederick de Berghe, while Verdugo himself had taken the field and was in the neighbourhood. Nevertheless, Maurice began the siege, although Vere had received positive orders to fall back. Very unwillingly he obeyed, and in the end of July he was at Doesburg, on the Yssel. In August he heard that Verdugo was threatening Maurice in his trenches. Orders or no orders, Vere flew to the rescue, and he was not a day too soon. Marching through the night, he came in sight of Coevorden at break of day on the 28th of August. He found a battle actually raging within cannon-shot of the trenches. Verdugo had organised a *camisado*. Dressing all his men in white shirts, he assaulted the camp of Maurice just before daybreak. The battle was at its height. Vere dashed into the thick of it, closely followed by his men. Young Count John of Nassau, writing to his father, said:

Vere fought with the enemy like a man. He came up half an hour after the fight began.— *Archives ou Correspondance inédite de la Maison d' Orange Nassau, recueil par G. Groen van Prinsterer. 2d^e Series, 1. 207, Lettre xciii.*

The assailants were at length repulsed, but there was a critical moment, and the Dutch infantry were giving way when Vere arrived so opportunely. Writing to Lord Burleigh, he said:

Considering the urgent necessity that drew me to the camp, I hope your Lordship will not disallow thereof.

On September 3, he reported that, Verdugo having made no further attempt to relieve the place, Coevorden was surrendered to Count Maurice. He concludes:

I will now hasten as much as shall lie in me to bestow the companies in garrison.—Vere to the Lords of the Council, July 23, 1592. Vere to Lord Burleigh, Aug. 29, 1592, and Sept. 3, 1592.

During the greater part of the winter he was employed on the uncongenial duty of shipping off companies which he had drilled and trained, to serve under other commanders in France and Ireland. Still there were 4,000 effective British troops in the Netherlands on the 1st of January, 1593.

The Duke of Parma died at Arras on the 3rd of December, 1592, after having commanded the armies of Philip II. in the Netherlands for thirteen years. He had reached the age of forty-six. Parma was undoubtedly the ablest general of his time. He was well versed in every branch of the military art, patient and cautious in arranging his plans, quick to strike, and persevering in following up a success. Latterly he had suffered from gout, but his intellect never failed, and to the last he showed his remarkable skill in arranging the details of a campaign. He was succeeded by the aged Count Peter Ernest Mansfelt, with whom Don Pedro Henriquez de Azevedo, Conde de Fuentes, was associated. Mondragon, verging on his ninetieth year, was still in command at Antwerp, and Verdugo at Groningen. The Spanish troops, once so formidable, were now no more than a match for the English and Dutch; while discontent caused by unrequited service, long banishment, and grievances with regard to pay, were fast undermining their discipline and sapping their efficiency.

CHAPTER 14

Sieges of Gertruydenburg and Groningen

The time was now fast approaching when the United Provinces, having driven the foreigners from their soil, and assured their independence, would be able to face their enemy on equal terms. In the midst of a harassing war, the people had made marvellous strides in material prosperity: their cities were becoming centres of industry and wealth; they were undertaking commercial enterprises on a great scale; and they appropriated some of their resources to the objects of the war. There remained two great strongholds which threatened the peace and welfare of the provinces, and which it was necessary to reduce before the liberated people could breathe freely. These were Gertruydenburg in Brabant, and Groningen in the north. The siege of the former place was undertaken on a scale which showed how rapidly the wealth of the provinces had increased, and how great were their present resources.

Gertruydenburg had been much strengthened since its mutinous garrison delivered it up to the Spaniards in 1589, and approaches were difficult, owing to the network of ditches and canals which surround it. Moreover, a besieging force would be exposed to attacks from the army under Count Mansfelt. An elaborate siege on a large scale was necessary, and the details were planned and matured by Prince Maurice. The first operations were to stop all roads by which an enemy could succour the town, and to fortify the camp against attacks from a hostile army in the field. This occupied all March, 1593, and in April the approaches against the town were commenced. The trenches were divided by ravelins flanking one another, each ravelin mounting two guns, and outside there was a wide water ditch. Instead of a counterscarp, rows of piles were driven into the ground, being left four feet above the surface, and pointed with iron. (Grimeston).

A hundred ships, forming a semicircle in the old Maas, completed the blockade, with light brigantines on the flanks. There were four main forts, connected by smaller forts in a double line, and upwards of 100 pieces of artillery were mounted on the works. The remarkable feature of these elaborate siege works was that as much care was taken to complete them for repulsing an enemy outside as for checking the sorties of the garrison. The camp arrangements were excellent, and the country people came to sell their produce just as if they were going to market in a peaceful town.

Prince Maurice, with Count Solms and Groenvelt, was posted on the western side; Sir Francis Vere conducted the approaches from the south; while Hohenlohe and Brederode were encamped at the village of Raamsdonk to the east. The River Donge, flowing from the south, supplied the moat with water. Two bridges over it connected the works, and on the 8th of April an outlying fort on the river was captured by Count Hohenlohe. During the siege the Princess Juliana visited her brother Maurice, on her way to be married to the Elector Palatine. She was conducted over the works, which were acknowledged to be the grandest that had ever been constructed in the annals of war.

Towards the end of May the approaches reached the counterscarp of the town on all sides. Meanwhile, the walls had been constantly battered, two governors in succession had been killed, and both ammunition and provisions were running short. On the 28th Count Mansfelt tardily appeared with an army of 7,000 foot and 2,000 horse, encamping in the villages of Capelle and Waalwijk, about six miles east of Gertruydenburg. On receiving this news, Sir Francis Vere observed:

> We may account that his coming hither cannot but turn to his loss and dishonour. For if he attempt to succour the town, he must needs be foiled, our advantages are so great; while in lying still he must endure great misery through want of vittayle, which they already begin to feel, having scarce any bread to put in their mouths.—Vere to the Lords of the Council, 29th May, 1593.

Vere advanced against Mansfelt with 600 English and 1,000 Frieslanders, and repulsed his infantry. By this time galleries had been run under the ramparts in three places; and on the 25th of June, the

Sieur de Gissant having been slain by a stone shot,—making the third governor who had been killed during the siege,—Gertruydenburg surrendered to Prince Maurice.

******

Grimeston, Meteren, Bentivoglio. Vere to the Lords of the. Council, 11th April, 29th May, 31st May, 16th June, 23rd June, 1593. Vere to Lord Burleigh, 23rd July, 1593. With this letter Vere forwarded a plan of the siege of Gertruydenburg, "hoping that it would be grateful to his Lordship."

******

Next day Mansfelt marched away, followed by the prince, whose troops occupied the Bommel-waart, in order to check any attempt in that direction.

Count William of Nassau, the *stadtholder* of Friesland, was holding his own with some difficulty against Verdugo and the Spaniards at Groningen and in the field. The Frieslanders had enlisted freely and fought valiantly in the patriot army, and had deserved well of their country. The States now felt anxious to send efficient aid to Count William, and to free the northern provinces from the presence of foreign invaders. Troops were sent into Friesland in July, and the States entrusted the command to Sir Francis Vere, of whose generalship a high opinion had been formed by Dutch statesmen.

The summer had been very dry, which facilitated the march of Spanish regiments to reinforce Verdugo; and Count William, not being strong enough to make a stand against them, fell back into Friesland. During September, Vere was manoeuvring in the neighbourhood of Groningen, sometimes repulsing an assault behind entrenchments, at others following or retreating before the enemy. It was an arduous and skilfully conducted campaign, but his force was quite insufficient for attempting a serious attack on Groningen. In October he returned to the Hague, and his troops went into winter quarters. (Vere to the Lords of the Council, 4th Sept., 12th Sept., 17th Sept., 22nd Sept., 30th Sept., 1593).

The States resolved to devote their whole power to the capture of Groningen during the season of 1594. The Archduke Ernest succeeded Count Mansfelt in command of the Spanish army, entering Brussels on January 31, 1594, while Verdugo, with a considerable force, was still in the northern provinces. Sir Francis Vere had been appointed General of all the English troops in the pay of the States, as well as Sergeant-major of the Queen's forces in the field. He marched with

Prince Maurice's army, and the united forces encamped before Groningen on the 20th of May, 1594.

The city of Groningen had declared for the Union of Utrecht, but the *stadtholder*, George Lalain, Count of Renneberg, was a traitor. He sold the place for 10,000 crowns and the Golden Fleece, arrested the principal citizens, and opened the gates to the Spaniards on March 3, 1580. Groningen was built with the angles of the walls nearly at the cardinal points. The centre of the town, from southeast to northwest, is occupied by the long Visch-markt, lined with quaint old gabled houses, and the Groote Markt, with its ancient "*Waag*" or weighing-house. The church of Our Lady, a lofty brick edifice built in 1246, is at one extremity of the Visch-markt. At the opposite end of the Groote Markt is the great church of St. Martin, with its gardens extending to the northeast wall. The stone tower of St. Martin's, built in 1482, is the most striking feature of Groningen. It is 300 feet high, of two stories, and a third forming an octagonal lantern. The church is of brick, and was once very imposing, with its lofty apsidal choir and ambulatory. The gates of the town, now demolished, were picturesque old mediaeval structures, with round flanking towers and pointed roofs.

The walls were protected by a wide, deep moat, whence a canal, called the Boter Diep, led from the northern angle to Delfziel on the Dollart. This was the main route of trade, and the way by which supplies reached Groningen from Germany. A few miles down this canal, on a lock, there was a strong fort, called Auwerderzyl. On the northwestern side of the town there were two fortified gates, called the Oude Boteringe Poort and the Ebbinge Poort. On the southwest side, facing Friesland, was the Aa Poort, in rear of the church of Our Lady. On the northeast side were the Porte du Garde and a curious old gate, erected in 1428, called the Poele Poort, which led to a suburb called Schuyten Diep. At the east angle was the harbour, where vessels chiefly congregated, and here a strong round tower rose above the walls, called the Drenkelaar.

The southeastern side had three gates, called the Ooster Poort, in front of which there was a strong ravelin; the Heere Poort, through which a road led southwards to the village of Haren; and a small sally-port called the Pas Dam. Approaching from Haren, these three gates were seen, breaking the line of the wall, with the frowning Drenkelaar on the right, and the towers of St. Martin and Our Lady rising high above the roofs. The walls were well supplied with artillery, and as Maurice approached a strong force under Lankama, Verdugo's lieu-

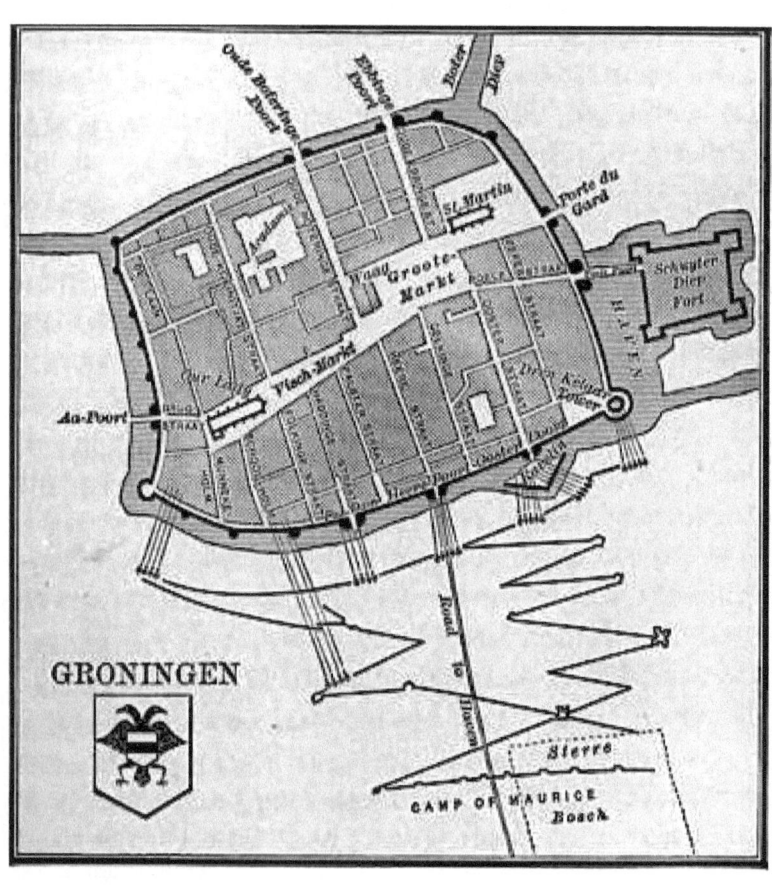

tenant, entered the town by the Poele Poort to reinforce the garrison. There was a small fort in the Schuyten Diep suburb to protect the haven.

★★★★★★

In 1879 I saw a collection of sketches of Groningen at the interesting maps, plans, and house of Mr. Backer, in the Groote Markt. The oldest was Spanish, with the date 1577. Another, entitled *Het Belegh de Stad Groningen in der Jaere MDXCIV.*, shows the siege works. There is a history of Groningen in two volumes, *octavo*, 1852, *Geschiedkundige Beschriving der Stad Groningen door Dr. C. T. Diest-Lorgion*. There are engravings of the old gates, now demolished.

★★★★★★

Prince Maurice had 125 companies of foot and twenty cornets of horse. His artillery was transported by water. It was not intended to blockade the town and make approaches on all sides, as at Gertruydenburg. The plan determined upon was to open trenches and attack on the south side. The Prince's headquarters were therefore established a little in advance of the village of Haren, nearly on the spot now occupied by the charming pleasure-grounds of the Sterre Bosch. From this position the approaches were made towards the several strong points of the enceinte. Five siege-guns were planted against the Drenkelaar tower, ten against the ravelin of the Ooster Poort, twelve against the Heere Poort, six against the Pas Dam, and three against the bastion at the southern angle. Count William captured the fort of Auwerderzyl by assault on the 29th of May.

Sir Francis Vere, with his English contingent, worked side by side in the trenches with the regiments of Friesland and Zeeland. When the guns opened fire there was a steady and continuous reply from the ramparts, and although the Drenkelaar was beaten down and half ruined, and much injury was done to the walls and gates, the defence promised to be stubborn and prolonged. Writing on the 27th of May, Sir Francis said:

> We have approached the town in divers places, and mean to pass by galleries to the rampart. The ditch is very broad and deep, and they ply with their artillery, so that, if they continue as they have begun, it will be very near a whole summer's work. Succour they cannot expect any, we being possessed of the passages.—Vere to Lord Burleigh, S. P. O., Holland, vol. lxxix.

Early in June Vere had lodged his men within the counterscarp and along the moat, where they were much exposed. One night there was a sudden sortie from the Heere Poort, when the English were surprised, and there was serious loss. Captain Wrey, standing at the head of the trench, was shot dead, and several men were killed and wounded. On the 18th of June Sir Edward Brooke was slain; Vere wrote:

> A gentleman if it had pleased God to spare him, would have done Her Majesty good service.

This caused another vacancy for Burleigh to fill up, and Sir Francis applied for the company for young Horace, he wrote:

> I cannot but recommend to your Lordship one of the fittest here for the place. My youngest brother hath, for his experience and trial made of his sufficiency, shown himself very capable of the charge. He has, for these three years, commanded my own company of foot. If it please your Lordship to enquire, I doubt not but you shall hear more good of him than I report; and if, according to the same, your Lordship be pleased to favour him, we shall think ourselves highly bound unto your Lordship.

Thus Horace Vere received his first company and became a captain. Soon afterwards, Prince Maurice and Sir Francis had a narrow escape. They were making a reconnaissance close to the walls, under a large buckler, when a shot struck it, and they were both hurled to the ground.

The mines were pushed under the strong ravelin in front of the Ooster Poort; and on the night of the 5th of July they were exploded, with excellent results, the work being carried by the besiegers before dawn, with a loss of 200 men to the garrison. A few days afterwards the principal citizens came into the camp, and terms of surrender were agreed upon. Lankama with his garrison was to march out, and the town was to receive magistrates appointed by Count William of Nassau, as *stadtholder* of Friesland. Prince Maurice with his principal officers made a triumphal entry into Groningen on the 15th of July, 1594. Maurice then returned, by way of Amsterdam, to the Hague. The loss of the garrison was very great, for of 900 only 400 sound men marched out. (Grimeston, Bor iii., Meteren, xvi., Vere to Lord Burleigh, May 27, May 31, June 18, July 6, July 13, 1594. Bodley to Lord Burleigh, July 10, 1594).

Among the losses during this campaign was the death of Sir John

Pooley, a brave cavalry officer, who had been Vere's companion in arms for many years and was a neighbour in Suffolk. The vacancy made Sir Francis a humble suitor to Lord Burleigh:

> For my brother Robert, that he may have your Lordship's favour for the company. He hath for this six or seven years served on horse, and for a good part of the time commanded my company. Were he not my brother I might well say that I know none of his rank that doth better deserve it. His sufficiency emboldens me to entreat your Lordship's favour, knowing he will not show himself unworthy the advancement.

★★★★★★

Another application for Sir John Pooley's company was made by young Griffin Markham, who was afterwards arraigned for high treason in 1603, with Sir Walter Raleigh, Cobham, and Brooke. He wrote a letter from before Groningen, dated July 25, 1594, to Sir Robert Knight, one of her Majesty's council.

> The death of Sir John Pooley hath given an unwished occasion unto your Honour to declare (by your favour with Her Majesty) your love which in particular you have unto my singular person which is a follower of the wars, May it, therefore, please your Honour (although there be many of better desert for service) to commend me unto Her Majesty as one worthy of this company.

★★★★★★

The three brothers had shared together the dangers of battle and siege, had held pleasant communion during long and weary marches, had sat and talked together before camp-fires; and now the eldest ventured to bring to notice the services of his young companions, that they might receive the promotion they had so well earned. The English companies, after the fall of Groningen, were distributed in various garrisons.

In the autumn Sir Francis Vere was engaged on an adventurous and somewhat perilous expedition. King Henry IV. had appointed the Duc de Bouillon as general in the country round Sedan, and it was resolved that young Count Philip of Nassau should march through the enemy's country and join him with a contingent. Sir Francis Vere, at the head of twenty-six cornets of horse and 5,000 foot, was requested to accompany him as an escort, see him safely at his destination, and return with all speed to the Netherlands. Count Philip crossed the

Rhine at Schenk's Sconce on the 22nd of October, 1594, and Vere followed the next day. They marched in parallel lines, the Count near the Rhine and Sir Francis towards the Meuse, until they formed a junction at a small town in the diocese of Treves.

Here they heard that the enemy was waiting for them, on the road they had to pass, with 5,000 foot and 1,800 horse. So they altered their route, crossed the Moselle, hurried forward with all speed, and reached Metz on the 7th of November. Next day they joined the Duke of Bouillon, who had a commission from Henry IV. to make war on the King of Spain. The original plan was that Vere should only go part of the way, but when he heard that the enemy was in force he did not feel justified in leaving Count Philip until he had formed a junction with Bouillon.

Hearing that Count Mansfelt and Herman de Berghe were waiting for him in the neighbourhood of Maastricht, Vere kept on the right bank of the Rhine during his return march. He crossed the river on November 19th, and reached Gelderland in safety, without the loss of a man. Maurice and the States were greatly relieved at his return, for he had with him the flower of their cavalry.

In the winter of 1594 the musters showed a strength of 4,500 men, including the garrisons of Flushing, Brill, and Ostend, and the companies which had served in the field, and were afterwards dispersed in various garrisons.

CHAPTER 15

Death of Robert Vere

Active service in the field, year after year, was but a small part of the work expected from Sir Francis Vere by the Queen's government. His position entailed upon him very heavy responsibilities connected with the administration of the forces. He was also required to conduct negotiations with Maurice and the States relating to the supply and transfer of troops and the conduct of the campaigns; and latterly he was called upon to correspond regularly with the government, and to submit full reports on all public events. Thus it came about that he who had hitherto passed his life almost exclusively in camps, with few thoughts of any matters apart from military business, was, by the force of circumstances, gradually educated in diplomacy and in the conduct of civil affairs.

Queen Elizabeth, while giving aid to the young republic of the Netherlands, in accordance with the treaty, had entered into a close alliance with the King of France, and had agreed to help him against the Catholic League with expeditionary forces, both in Normandy and Brittany. These engagements strained the resources of England to the utmost. Orders were sent to the Netherlands to transfer company after company to France. No sooner had soldiers attained proficiency in drill and some experience in the field, under the eye of Sir Francis Vere, than they were ordered away. He firmly believed that the best policy was to concentrate, and to strike at the heart of Spanish power in the Netherlands, and that the scattering of troops over France was a mistake, he wrote:

> Blows struck in this quarter are at the very root whence the danger springeth, while Normandy and Brittany are but at the very top branches.—Vere to Lord Burleigh, 16th June, 1593. S. P. O., Holland, lxxvii.

It was quite impossible that this business of drafting off his soldiers, carefully trained by himself, could be otherwise than very distasteful to Sir Francis Vere. He did his duty, and complied with the unreasonable demands upon his resources to the best of his ability, although that duty was a most unpleasant one. The government felt this, and increased his difficulties by incessant complaints of want of zeal in the queen's service, or of too much concern for the affairs of the States. If a company arrived in France deficient in the regulation number of men, after having been thinned by years of campaigning and sickness in the Netherlands, Vere was accused by Lord Burleigh of slackness in executing his orders, while the queen signified her heavy displeasure. In vain he explained that:

> The weakness groweth by the wars. . . the service must be considered where we had men hurt and slain, and our travail, whereof divers were sick. . . . these were the reasons for the weakness of those that went into France.—Vere, at Doesburg, to Lord Burleigh, 13th Jan., 1592.

The unreasonable complaints and unjust reprimands continued year after year, and had to be borne philosophically. Occasionally Vere had a chance of returning Burleigh as good as he gave. The Lord Treasurer granted leave of absence to captains without reference to Sir Francis, which was a great abuse. So Vere replied to his complaint of the inefficiency of companies sent to France:

> That one effectual means to beautify and strengthen a company is the presence of its captain, which is one of the greatest wants that I complain of some of them.—Vere to Lord Burleigh, 1st Feb., 1592.

Another hardship caused by the transfer of companies to France arose from the attractions of the young Dutch women. When the company of Sir Nicholas Parker was ordered to Brittany, it was found that several marriages had taken place; and there were so many men married in the country, belonging to Sir John Pooley's company, that the order for their removal was cancelled.—Bodley, at the Hague, to Lord Burleigh, 21st Sept., 1592.

In reality Vere displayed uncommon zeal in complying with the orders he received. In September, 1592, he was personally inspecting the men at Brill and Flushing, and superintending their embarkation. He did his best to explain to Dutch statesmen and to Prince Maurice the necessity under which the Queen was acting. But the denudation of the English contingent naturally caused discontent and alarm in Holland, (sent to Normandy, 1,250; to Brittany, 2,350: total, 3,600, about 1,250 returned from Normandy, but none from Brittany), and in 1594 Maurice wrote to the queen, entreating her to send more soldiers, without which the campaign could not be successfully undertaken. Another source of anxiety to the officer commanding the forces in the field was the extent to which he could rely upon help from the governors of the cautionary towns. Flushing and Brill were safe from attack, and there could be no excuse for withholding a moiety of their garrisons for service in the field during the summer. At Flushing, Sir Robert Sidney, and in his absence Sir Edmund Uvedale, always appear to have acted cordially with Vere; but at least on one occasion Lord Burgh, the Governor of Brill, showed another spirit.

******

At the setting forward of the enterprise of Grolle, the Count Maurice asked for some men from the Brill, which the governor sent conditionally that they should not be commanded by me; notwithstanding, if the service had gone forward, I was minded to have followed my commission. I know no reason why he should do it. This is the first complaint I have made since I have commanded, which I do more for other respects than for my particular, and yet I must humbly entreat your Lordship to let him know he hath done wrong to her Majesty's commission, which I have for the commanding of the forces employed in the field. (Vere to Lord Burleigh, Oct. 7, 1594.)

******

Ostend was differently situated. Its fortifications were for a long time in a very unsatisfactory state; it was in the heart of the enemy's country, and there were incessant alarms. A single incident shows how easily anxiety was excited in the minds of the officers at Ostend. A boy named John Coopman had been in the habit of going out into the swamps to catch fowl. One day he was captured by the enemy's cavalry, who took him to Nieuport, and asked him what artillery there was at Ostend. They also made him promise to go back, and then return to them with information as to where the sentries were stationed. He went home, and faithfully reported all that had happened to Sir Edward Norris, the Governor of Ostend. The incident excited great alarm. The boy's straightforward account of what had occurred should have cleared him of blame; but the apprehension of a sudden attack was so great that suspicion was aroused. The boy had been given orders not to go near the dunes where the horsemen from Nieuport might catch him, but to keep in the marshy ground. It was suspected that he might have escaped if he had chosen, as he was provided with a leaping-pole, and might have gone into drowned land, where horses could not follow him. It was recommended that he should be proceeded against by whipping. So the poor boy was whipped, while the whole case was seriously referred to the Lords of the Council. (Sir E. Norris, at Ostend, to the Lords of the Council, May 20, 1595. S. P. O., Holland, vol. lxxxi.)

Alarms such as these made Ostend a less reliable source of supply for troops than the other garrisons, but on the whole Sir Francis Vere worked well with the governors of the cautionary towns.

In 1593 there was a great improvement in Vere's position. He had proved himself to be so able and efficient as a military commander that Maurice and the Dutch statesmen were anxious to secure his services permanently. In July the States General began to fear that, as the queen had withdrawn so large a portion of the British force from the Netherlands, she might order Sir Francis Vere away also. So it was resolved to offer him 800 florins a month to secure his services. He accepted conditionally, believing that the arrangement might enable him to do her Majesty better service. The action he had taken was approved by the queen, he wrote:

> I have received no small comfort at the allowance of my proceedings with the States, which was with a dutiful reservation of my service to Her Majesty, as did become me. I take this offer of theirs to have proceeded from them, to witness unto the world their good acceptance of my small service, but chiefly to give Her Majesty some satisfaction; she having, at what time the companies were drawn from here, made mention of me by way of recommending me to their favour.—Vere to Lord Burleigh, July 2 and July 23, 1593.

Soon afterwards the States General obtained permission to recruit in England, and Sir Francis Vere was appointed general of all the English troops in their pay. In October, 1594, Vere himself received authority to raise 400 men in England, which he divided into three companies, and gave them to Sir Thomas Fairfax, Captain Constable, and Captain Heydon.

★★★★★★

Sir Thomas, afterwards first Lord Fairfax, had seen much service, and was knighted by Essex under the walls of Rouen. He was an old friend and comrade of Sir Francis Vere, as was his brother, Sir Charles Fairfax. The third brother, Edward, was a poet of eminence, and the translator of Tasso. In after-years the friendship between the two families was cemented by the marriage of Vere's niece with the grandson of his friend, Sir Thomas Fairfax.

Sir Christopher Heydon, who was knighted at Cadiz. He was the eldest son and heir of Sir William Heydon, of Baconsthorpe, in Norfolk, by Anne Wodehouse. Sir Christopher had taken his degree at Cambridge, and was a scholar as well as a soldier. He married Mirabel, daughter of Sir T. Rivet, of London, and had four sons, one of whom was slain at the Isle of Rhé. Sir Christopher died in 1623, and Baconsthorpe was sold by his son, Sir John Heydon.

★★★★★★

He also got recruits from among disbanded troops in the Netherlands. To the surprise of the army, the Queen ordered Sir Francis to disband the company of Sir John Pooley, who had died after the siege of Groningen. This was a laborious task. Mr. Sparhawke, the muster-master who had succeeded Mr. Digges, lived at Ostend, and it was some time before Vere could arrange a meeting with him at Bergen-op-Zoom, where the company was in garrison. It took a week to get the soldiers' accounts, which were in great confusion, into proper order. Vere reported that:

> He had much ado to content the poor men, which he did by granting them tickets under his hand for what the deceased captain remained in their debt, and by putting them in hope that the Queen would take further order for satisfying them.—Vere to Lord Burleigh, April 11, 1595.

Many were married in the country, and most of them determined to remain. They entered under Sir Francis Vere's standard, receiving pay from the States. In March, 1593, Sir Francis Vere sent forward a statement of the grievances of the soldiers, "which had been perused by the captains, but not devised by them." The clothing was not equal to the patterns, and of bad stuff; there was no fair rule for ransoming prisoners, and insufficient provision for sick and wounded. The paper was signed by Vere, and also by Sir T. Morgan, Sir T. Baskerville, and others. Vere strongly represented that if these grievances were not redressed, it would greatly hinder the course of martial discipline. These various details of military administration are mentioned as examples of the character of Vere's work, in addition to actual service in the field.

Although Sir Francis was now a general in pay of the States, as well as sergeant-major in command of the queen's forces in the field, he did not escape criticism, and even severe censure, for his military acts. The service of escorting Count Philip to Metz was hazardous, but it was successfully and ably performed, and it was undertaken at the request of the States and with their troops. Yet Queen Elizabeth saw fit to write him a very severe reprimand, and her letter, dated November 8, 1594, was put into his hands on the very day of his return. He was at a loss how to reply. Her Majesty said that "she nourished conceit of his evil carriage," on the ground of his want of prudence in his proceedings, of his slackness in obeying her commandments, of his over-great forwardness in matters concerning the States, and of rash venturing of the lives of her subjects. He answered that if he had not obeyed her orders exactly, it was from sincerity in her service; that his journey into France was sudden and was to protect the march of Count Philip; that all his men had returned safely and without loss. He concluded by saying boldly:

> If, in accepting this charge, being suddenly entreated thereunto, I have offended your Majesty, I humbly beseech I did so as part of my duty to yourself, since by your Majesty I am employed here to do the States service.—Vere to the Queen, Dec. 20, 1594. S. P. O., Holland, vol. lxxx.

Sir Francis was several weeks thinking over and preparing his answer to the queen's reprimand, and even then his heart failed him. He at last sent it under cover to Lord Burleigh, saying:

> I have presumed to reply, yet not being used to write to Her Majesty, neither knowing where I may be instructed what is fit, I have presumed to present your Lordship with a copy. I humbly beseech your Lordship to vouchsafe to read, and to provide either for the delivery or stay, as your Lordship shall judge for my good.—Vere to Lord Burleigh, from the Hague, Dec. 22, 1594.

The Lord Treasurer appears to have delivered the letter, and it did no injury to Sir Francis. The queen soon ceased to nourish "her conceit of his evil carriage," and her sound good sense led her to accept the explanation of one of the ablest and most loyal of her subjects.

Mr. Bodley and Mr. Gilpin were both at the Hague, yet the queen and Lord Burleigh required long reports from Sir Francis Vere on all political events, and on commercial and other enterprises which might be expected to come within his knowledge. Any neglect of this part of his multifarious duties brought down upon him a severe reprimand. This was excellent discipline. It called his powers of observation into play, and obliged him to reflect and ponder over the events, apart from military operations, which were passing around him. Since he landed with the Earl of Leicester at Flushing, a great nation had been created. The marvellous energy and intelligence of the Dutch people, during the last years of the sixteenth century, might well astonish contemporaries, as it has excited the admiration of posterity. They were fighting a powerful enemy who threatened their very existence, and at the same time they were engaged in a desperate struggle with the elements.

******

There hath been great loss in this last flood. The Betuwe and Bommel-waart were utterly drowned, the rivers being so swollen that the water ran over the dikes: 2 or 3,000,000 florins worth of damage. There hath not been such a flood in 400 years; caused by a sudden thaw after a long frost and great snow, while the tempest at S.W. stopped the river's mouth. (Vere, from the Hague, to Lord Burleigh, March 17, 1595.)

******

They lived, as it were, in a leaky, sinking ship, with enemies pouring in over the bows. Half the men were at the pumps day and night, while the rest of the crew repelled boarders. Yet, in the midst of this mortal struggle, they coolly prepared great commercial ventures, and dispatched expeditions of discovery.

It was the quality of calm intrepidity which at once raised this gallant people to a high position among the nations. Others have fought bravely for their independence. But no other people ever sent out Arctic expeditions and commercial voyages to the Indies, at a time when the sea was pouring wildly over their own homes, and a powerful enemy could hardly be kept from their doors. It was these glorious deeds which it was Sir Francis Vere's duty to watch and report upon.

In his letter of October 7, 1594, he related to Lord Burleigh the story of the attempt of Willem Barents to discover the north-east passage.

For the discovery of the passage to Chinay there were two ships sent hence at the country's charge with instructions, the one to search the passage along the continent, (by the Waigat), the other more to the northward, (round the north end of Novaya Zemlya), and when they had passed to the mayne to return. Either of them performed that he had in charge, both making the full discovery, and this report they make at their return. He who coasted the continent found a narrow passage, not so broad as that between Dover and Calais, where the greatest difficulty was that by reason of the narrowness it was soonest frozen, yet for six weeks it was open and navigable.

The other, which sailed more to the northwards, coasted that land which made the straight on the other side, and found an open sea to the northward. In comparing the courses which they held, they find the island lay between north and south 140 leagues. (Novaya Zemlya). The people like the greater sort of dwarfs, with great and flat faces, exceedingly active so that our men could not come near them. They are subtill enough, and their clothing skins. (Samoyedes, on the south coast of the Waigat). To this island they sailed in less than six weeks, and they hold it the better halfway to Chinay, so that if the passage were so long open, it were to be performed in six months. The next season they are to make the full discovery, being in great hope that a rich trade will be found that way.

In another letter Sir Francis reported the proceedings at Middelburg for the dispatch of the first Dutch voyage to the East.

They are sending forth two great ships to the East Indies by the ordinary way the Portugals use, the charge of which amounteth to 30,000 besides munition and artillery, which the States furnish.

In other despatches he reported upon the affairs of Hungary and of Persia.

After the resignation of Mr. Bodley in November, 1596, Mr. Gilpin became Her Majesty's envoy to the States, and from that time the employment of Sir Francis Vere on confidential and delicate missions to the States General, usually with Mr. Gilpin as a colleague, but sometimes single-handed, was frequent.

★★★★★★

Bodley was dissatisfied, and he declined to serve any longer in the States, owing to ill health. He wrote to Burleigh: "Never was any minister more faithful in Her Majesty's service nor no man living ever handled more hardly than myself. I will submit myself to any kind of rigour, rather than go again, for it will only work in Her Majesty further discontentment, and purchase more disgrace to all my actions in her service. (Bodley to Lord Burleigh, Nov. 18 and Dec. 18, 1596.) This man was not endowed with that patience and unselfish zeal which enable patriotic public servants to bear unreasonable censure as a part of the day's work.

******

The queen and her ministers were beginning to rely as much on his tact and judgment in the council-room as on his valour and conduct in the field. But they complained that his handwriting was illegible. In a letter to R. Cecil, dated Feb. 6, 1603, he says:

I do write unto your Honour with another pen, because I have heard your Honour cannot read my hand readily.

******

Yet his handwriting, though sprawling and unsightly, is very legible to modern readers, much more so than the hands of those who complained of it. He used two seals. One was simply the Vere arms, with a martlet charged with a crescent in the centre of the shield, to denote the second son of a fourth son. This was his usual seal. But he sometimes sealed his letters with a larger one, having a shield with eight quarterings: Vere, Bolebec, Sanford, Serjeaux, Badlesmere, Archdeacon, Trussell, and another; with an annulet in the centre.

******

Vere's private affairs fortunately required little attention. His mother and sister were entrusted to the efficient care of his elder brother John, and his two younger brothers were with him in the camp. But the head of the family had ruined a great estate. The Earl of Oxford had sold or mortgaged nearly every acre. By Lord Burleigh's daughter he had three daughters, (Elizabeth, Countess of Derby; Bridget, Lady Norris; and Susan, Countess of Montgomery), and the Treasurer was doing all in his power to save something out of the wreck for his grandchildren. John Vere and his mother had a long lease of Kirby Hall from the Earl, and Francis had a reversionary interest in the lease. Among other schemes, Lord Burleigh cast his eye upon this lease, in hopes of shortening it, or getting rid of it, in his grandchildren's interest. He applied to John Vere to surrender the lease, who demurred on the ground that the reversion belonged to his brother. Burleigh then addressed himself direct to Sir Francis. As that officer's advancement depended mainly on Burleigh's good will, this proceeding was in very questionable taste. The reply was satisfactory, Sir Francis wrote:

> As touching my brother's lease, which your Lordship desireth and he deferreth to part with in respect of me, it may please your Lordship to understand that I have signified unto him how greatly I desire your Lordship should be satisfied therein, so that I am out of doubt he will be conformable: and so much the rather for the entail your Lordship maketh to those ladies, whose honour and good, by all manner of obligation, we are bound to desire and further. I thought fit to inform your Lordship whereby my brother's slowness in resolution may be excused concerning this matter; that our mother nor any of us have where to put our heads but there; and myself, on whom a part of their hope is grounded, the greatest beggar of all, if by your Lordship's favourable patronage I be not supported.

A few months afterwards Burleigh wrote again on the same subject, and elicited a reply from Sir Francis that "as to the lease I will pass my interest therein fully to your Lordship." (Vere to Lord Burleigh, Nov. 7, 1593, and Jan. 7, 1594). Yet the scheme of taking the lease of Kirby Hall from this branch of the Veres, for the benefit of Burleigh's grandchildren, must have fallen through. For the old place continued to be the residence of their mother until her death, then of John Vere and his widow, and afterwards of Horace Vere's widow. Francis, being unmarried and in active service, gave the matter little thought Doubtless he was glad enough of the chance of complying with the request made to him by the powerful Lord Treasurer. During the winter of 1592-93 he was in England for a short time; but he had no opportunity of seeing his family again until he returned to Kirby Hall, bringing with him the tidings of a great sorrow.

The year 1596 opened with festivities, for in February Count Philip of Hohenlohe Langenburg was married to the Lady Mary, eldest daughter of William the Taciturn. The ceremony took place at the castle of Buren, in Gelderland, the States General and all the principal officers of the army being invited. In the same year her half-sister Elizabeth was married to the Duc de Bouillon. She became the mother of the famous Marshal Turenne. This year, also, saw the last of the two oldest English officers who had served in the war for freedom. Sir Thomas Morgan had continued to be governor of Bergen-op-Zoom until 1593, when old age obliged him to retire.

★★★★★★

He was deprived of the government of Bergen-op-Zoom very ungraciously. The Council of State, in Holland, took this resolution on the ground that a governor was unnecessary, and that the charge might be entrusted to the senior captain in the garrison, Bodley urged in opposition "that Morgan was the ancientest captain that had served in this country, and it could not but be taken very ill by Her Majesty." (Bodley to Lord Burleigh, April 12, 1593.)

★★★★★★

He was the very first volunteer to land at Flushing. Sir Roger Williams had been Morgan's companion when the volunteers first landed, and had served with distinction ever since. He was the most daring and headlong of all the English volunteers. In 1591 he had been transferred to France, where he continued his dashing exploits. Morgan and Williams both died in the same year. The funeral of Sir Roger Williams took place at St. Paul's, (Camden), and was attended by all his brother officers who were then in England.

★★★★★★

His writings were: *The Actions of the Lowe Countries,* printed by Humphrey Lownes in 1618; *A brief Discourse of War, with his Opinion concerning some part of Military Discipline.* London, 1590. *The Actions of the Lowe Countries* were reprinted in the *Somers Tracts*, 1. Grimeston's translation of the *History of the Netherlands* by Jean Francois le Petit (London, folio, 1609), contains additions from the *MSS.* of Sir Roger Williams. Williams also wrote *A Discourse of the Discipline of the Spaniards.* See Wood's *Athenae,* Oxon., 1. col. 643.

★★★★★★

In July, 1595, Maurice took the field with all his forces, including the English contingent under General Vere, and laid siege to Grolle. The Spanish forces were once more under the command of the ablest officer in Philip's service. Verdugo was dead; but Colonel Mondragon, the aged governor of Antwerp, took the field with the object of thwarting Maurice in any siege operations he might attempt, and closely watching his movements. The Count Herman de Berghe was

THE COUNTRY ABOUT WESEL.

nominally in chief command, but Mondragon, now actually in his ninetieth year, was the ruling spirit.

******

Count Herman of Berghe is in command, but Mondragon swayeth all. (F. Vere to Lord Burleigh, July 20, 1595. MSS. at Hatfield, vol. 31.

******

The works before Grolle were expeditiously begun, and the approaches had reached the counterscarp in several places, when Mondragon's army came in sight and offered battle. As Maurice was inferior in numbers, the States would not consent to a general action. The siege was consequently raised, and Mondragon, having relieved Grolle, fell back to a position on the Rhine, at Orsoy above Rheinberg, whence he could watch Maurice's every movement. The patriot army then encamped at Bislich, on the right bank of the Rhine, a few miles below Wesel, where it was strongly entrenched.

******

Vere to Lord Burleigh, July 10 and July 20, 1595, and Aug. 22. MSS. at Hatfield. Vere says that Maurice was resolved not to give battle. He adds: "Our drift is to hold the enemy here, and by lodging near to take such occasions as may be offered to give them a blow. For we hold it no small service to keep these men from making war in France."

******

The River Lippe, flowing from east to west, falls into the Rhine at Wesel. The army of Maurice was on the northern side of this river, with his headquarters at Bislich; Mondragon on the south side, with his headquarters at Rheinberg and Orsoy. On the south side, eastward from Wesel, the valley of the Lippe consists of a great moor called the Spellener Heide, bounded by a range of moorland hills called the Tester-berge, which approach the left bank of the Lippe. On the opposite bank is the little village of Crudenburg and the old castle of Schwarzenstein. The river is deep and rapid, and about twenty-four yards wide, with steep banks. Crudenburg is about five miles east of Wesel. On the south bank there are water meadows of no great width; then a very sandy heath with scrubby undergrowth, whence the hills of the Tester-berge rise abruptly. On the north side the country is a sandy moor, now partly cultivated, and with many pine and oak plantations.

It was observed by the Dutch cavalry outposts that the slopes of the Tester-berge were occupied by the enemy, but it was believed that the force did not consist of more than two cornets of horse. Young Count Philip of Nassau proposed a daring plan to cut them off, by fording or swimming the river with a body of cavalry, and charging across the moor. His scheme was approved with some reluctance, and he was allowed to organize a picked force of 500 men for the service. His brothers Ernest and Louis, and his nephew Ernest de Solms, Count Buchert de Kinski, Prevost de Sallandt, Godart de Balen, and Sir Marcellus Bacx led the Dutch troops, while the English were commanded by Sir Nicholas Parker and Robert Vere.

On August 22nd the reckless chivalry of Holland and England assembled along the banks of the Lippe. The project was wilder and more desperate than the Balaclava charge. They plunged into the river near Crudenburg, swam their horses over, and galloped across the moor. Mondragon knew all that was in preparation. The wily old fox had brought up his forces during the night, and, instead of finding two cornets of horse, Count Philip and his gallant followers encountered half the Spanish army. When this became evident there was only the choice between hasty retreat and a glorious death. Not a man hesitated. Putting spurs to their horses' flanks the 500 dashed into the enemy's ranks, and fought with desperate valour until they were overpowered by numbers. Count Kinski fell, mortally wounded. Count Philip and his nephew, Ernest Solms, had their horses killed under them, were badly wounded, and taken prisoners. Young Robert Vere nobly upheld the honour of his family on that fateful day. Fighting manfully in the thickest of the press, he was slain by the blow of a lance in the face.

******

Motley says that Robert Vere was taken prisoner and murdered in cold blood. But he does not indicate his authority. Sir Francis Vere, in his letter to Lord Burleigh, reported that his brother was slain in the battle by a blow in the face from a lance.

******

Sir Nicholas Parker and Marcellus Bacx conducted the retreat, which was covered by Prince Maurice with the reserves on the opposite bank. Count Philip and young Solms were conveyed to Rheinberg, where they were treated with all possible kindness and attention by old Mondragon. But they died of their wounds, and their bodies were sent to Maurice, in his camp at Bislich. (Grimeston. Meteren, Bentivoglio. Vere to Lord Burleigh, August 24, 1595).

The two armies continued to watch each other during September, and in October Mondragon, after ravaging the country of Juliers, marched into Brabant, (old Mondragon died the following winter, 1596), while Maurice went into winter-quarters. Sir Francis bore generous testimony to his ability and powers of organisation. ("His Excellency hath made his army exceeding perfect and fit for any hazard."— F. Vere to the Earl of Essex, October 1, 1595. MSS. at Hatfield.)

Sir Nicholas Parker, of whose conduct Sir Francis Vere spoke very highly in his despatch to Lord Burleigh, brought the melancholy tidings of the death of Robert to his two brothers. The loss was deeply felt. The three young men had scarcely ever been separated. From childhood they had studied and played together in their Essex home. Francis had gone to the wars first, but he had soon sent for his younger brothers, and they had been comrades for several years. Robert had first borne arms in 1589, for when Sir Francis returned, after his visit to England, he brought back his next brother with him.

Robert entered the cavalry, and continued to serve in that arm until his death. Horace joined them in 1590, and served in his elder brother's company of foot. Robert and Horace looked to their brother for guidance and advancement. They soon became useful officers, and there was always affectionate harmony between them. When the troops had been distributed into winter-quarters Francis and Horace obtained leave to visit England. It was a sad homecoming. They rode away into Essex as soon as they landed, to break the news to their mother and sister, (sister Frances was still living at home, she was married to Robert Harcourt, at Barking in Essex, on March 20, 1598), and to tell them that there must be a place vacant for evermore when the family assembled round the old hearth at Kirby.

During this visit Sir Francis Vere was taken more closely into the counsels of his sovereign. It had been decided that a great blow should be struck at Spain, that the war should be carried into the enemy's country; but the cooperation of the States General was necessary. Sir Francis was not only to have an important command in the expedition to Cadiz, but he was entrusted with all the negotiations on the subject with the States General.

Chapter 16

Cadiz

The resolution to carry the war into the enemy's country, and to strike a blow at Spain on Spanish ground, was arrived at, by the queen and her ministers, in the autumn of 1595. The Earl of Essex, then aged twenty-eight, and Lord Howard of Effingham were to be entrusted with the command of the expedition by land and sea, and they both advanced sums of money out of their private fortunes to help in its equipment. Preparations were made on a large scale, and with as much secrecy as possible; and it was considered that the United Provinces ought to furnish substantial aid for the common cause. Sir Francis Vere was entrusted with a confidential mission to the Hague, the object of which was to secure help from the States, in ships and troops.

On the 1st of March, 1596, Sir Francis, after a long and stormy passage, arrived at Middelburg, and hastened on to the Hague. He found the country full of alarms about Spanish invasions, and he anticipated that these alarms would be used as excuses for making difficulties about the queen's demands, but he was resolved to execute his mission by urging the reasons for compliance. He submitted her Majesty's wishes to the States on the day of his arrival at the Hague. On the 7th of March, Barneveldt waited upon him, to ask whether the queen's purposes were so absolute that no excuses nor allegations could be admitted. Vere, in reply, assured him that the demand was urgent, and implored him to induce the States to come to a speedy and favourable decision. After much discussion with Barneveldt during the ensuing days, the objects of Vere's mission were secured, and on the 20th the States announced to him that they would comply with the queen's wishes. The expenses would be heavy, but several deputies declared that:

There was no surer way of putting a good end to the war than to transport the same nearer to the heart of the great enemy.—Vere to Lord Burleigh, March 1, 7, 9, 20, 1596.

During his stay at the Hague, Sir Francis encouraged and incited Count Louis Gunther of Nassau to obtain the command of the Dutch contingent. The young count wrote for leave to his father, saying that:

> The enterprise will be of great importance to the good of all Christendom, and that such a voyage may never offer again for a young soldier like me, who will thus not only see England but all other countries.—*Le Comte Louis Gunther au Comte Jean de Nassau depart pour. Anglete*rre. (Prinsterer *Lettre xcvii.* 2nd Series, 1.)

He left the Hague with Sir Francis Vere, having obtained the appointment, and accompanied him to Middelburg, where active preparations were being made. Vere was to take with him a thousand of his English veterans, who were in the pay of the States, and at his earnest request they received a month's pay in advance. By the 22nd of April he was ready to sail from Flushing with them, to join the expedition. He found the whole fleet assembled at Dover.

The fleet was divided into four squadrons, under the command of Lord Howard of Effingham as lord admiral, the Earl of Essex as lord general, Lord Thomas Howard as vice-admiral, and Sir Walter Raleigh as rear-admiral. The lord admiral was in the *Ark Royal*, with Sir Ames Preston as his captain; and Captain Monson was the sailor and navigator in charge of the *Repulse*, with the Earl of Essex. Lord Thomas had the *Mere-honour*, and Raleigh the *Warspite*. Sir Francis Vere was lieutenant-general and lord marshal, and in command of the *Rainbow*. He was to be the chief adviser of Essex, and the conduct of operations on shore was practically entrusted to him.

Sir George Carew was master of the ordnance, and in command of the *Mary Rose*; Sir Conyers Clifford, in the *Dreadnought*, was sergeant-major general; Sir John Wingfield, in the *Vanguard*, was camp-master; Sir Robert Dudley had the *Nonpareil*, Sir Robert Southwell the *Lion*, Sir Robert Cross the *Swiftsure*, Sir George Gifford the *Quittance*, Captain King the *Tremontaine*. There were also twelve ships of London, and twenty-two Hollanders and Flushingers under Count William of Nassau. The council of war to advise the general consisted of the Earl of Essex, Sir Francis Vere, and four colonels of regiments, the Earl of Sussex, Sir Christopher Blount, Sir T. Gerard, and Sir John Wingfield.

The Earl of Essex went on board the *Rainbow* when the fleet got under weigh at Dover, in order to confer with Sir Francis Vere on the plan of the expedition; and, landing near Rye, they both went up to court, while the ships proceeded to Plymouth. After consultation with the queen and Burleigh, Sir Francis posted down into the west country, and set to work diligently with the organization of the troops. There were altogether 6,360 soldiers and 1,000 volunteers, besides nearly 7,000 sailors. The whole month of May was devoted to drilling the men and equipping the ships at Plymouth.

The army was regularly organised, with grades of officers from the general downwards. But the naval officers were in positions which were undefined. Sir Walter Raleigh, with all his great qualities and accomplishments, had a high idea of his own importance, and considered that his appointment of rear-admiral gave him superior rank to the lord marshal. Vere rightly held that the discipline and efficiency of the land force depended on his being next in rank to the General. Raleigh was a much older man. He had served with the Huguenots when Vere was a boy at school. He had since done good service in Ireland, had fitted out expeditions to Virginia, had commanded in a voyage to Guiana, and had risen to high favour with the queen. He considered himself a far more important personage than the zealous and hardworking general of the forces in the Netherlands, who was ten years his junior. He had several eager and not very wise supporters and admirers among the younger volunteers.

One evening, after dinner, when the officers were sitting over their wine, some words passed, on the question of rank, between Sir Francis Vere and Sir Edward Cooke, in the presence of the general and the officers of the Dutch fleet. The matter was taken up by a hot-headed youth named Arthur Throckmorton, "who used such words that my lords ordered him from the table."(Sir A. Standen to Anthony Bacon, May 23, 1596. Birch, ii.) This led to the question of military rank being seriously considered; and eventually the general ordered that Sir Francis Vere should have precedence of Raleigh on shore, and that Sir Walter Raleigh should be the superior officer at sea. Vere then assisted the Earl of Essex in drawing up the articles of war, (Birch, ii.), and at the same time they set down in writing the duties of each officer. (Vere's *Commentaries*).

All things being at length arranged, the fleet anchored in Cawsand Bay on the 1st of June, 1596, and made sail before a northeast wind on the 2nd, which carried them across the Bay of Biscay. There were high hopes and patriotic resolves in the hearts of those who manned that fleet. Philip's Armada had insulted the coasts, and filled the homes of England with alarm and dread. Eight years had passed away, and now the chivalry of England was about to return the compliment. Everything that was calculated to arouse the enthusiasm of young soldiers and volunteers seemed to unite in this memorable adventure. The lord admiral was the same dauntless seaman who had repulsed the great Armada.

Raleigh's very name was enough to call forth the ardour and zeal of his companions. For who among them had not heard of his deeds of valour and adventure in Guiana and the Spanish Main? Who had not read, with a thrill of pride and wonder, his narrative of the fight of the *Revenge*, and of the death of Sir Richard Grenville? The very ships which had basely triumphed then were in Cadiz now; and Raleigh, as he said, was on his way to 'revenge the *Revenge*.' There too was the gallant Sir Francis Vere, who had upheld the honour of England in the Low Countries for ten years, in numberless battles and sieges; who was covered with scars received in the fight for freedom; and under whose banner it was the dream of every brave English boy some day to learn the art of war.

With him was the flower of his army: his gallant young brother Horace; Oliver Lambart, who fought by his side in the romantic relief of Rheinberg; Wingfield, Parker, and many another good man and true from the Netherlands field force. And if the adventurers were justly proud of their leaders, they were equally proud of the glorious cause in which they were employed. They were to fight for their country and their beloved queen against the bitter and cruel enemy of both. They had all heard of the horrors of the Inquisition, and of the fate of the gentle Indians of America. What man could inform them more fully on such points than their rear-admiral? Their hearts overflowed with pity and indignation when these stories were recounted, and they believed that they drew their swords "for the good of all Christendom," as young Louis of Nassau expressed it. Yet they approached the Spanish coast in no savage mood. They would fight with those who resisted, but they would be full of chivalrous courtesy to the vanquished.

In this spirit the English adventurers rounded Cape St. Vincent. The ships had kept out of sight of land, while passing the coast of Portugal, lest the news of their approach should precede them. Their three best sailers—the *Litness*, *Lion's Whelp*, and *Truelove*—were sent on in advance to stop any small vessels which might spread tidings of the coming danger. By this precaution three fly-boats, bound for Cadiz, were captured and detained; and early in the morning of the 20th of June the fleet anchored off the spit of San Sebastian, on the southern side of the city of Cadiz.

The ancient city of Cadiz is built at the extremity of a narrow spit of land, six miles long, which forms a bay, a great part of which is very shallow. One deep channel, from half to a quarter of a mile wide, passes down its centre to Puerto Real, and there is another port, called Santa Maria, on the north side of the bay, which can only be approached by vessels drawing very little water. Cadiz was a walled town, with a small harbour called the Caleta, and a long spit at the end of which was the fort of San Sebastian, on the southern side. On the north side it was defended by the castle of San Felipe, which commanded the entrance of the bay; and the castle of Puntales further east, facing the narrowest part of the channel of Puntales, leading to Puerto Real.

To the west of the town, at the entrance of the bay, there are rocks, called Las Puercas and Los Cochinos; and near them was the anchorage where it was usual for the fleets bound for the Indies to assemble before taking their final departure. On that Sunday morning, when the English fleet hove in sight, there was a fleet of forty richly laden merchant ships at anchor off Las Puercas, about to sail for Mexico. They were to be convoyed by four large men-of-war, ("Four of the King's greatest and warlikest galleons."; Vere),—the *San Felipe, San Mateo, San Andres,* and *San Tomas,*—two great Lisbon galleons, two *argosies* which had great ordnance for ballast, and three war frigates. Nearer the town there were seventeen galleys, commanded by Don Juan Portocarrero.

The Spaniards were taken entirely by surprise. Hasty preparations were made for defence. The forty merchant ships were sent up the Puntales channel to Puerto Real. The four men-of-war were anchored in the narrowest part of the channel, with their broadsides to the sea. In their rear were the *argosies* and frigates. The galleys were ranged under Fort Puntales, with their bows, armed with long guns, pointing across the channel. By these dispositions the Spaniards hoped to repel the English attacking force, and save the merchant ships.

The English fleet had anchored off San Sebastian, outside the bay, and it had been hastily determined to attempt a landing at the Caleta. Troops were actually got into the boats, which were made fast astern of the ships, and the landing was only delayed by the heavy sea caused by a fresh gale. Spanish troops also were seen, ready to oppose the attempt. The *Warspite* had been behind the rest of the fleet, and when she arrived Sir Walter Raleigh went on board the *Repulse*, and protested strongly against the plan of landing at the Caleta. He said that unless the Spanish fleet was first defeated a landing would fail, and that therefore the English ships ought to come round into the bay. Essex was convinced, but he said that the lord admiral had the direction of operations at sea. Raleigh went on board the *Ark Royal*, and his arguments induced Lord Howard to alter the plan of attack. He then jumped into his boat, and pulled back to the *Repulse* to announce the change. Essex was eagerly waiting on the poop, and when Raleigh shouted *Entramos* to him as he came alongside, the excitable young earl threw his hat into the air for joy, and it dropped overboard.

The troops were all got on board again, but not before some of the boats had been swamped and a few men drowned. Towards evening the fleet was got under weigh, and anchored at the entrance of the bay, inside Las Puercas, ready for the attack next morning. Vere found himself to leeward of the other ships, and he hoped to get a better place by being under weigh first. So he began to heave up his anchor before the rest. There was a heavy sea, and he had forgotten to swift his capstan bars; this being his first command at sea. The ship was pitching, and the capstan proved too strong for the men, who were hurled backwards, and several were badly hurt.

So Vere cut his cable in the hawse, made sail, and worked to windward up the bay until he was able to anchor within range of the Spanish ships and forts. Late in the evening the lord admiral displayed the flag of council in his mizzen rigging, as a signal for the Earl of Essex and the other officers to come on board the *Ark Royal*. It was resolved to move up the bay with the tide next morning, and to board the Spanish ships; stations were arranged, and Raleigh was to lead the attack. But the eagerness to be first outweighed all other considerations. Vere submitted that the *Rainbow* drew less water than the larger ships, and that it was desirable that she should go in ahead of them. Essex replied sharply, "In any case you shall not go in before me."

Lord Thomas Howard shifted his flag to the *Nonpareil*, which was of lighter draft than the *Mere-honour*, and claimed the foremost place. Raleigh was determined to get ahead, and wrote afterwards that "always I must without glory say for myself that I held single in the head of all." They were all behaving like a pack of schoolboys, and it seemed likely there would be a regular scramble next morning.

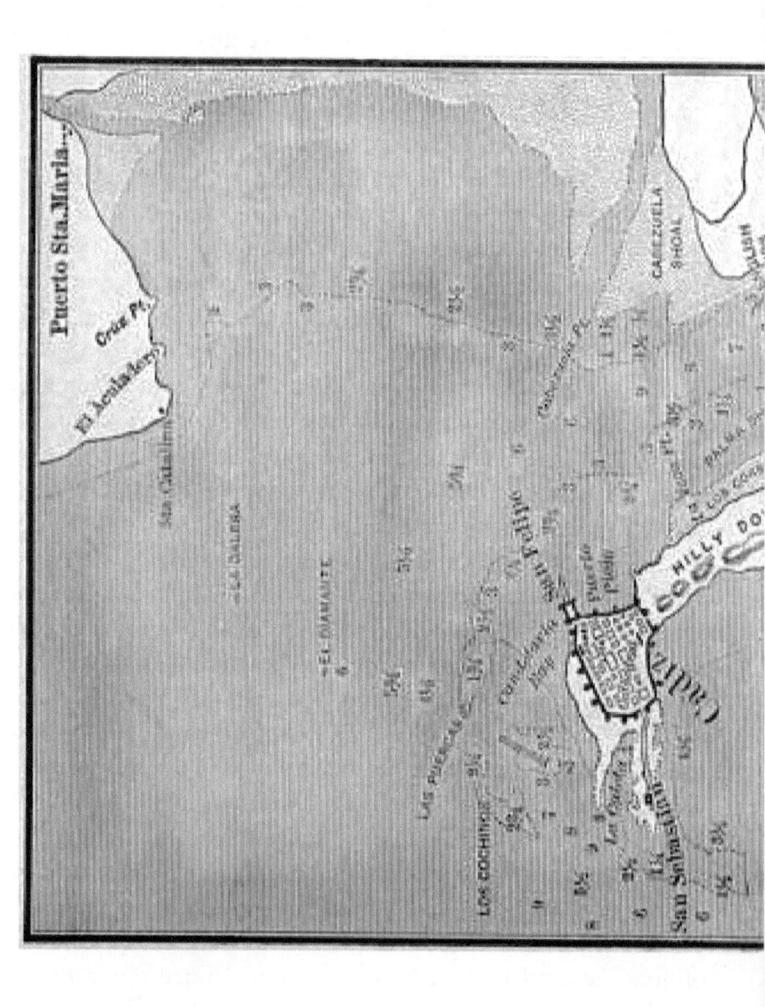

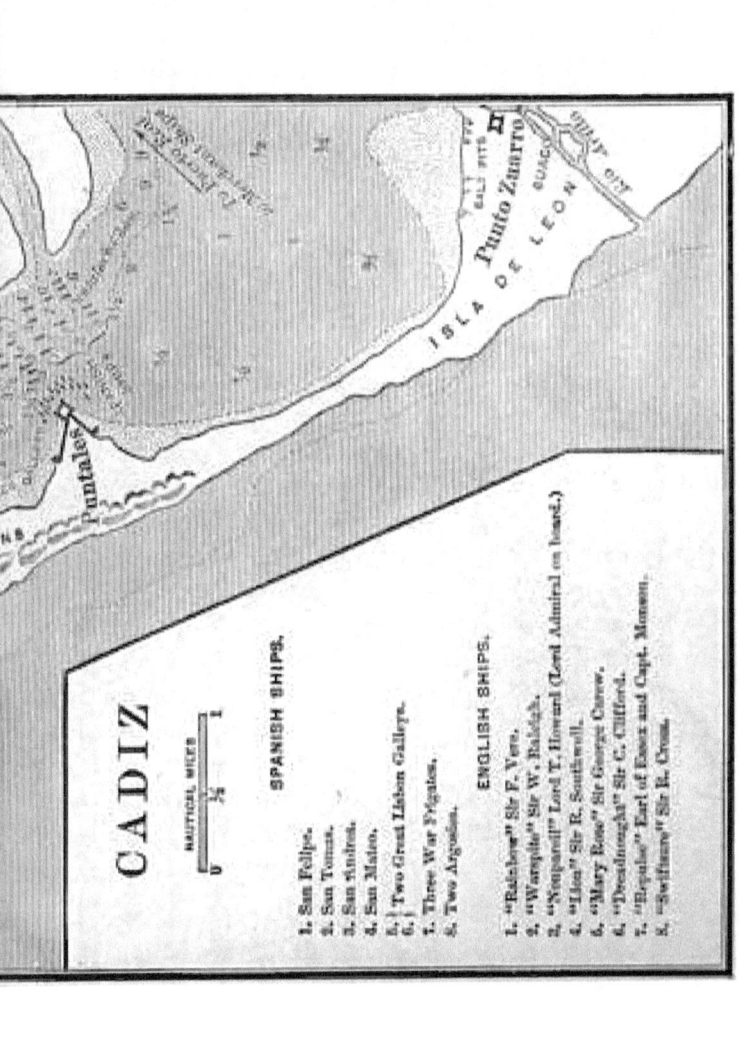

The four Spanish men-of-war remained with their broadsides across the passage, about in a line with the Puntales fort, and the seventeen galleys were close in under the land, to flank the enemy as his ships approached. Vere was much excited and interested in a conflict the nature of which was quite new to him; "having till that time been a stranger to actions at sea." During the night he brought the *Rainbow* up over her anchor, ready to make sail when the tide served next morning. He was the first to get into action, firing his heavy ordnance at the galleys, and driving them still further under the walls of the fort. He kept approaching them, with the lead constantly going, until he came within range of Puntales fort and the ships, and was exposed to a heavy fire on all sides, to which he promptly replied. The master of the *Rainbow* then anchored, being closer in shore than any of the other ships. The *Warspite* was next to him, and a little ahead, engaged with the large Spanish ships.

Next came Lord Thomas Howard in the *Nonpareil*, with the lord admiral also on board. Near the centre of the channel was Sir Robert Southwell in the *Lion*; and on the eastern side were Sir George Carew and Sir C. Clifford in the *Mary Rose* and *Dreadnought*. A little later Essex came up in the *Repulse* and Sir Robert Cross in the *Swiftsure*. Soon they were all closely engaged with the Spaniards, the cannonade lasting several hours, and the guns becoming very hot. Raleigh thought that if the firing continued his ship would be sunk, so he went in his boat to the general, to ask for fly-boats to board the enemy. While he was gone Lord Thomas got under weigh and shot ahead of the *Warspite*, and Sir Francis Vere sent a boat with a hawser to make fast to the *Warspite's* stern, in order to haul the *Rainbow* ahead. When Raleigh came back he cut Vere's hawser unceremoniously, and put his ship broadside across the channel, to prevent the others from getting ahead of him. The firing was then renewed, and continued until four in the afternoon, when the Spaniards gave it up in despair, trying to run the ships on shore. Their men abandoned them. Raleigh says:

> Heaps of sailors were tumbling into the sea, as thick as if coals had been poured out of a sack, some being drowned, others sticking in the mud.

The galleys slipped their cables, made sail, and ran up the bay. Three were taken by Sir John Wingfield in the *Vanguard*, but the rest passed through a narrow channel at the south end of the Isle of Leon, and got out to sea. Vere hurried on board the *Repulse* to urge the general to send boats with boarding parties to secure the grounded ships. Captain Monson went on this duty from the *Ark Royal*, and Sir William Constable, with some soldiers, from the *Repulse*, and two ships were captured, the *San Mateo* and *San Andres*. The Spaniards set fire to the flagship *San Felipe*, of 1,500 tons, and to the *San Tomas*. They were burnt to the water's edge. The *argosies* were taken by the Dutch ships under Louis of Nassau, and it was found that their ballast consisted of heavy ordnance. This hotly contested action had lasted from break of day until the afternoon. Sir Walter Raleigh was severely wounded in the leg by a splinter, and was unable to take part in the subsequent proceedings. He had been the true leader among the naval officers.

******

In discussing the question of ships versus forts, Sir Walter Raleigh said: "The fort St. Philip terrified us not, in the year 1596, when we entered the port of Cadiz; neither did the fort of Puntal, when we were entered, beat us from our anchoring by it, though it played upon us with four demi-cannons within point blank, from six in the morning till twelve at noon. (*History of the World, lib. v. cap.* i.)

******

Sir Francis Vere then took the lead in the land operations for the capture of Cadiz. The last half of a summer's afternoon was left, and there was not a moment to be lost. Boats were got ready, and the regiments of Essex, Vere, Blount, Gerard, and Clifford were told off as a landing party. The disembarkation was to be effected on a spit of land between Puntales and the town. The boats were placed in line and at equal distances: the regiments of Essex and Vere on the right and nearest the town, the other three on the left. The general and the lord marshal led in a boat some distance in advance, and gave the signals by beat of drum. They were closely followed by smaller boats, full of richly dressed young gentlemen volunteers. The bows of the boats touched the shore almost at the same moment, and the soldiers jumped out and formed in line without opposition. About 2,000 men landed.

On the land side, facing the spit, Cadiz was defended by a wall, with a gate in the centre and bastions at each angle, against which the sea washed at high tides. These fortifications and the strength of the garrison had taken away all idea, in the minds of the English Council of War, of taking the place without first landing heavy guns, placing them in position, and battering the walls. The first thought of Essex was, therefore, to select a site for the encampment.

Sir Francis Vere had a different plan. The spit of land was about half a mile across, and on the western side there were low hills, under which both cavalry and foot were seen to be hurrying into Cadiz. The three regiments of Blount, Clifford, and Gerard were sent southwards to the narrowest part of the spit, to guard the approach and prevent further communication between the town and the mainland. There remained a force consisting of the regiments of Essex and Vere and about 250 gentlemen volunteers, in all not quite a thousand men. The Spaniards were drawn up outside the walls, with some light horse thrown forward, apparently to invite a skirmish.

Vere then explained his plan for taking the town that night, pointing out that those very Spanish troops before the town would show the way into it, if they were properly handled. Essex, who when kept in good-humour was quite ready to listen to advice, and whose fiery valour made him eager for any hazardous enterprise, entered heartily into the scheme of the lord marshal. It was to lead the troops as near as possible to the town wall, under cover of the low hills on the west side of the spit, then to draw the Spaniards into a fight with what would appear to be an inferior force, drive them back in confusion and disorder, and enter the town with them.

Vere marched all the men over to the west side of the spit. He then picked out 200 soldiers, placed them under Sir John Wingfield, "a right valiant knight," and gave him his instructions. He was to march rapidly on the Spanish troops, drive in their skirmishers, and if the main body advanced against him he was to make a hasty retreat until he met his supports, and then to turn upon the enemy furiously. The supports consisted of 300 men under Sir Matthew Morgan, and they were to advance as soon as they saw Wingfield retreating. Essex and Vere were to follow with the main body. Count Louis of Nassau, the Earl of Sussex, Sir Robert Drury, and Christopher Heydon were with them.

The orders were so ably carried out that the Spaniards were fully engaged in chasing Wingfield before they discovered his supports. When fresh men suddenly appeared the Spaniards turned and fled. They were so closely followed that the cavalry abandoned their horses, and the fugitives saved themselves, some by the gates, which were hurriedly closed, and others by clambering over the walls.

The whole English force, led by Essex and Vere, then came up to the walls, which extended from sea to sea, with a broad dry ditch in front. The ramparts were massive and high, with a round bastion at either end; but they were not scarped, so that it was easy to mount them. These outer walls were, however, overtopped some six feet by the old wall of the town behind. Vere's veterans from the Low Countries, gallantly led by Essex himself, climbed up the outer wall, scaled the inner defence, and drove the enemy back with their shot.

Lieutenant Evans, of the regiment of Lord Sussex, was the first man over the wall. He had to leap down a pike's length. Arthur Savage followed close at his heels. Meanwhile, Vere sent a countryman of his, named Upsher, with a few men to see what guard was kept on the eastern side, towards the bay, and to report whether an entrance could also be effected in that direction. Upsher found a very slender guard, and entered the town on that side with slight opposition. Vere was on the ramparts, directing the operations. He saw that Essex was among the first to get over the wall, followed by the soldiers, that he was keeping no order, and that all were rushing recklessly up the streets.

He therefore determined to break down the gates, and to march in with a reserve force, which he could keep in hand. The gates were forced open with much difficulty and some delay. Sir Francis then marched in with his troops, (Camden says that Essex went through the gates with Vere), in good order, and advanced to the market-place, where he found Essex engaged with the enemy. Most of those who kept up any resistance retreated into the town hall, where they surrendered to Vere, and the Earl of Essex took possession. Vere then scoured the town and drove all the Spaniards out of the streets, either into the castle of San Felipe or the convent of San Francisco. Towards sunset about 200 Spanish cavaliers, who had taken refuge in the convent, surrendered, and the castle was delivered up the following day. Meanwhile, the lord admiral had landed with more troops, and guards were stationed along the walls, under Sir Edward Conway.

Thanks were offered up to God for this great victory, in the town hall, and afterwards the Earl of Essex conferred the honour of knighthood on Sir Samuel Bagnall, (he had received eight wounds, Arthur Savage was also wounded and knighted), for his special merit in the day's service. The loss was not very great on either side, but the English had to mourn the death of the gallant Sir John Wingfield, who fell mortally wounded in the market-place, just before all resistance ceased.

★★★★★★

Sir John Wingfield, brother-in-law of Lord Willoughby, was the same officer who was falsely accused and slandered by the

Dutch authorities when the mutinous garrison delivered up Gertruydenburg to the Spaniards. Wingfield was a man of honour and a valiant officer.

✶✶✶✶✶✶

When the people who had taken refuge in the castle of San Felipe surrendered next morning, they were treated with the utmost courtesy and consideration. The ladies received every sort of civility from their English captors, the memory of which is preserved in the old ballad of the "Spanish Lady."

✶✶✶✶✶✶

Percy's Reliques, ii. The hero of the story was supposed to be either Sir Richard Leveson of Trentham, or a Popham of Littlecote. But the late Mr. Charles Long fully established the claim of a young member of the family of Bowles of Swineshead. Jewels which belonged to the Spanish lady of the ballad were in possession of the Lees of Coldrey.

✶✶✶✶✶

About 5,000 Spaniards, including women and priests, were allowed to leave the town. Dr. Quesada, who knew English, remained to make terms and to obtain leave for non-combatants to depart. The terms were that citizens might depart with their clothes, that they should pay a ransom of 520,000 *ducats*, and that some of the chief citizens should remain as hostages for payment. All English galley-slaves were to be delivered up. All priests, women, and children who wished to go were taken across the bay to Puerto Santa Maria in boats.

✶✶✶✶✶✶

We have the testimony of Herrera on the subject of the conduct of the English at Cadiz: "In this affair the English behaved in divine matters as heretics, in human as politicians and men of war. They did not torture more than four or five to make them give up hidden treasure, they killed no one in cold blood, they ill used no woman, they took away no prisoners. The Earl of Essex ordered a man to be hanged for taking a cloth from a woman." (Lib. xii. cap. xii.)

✶✶✶✶✶✶

The forty merchant ships, all laden with valuable cargoes, had escaped up the channel to Puerto Real. Essex, when he landed, had sent a message to the lord admiral, by Sir William Monson and Sir Anthony Ashley the treasurer, entreating him to take prompt measures for the capture of these merchant ships. But the admiral, fearing that Essex's force was too weak, thought it necessary to land with reinforcements, in the first place. Meanwhile, the Duke of Medina Sidonia ordered all the ships and their cargoes to be burnt. The conflagration took place on the 23rd of June. The loss to the merchants of Seville and Cadiz was estimated at 20,000,000 *ducats*. (Camden. The report in the State Paper Office gives the loss at 8,000,000 crowns. The merchants had offered Essex 2,000,000 as ransom).

The English remained a fortnight at Cadiz. Besides Sir Samuel Bagnall, a number of officers received the honour of knighthood. Among them were the admiral's son William Howard, the lord marshal's brother Horace Vere, Christopher Heydon, Oliver Lambart, William Pooley, Nicholas Meetkerk, John Buck, John Aldrich, and Arthur Throckmorton.

★★★★★★

George Buck, the author of *The Life of Richard III.*, was also in the Cadiz expedition. But he was not knighted until 1603, when he became Master of the Revels.

★★★★★★

Sir Francis Vere received the ransoms of three wealthy prisoners: a clergyman, who was president of the Casa de Contratacion at Seville, and two cavaliers, named Don Pedro de Herrera and Don Geronimo de Avalos.

★★★★★★

I have received of certain Spaniards taken in Cadiz, for their ransoms, the sum of 12,570 *ducats* at 5s. 6d. the piece, moreover 50 or 60 of plate, and a suit of buttons which cost me 40 shillings each to see Sir Oliver Lambart. That is all I set down to the Commissioners at Plymouth. (F. Vere to the Earl of Essex, August 15, 1596. MSS. at Hatfield.) In the report of the commissioners appointed to inquire into the amount of booty taken at Cadiz, the value of Vere's share is set down at £3,638 15s. See *Archaologia*, xxii.

★★★★★★

The town was set on fire, and the fleet departed on the 5th of July. After stopping at a small port named Faroll, on the coast of Algarve, for fresh provisions, a course was shaped for England, and on the 8th of August the victorious expedition arrived safely at Plymouth. The fleet was increased by two large Spanish prizes, the *San Mateo* and *San Andres*, which were the more welcome because they formed part of the great fleet to which the little *Revenge* was forced to surrender in

1592.

As soon as the English expedition had made sail, Don Antonio Osorio entered Cadiz with 600 men, and he was soon followed by the Duke of Medina Sidonia. They found that the cathedral, the church of the Jesuits, the nunneries of Santa Maria and Candelaria, and 290 houses had been burnt. (Madoz). The most serious loss was the library of the Jesuits. Among that priceless collection was the manuscript history of the Jesuit Bias Valera, containing particulars respecting the Incas of Peru by one whose opportunities for collecting information were unequalled, and whose education and linguistic talent enabled him to profit by those opportunities to the full. The fragments that were saved from the fire were utilised by Garcilasso de la Vega in his *Royal Commentaries*. But the bulk was destroyed. The loss to posterity is irreparable. (See the introduction to my translation of the *Royal Commentaries* of Garci lasso de la Vega; Hakluyt Society, 1869).

The sack of Cadiz, with the destruction of the fleet, was a blow from which Philip II. and his government never recovered. It ruined the merchants and crippled the resources of the country, while it clouded the last years of the tyrant with mortification and shame. In proportion it raised the power and influence of the great queen, and filled the hearts of her subjects with joy and gratitude.

Sir Francis Vere passed the greater part of the winter of 1596-97 at the court of Queen Elizabeth.

******

The narrative of the Cadiz expedition is given in Camden's *Annals* and in Hakluyt. The naval action is fully reported in Vere's *Commentaries;* in Sir William Monson's *Tracts*; by Sir Walter Raleigh in a letter printed by his grandson, Philip Raleigh, at the end of an abridgment of the *History of the World* (8vo, 1700); and in Lord Essex's Report, S. P. O. Vere gives the fullest account of the land operations in his *Commentaries*. The narrative in the State Paper Office is headed "A Relation of the Winning of Cadiz." See also the ballad "The Winning of Cales," in *Percy's Reliques,* ii.

******

Chapter 17

The Island Voyage

An officer who had passed his life in training and leading soldiers on land was often called upon to become the captain of a ship, in the service of Queen Elizabeth, at a moment's notice. All his habits and ideas had to be changed for the time, and he had to learn new methods, a different science, and a strange phraseology. He had the help and advice of a professional seaman, who served under him as master; but the responsibility, the decision in all important cases, and the command rested upon the captain. Such demands on the powers of the Elizabethan officers must have had a tendency to put every faculty on the alert, to make men self-reliant, many-sided, and inventive.

Sir Francis Vere had passed the active season of 1596 in command of the *Rainbow*, learning the seaman's art and gaining a practical knowledge of what he called "sea cases." He was again to serve as a sea-captain in the following year. For King Philip was making great preparations to avenge the sack of Cadiz. A fleet was collected at Ferrol, an army was to be embarked, and it was believed that the invasion of Ireland was contemplated.

The queen resolved to meet this danger by equipping another fleet, with troops on board, to be commanded by the Earl of Essex, who this time was to be admiral as well as general of the land forces. Vere was again sent to the Hague, to arrange with the States for the services of a thousand of his veterans; and the Dutch statesmen were so well satisfied with the victory at Cadiz that no serious difficulties were raised.

The same old ships in which such glorious work had been done at Cadiz were refitted and commissioned once more. Essex at first took the *Mere-honour* as his flagship, but she was no longer fit for sea, and he shifted into the *Due-repulse*, with Master Middleton as his captain, and a dull, unlucky fellow named Cover as master. Lord Thomas Howard and Sir Walter Raleigh sailed again as vice and rear admirals in the *Lion* and *Warspite*. Raleigh had the accomplished Sir Arthur Gorges with him as captain and trusty friend, and Master Broadbent to navigate the ship. Young Lord Mountjoy had received the appointment of lieutenant-general; and he was to command the *Defiance*, with Sir Ames Preston as captain. Sir Francis Vere was lord marshal, on board the *Mary Rose*, his master being Captain John Winter, a companion of Sir Francis Drake. (John Winter was in Drake's voyage of circumnavigation, but returned home from Magellan's Straits).

Sir Christopher Blount was colonel-general, Sir Ferdinando Gorges sergeant-major general, and Sir George Carew master of the ordnance on board the great Spanish prize, the *San Mateo*. Three famous and gallant sailors had separate commands: Sir William Monson in the *Rainbow*, Sir Edward Michelborne in the *Moone*, and Captain Fenner in the *Tramontane*. The *Garland* was commanded by the young Earl of Southampton, the faithful friend of Essex, the *Bonaventure* by Sir William Harvey, the *Dreadnought* by Sir William Brooke, the *Swiftsure* by Sir Gilly Merrick, the *Nonpareil* by Sir Richard Leveson, the *Antelope* by Sir Thomas Vavasour, the Spanish prize *San Andres* by Captain Marcellus Throckmorton, and the *Foresight* by Sir Carew Reignall. Besides these seventeen queen's ships, there were several ships of London and numerous small tenders and victuallers. Vere's veterans numbered 1,200 men, and, in addition, about 7,000 soldiers were to be embarked.

******

Sir Thomas Wriothesley, Secretary of State in 1539, and afterwards Lord Chancellor and one of the executors to Henry VIII., was created Earl of Southampton in 1547, and died in 1550. He received the abbey of Titchfield from the Crown. His son, the second Earl, died in 1551. Henry, third Earl of Southampton, succeeded when he was very young. He was the friend of Shakespeare and of Essex, and he married a niece of the latter: This earl died in 1624. His granddaughter was Rachel, Lady Russell. The title of Earl of Southampton became, extinct in the Wriothesley family in 1667, when the fourth Earl died, who was Lord Treasurer.

Sir Thomas Wriothesley built "a right stately house" at Titchfield, chiefly with the materials of the abbey, where his descendants lived.

Sir Richard Leveson of Trentham married Margaret, daughter of the Lord Admiral C. Howard (Earl of Nottingham). He was a very distinguished naval officer. In this voyage he was aged twenty-eight. He died in 1605, and there is a monument, with his effigy in brass, in Wolverhampton Church.

★★★★★★

Having succeeded in his mission at the Hague, Sir Francis hurried back to England, and found the fleet at anchor in the Downs. The Earl of Essex was at Sandwich when Vere came to report himself. It was early in the morning; the luxurious courtier was still in bed, but the lord marshal was at once admitted, and was cordially received. Lord Mountjoy had been made lieutenant-general, an office which had been filled by Sir Francis Vere in the previous voyage. Essex declared that the appointment was forced upon him by the queen, that Vere would still be next to him, and that Mountjoy would have a title without an office.

Vere coldly replied that his duty would oblige him both to obey Lord Mountjoy and to respect his place; that he was not so ignorant of the earl's power as to suppose that Lord Mountjoy could be thrust upon him without his consent and procurement; and that in future he requested that Essex would not use him at all in any action wherein the earl was to go as chief. Essex looked upon this speech as the result of passing annoyance, and replied good-naturedly; but Vere had considered the matter, and spoke with a purpose. Essex had some fine qualities, but he was unstable and without judgment, and was not a man under whom Vere cared to serve. This "island voyage," as it was called, was the last in which the great general would serve under the Earl of Essex.

Some of the troops were shipped at the Downs. The fleet then got under weigh, and anchored in Portland Roads to embark more men, who were waiting there to meet the ships. There had been some misunderstandings between Sir Francis Vere and Sir Walter Raleigh during the Cadiz expedition. Essex was anxious that they should be reconciled. He therefore invited them both to come on board his ship, while they were at Portland, and asked them to shake hands in his presence. (Birch, ii. Vere's *Commentaries*). This they both very cordially consented to do, the more willingly as "nothing had passed betwixt us that might blemish reputation." Thence the fleet proceeded to Plymouth, where more troops were waiting, and a number of gallant young volunteers, "making a fine show with their plumes of feathers and rich accoutrements." (Camden). The orders were to attempt the destruction of the Spanish fleet in Ferrol, and then to cruise for the Indian galleons off the Azores. The expedition sailed from Plymouth on the 9th of July, 1597.

Those old ships, with their hulls high out of the water, and their poops towering still higher, looked gay and brave enough in Cawsand Bay, when flags and pendants fluttered from mast-heads and yardarms, and the decks glistened with the splendid dresses and bright arms of the adventurers. The trumpets and drums sounded, guns were fired, and the sea seemed alive with boats of all shapes and sizes, as the stately ships sailed out of the bay, and shaped a course westward, in a smooth sea. But the scene entirely changed when, a few days afterwards, they met with a storm in the Bay of Biscay.

The old ships were really dangerous in a heavy sea and a gale of wind. They were short in proportion to their beam and height above the water-line, and they answered their helms badly. They were made top-heavy by ordnance on their upper decks, and in very bad weather the guns had to be struck down into the holds. When the fleet of Essex reached the 47th parallel they encountered the full force of a furious gale. The ships strove obstinately against it until they were all more or less disabled. The Earl himself stood out until his ship sprang a dangerous leak, the mainmast was gone in three places and the foremast in two, the oakum worked out and the seams opened, the main beams were shivered, the upper works gave way, and the guns threatened to drop into the hold and make holes in her bottom.

Then Essex reluctantly shaped a course for England. The ships of Lord Thomas Howard, of Mountjoy, of Raleigh, of Shirley, of Blount, were all in the same plight. Shattered and disabled, they sought shelter from the storm at Falmouth or Plymouth. The mainmast of the *Mary Rose* was sprung in the partners, and shattered down to the step. Experienced old John Winter wanted to have it hove overboard, but Vere would not consent. He at length got back to Plymouth, and his mast was so effectually fished that it lasted out the rest of the voyage. On July 20 Essex sent a message to Robert Cecil, who had become Secretary of State, that he had removed from Falmouth to Plymouth, "to gather his scattered flock."

Never had smart young courtiers and gay volunteers been so bucketed about. It would be long before they forgot the Bay of Biscay. Sir Ferdinando Gorges and Sir Carew Reignall were so dreadfully seasick that they could not embark again. Sir A. Shirley took the place of the former, and Sir Alexander Ratcliffe, "a very forward and gallant young gentleman," (not long afterwards slain in Ireland), of the latter. The treasurer, Sir Hugh Biston, had also suffered so much from seasickness that he resigned his appointment. Many young gentlemen volunteers, including Lord Rich, secretly went home without taking leave. It was found impossible to provide for the large number of troops that had been embarked. All were dismissed, except Vere's 1,200 veterans. The supplies of provisions were not only deficient in quantity, they were bad in quality, and there were loud complaints of the beer especially. It was very vile and unsavoury, and the sickness was attributed as much to the bad beer as to the motion of the sea. Luckily, while the fleet was being refitted, a prize was taken and brought in, which was laden with Canary wine. This was served out to the different ships, instead of beer.

Essex and Raleigh went up to the court to consult respecting future operations, and it was resolved that an attempt should be made to burn the Spanish ships at Ferrol, and that the expedition should afterwards proceed to the Azores, to watch for the fleet coming from the Indies. Essex finally sailed from Plymouth on the 17th of August, 1597.

Again the fleet sailed southwards, across the Bay of Biscay, and again it encountered boisterous weather. The great Spanish prize, the *San Mateo*, with her spritsail set, carried away her bowsprit, and there was a great wreck under her bows. Then the foremast broke off close to the partners, hurling four men into the sea, who were keeping watch in the foretop. The gallant Sir George Carew was in command. He cleared away the wreck, and the Earl of Essex sent to propose that he and his crew should abandon the *San Mateo*, and be distributed among the other ships. Carew declined, declaring his intention to stand by his charge to the last. He rigged a jury-foremast, set a pinnace's sail on it, and, running before the wind, eventually reached a French port.

★★★★★★

Sir George Carew was a son of Dr. Carew, Dean of Windsor, He was afterwards President of Munster, did excellent service in Ireland, and published a book in 1633, called *Hibernia Pacata*. He was an accomplished scholar as well as a soldier. In 1605 he was created Baron Carew, and made master-general of the ordnance for life. 1625, created Earl of Totnes. He died in 1629, leaving an only child, a daughter named Anne, married to Sir Allen Apsley.

★★★★★★

Soon afterwards, on the 27th of August, Raleigh's ship, the *Warspite*, carried away her mainyard by the parral, and for some time was quite unmanageable, wallowing in the trough of the sea and rolling excessively. She was obliged to run before the wind, the *Dreadnought* keeping her company. These and other disasters led to the abandonment of the project for attacking Ferrol, and Essex decided upon shaping a course direct for the Azores, a run of 700 miles from the Portuguese coast. A fly-boat was dispatched to the *Warspite* and *Dreadnought* with the rendezvous.

After a voyage of eight days, the fleet came in sight of Flores and Corvo, the two most westerly of the Azores, where the inhabitants declared they were Portuguese and enemies of the Spaniards, bringing off fruit and fresh provisions. In a few days Raleigh and Brooke arrived, and a council of war was held on board the admiral's ship.

The Azores are nearly in the centre of the Atlantic, being 1,147 miles from the Lizard, and 1,680 from Newfoundland. They are between the 37th and 40th parallels, and the nine islands extend from W. N. W. to E. S. E. for four hundred miles. The small islands of Corvo and Flores are furthest to the west. Next come Fayal and Pico, Graciosa and St. George, which were originally settled by Flemings. Martin Behaim, of Nuremberg, the learned cosmographer, lived and was married at the town of Horta, the capital of Fayal. Farther east is Terceira, and still more to the south and east is St. Michael, the largest and most important island in the group. To the southeast of St. Michael is the smaller island of St. Mary. The richly laden fleets coming from the West Indies usually passed among the Azores, and stopped to take in water and fresh provisions.

When the fleet was assembled, the council decided that the Earl of Essex and Sir Walter Raleigh should attack Fayal, Lord Thomas Howard and Sir Francis Vere were to go to Graciosa, Mountjoy and Blount to St. Michael's; but the arrangement was not followed very exactly.

Raleigh, with the *Swiftsure*, *Warspite*, and *Dreadnought*, ran ahead of the rest of the fleet, and anchored off Fayal. He waited for three days, and then effected a landing at some little distance from the town of Horta. The Spaniards had fortified a steep hill, where the English were repulsed, suffering some loss. But they marched on, and entered the deserted town. It was built of stone, with red tiled roofs and a fine church, orchards and gardens being interspersed with the rows of houses. Raleigh was no sooner in possession than the rest of the fleet hove in sight, on the 22nd of September.

Essex was incensed with Raleigh for having presumed to land and engage the enemy without his knowledge and permission; and there were not wanting those who fanned the flame of his wrath. Sir Christopher Blount, Sir A. Shirley, and Sir Gilly Merrick were the leaders among those who strove to stir up dissension, urging that the rear-admiral ought to be put under arrest, and even cashiered, as well as the officers who landed with him. Raleigh was called before an assembly of principal officers, in the general's presence. Many spoke strongly against him. Vere gave his vote in Raleigh's favour. Lord Thomas Howard made friendly mediation, and the general was pacified. With a wise and noble admonition he forgave the offence, and Essex, with the principal officers, dined on board Raleigh's ship. (Camden says: "Essex reproved Raleigh sharply for acting without orders." Raleigh's defence was that he waited four days, wanted water, and was obliged to win it by the sword).

The Spaniards were still entrenched on the top of a steep hill overlooking the town of Horta, called the *Cerro de Carneiro*, with their flag flying. Sir Oliver Lambart received a sufficient number of men to guard the approaches to the town, and after sunset Sir Francis Vere prepared to make a close reconnaissance of the fort. He took with him the young Earl of Rutland, several other volunteers, and about 200 soldiers. On reaching the top of the hill it was found that the place had just been abandoned, and several English prisoners, including Captain Hart, were lying there with their throats cut. It was useless to attempt the pursuit of the murderers over the mountainous island, so fire was set to the town as a punishment. The fleet, after taking fresh provisions on board, sailed from Fayal.

Essex then cruised off and on, between the islands of Graciosa and Terceira, for three days, watching for the treasure fleet from the Indies. The people of Graciosa, like those of Corvo and Flores, sent fruit and fowls to the ships, submitted to all demands, and declared that, as Portuguese, they detested the Spaniards. Then, by a fatal error in judgment, Essex bore away to St. Michael's, leaving only four ships to cruise off Graciosa. Gorges says that this course was adopted by the advice of the master of the *Repulse*, "a dull, unlucky fellow, named Cover."

A pinnace was dispatched to the *Mary Rose*, with orders to Sir Francis Vere for that ship and the *Dreadnought*, on board of which was Sir Nicholas Parker, to cruise between St. George and Graciosa. The Earl of Southampton, in the *Garland*, and Sir William Monson, in the

Rainbow, were ordered to cruise off the north side of Graciosa. Vere received his orders at about ten p. m. A little after midnight the look-out men of the *Rainbow* heard signal guns. There was scarcely any wind, but Vere and Parker crowded all sail in the direction of the reports. The morning was very foggy, and nothing could be seen, but still the guns could be heard at intervals. At eight a. m. the fog rose, and disclosed to view a fleet of twenty Spanish ships, nearly hull down, making all sail for Terceira. Vere set every stitch of canvas, and kept wetting the sails, to make them draw, as the wind began to freshen.

The *Garland* and *Rainbow* were far ahead, and near the Spanish ships; and the Earl of Southampton did capture a lagging frigate, laden with cochineal. But the rest of the fleet got safely into Terceira, where the treasure was landed, and the ships were moored close under the guns of the fort. Among the Spanish fleet, which was commanded by Juan Gutierrez de Garibay and Francisco de Corral, there were six galleons laden with silver. The treasure amounted to 10,000,000, belonging to the crown and to private persons. The unfortunate Sir Richard Hawkins was on board one of the Spanish ships, being conveyed a prisoner of the Inquisition from Lima. He must have been sadly disappointed at losing this most tantalizing chance of escape. It was now evening, and the Earl of Southampton, Sir William Monson, and Sir Nicholas Parker came on board Vere's ship to consult. They resolved to send in boats to cut the cables of the outer Spanish ships; but the attempt failed, and they continued to watch the entrance, while a fast-sailing pinnace was sent to St. Michael's, to apprise the general.

Two days afterwards Essex arrived with the rest of the fleet, but the conclusion was that no attempt could be made on Terceira without extreme hazard; so the enterprise was abandoned. Provisions were running short, and it was decided that water and supplies should be taken in at St. Michael's, and, as the season was well advanced, that the fleet should then return to England. The plan was, that most of the ships, under Raleigh, should remain off the town of St. Michael's, while the soldiers, embarked in smaller vessels, were to effect a landing in the bay called Rostro de Can, near Villafranca, a town about fifteen miles southeast of St. Michael's, on the same side of the island.

Sir Francis Vere went ahead in his boat, to select a good place for disembarking; and the troops, led by the Earl of Essex, landed on a sandy beach in front of the town. Vere then occupied the town with 200 men, and found a good supply of corn and fruit. About 2,000 men were then marched up and quartered in the houses, where they were placed under the command of Vere. Essex and Mountjoy returned to the fleet off St. Michael's. Meanwhile, Raleigh had driven a large carrack on shore, and captured a ship laden with sugar and Brazil wood. The fleet then came to Villafranca to water; but it was tedious work, as the sea was shallow, and it was necessary to float the casks off to the boats. After watering for three or four days, Essex gave the order to embark. This, also, took a long time. The ships were at anchor at a considerable distance from the shore, and only one boat could come in at a time, owing to the surf. Essex was most of each day at the water-side, superintending the embarkation, and sending up to Vere for more men from the town, as he was ready to embark them.

At five in the afternoon of the 7th of October, the sentry on the church-tower reported masses of men approaching from the town of St. Michael's. Sir Francis Vere then sent up Sir William Constable, who corroborated the sentry's statement. There were still about 500 men on shore. Dispatching Constable to report the news to the Earl of Essex, Vere sent out thirty shot-men to a little wayside chapel, a long musket range from Villafranca, with orders to give the enemy a volley as soon as they came within range, and then to retire hurriedly towards the town, where Vere would be ready with the rest of his men to repulse and rout them.

As soon as these arrangements had been made, the Earl of Essex, with Lord Southampton and several others, came into the market-place, asking Sir Francis what he had seen. Essex was on horseback, the rest on foot, chatting round him, and giving little credence to the report. Essex called for tobacco, and he sat quietly smoking with his friends. Suddenly the sound of volleys of musketry was heard. The earl dropped his pipe, and listened intently. Another volley was heard. Evidently the soldiers at the chapel, instead of hastily retiring, in accordance with Vere's orders, were holding their own. (Herrera says that the Spaniards, commanded by Antonio Favella, killed 50 English, and took some prisoners).

The consequence was that the enemy halted. Keeping the advanced post in sight of the Spanish troops, the embarkation was continued after sunset, and at about midnight the last soldier stepped into the boat. Essex followed him. Then the outlying picket, commanded by Sir Charles Percy, was quietly withdrawn. Vere was the last man to leave the shore. Before sailing, Essex conferred the honour of knighthood on the Earls of Southampton and Rutland, Sir William Evers, Sir Henry Docwra, Sir William Browne, and a Dutch gentleman.

✶✶✶✶✶✶

Sir Francis Vere gives a full account of the "island voyage" in his *Commentaries*, and there is another in Camden. The official report is in Purchas, iv., lib. x. cap. xiv., which is followed by *A Larger Relation of the Island Voyage,* by Sir A. Gorges. Sir Walter Raleigh described his landing at Fayal in his *History of the World*. See also Sir William Monson's *Naval Tracts,* and Herrera, lib. xvi. cap. xxi.

✶✶✶✶✶✶

On the 9th of October the fleet shaped a course for England. It was soon scattered by a gale of wind. The *Mary Rose* very nearly ran into the *Warspite*, her stem tearing away the whole of the *Warspite's* port-quarter gallery. Then the *Mary Rose* sprung a very dangerous leak, and the men were kept constantly at the pumps until they reached Plymouth.

Fortunately, the same weather had scattered and almost destroyed the great Spanish fleet which had been fitted out at Ferrol for the invasion of England and Ireland. The intention of Philip II. had been to land an army of 10,000 men at Falmouth; but his ships were scattered, and as many as thirty-six were lost at sea.

✶✶✶✶✶✶

Vere had information from prisoners that the Spaniards intended to attack Ireland, and also that Falmouth was to be attacked, (Vere and Raleigh to Essex, Nov. 2 and 6, 1597. MSS. at Hatfield.)

✶✶✶✶✶✶

The English ships had suffered seriously, but they reached Plymouth at last, and the Earl of Essex posted to the court. Shortly afterwards a supply of treasure was sent down, with commission to Sir Walter Raleigh and Sir Francis Vere to pay the men, refit, and send the Queen's ships round to Chatham. Thus ended the unlucky expedition which is known in history as the "Island Voyage." The leader was a young man of distinguished bravery and zeal, but very deficient in judgment and knowledge. He was proud and irascible, yet generous and readily appeased; one who could take advice and was easily led, but who could not be driven. Both his virtues and his faults hurried the ill-fated Earl of Essex to his untimely end. He had around him the most renowned sailors and soldiers of their time, Raleigh and Monson, Vere and Mountjoy, and if experience and bravery could alone have won success, its attainment was certain. The elements which prevented the achievement of all that was intended, at the same time secured, in their own way, the main object of the expedition by scattering and destroying the Spanish fleet.

As soon as all his duties were completed at Plymouth, Sir Francis Vere set out on horseback for London, travelling post. He was galloping along near Marylebone Park, when he overtook a coach in which was Sir William Russell, the Lord Deputy of Ireland. (He was created Baron Russell of Thornhaugh in 1603, and died in 1613. He was great-grandfather of the patriot Lord Russell, who was judicially murdered by Charles II.)

They had not met for years; but Vere had seen Sir William charge at the head of England's chivalry near Zutphen, and Sir William had been governor of Flushing when Vere was defending Sluys. Vere jumped off his horse to salute his old friend with dutiful affection, and Russell stepped out of his coach to show the same cordial pleasure at the meeting. But Vere was in a profuse perspiration from having ridden hard; and standing bareheaded for some time in a bleak November afternoon, he caught such a violent cold in his head that he was confined to his lodging for three weeks. Meanwhile, the ears of Queen Elizabeth had been filled with ill-natured remarks about the Island Voyage, by the enemies of the Earl of Essex.

Sir Francis considered that this detraction was unjust, and as soon as he was able to go out he went to the court, which was then at Whitehall. He determined not to seek an introduction, but to be in attendance in the garden when the queen should come forth. Presently Elizabeth appeared at the head of a crowd of courtiers, and as soon as she set eyes on Sir Francis Vere she called him to her. Immediately she began to question him about the Island Voyage, appearing to be much incensed against Essex, and laying the whole blame of the failure upon him. In reply Sir Francis boldly justified the young earl, and answered all the objections that had been raised against him, in presence of his detractors. The queen was satisfied, and, having reached the end of the walk, she sat down, and continued to hold more confidential discourse with Vere alone, about the earl's disposition. Essex was afterwards made Earl Marshal of England; the lord admiral, who was his colleague in the Cadiz voyage, having previously been created Earl of Nottingham.

During the absence of Vere at the Azores, one of the oldest and bravest of his companions had passed away. Sir John Norris, second only to Morgan and Williams for length of service, and second to no one for gallantry in action, died in Ireland in 1597. He was President of Munster. Lord Burgh, the governor of Brill, had also died, and his successor, Lord Sheffield, resigned after a few months.

******

Thomas Lord Burgh of Gainsborough was descended from Sir Thomas de Burgh, who was created a Knight of the Garter by Richard III., and made Lord Burgh of Gainsborough in 1488. Lord Burgh succeeded Thomas Cecil as governor of Brill, and died in 1597. His widow was Frances, daughter of T. Vaughan. His gallant brother John was knighted by the Earl of Leicester, but came to an untimely end in a duel, in 1594, aged thirty two. There is a tomb to Sir John Borough (or Burgh) in Westminster Abbey.

******

Sir Francis Vere, after the Battle of Turnhout, in January, passed most of the winter and spring of 1598 at court, "gallantly followed by such as profess arms." (Rowland Whyte to Sir Robert Sidney, ii.) Every ambitious young gentleman sought employment under the greatest English captain of the time, and he received numerous applications whenever he appeared at court. He was himself desirous of obtaining the government of one of the cautionary towns, and that of Brill was now vacant. Many friends urged him to apply for it, and Sir Fulk Greville brought the subject to the queen's notice. Afterwards Sir Francis, when her Majesty was walking in the garden one evening, ventured to make the request to her in person. The Earl of Sussex was his only competitor, while he had a warm friend in Sir Robert Cecil, who had just become Secretary of State. The queen, in the summer of 1598, finally decided in favour of Sir Francis Vere. Towards the end of September he left England, and assumed the government of Brill, after taking the oaths of office.

******

Sir Francis Vere's lieutenant-governor at Brill was Sir Edward Conway, who had been knighted at Cadiz. Sir Edward was created Lord Conway of Ragley in 1624, and was Secretary of State in 1630. His father, Sir John Conway, died in 1603, and his mother was Elena, daughter of Sir Fulk Greville. Sir Edward married Dorothy, daughter of Sir J. Tracy of Toddington, and had Edward, 2nd Lord Conway, and Brilliana, born at Brill, and married to Sir R. Harley. The yearly cost of the Brill garrison of 500 men was, for officers, £2,244; men, £7,098; total, £9,342.

The governor received £1,241 a year, out of which a pension had to be paid to Lady Burgh. Vere's lieutenant was young E. Wilford, son of his old comrade Sir T. Wilford. The sergeant-major was Thomas Fawkes; water baily, Captain H. Fawkes; officer of musters, George Thoresby; master gunner, Gregory Gibbs; captain of a company, Sir F. Gorges.

★★★★★★

He was now governor of Brill, general of Her Majesty's forces in the Netherlands, and general of the English troops in the pay of the States.

CHAPTER 18

Battle of Turnhout

During the absence of Sir Francis Vere from the Netherlands on naval service, the activity and enterprise of Prince Maurice had been as conspicuous as ever; and there had been a change in the Spanish command. The Archduke Ernest died in February, 1595, and during the following year Don Pedro de Guzman, Conde de Fuentes, had been captain-general of the army of Philip II. The Archduke Albert, one of the younger sons of the Emperor Maximilian II., had been intended for the church, and had actually been appointed a cardinal and Archbishop of Toledo. But his career was changed; and his cousin, Philip II., selected him to represent Spanish power in the Low Countries. He was an amiable man, but was not remarkable for military talent. His very plain features are familiar to visitors to the Brussels picture gallery. The Archduke Albert entered Brussels on the nth of February, 1596, when he was thirty-seven years of age. In the following summer the siege and capture of Hulst gave some *éclat* to his government.

Late in the autumn of 1597 Sir Francis Vere came over to Holland and inspected the English field force, residing for some time at the Hague. On the approach of winter a division of the Archduke Albert's army, under the command of the Count of Varras, had advanced to the village of Turnhout, about twenty miles south of Breda. It consisted of 4,000 infantry and 600 cavalry, and it was evident that they were watching for an opportunity to undertake some exploit against the Dutch; probably their design was to surprise the town of Tholen. Sir Francis Vere saw a good deal of Barneveldt at the Hague, and one day, in the course of conversation, he remarked to the Dutch statesman that "the enemy did but tempt us to beat them." The idea bore fruit. Barneveldt discussed the matter with the other members of the States

General, and, towards the end of December, Maurice received orders to collect a force at Gertruydenburg, very secretly, to attack the enemy at Turnhout.

This enterprise was well planned, ably carried out, and was completely successful. It was an instance of the reward which attends upon vigilance and prompt action; and it served to display the special qualities of Sir Francis Vere to the best advantage.

A force of 5,000 foot and 800 horse, with two demi-cannons and two fieldpieces, under Heraugière, the governor of Breda, was secretly assembled at Gertruydenburg. Sir Francis Vere brought an English regiment, and he was to command one of the two troops into which the English cavalry was divided. Sir Robert Sidney came from Flushing with 300 of his garrison. Hohenlohe, with Marcellus Bacx under his orders, commanded the States cavalry. Brederode and Solms arrived with drafts from various garrisons, and Sir Alexander Murray with a regiment of Scots. At break of day on Thursday, the 23rd of January, 1598, the expedition marched out of Gertruydenburg in four divisions, with cavalry on the flanks. In the van were, six ensigns of foot under the colours of Maurice himself, next came 700 men under Sidney, then eight ensigns of foot under Sir Francis, and Murray brought up the rear with his Scots.

Marching all day, they reached the village of Ravels, near Turnhout, about two hours after dark. The distance from Gertruydenburg was twenty-four miles,—a long march. The rear guard did not reach camp until after midnight. It was a dark and bitterly cold night. Spies reported that the enemy was encamped at Turnhout, three miles from Ravels, without any entrenchments, and ignorant of their danger. Supper was hastily cooked, and the men rested after their long march. Maurice, Vere, and Sidney wrapped their cloaks around them, and lay down on the frozen ground. But Maurice was restless, walking up and down, and lighting fires of straw with his own hand, by the *corps du garde*. There was no sleeping by him, so Vere and Sidney went into a barn full of soldiers, and there got a little sleep. At length morning dawned.

The Count of Varras, brother of the Marquis of Warrenbon, "though an honourable knight, had more of magnificence, sumptuousness, and eloquence than experience in war." (Herrera). He had heard nothing of the threatening assemblage of troops at Gertruydenburg, and was encamped in the large village of Turnhout without any suspicion of danger. The small castle, surrounded by a moat, contained a garrison

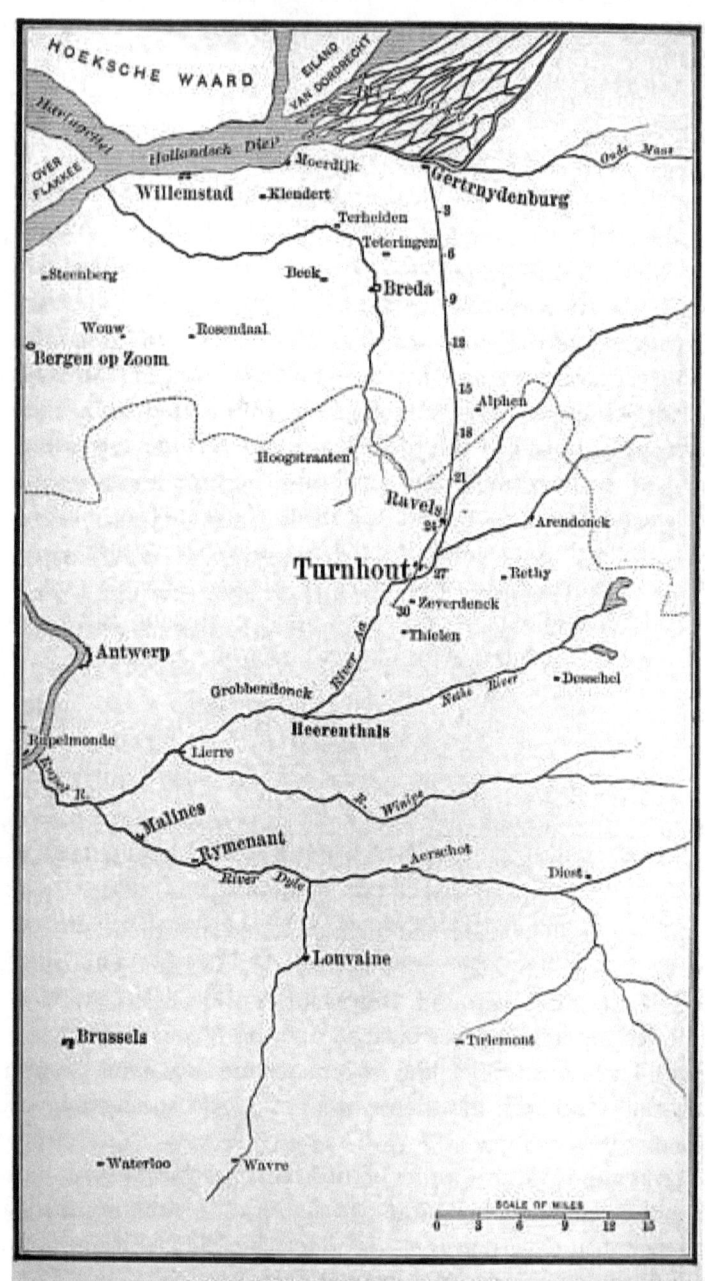

THE FIELD OF TURNHOUT.

of forty men. The force commanded by the Count of Varras consisted of four battalions of infantry,—the Germans under Count Solst, the Walloons and Burgundians under the Comte de Hachincourt and the Sieur de Barlaymont, and the Neapolitans under the Marquis of Treviso; and of five squadrons of cavalry, led by Nicolo Basta. The regiments of horse were commanded by Juan de Cordova, Alonzo de Mendoza, Juan de Guzman, Alonzo Mondragon, and the Flemings under the Sieur de Grubbendonck.

At about midnight the Count de Varras first heard of the proximity of Maurice's army. He immediately ordered a retreat to Heerenthals, twelve miles to the southwest, on the road to Malines. The baggage wagons were packed and sent off at once, escorted by the cavalry, the battalions of infantry following. Before dawn the retreat had commenced, and the whole force was well on the road to Heerenthals. In those days the country consisted of woods, with plenty of undergrowth, alternating with expanses of open heath. At a distance of a mile south of Turnhout, the little river of Aa crosses the road.

Maurice broke up his camp before dawn, and by break of day he reached Turnhout, and found that the rear guard of the enemy had just marched out of the village. On reaching the banks of the Aa, the wooden bridge had been broken down except one plank, and parties of the enemy were stationed on the other side. Maurice halted half-way between the village and the bridge. His council advised against pursuit, with the exception of Sir Francis Vere and Sir Marcellus Bacx. Vere not only insisted upon vigorous pursuit, but urged that if it were not immediate and sustained it would fail. Maurice concurred, and gave Vere 200 musketeers to dislodge the enemy's rear guard from the bridge-head. The country was intersected in all directions by hedges and ditches.

Sir Francis put his heavily weighted war-horse at a wide brook, where there was bad taking off, and it fell. Meteren says that the horse was killed under him. The general scrambled out on the other side, and continued to lead on foot, until he was remounted. The Dutch musketeers under his orders were commanded by Captain van der Aa, who, by a curious coincidence, had the same name as the river. Some crossed the bridge, while others, with the cavalry, got over the river by a very deep and dangerous ford. The enemy was now in full retreat, and it was evident that the pursuing infantry could take no further part in the operations. Vere saw at once that the only chance of delaying them was to keep constantly in their sight. He therefore rode on with a few officers. He saw some marching and others halting, as if there was some impediment in front, which he supposed to be caused by a block of wagons. They were marching along a broad lane, with trees and underwood on either side.

The English general took in the position at once. Assuming that the trees would conceal the smallness of his force, he called up his musketeers, and stationed them along the skirts of the wood, with orders to keep up a dropping fire, while he himself, with sixteen horsemen, followed along the highway, in full sight. He sent back a report to Maurice, with an urgent request that he would advance promptly and rapidly with all his cavalry, in which case victory was certain.

Meanwhile, Vere continued to keep touch of the enemy, whose rear guard maintained a skirmishing fire, and he was slightly wounded in the leg. Thus he kept them in play for three hours, when they emerged on an open heath, about three miles from the bridge. (Vere says five or six miles, Docwra two miles, an examination of the ground leads me to place the commencement of the heath at distance of three miles from the River Aa). This skirmishing caused considerable delay in the retreat, which was Vere's object, and it thus secured the victory. The open heath was about three miles across, with woods and enclosed fields on the left.

Along these Vere caused his musketeers to advance and fire upon the enemy; while he, now considerably reinforced, continued to follow in the open. The Count de Varras, now that he had sufficient space on the heath, formed his infantry in four solid squares of pikemen, with shotmen on the flanks. His cavalry and wagons had already crossed the heath, and entered the lane beyond, which had woods and enclosures on either side. The first square consisted of Germans led by Count Solst, then came Walloons and Burgundians under Hachincourt and Barlaymont, and the Marquis of Treviso brought up the rear with his Neapolitans. They were fast traversing the heath, and approaching the woods, where they would be in comparative safety.

Vere kept following them, anxiously watching the trees in the rear for the appearance of Maurice and his cavalry. At length, to his great relief, they began to come in sight. Then squadron after squadron emerged from the wood and formed on the open heath. There were very few minutes to spare. Vere galloped off to Count Maurice, and proposed to lead a charge at once; while Hohenlohe took up a position on the right. Then, almost at the same moment, Hohenlohe charged the enemy's right flank, while Vere dashed upon their rear.

After the first volley their shotmen broke and fled. The pikemen were injudiciously formed for receiving cavalry, and the English and Dutch soon broke their massed squares. Then several companies of horse galloped down the Heerenthal road, in chase of the enemy's cavalry and baggage.

Vere foresaw that these disordered and victorious pursuers would soon be routed by the well-ordered cavalry of the enemy, which had not yet been in action. He told Count Hohenlohe that he would do well to stop the pursuit. He then overtook Sir Nicholas Parker, who commanded his own English companies, and ordered him to station his men at the end of the heath, and check the counter-pursuit he anticipated. Sure enough, the disordered cavalry were soon seen to be returning as fast as they went, and galloped past Vere and Parker in wild flight. The enemy's cavalry were rapidly approaching in pursuit. But seeing fresh troops formed to receive them, they retreated without any further hostile attempt.

The destruction of the infantry battalions was complete. Out of 4,000, the number of killed was 300, of prisoners 600, and thirty-eight ensigns were taken. The Count of Varras was slain in the battle. Of the allied forces not above ten were slain; and the whole action was fought by under 800 horse. The infantry never came up. That night they rested at the village of Turnhout.

******

Turnhout is now, (1878), a growing manufacturing town. The church is in the centre of the Groot Markt. It is a modern cruciform building of brick, but contains a very fine pulpit of carved wood, like that at St. Andrew's in Antwerp,—the apostolic fishers in a boat, drawing their net, and at the foot the figure of Christ calling them. The banisters represent a vine with clusters of grapes on one side, and on the other an orange-tree with leaves and fruit. The old castle was at a short distance northwest of the market-place, a square building with an angle tower, surrounded by an unusually wide moat. It is now used as the prison. A street now extends south from the market place to the River Aa, and beyond it.

******

Next morning the castle of Turnhout capitulated, and the troops began their return march to Gertruydenburg.

******

The best account of the Battle of Turnhout is given by Sir

Francis Vere himself in his *Commentaries*; and in his official report, dated at Breda on January 27, 1597. (S. P. O., Holland, vol. lxxxv.) Sir Robert Sidney's report, dated from Flushing, is in the same volume, On February 28, 1597, Sir F.Vere sent a discourse of the exploit to Lord Burleigh, which had been published in French, Latin, and Dutch. At Hatfield there is an account of the battle by Sir Henry Docwra, dated January 30, 1598, which was sent to the Earl of Essex. I was supplied with a copy of this interesting document through the kindness of the Marquis of Salisbury. See, also, Grimeston, Meteren, Bentivoglio.

✶✶✶✶✶✶

Prince Maurice returned to the Hague on the 8th of February. Sir Francis Vere accompanied Sir Robert Sidney to Willemstad, whence the governor of Flushing intended to proceed by water to his charge. Vere wrote his official despatches, and gave them to one of Sidney's captains to deliver in England. Sidney's letter was sent home by the same opportunity. Both these gallant soldiers spoke generously of each other. Vere said: "Sir Robert Sidney deserved exceeding well in this service, being one of the first that charged." Sidney reported that the victory was due to Vere. Yet mischief was made between them, and Sir Francis was told that "his letters were kept back, and Sidney's delivered, that were far more partially written."

The news of the Battle of Turnhout was received in England with great rejoicing, and congratulations poured in on all sides. It was even dramatised in London, and introduced on the stage, all the officers who were present at the battle being personated.

> He that played Sir Francis Vere got a beard resembling his, and a watchet satin doublet with hose trimmed with silver lace. Sidney and the others were among the *dramatis personae*, and honourable mention was made of their services in seconding Sir Francis.—Rowland Whyte to Sir R. Sidney.

Queen Elizabeth wrote herself to Sir Francis Vere, on February 7, 1598, in the following terms:

> It is no news to hear, by the late defeat at Turnhout, that your presence and that of the other English in the service, has furthered both your own reputation and its success: yet we wish to signify our good liking of the report we hear of your services.

The receipt of this gracious letter from his sovereign gave no small comfort to her faithful and most loyal general, who warmly expressed his gratitude in a letter to Lord Burleigh. (Vere to Lord Burleigh, from the Hague, Feb. 20, 1598. (S. P.. O., Holland, lxxxv.) 2 Elizabeth did not shower titles and orders among her public servants, but they knew that she watched all they did with close and intelligent interest, that she appreciated their efforts and admired their skill and gallantry. She did not create her general a peer, because she held that the name of Francis Vere had become, through its owner's Merits, more illustrious than any court title that she could bestow.

CHAPTER 19

The Bommel-Waart

The long war was entering upon a new phase. Spain was becoming exhausted, and even Philip II. began to contemplate the necessity for peace and conciliation. The heretics, he unwillingly admitted, must be spoken fair. He determined to cede the Netherlands to his daughter Isabella, who was to marry the Cardinal Archduke Albert, and they were to be sovereigns, while the Spanish monarch only retained a suzerainty. Liberal terms were to be offered to the heretics if they would accept this arrangement, while proposals of peace were to be made to France and England. What a change since the days of Alva, or even of Parma! The once matchless Spanish infantry was no longer feared. The successes of the patriots, culminating in the battle of Turnhout, had produced a great moral effect both on the victors and the vanquished. Holland had grown rich and prosperous in the fight for freedom, while Spain had sunk deeper and deeper into debt and embarrassments. At last the haughty and exacting monarch of Spain and the Indies, who for years would listen to nothing but abject submission from his insurgent provinces, was fain to make the first overtures for peace.

The King of France, whose country was exhausted by a long civil war, listened to these overtures rather too eagerly, and without any regard for the obligation he had contracted with England and Holland in the time of his sore need. The English ambassador exerted all his influence to prevent the conclusion of a separate peace, but in vain; and the efforts of Barneveldt and Justinus of Nassau, who were sent on a special mission to Henry IV., were equally fruitless. The States General were convinced that there could be no lasting peace while Philip II. was alive. The Dutch envoys arrived in France during March, 1598, and they were in London, on their way home, in May; when they had several conferences with the queen and her ministers.

The Spanish overtures for peace, in whatever spirit they might be entertained by the English government, suggested a careful review of the position and of the relations between England and her ally. For fifteen years the brave queen and her loyal people had strained every nerve to help their neighbours in the death-struggle against despotism. The sacrifices made by England had been heavy and burdensome, and the time had come, now that Holland was no longer poor and in danger, when the propriety of concluding a new treaty between the allies might properly be considered. But Barneveldt and his colleague had no authority to enter into negotiations, and they merely expressed their individual opinions when they declared that:

> There should be no accord with Spain upon any conditions, and that the States ought not to hearken to any peace.

On the 31st of May the Dutch deputies left London for the Hague.

The government of Queen Elizabeth then came to the conclusion, that although the States could not be deserted, and that if they decided for a continuance of the war England must stand by them, yet that the overtures for peace ought to be carefully considered on their merits. It was also resolved that the relations between England and Holland ought to be revised, and that a new treaty should be negotiated, in accordance with the changed condition of affairs, and on a basis which should render the war somewhat less burdensome to England. This would entail the employment of a special envoy on a delicate and very confidential mission to the Hague.

The choice of the queen fell upon Sir Francis Vere. Since the victory of Turnhout he had been in England, had been most graciously received, and was fully acquainted with the course of the negotiations. He was a *persona grata* at the Hague, having always been a favourite of Olden Barneveldt. He had an intimate knowledge of all matters of account between his own country and the States, and had already shown his capacity as a diplomatist. He was appointed special envoy to the States General, with Mr. George Gilpin, the resident minister at the Hague, as his colleague. ("Sir Francis Vere is to go shortly with secret instructions to the Hague."—Chamberlain to Dudley Carleton, May 31, 1598).

Vere's instructions were carefully drawn up, and dated June 7, 1598:

> I will not fail to make all the haste I can over. Tomorrow I set forward if the wind is not very contrary. I have received my full

despatches.—F. Vere in London to R. Cecil, June 9, 1598. MSS. at Hatfield.

He was to remind the deputies that the queen had performed all the obligations of friendship in urging the King of France against a separate peace and in refusing to negotiate without the States, although she thus incurred the slander of being the main cause of the continuation of the war; and he was to inform them that, notwithstanding all the arguments she could use, Henry IV. had proceeded to proclaim his peace. He was then to urge upon their attention the extent to which the queen's own people had suffered from the long war, losing their lives and fortunes daily, until they were weary of such continual and endless vexations. The queen had loyally prohibited all traffic with the enemy. But the States had acted very differently, and their conduct had caused much indignation throughout England. Dutch ships had been continually employed for the Spaniards, not only in bringing their commodities from Brazil and other parts of the Indies, for gain and lucre, but in conveying all manner of grain to relieve their wants. Not longer ago than the previous April Dutch ships had come freighted with grain into the Tagus. (Spain and Portugal were then united).

The envoy was then to remind the States more fully of the sacrifices England had made for them, and of the benefits they had secured by this generous help. He was to recall to their memories how often they had been made acquainted with the heavy burden of the Queen's expenses for their country, and with the courses she had adopted to preserve their country from conquest since the fall of Antwerp; and that they had made solemn and confident promises to reimburse her. Yet it was then beyond expectation that she could have continued her charges as she had done. They knew full well that no prince of any realm of Christendom had ever done the like for any nation whatsoever; and they must consider that, by reason of help from England, they had settled their form of government, increased their traffic and commerce abroad, fortified and enlarged their cities and towns, filled them with rich inhabitants who had taken refuge from the enemy, increased their general wealth in every direction, and captured many places of notable strength.

Vere was then to remind the States that the Queen of England was accountable to God, in her own conscience, if she should needlessly grieve or expose her people. The peace with France would free the Spanish forces, and the queen's affairs could not be allowed any longer to hang in uncertainty. For Spain had offered peace to England, while the Spanish king possessed nothing of the queen's, "nor, God be thanked, has he any cause to boast of any pleasant fruit of any of his encounters with us." The answer Vere was to require from the States General, after pressing these considerations on their attention, was first whether they would assent to or dissent from a treaty of peace with Spain; and if they dissented they were expected to submit an exact comparison between their means and those of the queen since she first contracted with them, and to give her reasons why she should continue the war.

But her Majesty left the decision "to their own best liking, as she never had any intent to persuade them to anything but what might be best for their own preservation." The queen would not recommend any accord but on reasonable grounds, with all immunities and privileges preserved, and with no other acknowledgment of sovereignty but such as would be vested in a Duke of Burgundy, and not in a King of Spain. She desired Vere to assure the States that, in any dealings about peace, she would do her best to provide for them as those whom she held in dearest regard.

Finally, if the States continued in their resolution to make no peace with the King of Spain, then the Queen of England would still stand by them in that resolve. But in that case they must enter into a new treaty. Vere was to indicate certain points, "the better to lead them into the right accompte of what nature their offers ought to be made." They were to understand that the queen expected repayment of some good portion of the debt; that henceforward she should have no more charges either for auxiliaries or for the cautionary towns; that the States would be ready with good aid of ships and men if England was assailed; and that they would furnish supplies for the army in Ireland. ("Instructions to Sir Francis Vere, Kt., sent to the States, to be communicated with Mr. Gilpin," June 7, 1598. In the British Museum, Galba D, xii.; 20 pages, damaged by fire.)

These concessions the queen had a right to expect, in consideration of the greatly increased wealth of the provinces, and of the efficient help she had given them during many years.

Having received these detailed instructions and taken leave of the queen, Sir Francis Vere sailed for Flushing, but he was three days on the voyage "by reason of scant wind." He arrived at the Hague on the 16th of June, and next day he and Gilpin demanded an audience of the States General. (Sir W. Browne to Sir R. Sidney, from Flushing,

June 16, 1598. Sir F. Vere to Sir R. Cecil, from Middelburg, June 16, 1598, and from the Hague, June 21, 1598).

On the 18th they were received, and Vere delivered a speech embracing the various points of his instructions. The States acknowledged all the benefits that had been conferred on their country by the queen, and declared that they desired by all means to make their thankfulness manifest, and that they would do their uttermost to give her satisfaction. (Vere and Gilpin to R. Cecil, June 27, 1598. MSS. at Hatfield). As regarded the Spanish overtures, they were inclined rather to war than to a doubtful peace. (Grimeston; Meteren, Gilpin). Many conferences with Barneveldt followed, and Vere reported that the States would omit no possible means to yield Her Majesty all the contentment in their power. The resolution in favour of continuing the war made it necessary to examine the accounts between the two countries, and to obtain the concessions required by the queen. The States eventually acknowledged a debt to England of £800,000. They agreed to relieve the queen's government of expenses connected with auxiliary troops and the cautionary towns, to make an annual payment of £30,000, and to furnish aid, in ships and men, in the event of England being invaded. Barneveldt proceeded to London with the treaty, and it was ratified on the 16th of August, 1598.

******

S. P. O., Holland, vol. lxxxix. The English commissioners who signed this treaty were Egerton, Nottingham, Hunsdon, Essex, North, Knollys, Buckhurst, Robert Cecil; the Dutch signers were. Olden Barneveldt, Duvenvoord, Van Worck, Van Hottman, Heppela, and Noel Caron. The treaty is in French.

******

Lord Burleigh, who had served Queen Elizabeth with such unexampled fidelity and consummate ability during forty years, died, full of years and honour, on the 4th of August, 1598, twelve days before the signature of the treaty. He lived to see all his plans for the good of England succeed, all his patriotic aspirations fulfilled. A few weeks afterwards his equally industrious but far less able opponent breathed his last. Philip II. died on the 13th of September, 1598.

On the 6th of May Philip had formally ceded the Netherlands to his daughter Isabella, and on the 14th of September the Archduke Albert set out from Brussels to be married to the new sovereign, and to share with her the government of those provinces which still remained in the power of Spain. He left the Cardinal Andrew of Austria, and

Don Francisco de Mendoza, the Admiral of Aragon and Marquis of Guadalete, in charge during his absence. A vigorous attempt was made to gain some important success during the Archduke's visit to Spain. The admiral crossed the Meuse with a large army in September, 1598, and overran Cleves and Westphalia, in violation of the neutral rights of the Empire, and in November he battered the town of Doesburg. Shocking barbarities were committed by his soldiery, which aroused the indignation of the German princes, but he obtained no permanent advantage. Maurice had remained in an attitude of observation in the neighbourhood of Arnhem.

******

On December 30, 1598, the emperor published a mandate against the Admiral of Aragon, recounting the hostilities and pillaging of the Spaniards within the empire. (Meteren.)

******

Towards the end of the year Sir Francis Vere was called upon, in a letter from Queen Elizabeth herself, (dated December 15, 1598), to arrange with the States for the immediate dispatch of 2,000 English troops to Ireland. He promptly gave the necessary orders, and by January, 1599, the detachment was ready for embarkation at Flushing. The general had withdrawn 700 men from the cautionary towns, and 1,300 from the strength of eighteen companies. On this occasion the services of Sir Arthur Chichester, the future lord deputy, were transferred to Ireland. He had hitherto served in France and in the Ostend garrison.

By this time Queen Elizabeth had learned the value of Sir Francis Vere's services. He scarcely needed an advocate, for her appreciation of the merits of her general had been shown by entrusting to him the conduct of intricate negotiations, by giving him command of all English troops in the field, and by conferring on him the government of Brill. If such advocacy were needed, Vere had secured the confidence and friendship of Sir Robert Cecil, who had been Secretary of State since 1597. In March, 1599, Sir Francis expressed his thanks to Cecil for his labour to keep him in her Majesty's good opinion, in spite of the Earl of Essex, and also for his speeches at the council table in favour of his brother Horace. It was not until the early spring of 1599 that Vere was able to proceed from the Hague to Brill, in order to organise his new government; and in May he joined the army of Maurice, which was assembling along the line of the Maas, to oppose a formidable invasion of the Spaniards. He was accompanied by his brother Horace and by young Edward Cecil, a nephew of the Secretary, who now began his military career under the auspices of the greatest living master of the art. His father, Thomas Cecil, who had just succeeded as second Lord Burleigh, had been the first English governor of Brill. But he had soon retired, having shown no taste for the life of a soldier.

The army of Maurice was at first stationed along the line of the rivers, ready to succour Schenk's Sconce, Nymegen, Doesburg, or any other point that might be attacked. But the object of the Spaniards was to conquer the island of Bommel-waart, lower down the rivers, and thence to threaten Holland. Where the rivers Waal and Maas unite, at the eastern end of the Betuwe, there is a small island called Voorn, on which the Dutch had a strong position called Fort Nassau. The two rivers then separate again, to form an island called the Bommel-waart, which is twelve and a half miles long, and five across in the widest part. South of the Bommel-waart, the country of Brabant is drained by the rivers Aa and Dommel, which rise in an extensive morass, twenty-five miles long by six, called the Peel. The Peel yields excellent peat. Uniting at the important city of Bois le Due, the two streams form the River Dieze, which falls into the Maas, nearly opposite the centre of Bommel-waart island. At its mouth, on the Brabant site, was the strong fort called Crevecoeur. On the opposite side of the island, built along the left bank of the Waal, is the flourishing town of Bommel, with its lofty church-tower.

★★★★★★

> The old ramparts of Bommel are now, (1878), planted with avenues of lofty trees, chiefly horse-chestnuts, except along the quay facing the Waal. The church is near the inland or south end of the town; the lofty tower is of brick, with stone faced buttresses in four storeys, having a gallery and light balustrade round each. Thus the angle buttresses incline inwards and taper to the pinnacles. Formerly there was a spire. The church, dedicated to St. Martin, has spacious aisles, which are apsidal at the east end, and a loftier nave, with triforium and clerestory. The capitals of the pillars are richly carved with double chaplets of oak-leaves.
>
> At the west end of the south aisle there is an exceedingly pretty baptistery, and an old font, with the ark, tree of knowledge, and birth of the Saviour carved round it. There are two nearly obliterated frescos on the wall. From Bommel tower the whole

scene of the campaign of 1599 is spread out like a map: the broad waters of the Waal immediately below, Bois le Duc away to the south; Bommel-waart, with its bright green pastures, bounded by its two rivers, the Waal and the Maas; Rossum some three and a half miles to the east, and the famed forts of Nassau and San Andres just beyond.

Fort Crevecoeur is five miles to the south, in a line with Bois le Duc. A little nearer is the village of Hedel, and a mile to the east of it was the castle of Ammerzoden. Alst, where the Spaniards encamped before the siege of Bommel, is six miles to the east. There are several quaint and old houses, with rich carvings, in the town of Bommel.

★★★★★★

On the 4th of May, 1599, the Spanish Army crossed the Maas between Kessel and Theren, and invaded the island of Bommel-waart. Maurice rapidly concentrated his forces in the city of Bommel, throwing up entrenchments, while Bourlotte, in command of the invaders, encamped at the village of Alst. Following up this onward movement, the Admiral of Aragon captured the fort of Crevecoeur, and laid siege to Bommel. Nor did he rest content with this opening success. On the 16th of May he delivered a furious assault along the lines round Bommel, which was repulsed, the Spanish *maestro de campo*, Alfonso Davalos, being severely wounded. But the admiral continued his approaches, and planted guns, while skirmishes were of daily occurrence.

The States General strained every nerve for the defence of Bommel. They sent 280 vessels, several mounted with guns, to help in the river; 379 wagons were dispatched with provisions, and 356 horses were collected for dragging the guns. Their army numbered 10,000 foot and 3,000 horse. On the 13th of June Maurice was able to open a tremendous fire on the enemy's camp, which obliged the admiral to raise the siege. He retreated across the island and began the construction of a formidable fortress at the eastern end, facing the isle of Voorn, which he named San Andres in honour of his colleague, the Cardinal. His camp was moved to the village of Hurwenen. Maurice exerted himself to hinder the progress of Fort San Andres. Two bastions were to be raised towards the Waal, two towards the Maas, and a fifth inland, with connecting curtains, the rivers serving as a ditch. The works were designed by Velasco. Maurice planted guns on the opposite bank, and there was a heavy cannonade, but for many days the two armies were comparatively inactive.

THE BOMME

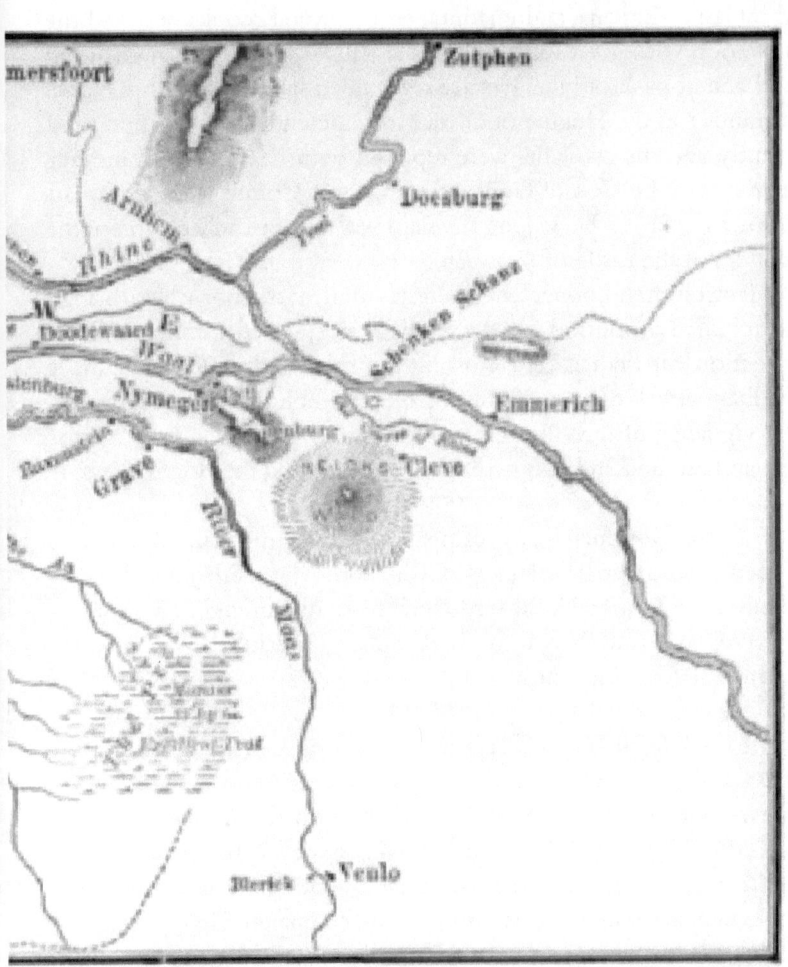

On the 24th of June a force under Count William Louis of Nassau and Sir Horace Vere crossed the river, and by break of day they had thrown up a half-moon of small extent at Heerewaarden, under a league from San Andres. Next day, 3,000 Spaniards and Italians, led by Jasper Zapena, and encouraged by several monks, attacked the half-moon with great fury, forcing the palisades, and fighting hand to hand and at push of pike. Horace Vere, aided by the Scottish Colonel Edmunds and the Huguenot De la Noue, defended the position most gallantly, and the assailants were repulsed with heavy loss. (Prinsterer. *Lettre clxxxii*. Le Comte Guillaume au Louis Comte Jean de Nassau, Voorn, June 26, 1599. Among the slain was Count Pacheco, son of the architect of the castle of Antwerp).

Maurice then connected Heerewaarden with Voorn by a bridge, and fortified a position on the Brabant side, called Lithoijen, for its protection. Sir Francis Vere, crossing the river with 6,000 men, made a brilliant attack on another Spanish fort, which they called Durango. The vigilance of the allies thwarted all the Spanish schemes of invasion, and on the 22nd of July the enemy evacuated the Bommel-waart.

******

For the Bommel-waart campaign see Grimeston; Meteren Bentivoglio; Sir F. Vere to R. Cecil, 26th May, 26th June, 23rd, July, 27th July, 1599: Edward Cecil to Lord Burleigh, 13th July, 1599; Rowland Whyte to Sir R. Sidney, 2nd July, 1599; Sir W. Browne to Sidney, etc.

******

Meanwhile, Sir Francis Vere had been struck down with a severe illness, and was confined for some days to his tent on the island of Voorn, "with no other troops about him than the musketeers of his own company." (Sir W. Browne to Sir R. Sidney, 20th July, 1599). On the 27th of July he sent Robert Cecil a plan of the island of Bommel-waart, showing the operations of the campaign. He reported that the Spanish army was so weaned and discontented that the soldiers disbanded in heaps, and that there was no likelihood of good government among them until the coming of the Archduke. In August another demand for troops arrived from the Queen, and Sir Francis Vere had the unpleasant duty of urging it upon Barneveldt, who was then at the camp. The Dutch statesman represented that the sword was now over their heads, and that the loss of more troops would be their ruin, but that the States would readily comply with the demand for ships. (S. P. O., Holland, vol. xci. Sir F. Vere to Robert Cecil, 1st Aug.,

1599). Vere then proceeded to the Hague, had an audience of the States General in full assembly on the 10th of August, and eventually obtained compliance with the queen's demands in full.

The truth was that a Spanish invasion was once more apprehended, and an army of defence was rapidly organised. (Chamberlain to Carleton, 1st Aug., 1599). The Castilian admiral was reported to be assembling ships and troops at Coruña. Sir Francis Vere was ordered to England with 2,000 of his best soldiers, and received the appointment of Lord Marshal of the army. He arrived in August, and was received in audience by the queen. (Rowland Whyte to Sir R. Sidney, 12th Sept., 1599). Rowland Whyte says that on reaching London:

> He came to Mr. Secretary's, who brought him to the queen, with whom he was long and very graciously used, and true it is that Mr. Secretary gives him all grace.

He and his men were kept on full pay until the danger of invasion had blown over. He was high in favour, and in September there was a rumour over London that Vere would be the next Lord Deputy of Ireland. (Rowland Whyte, 8th Sept., 1599: "Sir Francis Vere will have Ireland if Lord Mountjoy does not go.") In November he returned to the Hague.

★★★★★★

There is a letter in the State Paper Office (Persia) from Sir Francis Vere to Sir Anthony Shirley, which Mr. Evelyn Shirley has printed in his *Sherley Brothers*. It is dated at the Hague, on 18th Feb., 1600. Sir Anthony was an old companion in arms of Sir Francis, and was then at the court of Persia, in high favour with Shah Abbas. The letter is cordial and complimentary, but contains no news.

★★★★★★

The Archduke Albert had arrived in Spain some months after the death of Philip II. On the 18th of April, 1599, double marriages were celebrated at Valencia between King Philip III. and Margaret of Austria, and the Archduke Albert and the Infanta Isabella. The sovereign Archdukes, Albert and Isabella, then set out for their government, travelling by Milan, over the Alps to Basle, and thence by Besançon and Luxemburg. They entered Brussels on the 5th of September, 1599, and established a decorous, very dull Spanish court, representing a losing cause. Early in the following year the Spanish garrisons of San Andres and Crevecoeur sold those important fortresses to Prince Maurice for their arrears of pay. (£22,500 for the forts, with ordnance and munitions.—Letter from Sir F. Vere, at the Hague, 29th April, 1600.)

They had been in a mutinous, discontented state throughout the winter. All the fruits of the Bommel-waart campaign were thus lost to the Spaniards, and the prospects of the Archdukes were gloomy and disheartening. On the other hand, the new century opened to the allies with bright anticipations of independence and prosperity.

CHAPTER 20

The Eve of the Battle of Nieuport

The States General, guided by the advice of Olden Barneveldt, resolved to carry the war into the enemy's country in the summer of 1600, believing that the Archdukes were embarrassed by want of funds and by mutinous troops. Ostend was held by their ally, the Queen of England, and it was determined that the bulk of their army should be landed on the Flemish coast, and should lay siege to the town of Nieuport, west of Ostend, and afterwards to Dunkirk. Prince Maurice considered this enterprise to be extremely hazardous, and Sir Francis Vere held the same opinion. But the military authorities were overruled, and a large fleet was assembled off Flushing, to embark the troops and land them on the opposite shore.

The army consisted of 12,000 infantry, 1,600 cavalry, and 10 pieces of artillery. It was divided into three divisions: the van led by Sir Francis Vere, the battle by Count Everard Solms, and the rear by Count Ernest of Nassau and Olivier de Tempel. Count Louis Gunther of Nassau was general of cavalry. Vere's division consisted of 1,600 English veterans, 2,500 Frisians, 250 of Prince Maurice's guard, and 10 cornets of horse, making a total of 4,500 men. His brother, Sir Horace Vere, was with him, and his trusty friend and counsellor, Sir John Ogle, who was lieutenant colonel. There, too, were Sir Robert Drury, Sir Charles Fairfax, Captains Holies, Gilbert, Sutton, Lowell, and Morgan, while Sir Edward Cecil commanded Vere's regiment of horse. Vere's Frisians were led by Generals Taco Hettinga, Arusma, and Ripperda. Maurice, who commanded in chief, had with him his young brother Frederick Henry, Counts Frederick, Albert, and Otto Solms, his half-brother Justinus of Nassau, two sons of Admiral Coligny, and Lord Grey de Wilton.

Young Ernest of Nassau occupied Fort Philippine on the 21st of

June, this being the point selected for the disembarkation of the army on the Flemish coast. Philippine is near the head of a large shallow inlet, with many sandbanks, dry at low water, called the Braakman.

★★★★★★

The Braakman penetrates to within a few hundred yards of the Belgian frontier, and thus divides Dutch Flanders, on the south side of the Scheldt, nearly in two. It is about five miles deep and two across, and contains two islands, called Kleine Stelle, on which there is a farm, and Angeline Polder. Philippine is on the western side,—a little fishing village of one street, running up from the tiny harbour, where over twenty boats come in on a Saturday night, and gayly fly the Zealand flag from their mastheads all Sunday. These boats busily unload their cargoes of mussels, which is the great trade of the place.

The mussel spat is obtained from Dunkirk, and put on regular layings near the mouth of the Braakman, or in the Scheldt. Next year it is brood, and in the third year the mussels are taken up. Carts come in from Belgium to take away the sacks of mussels, with strong net bottoms, so that the wet from the mussels can easily drip out. They are sent to all parts, but principally to Paris. The men fish, the women cultivate the vegetable gardens. The Protestant church at Philippine probably dates from the time of the Synod of Dort, or thereabouts, judging from the style of carving of the pulpit. There mains of the old ramparts form a breezy promenade on soft turf, but they are not planted with trees. At high tide the Braakman is one sheet of water, with bright green shores, and extensive flats covered with equisetum and other marsh plants. In winter these flats are frequented by wild ducks and many other aquatic birds.

★★★★★★

It is now a fishing village, with a thriving trade in mussels, but in those days there seems to have been nothing but a small fort. The fleet arrived on the 22nd, and the whole of that day was occupied in landing the army.

When Maurice disembarked there was only a small force of Spaniards in the neighbourhood, under an officer named Rivas. But as soon as the news reached the Archduke Albert at Brussels, he rapidly concentrated his army round Ghent, and prepared to march against the invaders. This aggressive campaign was a bold and hazardous step on the part of the States General. The destruction of their army, thus isolated in a hostile country, would have left Holland open to invasion, and might have led to the annihilation of her recently acquired liberties. On the other hand, a victory in a great pitched battle between Maurice and the flower of the Spanish forces in the Netherlands would have a moral effect throughout Christendom of the utmost importance to the cause of liberty, quite apart from its immediate consequences.

The army of Maurice advanced from Philippine to the neighbourhood of Ostend by rapid marches, and captured the forts and redoubts of the enemy round that city, including Oudenburg and St. Albert. The latter was in the *dunes*, about two miles to the south of Ostend. A body of 2,000 men was left to garrison these important positions, which were on the line of march that the Archduke must take from Bruges to Nieuport; and on June 30 Maurice resumed his advance upon the latter town. Solms had been detached to capture Fort St. Albert. The rest of the army first advanced somewhat inland, apparently along the line of the present, (1878), canal between Bruges and Nieuport; but finding the country in a swampy condition and unfit for the passage of artillery, they passed over a stream called the Yper-leet, at the village of Leffinghe, and made their way across the meadows to the seaside with much difficulty, filling up ditches, laying bridges, and making a road practicable for field-guns as they advanced.

Crossing the dunes, they reached the shore at about a cannon-shot from Fort St. Albert, which had already surrendered to Solms, and early in the morning of the 1st of July they marched along the beach to Nieuport Haven, which was waded by the greater part of the army at ebb tide, about eight a. m. The division of Solms arrived a day or two earlier. He had advanced direct along the sands, after taking Fort St. Albert on the 28th. He crossed the haven with half his force, leaving 3,000 men on the Ostend side. This part of the army was before Nieuport for two or three days, and the rest for one day, busily engaged in making a bridge over the haven, selecting points of vantage for the siege, entrenching, and preparing an encampment. The fleet arrived on the morning of the 1st of July.

******

Mr. Motley (in his *United Netherlands*, iv.) represents Sir Francis Vere in a very unfavourable light. He has, most unfortunately, taken an erroneous view of Vere's character and conduct. He writes of Sir Francis as one whose advice was so bad that it could scarcely have been given in good faith (iv.), whose only virtue was personal courage, and who published a party pamphlet marked by "spleen, inordinate self-esteem, and wounded pride of opinion," upon which no reliance can be placed. These, it must be admitted, are grave charges expressed in very strong language, Mr. Motley has added a *Special Note,* with the object of justifying his censures on Sir Francis Vere.

It will be my duty to refute entirely every single point which Mr. Motley has raised against Vere. I propose to deal with each accusation of Mr. Motley as it occurs in the course of the narrative.

Mr. Motley's first charge is (iv) that all other authorities agree that Maurice's army came before Nieuport in the morning of the 1st of July, and that the battle was fought on the 2nd, while Vere gives the time occupied in quartering and entrenching before Nieuport at two or three days. On the strength of this imaginary discrepancy Mr. Motley pronounces Vere's narrative to be untrustworthy. Both accounts are correct. The main, body, under Maurice, was, it is true, only before Nieuport during the 1st of July and the early morning of the 2nd; altogether about twenty-four hours, But the division of Solms arrived on the 29th. Vere is quite accurate in giving the whole time during which the troops were before Nieuport at two or three days, (Vere's *Commentaries*) Considering that he was writing from memory, some years after the event, Sir Francis Vere's precise accuracy on this and all other points is very remarkable.

******

Nieuport is a quaint and interesting old Flemish town, between Ostend and Dunkirk, with a wet ditch supplied by a canal from Bruges and by the River Yser, which here falls into the tidal estuary forming the haven. Nieuport was originally a village, called Sandhoofd, depending on a seaport town founded in very ancient times by a Lombard colony, called Lombaertzyde. But this port was swallowed up by the sea, and the approach to it choked with sand in 1116. The change seems to have opened the present haven, for Sandhoofd was erected into a town, with the name of Nieuport, in 1160, and Lombaertzyde became and still is a little rural village, a mile from the haven and from Nieuport. The town of Nieuport was strongly fortified with a brick wall, having high, circular towers at intervals, with conical tile roofs and a lofty and solid square keep at the southeast angle, which is still standing, (1878).

The place was taken by the English under the Bishop of Norwich in 1383, (Froissart), but stood a long siege from a French Army, resisting three assaults, in 1489. The Hotel de Ville, built in 1710, contains a curious and ancient but very inaccurate plan of the Battle of Nieuport; a large modern picture, by L. Moritz, representing the Admiral of Aragon surrendering himself prisoner to Prince Maurice after the battle, which was given to the town by the late King William I. of the Netherlands, in 1820; and a painting on panel of the town as it was in 1600. The haven is now artificially deepened, so that timber-laden brigs and other small craft come up to the town. This channel connects Nieuport with the sea, a distance of a mile and a half. It could easily be waded across during the greater part of the time between half ebb and half flood. On the left bank of the haven, halfway between the town and the sea, there were two lighthouses, built by Count Guy de Dampierre in 1284, at a place called Vterboede. They are shown on the old map at Bruges. One still remains,—a picturesque hexagonal tower surmounted by a short steeple, which has recently been carefully restored.

From the Texel to Dunkirk the flat and fertile plains are protected from the sea by the dunes, a line of hills of fine sand and varying height, thrown together in an apparently confused mass of crests and ridges. There is evidence that the dunes were once much further to the westward, and that they have gradually encroached on the land. In some places the same soil as forms the fields within the dunes crops out on the seashore, and at others the roots of trees are uncovered and fishermen's nets get entangled in them. In 1520 a castle built by the Romans at the mouth of the Rhine, inside the dunes, appeared, uncovered, on the seaside, with walls eight feet thick. In 1674 these old Roman walls were 1,600 paces out at sea, beyond the shore line of Katwyk; and in 1752, at very low water and after a long continuance of easterly winds, the last remnants of them were seen.

In 1460 the church of Scheveningen was destroyed by the sea. It stood 1,900 yards more to seaward than the present church, which was built on the inland side of the village, and is now nearly on the seashore. The coast of North Holland loses, on an average, about eight feet every year, the dunes being blown inland; but dunes can be artificially raised by making a sand dike, against which the blown sand accumulates. Part of the dunes on the coast of North Holland were thus formed by order of Olden Barneveldt in 1610, soon after the battle of Nieuport. In South Holland the dunes are from thirty-two

NIEUPORT AND AD

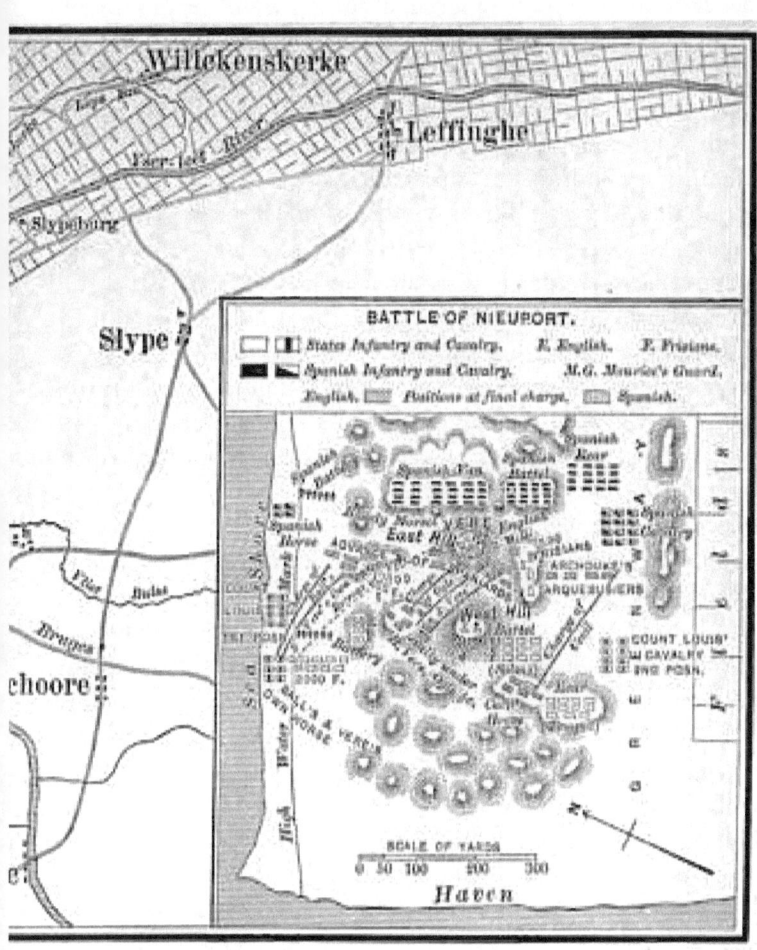

to forty-eight feet above high-water mark, and the highest dune in North Holland attains a height of one hundred and twenty feet. Their width in Walcheren varies from one hundred to six hundred yards, but on the Flemish coast, west of Ostend, it is less. They have, in some parts, a motion from the sea towards the inland, and it is possible that the dunes at Nieuport may have receded; but this seems very doubtful.

There is a large bird's-eye map of Flanders in the Hotel de Ville at Bruges, which shows the position of the dunes before the battle. This map was made by Pierre Clarissius in 1597, and is a copy of the original map, on a very large scale, constructed by Pierre Pourbus in 1566. Here the position of the dunes, their distance from the haven and from Lombaertzyde, and their width, are shown much as they appear now. It is not a little remarkable that the ridges and bottoms, the hilltops and valleys, are precisely as Sir Francis Vere described them; so that the relative distances and the general features have continued nearly the same to the present day. The dunes have been sown, since 1820, with a peculiar tough grass, called *helm* (*Psamma arenaria*, P. B.), which takes deep root in the sand, and is very useful in checking the drift, but it fails in preventing the sand from being, to some extent, blown inland by strong westerly gales.

The section of dunes between Nieuport and Ostend, a distance of nine miles, has the peculiarity of containing small oases or valleys, surrounded by the sand-hills, where ragwort, wild pansy, plantain, and clover grow luxuriantly; and from their inner edge a grassy slope extends to the line of cultivation. The whole place swarms with rabbits. The view from the higher ridges of these dunes, looking inland, is very picturesque. To the right is the town of Nieuport, with its massive church-tower, embosomed in trees, and all along the line of the horizon are the Flemish villages, with their red-tiled, white-walled houses and church-spires, surrounded by fruit orchards, and wider outer circles of waving crops and emerald pastures. It was in these dunes, and within sight of the peaceful villages of Lombaertzyde and Westende, that the memorable Battle of Nieuport was fought, on July 2, 1600.

During the whole of the 1st, Prince Maurice's army was hard at work completing the bridge and preparing for the siege of Nieuport Many vessels of the fleet had come up the haven, and at low water were high and dry on the mud. Towards evening Maurice received news from Ostend that a large force of the enemy was before the fort of Oudenburg. A council of war was called, and most of the officers declared that it was a mere piece of bravado on the part of Rivas, at the head of a small body of infantry, with which he had advanced from Sluys. But Sir Francis Vere maintained that it was the main body of the Archduke's army. He advised Maurice to retrace his steps with his whole force before the enemy could have time to retake the forts, and so attack him at a disadvantage, with the forts in his rear. The advice was excellent, and recommended itself to Maurice; but, as Vere says, the Prince was usually slow in resolving, and he waited for further news.

※※※※※※

In commenting on this council of war, Mr. Motley makes his second charge against Sir Francis Vere. He says: "The advice of Vere involved an outrageous impossibility, and it seems incredible that it can have been given in good faith; still more amazing that its rejection by Maurice should have been bitterly censured. Two thirds of the army lay on the other side of the harbour, and it was high water at about three o'clock." (iv.) He goes on to say that it would take longer to cross by boats and temporary bridges than to wait for low water in the morning; and that if the enemy made his appearance while they were crossing, the army would be hopelessly lost. The answer to all this is conclusive. Maurice did not reject the advice, but merely procrastinated; and Vere certainly never censured his old comrade in arms, of whom he invariably speaks in respectful terms. It was nearly dead low water when the first news arrived, before dusk, and the army could have waded across the haven with ease, without danger from an enemy, who was then upwards of ten miles off.

※※※※※※

The same evening another messenger arrived, followed by a third, who reported that the forts had surrendered to the Archduke. Maurice again sent for his trusty councillor, Sir Francis Vere, who gave the same advice, with this change: that, whereas his first project was to attack the enemy under cover of the forts, he now, that chance being lost, proposed an advance to the road from Leffinghe to the Dunes, which the army had constructed on the 29th, through the low ground. In that advantageous position he would await the attack of the Spaniards, with the River Yser-leet in their rear.

Maurice saw the importance of Vere's advice, but, instead of advancing with the whole army, as Vere intended, and as was essential to success, he detached the portion of the division of Solms which had remained on the right bank of the haven, consisting of 2,500 infantry, 500 horse, and two guns, under the command of his cousin, Ernest of Nassau, saying he would follow with the rest of the army in due season. Vere was strongly opposed to this division of the forces. (*Commentaries*). He urged that so small a number of men could offer no effectual resistance, whereas, if the whole army advanced at once, their position would be improved under any circumstances. If the enemy had already crossed the low ground, the army could give him battle better there than at Nieuport, with the haven cutting off all retreat. If part of the enemy's force only had crossed, which was most likely, the victory would be easy.

But at midnight the detachment was dispatched under Count Ernest, and it fell out exactly as Vere had predicted. The enemy was crossing the stream at Leffinghe when Ernest came up. His men broke and fled at the first fire, being daunted by the overpowering numbers of the enemy, and 2,500 men were thus lost, without checking the Archduke's advance for a moment. Fortunately, that personage marched slowly, and with long halts, or the position of Maurice would have been very critical. As it was, the invaders were placed in a most hazardous position. They must give battle in the dunes, with Nieuport in their rear, and with the certainty that a reverse would be little less than annihilation.

Maurice ordered the rest of the army to march down to the haven side by break of day, in readiness to cross at the first ebb. (Vere's *Commentaries*). Sir Francis Vere commanded the vanguard, and was at the water side by dawn; but the haven was not yet fordable. He therefore joined Prince Maurice again, and was with him when news came that the Archduke had crossed the dunes, and was marching along the seashore. Vere urged the necessity of crossing with all possible speed and taking up a position in the dunes before the enemy was upon them. He then returned to his troops. The soldiers would have stripped to keep their clothes dry, as they had done the day before, but Sir Francis thought it inexpedient, the enemy being so near at hand, and therefor:

> Willed them to keep on their clothes and not to care for wetting them, for they should either need none, or have better and dryer clothes to sleep in that night. (Vere's *Commentaries*).

The cavalry, commanded by Count Louis Gunther of Nassau, who had been placed under Vere's orders, crossed the haven at about 8.30 a.m.,—"*à demy à nage, à demy à gue*," as the Count told his father,—and the infantry of the vanguard followed, taking up their positions on the seashore and in the dunes.

******

Mr. Motley bases his third charge against Sir Francis Vere on his account of the passage across the haven. He says that it is inaccurate, and that these misstatements render Vere's evidence untrustworthy, and make him unworthy of credit. Mr. Motley alleges that Vere's words are that he ordered them "*to cross the haven at dawn of day, at the first low tide*" The italics are Mr. Motley's. Here is certainly a mistake, but it is not made by Vere. Mr. Motley goes on to show that it was high tide at dawn of day on July 2, 1600, while the crossing took place at eight a. m., and that consequently Vere's statement is erroneous.

Now, Sir Francis Vere not only does not use the words which Mr. Motley puts in his mouth, but gives an entirely different and perfectly accurate account of the passage. His words are: "The rest of the army was commanded to march down to the haven's side by the break of day, to pass at the first ebb tide." He does not imply that the ebb tide was at break of day, and what follows completely disposes of Mr. Motley's accusation. Sir Francis goes on to say that the water was not then passable, that he therefore returned to Prince Maurice, and that he afterwards went back to his troops, "and, so soon as the tide served, I passed my men as they stood in their battalions." (Vere's *Commentaries*.)

******

When Sir Francis Vere and Count Louis reached the seashore, they could see the enemy afar off, marching along close to the edge of the breaking waves. There was not a moment to be lost, and Vere at once proceeded to select the most advantageous positions in the dunes to post his troops of the vanguard, and prepare for battle.

The haven makes a break in the dunes, and they begin to rise, at first in very gentle grassy undulations, at a distance of 180 yards from the haven's margin. Here they are of considerable width, but their breadth is much less a few hundred yards further towards Ostend. At this narrow point Vere resolved to give battle. Towards the haven, and 250 yards within the dunes, there is a high, rounded sand-hill, 50 feet above the sea, with ridges sweeping round from either shoulder and forming a circle. In the centre of this circle there is one of those flat plains already referred to, now called the "Oasis Valerie." Directly across this oasis, and in front of the first, or West Hill, there is a second, or East Hill, the distance between them being 120 yards. Vere, judging by eye, calls it about 100 paces. In front (east) of the East Hill the dunes are intersected by a hollow bottom, the sand ridges being higher to the seaside, or north, than towards the inland, or south.

The bottom runs clean across the dunes, which are here only 368 yards wide, from the seashore to the inland plain, so that Vere could conveniently occupy them with his vanguard. On the hither or western side of the bottom, where the East Hill stood more advanced than the rest, he resolved to await the enemy. The ridge and hill tops vary in height from 30 to 50 feet above high-water mark. The above is Vere's description, and exactly similar features can be traced in the present dunes.

The vanguard consisted of 4,350 men, of whom 1,600, (not 2,600, as stated by Motley, iv.), were English, 2,500 Frisians, and 250 of Prince Maurice's guard. From this force Sir Francis selected a thousand picked men,—250 English, 250 of Maurice's guard, and 500 Frisian musketeers. He posted the 250 English and 50 of the guard in the very front of the position on the East Hill, which is steep and sandy, and at the top so hollow that the men, when lying down, were covered from the sand-hills on the other side of the bottom as by a parapet.

On the top of the loftier West Hill the remaining 200 of the guard were posted, and Maurice caused two demi-culverins to be placed there. The semicircular ridge connecting the East and West Hills on the land side is rather lower than the West Hill, and very steep on the side facing inland, with loose sand. Here Sir Francis posted the 500 Frisian musketeers, with orders to fire only to the south, as they commanded all the ground by which the enemy's cavalry could pass on that side. On the other ridge, between the two hills facing the sea, and concealed in the sandy ravines, were 700 English pike and shot men, ready to support the forlorn hope on the East Hill.

Prince Maurice placed the rest of his artillery, consisting of six pieces, on the seashore at the foot of the dunes, nearly in a line with the West Hill; and the remaining troops of the vanguard, consisting of 650 English and 2,000 Frisians, were stationed on the outer slopes of the dunes, near the battery, ready to reinforce the advanced party. The cavalry were at first on the extreme left, close to the sea, Count Louis being on the right by the dunes, and that dashing cavalry officer, Marcellus Bacx, on the left, near the sea. The divisions of Solms and Tempel were also on the seashore, in the rear of the West Hill.

As soon as Sir Francis Vere had completed his arrangements, Prince Maurice rode to the front with the other commanders to consult whether the army should advance or abide the coming of the enemy. They all counselled an advance except Vere. That experienced veteran expressed an opinion that:

> The archduke's forces had been gathered in haste, that they had no provisions with them to last for any time, and that they had no alternative but to advance and give battle.

> He therefore strongly advised that the army should await the attack of the enemy in the excellent positions he had selected. This advice was adopted by Maurice, and a decisive victory was the consequence.

★★★★★★

> Such was Vere's advice, as stated by himself. Mr. Motley says that Vere's advice was to throw up entrenchments to the northeast, and refuse the battle that day, if possible; and that Maurice replied that there would be no entrenchments that day but those of pike and arquebus (iv.). Nothing of the kind ever happened. Vere would not have posted his vanguard in carefully selected positions if he had not in tended to fight that day. The proposal to entrench in shifting sand would have been absurd, if it had ever been made.

★★★★★★

> The archduke's army numbered 10,000 infantry, 1,600 horse, and six guns. Zapena, an experienced officer, was marshal of the army, and the cavalry was commanded by the Admiral of Aragon. The archduke's chief strength was in his infantry, composed of old and trained soldiers, who, up to that date, were "unfoiled in the field." After they were in full view they rested for two hours on the inner slopes, waiting until the rise of the tide should render the sands unserviceable for cavalry, their chief trust being in their foot. At about half flood they again crossed to the sea-sands, and marched forward, with some light cavalry in advance. As these horsemen were well in front, Vere wished to send forward the cavalry of the vanguard, with the object of drawing the enemy's horse away from the foot until they were within range of the battery on the beach, and then to have opened fire, and afterwards charged them vigorously.

But Count Louis of Nassau, through some misunderstanding, did not charge, and when the enemy's horsemen came within range, Vere ordered the guns to be fired. The artillerymen did their work so well that the enemy's horsemen were scattered and thrown into confusion, eventually taking refuge in the dunes.

✶✶✶✶✶✶

Vere's *Commentaries*.

This little skirmish gives occasion for the fourth charge which Mr. Motley brings against Sir Francis Vere. Count Louis Gunther, in a letter to Count John of Nassau (Prinsterer, Lettre ccviii. ii.), said: "Vere judged that I had advanced too far, and thought I should fall back nearer the infantry. I feared this movement might cause confusion, the enemy being so close, and dishearten the men." Mr. Motley turns this into Louis having wanted to charge, and Vere having ordered him to fall back. Upon this Mr. Motley at once assumes that Vere's account is false. His ground for this assumption is that Vere made inaccurate statements as to the length of time the troops were before Nieuport, and as to the tide when they crossed the haven. It has already been shown that Vere's statements on both points were strictly accurate, so that these reasons for discrediting the English general are invalid.

The truth is clear enough. Mr. Motley states (iv.) that, by Vere's order, the cannoneers fired a volley before the cavalry had time to make the proposed feint, "thus precipitating the action, and almost in an instant changing its whole character and defeating its original plan." Now what was the object of this proposed feint on the part of the cavalry? It was to draw the enemy's cavalry within range of the guns. It is admitted on all sides, that, when Vere opened fire, the enemy's cavalry actually was within range, and was thrown into confusion. It is clear, therefore, that the guns were not fired too soon, but exactly at the right moment. Young Louis simply misunderstood the order, which was to advance, not to fall back. But no harm was done, and there was no intentional misstatement on either side. The action was not precipitated, its character was not changed, and the original plan was not defeated, but was carried out to the letter.

✶✶✶✶✶✶

Soon afterwards it was high tide, when there is barely a space of thirty yards between the sea and the steep sand-hills. The enemy, therefore, marched all his infantry into the dunes, while his horse crossed over to what Vere calls the "Greenway," between the dunes and the cultivated fields inland. The remaining portion of Maurice's army executed a similar movement. The 2,000 detached to garrison the forts near Ostend, and the 2,500 sent away with Count Ernest, had reduced the infantry to less than 7,500 men. Of these, 4,350, or more than half, composed the vanguard under Sir Francis Vere, which really fought the battle. The centre under Count Solms, numbering about 1,000 men, was stationed in the dunes, about a musket-shot to the right rear of the vanguard, and the rear, of 2,150, under Tempel, was at the same distance to the right rear of the centre, so that the three divisions were posted en echelon across the dunes.

The rear was never engaged at all. The whole of the cavalry, except Sir Francis Vere's own troop and that of Ball, which remained by the battery on the beach, was moved to the "Greenway "facing the Spanish cavalry. This "Greenway "is an undulating grassy lane, sloping from the dunes to the dry hedge which fences in the fields of corn and beans, and is 150 yards in width; so that, as Vere says, the cavalry was not formed "in any large front, but one at the tail of the other, as the narrowness of the passage enforced." (There are not, and never can have been, any ditches across this sloping "Greenway," as Mr. Motley tells us (iv.), unless water could run up hill). The "Greenway "was fully commanded from the southern ridge, where Vere had posted the Frisian musketeers.

Maurice heartily approved of all the arrangements made by his trusty English colleague; and when the battle was about to commence, he was urged, for many reasons, to keep in the rear of all. To this he agreed; while Sir Francis Vere took his post on the top of the East or foremost hill with his 250 gallant Englishmen. Soon the Spanish forlorn hope of arquebusiers appeared on the crests of the ridge on the opposite side of the bottom and opened fire, while their vanguard advanced down the slopes.

CHAPTER 21

The Battle of Nieuport

The Battle of Nieuport began at about half past two in the afternoon of the 2nd of July, 1600. Vere's plan was to hold the advanced positions as long as possible with his forlorn hope of the vanguard, bringing up the 700 men on the north ridge and the 650 English reserves gradually as required, and fighting with bull-dog tenacity. He thus intended to wear out the Spaniards, who were already tired by the long march from Leffinghe. Then, at the last moment, and when overborne by numbers, he intended to send for fresh reinforcements to fall upon the exhausted enemy.

After exchanging fire from the hills on either side of the bottom, 500 of the flower of the Spanish infantry rushed into the hollow and charged the East Hill, on which Vere was posted. The 250 Englishmen and 50 of Maurice's guard received them on its sandy slope at push of pike, and a desperate struggle ensued, which was obstinately continued for half an hour; the Spaniards being at last obliged to fall back behind some low ridges in the bottom. At nearly the same time the enemy's cavalry advanced down the "Greenway." But the two demi-culverins on the West Hill, and the 500 Frisian musketeers on the south ridge, so galled them, that, at the first appearance of a charge by the horse under Count Louis, they fell back to their infantry supports, followed for some distance by the young count.

At the same instant, and while the Spanish forlorn hope was falling back from the assault on the East Hill, Vere ordered 100 Englishmen from the north ridge to advance as covertly as possible and attack the Spaniards in the bottom on their right flank, while 60 men charged down the hill and engaged them in front. The Spaniards broke and fled to the main body of their vanguard, where they rallied, were reinforced, and seized a round sandy hill in the bottom, near the West

Hill, which Vere considered to be an important post. He therefore brought up more men from the north ridge, and strove to dislodge them. Vere describes the struggle as a "bloody morsel." The position was an isolated eminence, and the men came to hand-blows upon the whole circle of the hill, with much slaughter on both sides; but in the end the enemy was forced to retire.

At this juncture the archduke advanced his centre in line with his vanguard, and strove to drive the English from their points of vantage in the bottom, sometimes gaining and sometimes losing ground. Vere continued to draw from his 700 men on the north ridge, and persisted in the desperate struggle, his design being to draw down the bulk of the enemy on his handful of men, and so spend and waste them as that they should be unable to withstand the reserves. The ensigns of the van, centre, and rear of the Spaniards were now brought up in line on the hills to the east of the bottom, but rather to the right of Vere's hill, and directly fronting the more distant centre and rear of Maurice's army. In this order the Spaniards advanced until they received a check from the fire of the Frisian musketeers on the south ridge, and their leading columns took shelter in the hollows, sending out skirmishers.

Then the Spaniards turned their main force upon Vere, the fight continuing hotter and hotter, without intermission, in the bottom, until the whole of the 1,600 English were engaged. They were overborne by the overwhelming numbers of the Archduke's soldiers. Vere now saw that the time had arrived for the reserves to come to the front, and that a charge of cavalry could alone settle the day; for even if driven back by infantry, the enemy would have time to rally. He therefore sent orders for his 2,000 Frisians, posted near the seaside battery, to advance; and he also sent to ask Maurice for part of the cavalry of the centre. He sent messenger after messenger, but no aid arrived. At last he himself rode down into the bottom amongst his men to cheer them on, doing the work of a common soldier as well as of a general.

Thus, with extreme difficulty, the little band and its heroic leader continued to hold the enemy in check. Still no help came. Vere received a musket-shot in the thigh, and soon afterwards another in the leg. He concealed his wounds from the men and fought on, hoping for succour, but none came. At last his men were overwhelmed by numbers, and fell back slowly and in good order towards the battery on the seaside. The Spaniards followed at a respectful distance, though a few of the enemy's skirmishing cavalry came close up, and killed some men by thrusting rapiers under their armour. During the retreat

Sir Francis Vere's horse fell dead under him and upon him, so that, sorely wounded as he was, he could not move. His lieutenant-colonel, Sir John Ogle, Sir Robert Drury, and a gentleman named Thomas Higham, came to his assistance. They extricated their chief and put him up behind Sir Robert. Ogle's clothes were stained by the blood from his general's wounds. The fact that there should have been time for this shows how cautious was the Spanish pursuit, though Ogle says that there was only just time, and that they ran considerable danger of being captured.

******

Here Mr. Motley makes another attack upon Sir Francis Vere (iv.). He says: "Vere complained that he was not sufficiently seconded, and that the reserves were not brought up rapidly enough to his support. He was manifestly unjust; for, although it could not be doubted that the English and the Frisians did their best, it was equally certain that every part of the army was as stanch as the vanguard. It may safely be asserted that it would not have benefited the cause of the States had every man been thrown into the fight at one and the same moment."

The answer to this charge is conclusive. Vere not only made no complaint, but he distinctly disclaimed anything of the kind. His words are: "I will charge and accuse none but the messengers of their slackness." Yet never was complaint more justifiable. The delay in sending succour as nearly as possible enabled the Spaniards to gain a complete victory. Mr. Motley speaks of the Frisians having done their best. Why, the 1,000 Frisians composed the very reinforcement for which Vere sent messenger after messenger, and which never came! Mr. Motley continues, that "every part of the army was as stanch as the vanguard." But he forgot that a large part of the army was never engaged at all! It was very easy for troops to be stanch when they were out of range. Mr. Motley's last sentence, in the passage quoted above, is also calculated to convey an erroneous impression. Vere was the last man to desire that "every man should be thrown into the fight at one and the same moment." His whole plan was the very reverse of such tactics. It was to hold the enemy in check and tire him out with the smallest force possible, bringing up reserves gradually, and only at the moment they were needed. He and his men performed prodigies of valour: the 1,600 picked men from the vanguard kept the whole Spanish Army at bay for hours; half their number fell; Vere's repeated and urgent entreaties for aid were unanswered; and yet he made no complaint, imputing blame only to the slackness of messengers.

★★★★★★

On reaching the battery on the sands, Vere found the 1,000 Frisians, who might have turned the scale, still there. They had received no orders to advance. There were also 300 foot under Sir Horace Vere, and some cavalry under Captain Ball. Sir Francis ordered the cavalry, supported by Horace, to charge the Spaniards, who were now streaming out on to the beach. The enemy's troops were routed on the sands, and fled back into the dunes. Then, at length, the worn-out hero, who was suffering from severe illness as well as from two bleeding wounds, put himself into the hands of his surgeon. (Ogle's *Narrative*).

The Spaniards now carried the East Hill and advanced into the valley beyond, where 2,000 of their number formed in *tercios*. Others drove back the Frisian musketeers from the south ridge, and the archduke's own arquebusiers advanced along the Greenway. This was the most critical moment in the battle. The fate of the army of the States was hanging on a thread. Maurice now took his stand on the West Hill, where the two demi-culverins were planted, whence he had a better view of the field. The Spaniards, though momentarily victorious, were tired and worn out with fighting. There was still hope.

The English officers began to rally their men in the sheltered hollows between the West Hill and the beach, almost overlooking the valley where the 2,000 Spaniards had formed. Hither Sir John Ogle brought 30 men. (Ogle's *Narrative*). He was soon joined by brave Charles Fairfax. Then came young Gilbert, slain immediately afterwards, with more men. Seeing this force gradually increasing, the Spaniards sent out 150 men against them from the main body of 2,000. At that moment Sir Horace Vere rode up from his victorious charge on the beach, bringing further reinforcements, including the companies of Captains Lowell, Sutton, and Morgan.

Seeing this, the 150 Spaniards fell back again to the main body. Prince Maurice also saw it, and joyfully exclaimed: "*Voyez, voyez, les Anglais qui tournent à la charge!*" He gave orders to Dubois, the commissary-general of cavalry, to bring the remaining horse forward, under Sir Edward Cecil, to be ready to charge in any direction that might be required. All these movements took place more rapidly than they can be related, and amidst shouting and uproar.

Then Sir Horace Vere, Ogle, and Fairfax, with their rallied men, charged furiously down the slope and across the valley, just as the main body of Spaniards was thrown into slight confusion by the retreat of the 150 skirmishers. The renewed fight was short and decisive. The Spaniards were tired and worn out. They broke and began a retreat which ended in flight. Maurice, "whose vigilant and judicious eye was upon our actions and motions all this while," as Ogle tells us, ordered Sir Edward Cecil to charge with his cavalry. The regiments of Marcellus Bacx and of Ball also charged. The Frisian musketeers rallied; Maurice advanced the centre division under Solms, and plied the enemy with shot from the demi-culverins. By a second charge Cecil scattered the Archduke's arquebusiers on the Greenway. Ogle says:

> These charges, by the hand and favour of God, gave us the day.

The Spaniards broke and fled in all directions. The archduke never drew rein until he reached Bruges. Zapena and the Admiral of Aragon were taken prisoners, and about a third of the Spanish army was killed or wounded. Of the 1,600 English, no less than 800 were killed or wounded; eight captains we're slain, and all the rest but two were wounded. But the victory was complete.

The terrible slaughter of the English proves, as Vere expresses it, that "on our side in a manner the whole loss fell on the English"; that is to say, that they bore the brunt of the fight, and that the heaviest share of the loss was theirs. He adds:

> I dare not take the whole honour of the victory to the poor English troop of 1,600 men, but leave it to be judged by those that may give their censure with less suspicion of partiality.

✶✶✶✶✶✶

Mr. Motley's attacks on Sir Francis Vere have now been disproved and shown to be without any justification. We next come to that eminent historian's remarks on Vere's writings. He says: "The narrative of Vere is marked throughout by spleen, inordinate personal and national self-esteem, undisguised hostility to the Nassaus and the Hollanders, and wounded pride of opinion." He then accuses the great general of "looseness and recklessness of assertion, which would be almost impossible had Maurice or his cousins been likely to engage in a controversy concerning the Nieuport expedition" (iv.). He finally remarks that, while the letters written by the Counts Louis and Ernest concerning the battle of Nieuport remained in the family archives for two centuries and a half, so that "the controversy with Vere" is an "all unconscious one on the part of those buried warriors," Sir Francis Vere's narrative "was a publication,—a party pamphlet, in an age of pamphleteering."

In reply to this formidable indictment, it may be observed in the first place, that Mr. Motley appears never to have read Vere's narrative, for he quotes from an incomplete French abridgment. The narrative to which he refers is contained in Sir Francis Vere's *Commentaries*. Its whole tone is diametrically opposite to what Mr. Motley represents. It is a calm and remarkably accurate statement of facts relating to actions in which Vere was personally engaged, written from memory at the close of his life, and not intended for publication. Its accuracy can be proved by comparison with his own letters and those of others describing each action, and written at the time, which are still preserved; but which were not before Vere when he wrote his Commentaries.

The members of the House of Nassau are never mentioned but in respectful, sometimes in affectionate, terms. Vere's fondness for the Hollanders and devotion to their cause are conspicuous in all his writings. This strong and natural bias not unfrequently brought down upon Vere the censure of the Queen and Burleigh. The expressions of affection and gratitude in the grant of a pension to Sir Francis Vere, by the States-General, bear strong testimony to the cordial relations between them. Thus the Dutch themselves conclusively refute Mr. Motley's assertion that Vere felt hostility towards them. There is no sign of spleen or inordinate self-esteem in his writings, and certainly there could be no wounded pride of opinion, for Vere's advice was always taken.

The accusation that Vere was guilty of looseness and recklessness of assertion has already been refuted with reference to the five cases put forward by Mr. Motley. The controversy between Vere and the House of Nassau existed only in Mr. Motley's imagination. There was no such controversy. On the contrary, Maurice gave Sir Francis Vere full credit for his conduct of the battle of Nieuport, and said, in his letter to the Queen, that the victory was due to her general (*Sidney Papers*, ii.). Surely Maurice himself was a better judge, on this point, than Mr. Motley! The narrative of Vere was no more a publication or a party pamphlet than were the letters of the Nassaus. Neither the one nor the others were intended for publication, nor were published until many years after the deaths of the writers.

Mr. Motley finds fault with Vere for not mentioning the rout of Count Ernest at Leffinghe, and the charges of cavalry led by Count Louis. In the first place, Vere does mention the charges of cavalry; and in the second, his avowed object in writing was to describe the operations of troops under his own personal command only.

It is with great regret that I feel obliged to refute these persistent attacks by Mr. Motley on the good name of a great general. But the reputation of such a man as Sir Francis Vere belongs to posterity, and it is a bounden duty to defend it when unjustly assailed. It is difficult to understand how so strong a prejudice can have arisen in Mr. Motley's mind. It is curious that Mr. Motley's daughter should since have married a lineal descendant of Sir Francis Vere's sister. Sir William Vernon Harcourt, descended from Frances, sister of Sir Francis Vere and wife of Sir Robert Harcourt of Nuneham, was married to Elizabeth, daughter of John Lothrop Motley, in 1876. They have a son Robert, born in 1878, who is grandnephew of Sir Francis Vere, and grandson of Mr. Motley. "*Blood is thicker than water,*" and if the great historian had been spared longer, he would probably have reconsidered his estimate of Sir Francis Vere. In that case a different conclusion might confidently have been anticipated, based on the merits alone.

******

Mr. Edmonds, with Sir Francis Vere's despatch, and another from Lord Grey de Wilton, arrived in London on the 4th of July. The news of the victory had preceded him; for Caron, the Dutch envoy, galloped out to Richmond on the previous day and reported what he had heard from Barneveldt. The queen was highly pleased, and sent warm congratulations to Prince Maurice, who, in his letter to her Majesty, did full justice to her general, "attributing the victory to the good order and direction of Sir Francis Vere."

******

Rowland Whyte to Sir Robert Sidney, July 5. 1600, ii. There was great surprise at the conduct of Sidney. He was at Nieuport on the 1st, but went off to Flushing in a ship on the morning of the battle. His brother Philip would certainly have been in the thickest of the fight. Sir Robert Sidney's own explanation was merely that he withdrew himself out of the fight, being wholly unprepared for such a day.

******

The name of Vere was in every man's mouth, and just pride was felt that the work was done so well by the English contingent. The queen was very often heard to say that she held Sir Francis to be the worthiest captain of her time. (*Sidney Papers*, ii.). Fifteen years of faithful and steadfast work had wrought a change which must have seemed marvellous to those who watched the course of events. No one did so more intently and with fuller knowledge than Queen Elizabeth herself, and no one knew better to whom it was mainly due that the successors of the men who fled like sheep at Gemblour, were able to turn the dreaded *tercios* of Spain into mobs of panic-stricken fugitives among the sand-hills of Ostend.

Sir Francis Vere's wounds proved to be very serious. He was carried to Ostend, where, while still confined to his bed, he was gladdened by the receipt of a most gracious letter from the queen herself, which was delivered to him by the Earl of Northumberland. In August he was conveyed to Ryswick, where he was lodged in a pleasant house belonging to the Prince of Orange, and in this suburb of the Hague he slowly recovered; but he was suffering from his wounds for several months. He, however, had the great pleasure of knowing that the military success of the allies went hand in hand with cordial diplomatic relations. In the autumn of 1600 he was able to report that:

> In all the time I have served on this side, I have never seen so much willingness to accomplish the wishes of her Majesty, nor so absolute a belief in her singular care for their provinces as now of late, which they generally acknowledge with no small applause of her Majesty's courses.—Sir F. Vere to Sir R. Cecil, from Ryswick, 10 Sept. 1600. S. P. O., Holland, vol. xcii.

Chapter 22

The Siege of Ostend

Sir Francis Vere enjoyed the hospitality of Prince Maurice while he slowly recovered from his wounds. His health had been seriously impaired. But he was obliged to give constant and close attention to the efficiency of the force under his command; for a time of trial was approaching. Ostend was seriously threatened with a siege.

One of the general's chief troubles had been the way in which useless officers were forced upon him by powerful relations at home. These fine gentlemen did not object to an exciting skirmish, or even to a battle, if they could go home to swagger about it immediately afterwards. In ordinary times they were constantly absent. They had a strong dislike to hard work, and were useless as regimental officers. The general naturally deprecated their presence in his army. Among these encumbrances were the Earl of Northumberland, a consequential, pompous nobleman; and Sir Callisthenes Brooke, who thought he could do as he pleased because he was a cousin of Lord Cobham. Brooke chose to absent himself without leave, and we gather from one of Sir Dudley Carleton's gossiping letters that:

> Sir Callisthenes is likely to be displaced unless he is well seconded by friends in England.—Carleton to Chamberlain, from the Hague, Feb. 14, 1601. S. P. O., Holland, vol. xciii.

Sir Francis was not a man to brook interference of this kind. He wrote to Lord Cobham:

> My care for Sir Callisthenes has been great, but on the other side he hath not answered any part of my expectations of his affection and towardliness to the wars, insomuch that the States themselves are highly offended with his long absence.

Instead of at once resuming his duties on his return, he went off with Sir Dudley Carleton to see the sights at Amsterdam. At last the general was obliged to dismiss him from his company. Captain Lower, a creature of the Earl of Northumberland, was another inefficient officer whose services were dispensed with.

Sir Dudley Carleton's barrack-yard gossip was, that the general:

> Held himself *haut a la main* to all his captains, which breeds a general discontentment among them.

Sir Francis Vere explained the position to Secretary Cecil in a subsequent letter. He wrote:

> I have done nothing out of spleen to Sir Callisthenes, but constrained thereunto by his own carriage, after long toleration of his courses. I am, I confess, very curious to have worthy officers, and to that curiosity I impute chiefly the good success it pleaseth God to give to our actions; and though my changing of men may bear with divers a hard interpretation, it shall never be found I discharged any without just cause.

Sir Francis Vere "bred general discontentment" among the Callisthenes Brookes of his army, but he was revered by officers like Lambart and Parker, Ogle and Fairfax. Such men as those whose statues kneel around his monument in Westminster Abbey were ready to live and die for their beloved general.

While Sir Francis was still convalescent at Ryswick, he received tidings of the rebellion of the Earl of Essex, (7th and 8th of February, 1601), and a copy of the queen's proclamation.

> I caused it to be printed in Dutch, and by that means things are generally understood according to the truth. This conspiracy is likened to that of Catiline. My Lord Admiral and my Lord Burleigh, the one for entering the city and proclaiming the Earl traitor to his face and in the heat of the stir, and the other for his exceeding diligence in raising forces and taking the earl, are greatly reputed.

★★★★★★

Essex was tried on the 19th, and executed on the 25th. On this occasion, Queen Elizabeth yielded to the importunities of her ministers with the utmost reluctance.

★★★★★★

Vere had been an object of Essex's dislike and hostility ever since the Island Voyage. He had generously defended the earl to Queen Elizabeth, and had received nothing but ingratitude for his pains.

The Battle of Nieuport was the most signal victory gained by the Dutch patriots and their allies during the long struggle for independence, and its moral effect was very great. But the siege of Ostend was of even higher moment The desperate tenacity with which the heroic defenders held out, by fully occupying the main army of the Archdukes, enabled Prince Maurice to capture strong places and gain advantages in the field in one campaign after another, without a check. The States General appear to have been mainly influenced by a desire to retain the Flemish port, but the result of their policy was to bring the most memorable struggle in modern history to a close. The siege of Ostend led directly to the twelve years' truce.

Ostend was originally a little fishing-town facing the sea, with a haven on its western side, formed by the mouth of the Yper-leet, the sluggish river which flowed under the bridge at Leffinghe, where Ernest of Nassau was defeated. The old church and town faced the sea, on the site of the present esplanade and Kursaal, but in 1583 the new town, more inland, was regularly fortified with ramparts, counterscarps, and two broad ditches. The dunes were cut away, and the sea was allowed to fill the ditches and surround the town; and a wide gullet, called the "*Geule*" was beginning to form a new harbour on the east side, towards the end of the sixteenth century. This is the present harbour. To the south the country was intersected by a network of canals, and was often flooded; and the land rose slightly towards the dunes, on either side of the town.

On the 5th of July, 1601, the Archduke Albert began the siege of Ostend with 20,000 men and 50 siege-guns in position; while the small garrison of under 2,000 was at first commanded by stout Governor Vandernood. The States General held that the defence of this outlying post was a matter of vital importance. They looked round for the ablest commander in their service, to whom the post of danger and heavy responsibility might be entrusted. The choice naturally fell upon the hero of Nieuport. Sir Francis Vere received his commission from the States, not as governor, but as general of the army employed in and about Ostend, with very ample powers.

Sir Francis first dutifully proceeded to England to obtain the approval of Queen Elizabeth, and to raise a body of 3,000 recruits. His brother Horace was detached from the army of Prince Maurice with eight companies of veteran English to reinforce the Ostend garrison.

OSTEND.

On the 9th of July Sir Francis landed, with these troops, on the sands opposite the centre of the old town of Ostend, for the besieging enemy commanded both havens with their guns. Governor Vandernood met him at the water's edge, and delivered up the keys of Ostend. The garrison then consisted of thirty companies of Netherlanders in two regiments of 2,600 men, under Vandernood and Uchtenbroek, to which Vere added his eight companies of English of 100 men each, which brought up the total to 3,500 men. (Vere to Cecil, July 17, 1601. S. P. O., Holland, vol. xciii.).

The enemy had an army of 20,000 men, three parts of which were encamped round Fort Albertus, under the immediate orders of the archduke, while a fourth was on the east side under Count Bucquoy. Thirty pieces were in position on the west, and ten on the east side, which kept up an intermittent fire, .and did much damage, even at this early period of the siege.

Ostend was not possessed of any great natural advantages for defence, beyond the facilities for letting the water from the sea into the numerous ditches and canals which intersected the country. The siege was a desperate struggle for the possession of the sandhills and marshes on the bleak shores of the North Sea. Yet the whole civilized world watched with bated breath for the result. Landward—that is, to the south—the town was well protected by an intricate network of ditches and marshy ground, overflowed at spring tides. To the east was the "*Geule*," or gullet, corresponding with the present harbour; to the west, the old harbour, then fast filling up; and to the north, the old town with its palisades facing the seashore.

The vulnerable points were on either flank of the old town, where, the land rising towards the ridges of the dunes near the sea, the besiegers were enabled to approach with their parallels and batteries. On the east flank the "*Geule*" was broad and deep, but on the side of the old harbour the water was fordable for four hours at every tide; and the defences on the west side of the old town consequently formed the key of the position. The ditch passed between the old and new towns, which were connected by bridges, and round the new town, parallel to the "*Geule*" on one side, and to the old harbour and Yperleet River on the other. It was broad and deep, and had ramparts and bulwarks (or bastions) on one side, and a counterscarp with ravelins on the other.

The most important point for defence was the northwest angle, near the mouth of the fordable old harbour. This was the only place where an approach could be made to the walls on firm ground. Here the enemy concentrated his efforts. The defence at this hotly disputed corner consisted of a strong ravelin in the counterscarp called the "*Porc-espic*," and a bastion in its rear known by the name of the "*Helmund*," (Hell's mouth). On the other side of the ditch, in the old town, and still closer to the mouth of the old harbour, a fort called the "Sand-hill" was formed on a portion of the dunes that remained when the rest was cut away. Its site is to the right rear of the present Kursaal. These three works formed the key of the position. From the "Sand-hill," along the sea-face, the old town was protected by strong palisades forming bastions with connecting curtains, and a succession of three small forts, called respectively the "Schottenburgh" next to the "Sand-hill," the "Moses Table," and the "Flamenburgh," defending a cut from the town ditch into the "*Geule*," at the eastern corner.

On the eastern side of the town facing the "*Geule*," the defences consisted of the "North Bulwark" at the northeast angle, with a corresponding ravelin in the counterscarp; the "East Bulwark" or "*Pekell*," in the centre of the eastern wall; and the "Spanish Bulwark" at the southeast angle, with an outwork called the "Spanish Half-moon" on the other side of the "*Geule*." In the centre of the south wall was the "Southeast Bulwark," flanked to right and left by the "Spanish" and "South Bulwarks," all with corresponding ravelins in the counterscarp. On the west wall, facing the old harbour, were the "West Bulwark" and "Southwest Bulwark" and ravelins.

Between the "South" and "Southwest Bulwarks," and beyond the counterscarp, there was an extensive outwork near the point where the River Yper-leet flows into the old harbour. It was called the "*Polder*," and had formerly been a field from which the water had been pumped by means of windmills. It was necessary, from its position, to include it in the system of defences. These details, which would be tedious and scarcely intelligible without a map or plan, become perfectly clear when the necessary illustration is supplied; while it will not be possible to retain a sufficiently correct notion of the works, so as to follow the events of the siege, unless the system of defences is kept in the mind's eye. (There were five main guards).

Sir Francis Vere, after a careful examination of the fortifications, came to the conclusion that his first care should be to strengthen and secure the "*Polder*," and his next to provide a safe place for the shipping to unload. The "*Polder*" at the southwest corner of the works was a space of some extent, surrounded by water, the old haven washing it on one side, and the ditch of the counterscarp on the other. Vere saw at once that if the enemy got possession of it, he might drain the water out of the ditches and so make an easy approach to the town wall. The general, therefore, set the garrison to work entrenching the "*Polder*," the outer wall of which was well flanked by the "West Bulwark "and ravelin, raising the ramparts to resist cannon, and constructing two works called the "Polder Square" and the "Polder Redoubt," the latter at the extreme southwest angle, and another called the "West Square," or "*Quarrier.*" He also threw up a work beyond the southern counterscarp, called the "South *Quarrier.*" The "*Polder*" was thus assured from sudden attack. In order to protect the shipping, Sir Francis cut a passage in the counterscarp at the southeast angle of the works, by which the water from the "*Geule*" flowed into the town ditch, and here a hundred vessels at a time could lie and unload, safe from the annoyance of the enemy's shot. But to reach this place the vessels had to run the gauntlet of Count Bucquoy's batteries on the "*Geule.*" To escape this danger, another cut was made near the sea, between the "Flamenburgh" and the "Northeast Ravelin."

Having strengthened the "Polder" and provided for the safe entry of ships with supplies and troops, Sir Francis Vere conceived the idea of drawing the enemy into the low marshy ground to the south of the Yper-leet, which he knew would entail upon them great expense, delay, heavy labour, and much loss. With this object he determined to occupy a rising ground surrounded by swamps and ditches, whence he could annoy the enemy's boats coming with supplies from Bruges, and probably draw part of the archduke's forces away from the real key to the position on the dry land of the dunes, near the mouth of the old haven, and into the water-covered swamps to the south.

Accordingly 200 Englishmen occupied the post thus selected by Vere, and a heavy fire was opened upon them from one of the enemy's forts called "*Grooten-dorst*," doing little harm. Then, as Vere had intended, the Spaniards advanced in force from the dunes, and the English general withdrew his men, leaving eighty to decoy the enemy farther into the swampy lands, with orders to fall back into the "South Ravelin." This was a successful little piece of strategy. The enemy would have been deluded with other feints and surprises, and worn out by continuous heavy marching, had not their antagonist been temporarily disabled.

The Spaniards kept up a tremendous fire on the town from all their batteries, and on the 4th of August Sir Francis Vere was severely wounded in the head. His condition became so critical that complete rest was ordered for him. Writing to Secretary Cecil on the 17th, his brother Sir Horace said:

> My brother left this town the 10th of this present, being grown into extremity of illness, altogether inclined to a fever, so that his hurt, accompanied with a fever, and the offence our turbulent neighbours gave him with their artillery, made that by no means he could take his rest, so that weakness grew upon him very fast, and by the judgment of the doctor and chirurgeon if he did not remove there could be no likelihood of his recovery. It was very apparent that his stay would endanger his life. But now I hope he will, in few days, be in good forwardness to resume his post.—Sir Horace Vere to Cecil, August 17. 1601.

Sir Francis went to Middelburg to be cured of his wound, and in a few weeks he was convalescent. In September he returned to Ostend with Sir R. Drury.

★★★★★★

> Sir Francis Vere, as I conceave, is by this day in the town, and although his wounds are as yet nothing well cured, yet his honour carries him thither. Sir R. Cecil to Sir J. Carew, September 5, 1601. (Camden Society, 1864.)

★★★★★★

Meanwhile the fire from the besiegers was continued with unabated fury; and the soldiers of the garrison dug underground quarters in the marketplace and near the "Pekell" bastion, for protection against the hail of shot. The queen and the States were steadfast in their resolution to defend the place. Recruits arrived on the 1st of August from England, and the Queen's government had taken praiseworthy care for their equipment. Vere reported that:

> The men were very well apparelled and the arms are very serviceable.

On the 8th of August 1,200 more were landed, of whom Sir Horace said:

> For the soldiers, in my time, I have not seen their like for proper men, well armed and apparelled.

Sir Horace led out several sorties, and there was some loss.

★★★★★★

Sir Horace reports: "Captain Madison was sore hurt. We have

indeed lost a good number in our commonwealth here, and one exceedingly devoted to the service, in Captain Holcroft. This bearer, Captain Brett, has had the reputation among us of an honest understanding soldier."

******

But the enemy, no longer distracted by puzzling manoeuvres of the veteran Sir Francis, steadily advanced his approaches to the margin of the old haven, opposite the "Sand Hill" fort, between which and the water's edge seven rows of palisades had been fixed. Soon the sides of the "Sand Hill" were sown so thick with shot that they formed an iron wall, against which the fresh shot struck and were shattered, the pieces flying into the air. One day the Dutch Colonel Uchtenbroek and the Sieur de Chatillon, the gallant young commander of a French contingent, were standing on the "Sand Hill" watching the iron hail, when Chatillon's head was struck off with a cannon-shot, and the brains were dashed upon Uchtenbroek's left cheek.

On the 19th of September, to the great relief and joy of the garrison, Sir Francis Vere returned. In the interval, contingents of French, Scots, and Frisians had arrived, besides 2,000 English recruits. The siege of Ostend was becoming the military school of Europe. Young noblemen and gentlemen from England, France, and Holland flocked here to learn the art of war from the renowned Sir Francis Vere. Those who came to learn and to work were cordially welcomed by the general as pupils and comrades in arms. Those who came to swagger and indulge their personal vanity were soon made to know that their room was preferred to their company. Among the latter class was the Earl of Northumberland, who passed his time in fancying that he had been slighted, and in standing upon his dignity, while all good men and true were fighting and working heart and soul under their great commander. If a man under his command was no use, Vere let him know it, whether he was a peer or a pikeman.

******

The Earl of Northumberland went hence yesterday, weary enough of the discommodities of this place, and of the little observance done him. (Vere to Cecil, September 22, 1601).

On September 22nd the garrison consisted of 29 English companies, 29 Dutch companies under Colonel Van der Noor, 22 French and Scots who came with Chatillon; total, 80 companies. The companies consisted of 250 men each, except those of Sir Francis and Sir Horace Vere, which numbered 300. These were the original complements, but on September 22nd the whole number was reduced to 2,440, there being often no more than 80 in a company. The whole garrison numbered 4,480.

★★★★★★

Meanwhile the Archduke Albert was fighting with other weapons than pike and shot. He engaged a traitor named Conisby, who went to England, procured letters to General Vere, and crossed over to Ostend. He then began to convey intelligence to the besiegers of all that took place in the town, under an agreement with Albert. There was a boat sunk in the mud, on the banks of the old haven, near the "Southwest Redoubt." His habit was to deposit letters there, whence a Spanish soldier took them during the night. At last Conisby grew bolder, and tried to bribe a sergeant to blow up the powder magazine. The sergeant revealed the plot. (Vere to Cecil, November 11, 1601). The traitor confessed everything, and was sentenced to be whipped out of the town. After this disclosure, the Archduke Albert could lay but slight claim to any extremely punctilious etiquette when stratagems were planned, and this matter of Conisby should therefore be borne in mind.

It was not until the 4th of December that the Archduke was prepared to storm. For months the Spaniards had been at work advancing their batteries, forming foundations in the haven by sinking huge baskets of wicker-work filled with sand, and building floating platforms, on which guns were mounted in the "*Geule.*" But at last, on the night of the 4th, there was an alarm that the enemy was assaulting the walls. The general rushed out unbraced, followed by Captain Caldwell and some soldiers, and found his own company at push of pike with the Spaniards. A fierce struggle ensued, and the besiegers were driven back. Vere ordered wisps of straw to be set alight and fixed on the ends of the pikes, that the retreating foe might be fired upon with effect as they fell back; 500 remained behind to pay for their temerity. Then Sir Francis called his young page, Henry Hexham, who tells the story, and said, "Boy, come now, pull up my stockings and tie my points," and so he returned home again to his rest.

★★★★★★

Henry Hexham afterwards became an officer of distinction, quartermaster of Lord Vere's regiment, and a military author. His brief supplement to Sir Francis Vere's account of the siege of Ostend is very useful. It furnishes undesigned evidence which serves to refute the attacks of Mr. Motley.

******

On the 12th of December there was a hard frost, and it continued to blow a gale of wind from the southeast until Christmas. No succour could reach Ostend in all these dreary weeks, either in the form of supplies or men. The garrison was wasting daily. Ammunition was falling short. The places to be guarded were very numerous, and the numbers were alarmingly small. It was known that the archduke soon intended to make an assault upon the town with his whole power, and Vere's only hope was to gain time. The welfare of a great cause, one of the greatest for which brave men ever fought, depended on the prolongation of the defence of Ostend. Vere saw the power of the besiegers and his own weakness. The strength of the garrison had dwindled to 2,100, while 4,000 men were barely enough to man the works. The industry of the general slept not; his vigilance was shown by his daily and nightly rounds about the town and works. Yet there was no hope but in recourse to some stratagem, such as has always been held to be within the rules of honourable warfare, if not accompanied by any breach of word or faith.

One day, after Sir John Ogle had gone his rounds, the general called him into his lodgings and said:

> Rather than you shall see the name of Francis Vere subscribed to the delivery of a town committed to his custody, or his hand to the least article of a treaty, had I a thousand lives I would bury them all in the rampier.

He was strongly moved, but he said nothing more at that time. Soon afterwards he called a council of colonels and chief officers, and asked their advice on two points: first, whether, with the present numbers, all parts of the works could be manned in case of an assault; and second, if not, whether it would be advisable to withdraw the guards from the "*Quarriers*," to strengthen the garrison within the walls. The officers said that the numbers were too few, but that the "*Quarriers*" ought not to be abandoned, though no one could suggest any plan for holding them. Sir Horace Vere and Sir John Ogle alone gave their advice to abandon the "*Quarriers*" rather than endanger the loss of the town.

******

In commenting upon this incident, Mr. Motley renews his attack upon the character of the English general. He says that "Sir Francis

Vere called his principal officers together, announced his intention of proposing at once to treat, and to protract the negotiations as long as possible, until the wished-for sails should be discerned in the offing, when he would at once break them off and resume hostilities" (iv.) Mr. Motley calls this statement "a cynical trifling with the sacredness of trumpets of truce and offers of capitulation, such as in that loose age *were* (*sic*) deemed far from creditable." He goes on to assert that "the Council of War highly applauded the scheme, and importuned the general to carry it at once into effect." Further on he characterizes this alleged conduct as "Vere's perfidy" (iv.), and as "gross treachery" (iv.).

Mr. Motley's accusation is disproved by the evidence of Sir John Ogle, a man of unimpeachable integrity and stainless honour, which evidence is undesignedly corroborated by that of young Hexham, the general's page. They relate exactly what took place at the council, as narrated in the text. No such proposal as Mr. Motley describes was made by Vere to the council. As the scheme was never propounded to the council, it follows that the council never highly applauded it, and never importuned the general to carry it into effect. Mr. Motley appears never to have read the narratives of Ogle and Hexham.

★★★★★★

Some days elapsed, and the archduke had completed his preparations for an assault, and was only waiting for low water. Then, and not till then, it was that Vere bethought him of a stratagem. *He took no counsel.* He sent an officer, who spoke Spanish, into the "*Porc-espic*" to ask for a parley. The officer called, but got no answer. He then sent Sir John Ogle, who went to the side of the old haven with a drummer. Don Mateo Serrano, the governor of Sluys, came forward, and Ogle gave the message, which was "that General Vere wished to have some qualified person to speak with him." (Not a word about treating for a capitulation, as Mr. Motley incorrectly states). Serrano reported this to the archduke, who agreed, and it was settled that Ogle should be a hostage for the Spanish officer, and that each should bring a colleague.

Ogle took his tried companion-in-arms, Sir Charles Fairfax, the brave young officer who helped to rally the English at the battle of Nieuport. The two Spaniards were Governor Don Mateo Serrano and Colonel Don Simon Antonio. They crossed to the Ostend side, while Ogle and Fairfax were conducted to the presence of the Archduke. Albert conjured Sir John Ogle to tell him "if there were any deceit in this handling or no?" Ogle answered: "if there were it was more than he knew"; for Vere had told him nothing. The Archduke then asked what instructions Ogle had, who replied that he had none, and that he and Fairfax had merely come as pledges for the return of the Spanish officers. He next asked whether Ogle thought the general intended sincerely or not; and the English hostage answered that he was altogether unacquainted with the general's purpose.

★★★★★★

This was quite true. Vere had not divulged his intentions to a soul. Yet Mr. Motley remarks, "Although Captain Ogle had been one of the council, had heard every syllable of Vere's stratagem, and had heartily approved the whole plot." It has been seen that the subject was not mentioned at the council. Ogle and Fairfax were ignorant of the general's plan, and Ogle spoke the simple truth to the archduke.

★★★★★★

Next morning the news arrived that Serrano and Antonio had returned without speech of Sir Francis Vere. Then it was that Ogle, calling to mind the speech of the general in his lodgings, said to Fairfax: "he verily believed he meant to put a trick on them." Fairfax's rejoinder was;

The trick is put upon us methinks, for we are prisoners and in their power, they at liberty and our judges.

Ogle said there must be some mistake, and offered to write to Vere. The object of all this was to gain time. The Spaniards were sent back on pretext of some irregularity, but they were sent to Count Bucquoy on the east side, so that they had to make a long round, and a night and day were thus gained. Next day, towards evening, Serrano and Antonio were once more admitted into Ostend, and this time Sir Francis received them very hospitably. He feasted them, and drank many healths; but the terms he had to propose to them were, not that he should surrender Ostend, but that the archduke should raise the siege. He then led them into his own chamber, and laid them on his own bed to take their rest. Meanwhile Captains Clark and Ralph Dexter were at work all night in the old town—the vulnerable point—strengthening the palisades. After break of day the sentries saw, to their great joy, five men-of-war from Zeeland at anchor off the town. They brought 400 men, besides provisions and materials of all kinds.

The troops were immediately landed under a heavy fire from the enemy's batteries on either side, but only three sailors were hurt. The noise aroused Serrano from a heavy sleep after his debauch, and he asked the reason for the firing. When he was told he was amazed, and would not believe it until a certain Captain Pottey, who had come with the ships and whom Serrano knew well, assured him that it was so. The general politely informed the Spanish officers that, as succour had arrived, the negotiation must be broken off. They were sent back, while Ogle and Fairfax returned to Ostend. The Archduke was naturally much discomposed at so unexpected a disappointment. He thought the place was his. The Infanta Isabella, gorgeously attired, with twenty ladies and gentlemen in her train, had walked before the walls of the town. They would have to wait a long time before they could come in. The stratagem had saved Ostend.

★★★★★★

Vere reported the whole transaction to the States, in a letter in French dated Dec. 25, 1601, and to Cecil on Dec. 22. The council of war knew nothing of Vere's intention, nor did Sir John Ogle. The general consulted no man. He simply asked for two Spanish officers to speak with them. He offered no terms, made no proposal, and there was no breach of faith. If the archduke chose to assume that a surrender was intended it was his own lookout, and he little knew of what stuff Vere was made. The employer of the traitor Conisby was "hoist with his own petard."

★★★★★★

Sir Francis now set to work in good earnest to prepare for the assault. He had 1,200 men busily employed for the eight following days, and at time of low water, in the night, the time of greatest danger, he stood on guard in person, which conduced much to the encouragement of the men. Early in January, 1602, he received intelligence that the enemy was preparing for a general assault; and during the whole of the 7th two of the besieging batteries, consisting of eighteen cannon, sending balls of forty to forty-six lbs. weight, kept up a crushing fire on the "Porc-espic," "Helmund," and "Sand-hill." The Spaniards had by that time sent 163,200 cannon-shot into the town, and scarcely a whole house was left standing. The "Sand-hill" was more thickly lined with iron than ever, and the shot, striking against each other, rolled into the *fausse braye*, or, breaking into pieces, flew into the air as high as the steeple of the old church.

Towards evening the enemy was seen bringing down scaling-ladders, hand-grenades, and ammunition to the farther bank of the haven, and the archduke's army was marshalled for the assault Count Farnese, with 2,000 Italian and Spanish troops, was told off to attack the "Sand-hill "and the curtain of the old town wall. The governor of Dixmunde, with 2,000 Spaniards, was to assault "Helmund" and the "Porc-espic." A force of 500 men, under another captain, was to scale the west ravelin, while a similar number attacked the "South Quarrier." On the east side Count Bucquoy was to deliver a general assault, specially attacking the east ravelin and the defences of the new haven.

Vere watched these preparations with unceasing vigilance. He never slept, and all that day he was preparing for the defence. Several houses, which had been ruined by the enemy's fire, were pulled down for the sake of the beams and spars, to be used as palisades. At high water the general caused the west sluice, which let the water into the town ditch from the old haven in the rear of "Helmund," to be shut, in order to retain as much water as possible for an object which will appear presently. He then stationed his little garrison in the best possible way. But the works were numerous, and his numbers very inadequate.

Sir Horace Vere and Sir Charles Fairfax, with twelve weak companies, some of them not above ten or twelve men strong, armed with pikes and muskets, were stationed in the "Sand-hill." Farther east, along the wall of the old town, the Schottenburgh and adjoining curtain had been much damaged by the action of the waves during recent gales, and by the enemy's shot. This was a most critical point. Here Sir Francis Vere himself took his stand, (not in the "Sand-hill," as stated by Motley), with six weak companies. Two more companies, under Captains Haughton and Utenhoven, occupied the Schottenburgh redoubt.

From the Schottenburgh to the old church, which the enemy had shot down, there were 300 of the Zeelanders who had arrived on the day that the parley was broken off. From the church to "Moses Table" were six weak companies under Captain Zittan. In the work called "Moses Table" was a worthy French captain named Montesquieu de Roques, "whom Vere loved entirely for the worth and valour that was in him." He had two French companies and five weak Dutch companies to second him. Captain Charles Rassart occupied the north ravelin with four companies, and there were two whole cannon and two fieldpieces in the "Flamenburgh." These works protected the new haven where the ships were lying, and thus the defence of the old town was provided for.

The two most important works, flanking the breach by which the enemy must approach, were the "Porc-espic" and "Helmund." Four of the strongest companies garrisoned the former work, and in the latter were ten weak companies and nine pieces loaded with musket-bullets. This post was entrusted to Sergeant-Major Carpenter and Captain Meetkerk. Here also was Auditor Fleming (one of the historians of the siege). In the "West Bulwark" were two whole and two demi-culverins, to sweep the old haven. The rest of the works, especially to the south, were weakly guarded, because the enemy must necessarily first carry the keys of the position, which had been so long battered by his guns.

Along the curtain of the old town, and on the breach which had been made under the "Sand-hill," were collected firkins of ashes to blind the assailants, little barrels full of tenter nails to pour on them, heaps of stones and bricks from the ruins of the old church, hoops bound with squibs and fireworks to throw over their heads, ropes of pitch, hand-grenades, and clubs.

At dusk, and a little before low water, the besiegers rested to cool the guns which had been playing on the breach all day. There was an ominous pause,—a lull before a still more terrific renewal of the tempest. Taking advantage of this precious time, Vere ordered his trusty engineers, Captains Dexter and Clark, with fifty stout sappers, who each had a rose noble for every quarter of an hour's work, to get on the breach and rapidly throw up a small breastwork, driving in palisades. In defending this vital point Horace Vere and Fairfax would thus have some slight shelter. Then the general himself went down into the "*fausse braye*," and called for an officer to go out "*sentinel perdu*" and creep to the margin of the old haven between the gabions. He crept out on his belly, and discovered Count Farnese wading across with his 2,000 Italians, and drawing them up in battalions on the Ostend side. Then he crept as silently back to Vere.

"What news?" whispered the general.

"My general," he answered, "I smell good store of gold chains, buff jerkins, Spanish cassocks, and Toledo blades!"

"Ha!" exclaimed his chief, "sayest thou me so! I hope thou shalt have some of them *anon*."

Vere then went to the top of the "Sand-hill" and issued orders to have everything in readiness, but not to fire until he gave the signal, and then to open with both ordnance and small shot.

The lull was succeeded by a deafening storm. The archduke fired a gun as a signal to Bucquoy, and the besiegers rushed to the assault from all points just as the darkness of night set in. Vere at once opened a hot fire, raking through their battalions, and making lanes amongst them as they formed on the sands. In another minute they dashed onwards to the foot of the "Sand-hill" and along the curtain of the old town, halted for a moment, and poured in a volley. All the parapets had been crumbled down by the fire during the day, so Vere ordered the men to fall flat, and the volley passed over their heads. Then the Spaniards rushed into the breach where Sir Francis Vere stood, brandishing his sword, and calling to them, in Spanish and Italian, to come on. As they climbed up, the firkins of ashes, stones, and clubs were hurled at them, and flaming hoops were cast over their necks. The ordnance thundered on them from the bulwarks, and all the walls of Ostend were alight with fire.

The brave assailants no sooner climbed to the crest of the "Sand-hill" or the "Schottenburgh" than they were knocked on the head or run through. Three times they rallied to the charge, and three times they were beaten back along the curtain, while the struggle on the breach waxed hotter and hotter during the space of an hour. Similar assaults were made on the "Porc-espic," on the west ravelin, and on the "South Quarrier." On the east side three strong battalions of the enemy were formed on the margin of the "Geule," and attacked the outwork known as the "Spanish Half-moon." Vere resorted to another stratagem. A soldier was ordered to jump out and give himself up, telling the enemy that the "Half-moon" was slenderly manned, and offering to lead them in.

This was done, and the Spaniards took the place easily. The general's object was to draw them away from the support of their comrades on the western attack. He contented himself with guarding the points of most importance, feeling sure that he could recover the others at his leisure. In fact, the "Half-moon" was quite open towards the town. The tide was rising, a heavy fire was opened on the intruders from the "Spanish Bulwark," and finally Captain Day, at the head of a company, drove them out with a loss of 300 men.

At length the besiegers were repulsed at all points. The columns on the west side beat a doleful retreat to the ford over the old haven, while the strong south wind bore the tidings of Vere's glorious victory to friends in England and Holland.

The beaten assailants were no sooner in the ford than Vere caused the west sluice to be opened, and the waters he had stored in the town ditch, by closing them in at high tide, rushed down the haven in a torrent while the enemy were wading across, and carried many away into the sea.

★★★★★★

It is with reference to this incident that Mr. Motley aims his final shaft at Sir Francis Vere. It is a small matter, but it should be put right. Mr. Motley says: "Cool Auditor Fleming, whom nothing escaped, quietly asked the general's permission to open the western sluice. Vere's consent was at once given. The historians Bentivoglio, Grotius, and many others, give Vere, as a matter of course, the credit of this feat. But Fleming was a man whom I should judge incapable of falsehood "(iv.) Nevertheless Fleming was not without capacity in that line. The historians are undoubtedly right, and "cool Auditor Fleming" made a very cool statement by giving himself credit to which he has no claim whatever. The previous order of Sir Francis Vere indicates that the plan was entirely his own. But the matter is set at rest by the undesigned corroboration of young Hexham, the general's page. He says: "General Vere, perceiving the enemy to fall off, commanded me to run as fast as ever I could to Sergeant-major Carpenter and Auditor Fleming, who were upon 'Helmund,' that they should presently open the west sluice, out of which there ran such a stream and torrent down through the channel of the west haven that upon their retreat it carried away many of their sound and hurt men into the sea."

★★★★★★

The defenders then poured over the walls and secured an immense amount of plunder. There were Spanish pistols, cassocks, swords, gold chains, targets, and among them a shield on which were enamelled the seven worthies. There were heaps of dead under the "Sand-hill" and along the wall of the old town, goodly young men Spaniards and Italians amidst broken scaling-ladders, axes, spades, and shovels. Among the slain there was the body of a young Spanish girl in male attire, who had fallen in the assault. Under her dress was a chain of gold set with precious stones, besides other jewels and silver. Her name is unknown, her history unwritten. Doubtless it was not less romantic than that of Catalina de Erauso, "the Nun-Ensign," who, born in 1585, was the contemporary of the nameless heroine of Ostend. The enemy lost 2,000 men, including the Count d'Imbero and Colonel Antonio, the envoy.

The loss of the garrison was 30 killed and 100 wounded. Charles Fairfax fought gallantly in the breach.

******

Sir Charles Fairfax was brother of Thomas, first Lord Fairfax, and of Edward Fairfax, the translator of *Tasso*. In the Fairfax *Correspondence* (i.) it is stated that Charles was slain by a wound in the face, from a piece of the skull of a marshal of France, who was killed close beside him by a cannon-ball. This is evidently a confused version of the death of Chatillon (see *ante*) applied to another person. There was no marshal of France at Ostend. Fairfax was not slain at this time. We learn from a letter from him to the Earl of Northumberland, dated June 14, 1604, that he was badly wounded in the right arm during this assault, that he was afterwards at the siege of Sluys, and that he was sent back to Ostend to command the English companies towards the end of the siege.

******

Horace Vere was wounded in the leg with a splinter. Captains Haughton and Madison and Nicholas Van den Lier were killed, and four other officers. Among these was Master Tedcastle, a gentleman of Sir Francis Vere's staff, who was killed when standing between the general and his page. He called to young Hexham to take off his gold ring and send it to his sister as his last farewell, and then he died.

The besiegers had had enough to last them for some time. The general remained for a few months longer, when he was called away by the States General to assume an important command in the field. Sir Francis Vere left Ostend on the 7th of March, 1602, accompanied by his brother Horace, "both carrying away with them and leaving behind them the marks of true honour and renown." Sir John Ogle also went with the general. Sir Francis had conducted the siege of Ostend for the first eight months. With uncommon engineering ability he put the town into an excellent posture of defence; he showed admirable skill and activity in drawing the enemy from the main attack; his splendid example inspired his garrison with confidence and courage; and in the arrangements for the defence against the grand assault, and his conduct of the action itself, he displayed all the qualities of a consummate general.

After the departure of Sir Francis Vere, the garrison of Ostend, thanks to the heroic valour of a succession of Dutch governors, held out for two years and a half. Their constancy was of the utmost moment, for the siege continued to occupy the great mass of the Spanish Army, and so led to the recognition of the independence of the Dutch Republics. Vere was succeeded by Frederick van Dorp, who gallantly repulsed an assault on the "Porc-espic" in April, 1603, but the Spaniards captured and retained the "Polder." The loss during that year, from wounds and sickness, amounted to 4,000. Van Dorp was followed by Charles van de Noot; and in October, 1603, the renowned Spinola assumed the conduct of the siege. In December, 1603, Peter van Gieselles became governor. He repaired the "Sand-hill," "Porc-espic," and "Helmund."

He was slain on March 12, 1604, in repulsing an assault from the Polder. The two next governors were slain; and in June, 1604, Colonel Uytenhoove made an heroic attempt to hold the place by throwing up an inner line of defences on the west side, which were called "Little Troy." The last governor was Daniel de Hartaing, Lord of Marquette. The place was a mass of crumbling ruins. On September 13, 1604, the "Sand-hill," the true key to the whole position, fell into the hands of the Spaniards, and on the 20th the governor capitulated to his generous enemy, the Marquis Spinola. When the Archduke Albert entered upon possession of this long-sought prize it was a confused heap of smouldering ruins. The bleak Flemish sand-hills were his, but Holland was lost forever. Freedom gained an enduring triumph through the glorious defence of Ostend.

Chapter 23

Death of the Queen, and Resignation of Sir Francis Vere

Sir Francis Vere was recalled from Ostend by the States General to be consulted on an urgent question. He was received at the Hague at an assembly of all the deputies, when he reported fully on the state of the beleaguered town, and the prospects of the defence. He was then referred to a special committee consisting of Prince Maurice, Barneveldt, and a few others, to whom, for speedier dispatch and greater secrecy, the succouring of Ostend was committed. There was great difficulty, owing to the intolerable cost of the defence, in levying a force with which to carry on an offensive war, and draw the enemy from Ostend. The object of the States was to raise an army of 20,000 foot and 5,000 horse; but they needed further help from England to complete the numbers. (Sir F. Vere, at Ryswick, to Sir R. Cecil, March 21, 1601. S. P. O., Holland, vol. xciv.)

Vere was therefore requested to undertake a special mission to the Queen, to obtain her sanction for raising more recruits, and then to return with all possible speed to Holland, to assume command of the English contingent in the field. Noel Caron, the Dutch envoy in London, was joined with Sir Francis Vere in this mission. The great general was cordially welcomed by the queen, and the wishes of the States were complied with at his request.

During this rapid visit to England on urgent affairs of state, Sir Francis was subjected to some annoyance by the Earl of Northumberland, who thought that he had been treated with less respect than his rank demanded while he was at Ostend.

★★★★★★

Henry Percy, ninth Earl of Northumberland, was a cousin of Sir

Francis Vere, his maternal grandmother having been a Vere. His father had committed suicide in the Tower in 1585, to avoid trial and sentence for high treason. His uncle, the seventh earl, was beheaded at York for treason in 1572; and his grandfather, Sir Thomas Percy, was executed at Tyburn in 1537.

★★★★★★

As soon as he heard that Vere had been at court he watched an opportunity to insult him, and eventually sent him a foolish challenge by a certain Captain Whitlock, on the 24th of April. The earl's letter was as follows:

> You love to take the air and to ride abroad: appoint, therefore, a time and place to your liking that I may meet you. Bring your friend with you. I will be accompanied with another that shall be witness of things I shall lay to your charge. If you satisfy me we will return good friends; if not, we shall do as God shall put in our minds.

Sir Francis said he would not answer it at once, but would consider the matter. On Sunday, the 25th, he sent his friend Sir John Ogle with a letter which the earl would not receive, using violent language, and threatening Ogle if he offered it to him again. Sir Francis then sent to suggest a meeting in London, each accompanied by a man of gravity and some rank in the state. Vere named Sir Edward Stafford. (The queen's ambassador in France). The earl rejected this proposal, demanding a private meeting. A third time Sir John Ogle went to this foolish brawler and informed him that the general thought it not reasonable to satisfy him after the manner he required, and therefore he would not do it. But he desired to have, under the earl's hand, the particular causes for which he considered himself aggrieved. Northumberland replied that to write would be tedious; that by his refusal he was thoroughly persuaded Sir Francis had done him those wrongs which he meant to lay to his charge; that he would lay up the general's injurious dealing in his heart, and right himself thereafter as he should think fit.

The matter rested for three days, and meanwhile it came to the ears of Noel Caron, the Dutch envoy, who reported it to the queen in council. Her Majesty commanded Northumberland to forbear any attempt against Sir Francis, as he was then employed on her service. The earl submitted, but he declared that Sir Francis was a knave and a coward, and that:

In fleering and geering like a common buffoon he would wrong men of all conditions, and had neither the honesty nor courage to satisfy any.

Sir Francis Vere then drew up the following note:

The Earl of Northumberland makes profession to hate Sir Francis Vere upon divers sinister reports made by base and factious persons, but never called him to account at the time. Sir Francis admits that upon the certain knowledge he had of the countenance and favour the Earl showed to certain mean persons, and the contentment he took in their backbiting Sir Francis Vere, he grew into contempt of this humour of the earl's and afforded him little respect. Their first meeting in England was at the Court, on April 12th, Sir Francis Vere being sent to Her Majesty by the States as a public person upon very weighty and important affairs. On the 23rd of April, at 6 in the evening, Captain Whitlock came with a challenge. Sir Francis framed an answer and sent it by Captain Ogle, his Lieutenant Colonel, from his lodging in Aldersgate Street, on the 25th. The earl refused the letter.

The Earl of Northumberland, although bound in honour to defer his quarrel until the general was free, published a scurrilous paper in English, French, and Italian, calling Sir Francis a knave, a coward, and a buffoon. Vere was on the very eve of starting on his return to Holland. He addressed the following letter to the earl, in reply to his disgraceful slander:

Because I refused to meet you on your peremptory and foolish summons, you conclude me, in a discourse sent abroad under your name, to be a knave, a coward, and a buffoon; whereupon you have procured me to set aside all respect of your person and to say you are a most lying and unworthy lord. You were bound by Her Majesty's commandment not to assail me, and I, by the business committed to me, not to seek you. When we shall be freer, as God shall make us meet, I will maintain it with my sword.

Francis Vere.

******

The correspondence between the Earl of Northumberland and Sir Francis Vere, from the *Cotton MSS.*, is published in the supplement to *Collins's Peerage* (8vo, 1730), and also in the *Somers Tracts*, i. A manuscript copy of Northumberland's challenge and the answer is in the possession of the Duke of Westminster at Eaton. The Duke of Sutherland has another copy of the challenge.

✶✶✶✶✶✶

Mr. White, the general's servant, brought this letter to the earl on the day his master sailed for the Low Countries. Three years afterwards the Earl of Northumberland was committed to the Tower on charges connected with the Powder Plot, and there he remained for many years, safe from Vere's sword, and from the punishment for his insolence, which he so richly deserved.

✶✶✶✶✶✶

The earl's imprisonment by the Star Chamber was illegal and unjust. The pretext was that his namesake, Thomas Percy, was a gunpowder-plot conspirator, but the earl himself was quite innocent. He was not only imprisoned for fifteen years, but fined £30,000. During his confinement he patronised the mathematicians Robert Hues and Thomas Harriott. But his character was not changed by adversity. When he came out of prison in 1620 he was as silly and pompous as ever. Hearing that the favourite Buckingham drove in a coach and six, he went down to Petworth in a coach and eight. He died in 1632, aged seventy, leaving by his wife Dorothy, daughter of Walter Devereux, Earl of Essex, a son Algernon, tenth Earl of Northumberland, who naturally became a stanch Parliament man.

✶✶✶✶✶✶

In this unpleasant affair Sir Francis Vere kept his temper, and acted with dignity and sound judgment. While refusing to gratify the foolish lord's whim, at a time when he was engaged on important public duty, he offered to make any explanation that might be right, with persons of gravity and position to decide between them.

On arriving at the Hague, Vere at once joined the army of Maurice, and in the hurry of preparation for the campaign he must have soon forgotten the annoying piece of folly which wasted some of his precious time in London. He was at the head of 8,000 Englishmen in the pay of the States, who formed nearly half the infantry of the patriot army. In Vere's absence the command of the English companies of horse had been given to Sir Edward Cecil, an appointment which had his full approval. ("One very worthy of command." Vere to R.

Cecil, May 26, 1602).

Maurice named Schenken Schanz as the rendezvous, and as soon as the army had assembled, he crossed the Waal at Nymegen, and the Maas at Mook, advancing thence into the heart of Brabant. There had been some delay owing to negligence in sending forward provisions for the English contingent. (F. Vere to Secretary Cecil, July 11, 1602). Maurice found his progress opposed by the Admiral of Aragon, who was strongly entrenched; so he retraced his steps, and laid siege to Grave on the 9th of July, 1602.

******

The distance across the country between the Waal and the Maas, from Nymegen to Grave, is seven miles. Grave is a small town, surrounded by disused fortifications, on the left bank of the broad stream of the Maas. These defences are of the Coehorn period, and there are no traces of the walls which existed in Vere's time. It is now a quiet little Dutch place, with its *Groot-markt,* town hall, lofty church, and avenues of trees round the grassy ramparts. The church dedicated to St. Elizabeth has its western end facing the *Groot-markt.* It consists of a choir and transepts, but the nave has been destroyed. There is a tomb of Arnold, Duke of Gelders, a great-grandson of Edward III., and father of Mary, wife of James II. of Scotland. Arnold died in 1473. The church also contains some fine oak carving, and curious pictures representing the martyrdom of some white friars.

******

This was the last military operation in which Sir Francis Vere was engaged. When, as a young man, he began his military career under the Earl of Leicester, the first event in the campaign was the loss of Grave. And now the last service he performed was connected with the recovery of Grave. At about noon on a Thursday in August, Sir Francis was in the trenches, directing the siege works, when he was wounded in the face. A bullet struck him under the right eye and passed towards the ear, where it lodged. (Sir R. Sidney to Cecil, Aug. 15, 1602).

The old warrior was conveyed to his former lodging at Ryswick. There he remained in a critical condition for many weeks, and it was the end of October before he was able to go out and attend to business. (F. Vere, from Ryswick, to Cecil, Oct. 19, 1602. "I am a stranger to affairs by reason my hurt suffers me not to go abroad."). The organisation of the States army was under revision, and the changes made it necessary for General Vere to maintain his own position, and to advocate the rights and interests of his countrymen in the pay of the States. It was not until the end of the year that these weighty affairs began to be discussed, and in the mean while Prince Maurice had returned from the capture of Grave.

★★★★★★

Sir W. Browne, who was then acting governor of Flushing for Sidney, was a very fine old warrior, but he was sadly given to spreading unauthenticated and improbable gossip. On November 29, 1602, he wrote: "I hear that of late Sir Francis, abroad in his coach, met his Excellency's (Prince Maurice) coach, and passed by without saluting him, and that afterwards he sent his excuse, saying that he was sorry, that he saw not his Excellency, as it was on his blind side. I hear that his Excellency's answer was that it was a blind excuse." *Sidney Papers*, ii. Sir Francis Vere and the prince were in reality on perfectly amicable terms.

★★★★★★

In September, 1602, Mr. George Gilpin, the Queen's agent at the Hague, died rather suddenly, and it was some time before Sir Ralph Winwood was sent to succeed him. (He did not arrive at the Hague till July, 1603). Sir Francis Vere was left to fight his battle single-handed. He contended that he ought to have sole command over his own men, with suitable jurisdiction, so as to ensure their being dealt with according to their own laws. He sent his friend Sir Edward Conway, who thoroughly understood the position, to explain the grounds of his contention to Secretary Cecil.

On the 22nd of January, 1603, Sir Francis was received in audience by the Assembly of the States General, when he delivered a strong and peremptory speech, claiming better treatment for his soldiers. He implored the queen's government to support him in the line he was taking, (F. Vere, at the Hague, to Cecil, February 6, 1603), especially with regard to his men being subject only to their own laws and ordinances, and to the English general being judge of causes concerning his people.

The negotiation was delicate and rather intricate, but Maurice understood the points at issue and was well disposed, while Barneveldt was Vere's friend and upheld him. (*Sidney Papers* ii). He was well supported by Cecil and the English government, and in January, 1603, he wrote: "On the point most debated I do think they will give me contentment." By February Vere had gained his point, and was able to report that "the States have granted my request, which is an addition to my former authority." (F. Vere, at the Hague, to Cecil, February 27,

1603).

Vere reported, at this time, that the power of the Stadtholder was increasing. He wrote:

> The Prince Maurice groweth daily more powerful in this State, and taketh upon himself more princely greatness than heretofore. As long as the States can endure the charge they are now at, in all appearance he will defend their country from the power of Spain.

Wearied by these long negotiations, and still suffering from his wounds, Sir Francis Vere had retired for a little rest to the pleasant suburb of Ryswick. Over him was the shadow of a great national calamity. On the evening of Monday, the 21st of March, one of Prince Maurice's pages was ushered into the English general's presence. He brought a letter which the prince had received from the States of Zeeland, reporting that the queen was dangerously ill and past all hope of recovery. The news had been brought over:

> By the captain of a Zeeland man-of-war, named Cornelius Lensen, who was desired by a Dutch merchant of good repute to hasten into these parts lest, by a general arrest, both he and his ship might be stayed.

The page also had instructions from Maurice to tell Vere that he had news of the death of Her Majesty. Sir Francis immediately hurried to the prince's house, and found that this news was grounded on the report of the same Cornelius Lensen. He therefore allowed himself to indulge in hope, and tried to think no more of it. But this was impossible. Elizabeth was the object, not of devoted loyalty only, but of affection and love, to all true Englishmen. She was their ideal of a great queen, loving her subjects, devoting herself to their good, wearing out her life in their service.

Vere was plunged in grief. He could not rest. Next morning he flew to the house of his friend Barneveldt for more news. A letter had just been received from Noel Caron, the Dutch envoy in London. He reported that the Queen was ill at ease, and that, in his opinion, this was caused by trouble of mind at having pardoned Tyrone, and at the marriage of the Lady Arabella.

******

The queen's grief had been caused by the death of her cousin and life-long friend the countess of Nottingham. Arabella Stuart was at Sheriff Hutton. The queen had been annoyed at a report that this lady was said to be in treaty of marriage with William Seymour; but the report was denied, and had had no effect upon the queen's health, as Vere rightly judged. Nothing of that sort was capable of giving a shock to one of the most truly brave women that ever lived. Physical causes alone accounted for her death.

★★★★★★

On this Vere observed:

> Her Majesty's most princely wisdom and magnanimity were warrant to me that no deed of hers and no accident could so far distemper her mind. So I concluded with myself that the Queen was not sick, in which belief I remained for two days. Then the wind became fair to come out of England, and advertisements came on all hands from our private friends that Her Majesty was dangerously sick. Now there are letters from M. de Caron, wherein he writeth that he, being betwixt the cofferchamber and Her Majesty's bedchamber, did see great weeping and lamentation among the lords and ladies as they passed to and fro, and that he perceived by them that there was no hope that Her Majesty should escape. This hath made me doubtful of Her Majesty's welfare, and perplexed me in my mind, no less than I have cause and more than I can express. And yet I have been so far from thinking that I should live to see that dismal day, that I cannot thoroughly keep from my mind the suspicion I have that this bruit is altogether false, or at the least the malady is not so serious as is given out. I end with my most humble prayers to the Almighty to deliver Her Majesty from the present danger, and lengthen out her days to the uttermost course of nature. (F. Vere, at the Hague, to Cecil, March 24, 1603).

For a few days longer Sir Francis Vere continued to hope against hope that the life of his beloved sovereign might be spared. But on the 20th of March official news, which could not be doubted, arrived of the great queen's death. Vere then reported that;

> Although I was full of grief for the loss of so gracious a Sovereign, I instantly sent to the magistrates and my officers in the Brill to cause the king to be proclaimed.

He also sent his brother Horace with a letter to his new master, a copy of which he forwarded to Cecil.

The queen's death was a greater public calamity than was at first understood. Yet the grief, not only of men like Vere who knew her well, but of the whole people, was deep and real. She had loved them, and was in perfect sympathy with them. Never was this more strikingly shown than at the meeting of her last Parliament, in 1601, when she conceded their demands before they were presented to her, almost as if by instinct. All her great undertakings for the good of her people, and on behalf of causes which they held dear, had succeeded. Spain, the mighty enemy, was defeated and humbled. The Dutch allies had gained their freedom. Ireland was conquered. The East India Company was founded. Trade and commerce flourished. Elizabeth had worked harder than most strong men could do. The incessant toil and anxiety, the constant strain on her faculties, had at length worn her out. She disregarded the warnings of approaching collapse.

At the opening of her last Parliament she could scarcely bear the weight of her robes, and needed actual support of those around her. Yet she delivered the noblest speech that constitutional sovereign ever uttered. Only six weeks before her death she received the Venetian ambassador in state. She continued to work long after prudence would have prescribed absolute rest. At last she broke down suddenly and utterly, and died three weeks afterwards. She literally died of overwork in the service of her people. A nobler end no sovereign ever made. No wonder she was beloved. No wonder that the people cherished the memory of the great queen who had loved them so devotedly, had worked for them, and died for them. Nearly all her early friends had died before her: the unworthy Leicester, the only man she ever loved; Burleigh, the life-long friend and adviser; her cousins Kate Gary and Lord Hunsdon; her old friend in adversity, the Lady Norris—"my own crow," as the queen called her; fair Isabel Harington, her cherished bedfellow,—all had passed away.

One of the lovely maids of honour who attended the Princess Elizabeth at Hatfield in Mary's days, was still by the great queen's side in her saddest hour and her death. Sweet Margaret Willoughby was faithful to the end. (She had become Lady Arundell of Wardour). The children of her old friends were also faithful to the end, in most instances, and cherished the memory of their queen and their benefactress. To those around her the loss was heavy. To the country the news came as a stunning blow. How much greater would the grief have been if all the shame, dishonour, and mean tyranny of the next forty years could have been foreseen!

James I. began his reign by making a treaty with France, which included promises of aid to the States General. This was in July, 1603. In 1604 the perfidious pedant made a treaty of peace with Spain and the Netherlands Archdukes, leaving the Dutch patriots to fight their battles alone. The people of England submitted to the reversal of their great Queen's policy with undisguised regret and shame. The English companies continued to serve the States, and volunteers were as abundant as ever.

No one felt the shame more deeply than Sir Francis Vere. James had confirmed him in the government of Brill, (by Patent, April 16, 1603), which town was to be retained until the debt of the States General was paid. He was general of the English troops in the pay of the States, with enlarged powers, enjoying the confidence and friendship of Prince Maurice and Barneveldt. Sir Edward Cecil tells us that the soldiers reverenced and stood in awe of him.

> He was the very dial of the whole army, by whom we knew when we should fight or not.

He loved the States, and was devoted to their cause. His twenty years of service had cemented many friendships, not only among his own comrades in arms, but also among the people for whom he had fought so long and valiantly. He was at the zenith of his fame, and second only to Maurice in the army of the States.

But it was at this time that Sir Francis Vere resigned his honourable employment in the service of the States General. His health was failing, he was covered with wounds, riddled with bullets, and they had left their effects on his powers of endurance and of application. Exposure, incessant toil, attacks of ague, and mental strain had done their work. He felt that at the early age of forty-four he was past his prime. He knew that his younger brother Horace would ably fill his place. Moreover, the death of his beloved sovereign and the disgraceful peace had taken the heart out of his work. So he retired from the service of the States in the summer of 1604, amidst expressions of regret and cordial wishes for his future welfare. The States insisted upon his retaining honorary command of his regiment of horse. Sir Francis returned to England, and went to live on his own property at Tilbury, close to Kirby Hall, the home of his mother and elder brother.

In August, 1605, the old warrior became tired of inaction, and wrote to his friend Secretary Cecil, who had been created Earl of

Salisbury in the previous May, for leave to proceed to his government at the Brill. Sir Edward Conway had been acting as his deputy. He could not bear to frequent the court, where he would be reminded of the change at every turn. Nor would James be likely to desire the company of warriors such as Vere, infinitely preferring the society of such creatures as Carr or Villiers. Writing to Salisbury, the great general said:

> Your Lordship knoweth how unfit I am for the court, and hope in your favour to excuse my backwardness that way. I am and shall always be most ready, with my best industry, to perform what shall be commanded of me. (F. Vere, at Tilbury, to the Earl of Salisbury, May 2, 1605. MS. at Hatfield).

Salisbury, in a friendly and very complimentary letter, informed Sir Francis that there was no necessity for his going to his government at the Brill, so far as the king's service was concerned. But he was entrusted with an honourable mission to the Hague, and with letters from James which would be very acceptable to the States General, for they contained a promise that the Archduke Albert should be restrained from recruiting in the dominions of the British King. Vere arrived at the Brill on the 2nd of December, 1605, (Vere to Salisbury, December 15, 1605. *Papers at Hatfield*, vol. 1), on which event that incorrigible old gossip, Sir William Browne, observed:

> We shall understand shortly how the States and he will agree. (*Sidney Papers*, ii.)

He proceeded to the Hague, and delivered his Majesty's letters to Prince Maurice and the States General in solemn assembly. All were glad to see their faithful old friend again.

> They gave me a very good welcome, seeming to be glad of my return into these parts, and of my affection to their service.

Sir Francis Vere had the pleasure of hearing the praises of his brother Horace for his gallant services at the recovery of Sluys in 1604, and for his skill and bravery in saving the army of the States in the retreat from Mulheim in 1605. Horace had been brought up as a soldier by Francis, had learned the art of war from him, and had been his comrade for many years. They were more than brothers, and the successes of one were sources of deepest pleasure to the other. This last visit of Sir Francis Vere to the Hague was, in all respects, most agreeable and satisfactory. He took his final leave of his old comrade in arms, Prince Maurice, and of the States General, in May, 1606, and returned to England in June, bringing with him a substantial proof of the regard and affection in which he was held by his old masters. He thus announces it to Salisbury:

> An annual liberality the States have laid for me, and desired I should take as a testimony of their favour, whereof I thought it my duty to advertise your Lordship.—F. Vere, at the Brill, to Lord Salisbury, May 31, 1606. MSS. at Hatfield, vol. 1.

The announcement of this "annual liberality," as Vere calls it, is preserved in the British Museum, and is expressed as follows:—

> The States General of the United Provinces.
> Whereas the noble valorous Sir Francis Vere Knight, governor of the town and forts of Brill, did many years well truly commendably and beneficially serve the United Low Countries not only in the said quality but also in divers other qualities as well as Commander General of the forces by the most laudable goodness of the Queen's Majesty of England France and Ireland to those countries kindly granted. Also as Colonel of a regiment of English companies levied at the charge of this country likewise as Commander General of troops of horse and foot of divers nations used under his conduct in many exploits, and after the last agreement made with the most honourable the Queen's Majesty of England in the year 1598, as General of the Englishmen of war both horse and foot being in the service of the Low Countries.
> Also of a third part of the army in divers expeditions and besiegings, and within and without the city of Ostend in the renowned siege of the same town in 1601 and 1602 as otherwise; and that we always have noted his honour and perfect and steadfast affection for the welfare of the United Low Countries in general and particular. To acknowledge the said continual great and notable services and affection, we, after perfect deliberation, in recompense of the said services, as well for his person in the aforesaid qualities and as Captain of his two companies of horse and foot, as also for the services of his officers and soldiers of the same, until the day of the purchase thereof made (of the which he hath delivered us over the acknowledgment and acquittance) have granted and ordained, and do grant and ordain

by these presents to the said Sir Francis Vere a pension during his life time of three thousand pounds of 40 pence (£500 sterling a year), the pound,—a coin of these countries, yearly.

The first year shall expire on June 8, 1607, so forward from year to year during the life time of the said Sir Francis Vere; and to shew yet further to the said Sir Francis Vere how acceptable we did hold his services, we have, at his earnest instance, granted and consented, and do grant and consent by these presents, that if, at the time of his decease the honourable Lord, Henry Vere Earl of Oxford, being the head of his House, be alive, the payment of the said pension of three thousand pounds yearly during the life of the same Lord shall be continued so long as the said Earl shall be alive.

In's Graven Hage, the 6th day of June, 1606.

******

Edward, seventeenth Earl of Oxford, died and was buried at Hackney on July 6, 1604, after having run through nearly all his estates. His son Henry succeeded as eighteenth Earl, but was very poor.

Cotton MSS., Titus, cvii. 132. The signatures are gone. Motley and other writers allege that Vere was not on cordial terms with Maurice and the States General, and that there was no love lost between them. Maurice and the States General could not offer a better refutation of these erroneous statements than the above document affords. In every line it shows the cordiality and friendship which existed, from first to last, between Maurice and the States General on the one hand and Sir Francis Vere on the other.

******

Long and faithful service was thus suitably rewarded, and the grand old champion of liberty could have had nothing but pleasant reminiscences and kindly feelings towards the rulers and people of Holland when he sailed from the Brill, and took his last farewell look of the Dutch coast in June, 1606. On returning to his native land to end his days there, he was welcomed with the news that further well-won rewards had been conferred upon him by the English government. On June 15, 1606, he was appointed Governor of Portsmouth and the island of Portsea, Constable of Porchester Castle, and Keeper of East Beare forest for life.

******

In succession to the Earl of Devonshire, who died in April, 1606. Devonshire was the Lord Mountjoy of the "Island Voyage."

Sir Thomas Cornwallis was appointed Deputy Keeper of East Beare forest, under Sir Francis Vere. His tomb is in Porchester church.

★★★★★★

And so the old warrior rested from his labours. He saw the complete success of all his toils and services a few months afterwards, when the armistice practically acknowledged the independence of the United Provinces.

CHAPTER 24

Marriage and Death of Sir Francis Vere

When Sir Francis Vere finally returned to England, after twenty years of glorious service, he found that a home had been made ready for him within a short walk of Kirby Hall, where his brother John lived with their mother, and almost in "sight of the ancient keep of Hedingham Castle. This residence, prepared for the great general, was called Tilbury Lodge. The estate of Tilbury near Clare, in the valley of the Stour, (called Tilbury near Clare, to distinguish it from East and West Tilbury on the Thames), had belonged to the Veres for centuries, when the seventeenth Earl of Oxford sold it to Israel Ames in 1583, who made it his place of residence. Ames had married Thomasine, daughter of William Carew of Stone Castle, near Greenhithe in Kent, and Mr. and Mrs. Ames thus became neighbours of John Vere at Kirby Hall.

******

> Tilbury was granted to Alberic Vere, first Earl of Oxford, by the Empress Maud. The parish contained the manors of Tilbury, Skeyes, Brays, and North Tofts.
> Israel Ames was a son of Roger Ames, by Elizabeth, daughter of George Lawson, of Yorkshire.
> There is a gravestone of black marble in Stone church, to the memory of William Carew, brother of this Thomasine, who afterwards married John Vere. He is said. to have died in 1625, aged about thirty-five.

******

There they resided for twelve years, but in 1593 Israel Ames sold Tilbury to Edward Cotton, who merely held it until another purchaser could be found. At this time Sir Francis Vere was anxious to acquire a home for himself in his native county, and he had requested his brother to look out for any estate in his neighbourhood that was for sale. The opportunity soon offered. In December, 1598, Cotton sold the estate of Tilbury to John Vere of Kirby in trust for his brother, and John conveyed it to Sir Francis Vere on May 1, 1604. (Morant's *Essex*, ii.). The estate included the manors of Tilbury *juxta* Clare, Skeyes, and North Tofts, and the advowson of the living.

※※※※※※

In the *Inquisitio post mortem* of Sir Francis Vere (No. 7, James I., 1st Pt, No. 182) lands are mentioned, as part of the estate, in the parishes of Belchamp St. Paul and Great Yeldham. Sir Francis is also said to possess the manors called Little Bromley Hall, *alias* Church Hall, and Ovington, and several fields in the parish of Ashen-on-Esse.

※※※※※※

The house, usually called Tilbury Lodge, was surrounded by a park, and near it was the church, the tower of which was built by the Countess of Oxford in 1519. It had the badges of the Veres cut in stone and let into the brickwork. (*Holman MS. Coll.* "Now defaced by time. *Vidi* August 5, 1825."). A pleasant, well-timbered expanse of country extended from Tilbury Park to Kirby and Hedingham Castle. One result of the negotiations for the purchase of Tilbury was that John Vere married the widow of Israel Ames, its former owner, and brought her home to Kirby.

The old soldier, covered with honourable wounds and prematurely aged by exposure and hardships of all kinds, certainly needed repose. He found rest at the pleasant lodge in Tilbury Park, close to his relations, and surrounded by the haunts of his childhood. He avoided the Court, so changed and degraded since the days of the great queen; but his office of Governor of Portsmouth and of the island of Portsea occupied much of his time. The last years of his life were passed between his official post at Portsmouth and his home at Tilbury. He actively promoted the repair and completion of the Portsmouth defences, and reported the defects to Lord Salisbury. At the same time he was anxious to prevent the garrison rules from interfering with the trade of the town. He wrote to Lord Salisbury that:

> The magistrates complain of difficulty in having passage to their shipping in the haven at all times of the night, as tide and weather require.

The consequence being that seafaring men for the most part resorted to Gosport. Sir Francis recommended that the rules should be relaxed. (Vere to Salisbury, March 13, 1607, August 16, 1609. MSS. at Hatfield).

A contemplation of the life of Sir Francis Vere leads to the conclusion that during his active career he had been wholly wrapped up in the duties of his profession, to the exclusion of all softer feelings. We meet with no indication of a love passage of any kind, throughout his own correspondence and that of his contemporaries. If there had ever been anything of the sort, it is almost certain that Sir William Browne or some other gossiping letter-writer would have put it on record. But now that he had leisure, Sir Francis turned his thoughts to matrimony, and it was not long before he was engaged to a very young lady, who no doubt conceived a romantic affection for the great general.

The pleasant Surrey village of Mitcham, on the edge of the Downs, was on the road from London to the queen's palace at Nonsuch; and the handsome residences there often served as halfway houses, where hospitality was dispensed to the numerous courtiers and public servants who frequented the road. Sir Henry Burton was Lord of the Manor of Mitcham, and Sir Walter Raleigh had a house and estate there. Another goodly house by the roadside at Mitcham was the property of Mr. John Dent, a citizen of London belonging to the Salters' Company, whose place of business was in St. Bartholomew's parish by the Exchange. (Where the Bank of England now stands; 1878).

He came from Leicestershire, his father having owned property at Halloughton, in that county. His second wife was Alice, daughter of Christopher Grant, of Manchester, by whom he had a son, Thomas, and two daughters, Mary and Elizabeth. The position of Mr. Dent's house on the road to Nonsuch procured a great honour for its owner. In 1592 the queen not only stopped at Mitcham, but paid Mr. Dent a visit which lasted three days, from Friday the 28th to Monday the 31st of July.

******

This appears from the baptismal entries for 1592, an unexpected place to find the sole record of a royal visit: "Edward son of Henry Whitney Esq. born Friday July 28th, the same day yt' her Majestie came to Mr. Dent his house, and baptized Monday 31st the same day that her Matie wente from hence to Nonsuche. (I am indebted to Colonel Chester for this interesting extract).

★★★★★★

Three years after the queen's visit Mr. Dent died, and was buried in the church of St. Bartholomew by the Exchange on the 30th of December, 1595. His widow was soon consoled. Less than three months after his death, on April 10, 1596, she was married, at Mitcham, to Sir Julius Caesar, an eminent lawyer and Master of Requests. (She bore him two sons, Robert and Edward. See *Life of Sir Julius Caesar* by E. Lodge; 4to, 1827).

Sir Julius was the son of Dr. Caesar Adelmar, the Italian physician to Queen Mary and Queen Elizabeth, who had the name of Caesar from his mother, a daughter of Giovanni Pietro Cesarini. Queen Mary ordered his posterity to adopt the name of Caesar. Julius was born at Tottenham in 1557, and lost his father in 1569. He was educated at Oxford and at the University of Paris, and soon distinguished himself at the bar. He became judge of the High Court of Admiralty in 1583, Master of Requests in 1590, Chancellor of the Exchequer in 1606, and Master of the Rolls in 1614. By his first wife, a daughter of Alderman Martin, whom he married in 1582 and buried in 1595, he had a son Charles, who was his heir. His town house was on the north side of the Strand, but after his marriage with Mistress Alice Dent he frequently resided in her house at Mitcham.

★★★★★★

In the article on Sir Julius Caesar, in the *Dictionary of British National Biography*, it is erroneously stated that he inherited the house at Mitcham from his first wife, and that his second wife's maiden name was Green. Her name was Grant. See Lodge's. *Life of Sir Julius Caesar* (1827).

★★★★★★

The queen had found this house a very pleasant and hospitable resting-place on her way to Nonsuch. So she repeated her visit. Sir Julius Caesar had the honour of entertaining her there on Tuesday the 12th of September, 1598. She supped and lodged, dined next day, and went on to Nonsuch "with exceeding good contentment."

★★★★★★

Sir Julius Caesar enumerates the presents he gave to Her Majesty on this occasion, and plaintively remarks that the visit cost him £700.

★★★★★★

We may suppose that Sir Francis Vere, in his frequent rides to court, occasionally enjoyed the hospitality of the house at Mitcham. He was acquainted with Sir Julius Caesar, and after his retirement from active service he became intimate with the other inmates of the house; for the worn-out veteran, the hero of so many glorious deeds, England's greatest and most renowned general, became the lover of young Elizabeth Dent, a girl who had only just passed her sixteenth birthday. (Baptised at the church of St. Bartholomew by the Exchange, London, on October 18, 1591). For her there was doubtless a romance in having won the love of so famous a warrior. Her sister Mary was engaged to Sir Henry Saville, of Methley, a young gentleman twenty-eight years of age, while Elizabeth's lover had reached the maturer age of forty-eight.

Sir Julius Caesar, (in Sir Francis Vere's marriage settlements he is called "Sir Julius Caesar *alias* Adelmar."), arranged a grand wedding for his stepdaughters. They were to be married in Mitcham church on the same day and at the same time. (This church was destroyed by lightning in 1627, and its ten bells were melted). On the 26th of October, 1607, the following entry occurs in the Mitcham register:

> Sir Francis Vere and Elizabeth Dent, Sir Henry Savill and Mary Dent were maryed the same day and at ye same tyme: they were both the daughters of Mr. John Dent gentleman, and of the right worshipful ye Lady Caesar, now wife to the right honourable Sir Julius Caesar, Chancelor of ye King's Majesties Exchequere and one of the Lordes of his privie Counsell.

******

Sir Henry Saville was created a baronet in 1611. By Mary Dent he had one son, John, who died in France just after he had reached his majority. Sir Henry died on June 23, 1632, aged fifty-three. His widow was married secondly to Sir William Sheffield,

******

By the marriage settlement, Sir Francis Vere received £2,000 with his wife, and he settled all his landed property on her for her life. During the very brief interval of twenty-two months between the marriage and death of Sir Francis there was scarcely time for the young girl's romance to wear out, and when she was left a widow, at the early age of eighteen, the deep grief recorded on her husband's monument was doubtless sincere. It was no slight honour to be the cherished wife of so great a man.

******

The peerages say that Sir Francis Vere had five children, and even give their names—John, Edward, Henry, Dorothy, and Elizabeth. This is obviously impossible, as he was only married for twenty-two months and three days, and I can find no trace of his having been married previously. He may have had one child, which died before him. The authority for the names of Sir Francis Vere's imaginary children, as given in the *Biographia Britannica*, is the Visitation of Essex in the Herald's Office, No. 124. His widow, in August, 1613, married Sir Patrick Murray, third son of John, Earl of Tullibardine, and had two sons.

Lady Caesar (Alice Dent) died on the 23rd of May, 1614. She was buried with great pomp on the 30th of June at St. Helen's church in the city, being aged forty-five, Sir Patrick and Lady Murray and Sir Henry and Lady Saville attended the funeral. Sir Julius Caesar married a third time in 1615, and died on April 18, 1637, aged seventy-nine. He was also buried at St. Helen's, where his monument still exists. The inscription is wrought in the device of a deed with pendant seal, the attaching cord being severed.

******

In the last years of his life Sir Francis Vere amused his leisure by writing, from his own point of view, some account of those actions in which he was specially engaged, and the results of which were due either to his advice or to arrangements made or suggested by him. These notes were jotted down as reminiscences for himself and his friends, and were not intended for publication.

******

These notes were published by Dr. William Dillingham in 1657, nearly fifty years after the death of the writer of them, with the following title: "*The Commentaries of Sir Francis Vere*, being diverse pieces of service wherein he had command, written by himself by way of commentary, published by William Dillingham, D.D., Cambridge, 1657. Small folio, pp. 209," and eight pages of introductory matter unpaged. The volume is illustrated by very fine engravings of the battles of Turnhout and Nieuport and several maps. It also contains engraved portraits of Sir Francis and Sir Horace Vere and Sir John Ogle, and an engraving of the tomb in Westminster Abbey. It is dedicated to Sir Horace Townshend, Bart., a grandson of Sir Horace Vere. Dr. Dillingham, in his address to the reader, explains that he met with a manuscript copy of Sir Francis Vere's Notes in the library of a friend, which had been transcribed from one in the possession of General Skippon. He at once concluded that a work of such value ought not to remain in manuscript. He therefore sought for other copies, with a view to obtaining an accurate version, and found one in the library of the Earl of Westmoreland which had been transcribed from the original, and another in the possession of the great Lord Fairfax.

He also obtained the original, which was the property of the Earl of Clare. Dr. Dillingham made his volume more complete by adding Sir John Ogle's accounts of the last charge at the Battle of Nieuport and of the parley at Ostend, as well as a short narrative of events at the siege of Ostend, written by young Hexham, Sir Francis Vere's page. After the brief epistle to the reader, Sir Robert Naunton's eulogium on Sir Francis Vere (from his *Fragmenta Regalia*) is given. Lastly, there is inserted at the end of the volume a Latin translation of Vere's account of the battle of Nieuport, by the learned Dr. Dorislaus. The actions treated of by Sir Francis Vere include but a small fraction of those in which he was engaged. They are:

1. Bommel-waart.
2. Relief of Rheinberg.
3. Second relieving of Rheinberg.
4. Relief of Litkenhoven.
5. Surprise of Zutphen Sconce.
6. Siege of Deventer.
7. Defeat of Parma at Knodsenburg.
8. Cadiz Journey.
9. Island Voyage.
10. Government of the Brill.
11. Action at Turnhout.
12. Battle of Nieuport.
13. Siege of Ostend.

Some of the manuscripts referred to by Dr. Dillingham are probably still extant. There is a manuscript folio of the "Cadiz Journey," by Sir F. Vere, at Kimbolton Castle. Lord Calthorpe possesses a complete manuscript copy of the *Commentaries*. The Duke of Northumberland has a manuscript comprising the Cadiz Journey, Island Voyage, and battles of Turnhout and

Nieuport; and Lord Leconfield, in a thick MS. folio, has copies of the chapters on the battles of Turnhout and Nieuport and the parley at Ostend.

★★★★★★

They only relate to a fraction of the actions in which he was engaged. To one who has also read his letters and despatches written on the spot, and the letters of others describing the same events, the most striking feature of these notes is their accuracy. With the exception of discrepancies in numbers of men or guns,—and even these are of rare occurrence,—the agreement of the notes, written from memory long after, with narratives prepared at the time, is very remarkable. Another point worthy of remark is the proof afforded by the notes, of the modesty and absence of self-assertion in Vere's public despatches. We hear for the first time in the private notes of wounds received in battle and of horses killed under him, incidents which receive no notice in his official reports. The notes are, to a great extent, in the form of commentaries on the actions treated of, interspersed with remarks which illustrate the development of events. The narrative portions are clearly written and very interesting, and as historical evidence they are invaluable.

★★★★★★

If it is borne in mind that Vere's *Commentaries* were only intended to discuss those actions in
which he took a leading part, that they were not intended for publication, and were not published until fifty years after the author's death, the injustice of some of the criticisms which have been made upon them will be apparent. Johnson, in his *Historia Rerum Britannicarum*, says: "*Inimici ejus dixerunt obtrectare alienee glorias solitum.*" Dr. Birch, in his *Memoirs of the Reign of Elizabeth*, says: "Vere never fails, in his *Commentaries*, to claim the chief merit in all the actions in which he was concerned." The answer to this is conclusive. Vere does not mention half the actions in which he was concerned, in his *Commentaries*, so that it is simply impossible that he can claim the chief merit in all. The avowed object of the *Commentaries* is to discuss such actions as were conducted by himself or by his advice; surely a natural and reasonable subject for the chief actor to take in hand. The only fair course for a hostile critic to adopt would be to dispute Vere's facts. This is what Mr. Motley has attempted, and a perusal of the footnotes in the chapters on the battle of

Nieuport and the siege of Ostend, in the present work, will show with what success. Mr. Motley also accuses Sir Francis Vere of publishing a party pamphlet in an age of pamphleteering. This is not the case; he never did anything of the kind. The *Commentaries* were written for himself and his immediate friends, and were never intended for publication. They were not published until half a century after Vere's death, and then only owing to the accidental circumstance of a copy having fallen into the hands of Dr. Dillingham.

******

Sir Francis Vere lived to see the great work of his life crowned with complete success. The mighty battle for freedom had been won. In April, 1609, the truce for twelve years was signed, and the independence of the Dutch Republics was secured. The great general continued to perform his public duties to the last. There is a letter of his from Portsmouth, written within a fortnight of his death, in which he discussed various details respecting the affairs of the garrison. The date of this letter, showing that he was then transacting business at Portsmouth, seems to point to the conclusion that his death was rather sudden. He died in London on the 28th of August, 1609, and was buried next day.

The remains of Sir Francis Vere were interred in Westminster Abbey, in the chapel of St. John the Evangelist, on the eastern side of the north transept. Near his tomb rest the bodies of several companions in arms, among them those of the gallant Norrises, under a splendid tomb, and that of Sir George Holles, over which there is a statue in the costume of a Roman soldier. The funeral, which took place on the 29th of August, 1609, was attended by his brothers and by all the friends and brother officers who were then in London. (Sir Francis Vere's name is the eighth in the Westminster Abbey register of burials, which only begins in January, 1607, see Colonel Chester's work).

Soon a noble monument was raised over his grave by the young widow, doubtless under the advice and with the assistance of her accomplished stepfather, Sir Julius Caesar. It is in imitation of the beautiful tomb erected over the grave of Engelbert of Nassau, at Breda, which Sir Francis Vere must have seen and admired. The effigy of the great general lies on a platform of black marble. The eyes are closed, the beard cut square, the forehead broad and high, the nose straight. The dress is a civil magistrate's cloak and a shirt. The feet rest on a wild boar, the crest of the Veres. At each angle of the platform kneels the full-sized figure of an officer in armour, with sword and sash passed over the left shoulder. These figures support another slab of black marble on their shoulders, on which rests the general's armour, a helmet with plumes, breastplate, a shield with eight quarterings, pouldrons, vantbraces, gauntlets, taces, and spurs, all carved in white marble. The inscription is as follows:—

> *Francisco Vero, Equiti Aurato, Galfredi F. Joannis Comitis Oxoniae Nepoti, Brieliae et Portsmuthae Praefecto Anglicarum copiarum in Belgio Ductori summo. Elizabetha uxor viro charissimo, quocum conjunctissime vixit hoc supremum amoris et fidei conjugalis monumentum maestissima et cum lacrymis gemens posuit. Obiit xxviii Die Augusti anno salutis MDCVIII et anno Ætatis suae liiii."*

★★★★★★

The inscription errs both as regards the year of Vere's death and his age. He was forty-nine, not fifty-four, when he died. The latter figure would make him older than his elder brother John. The year 1608 should be 1609. This is proved by the Abbey register, by the entry at the Herald's College, and by the existence of letters written by Sir Francis Vere in 1609. The *Biographia Britannica* gives 1608 as the year of his death, and his age fifty-four, quoting from the epitaph,

★★★★★★

The post-mortem inquisition of Sir Francis Vere's property was taken at Stratford Langthorn, in Essex, on the 4th of November, 1609. (Public Record Office. *Chancery Inquisitions Post Mortem,* No. 7, James I., 1st Part, No. 182.)

The story of the life of Sir Francis Vere clearly points out the main features of his character. He was earnest and persevering. He put his shoulder to the wheel when he was a young man, and he never faltered nor turned aside until the work was done. And such work! It demanded every faculty, every power of mind and body, and he gave them all lavishly and without stint. He lived for duty. He devoted his life to the service of his country. That service consisted mainly in fighting for the cause of an ally, and Vere naturally came to love the cause which was dear to his countrymen, and the people among whom he lived for so many years. They trusted him in return. Maurice invariably consulted him, and relied upon his advice. Barneveldt was his firm and constant friend. The one romance of Vere's life was his devoted loyalty to Queen Elizabeth. It may seem that his devotion was poorly requited, but it was not so. The queen, who was a good judge of character, considered Vere to be the best general in her service. She entrusted him with diplomatic missions, made him commander of her forces, and governor of the Brill. She was urged to do more, and to make him a peer. This was her reply:

> In his proper sphere, and in my estimation, Sir Francis Vere is above a peerage already. All that could be expected from such an addition would be the entombing of the spirit of a brave soldier in the corpse of a less sightly courtier; and by tempting him from his charge, hazard that repute upon a carpet which his valour has dearly purchased him in the field.—Osborne's *Traditional Memoirs of Elizabeth*, Art. 17, quoted by Cayley in his *Life of Raleigh*, i.

The only portrait of Sir Francis Vere is a half length, painted when he was a young man, a profile to the left. It is now in the collection of the Duke of Portland, at Welbeck. It was engraved by Faithorne, and is given in Vere's *Commentaries*.

PART 2: SIR HORACE VERE

CHAPTER 1

The Recovery of Sluys, and the Battle of Mulheim

There had been intimate companionship between the two brothers, Francis and Horace Vere, during their military life. Horace had come to the Netherlands to learn the art of war, after his brother had been five years in active service and had attained to the command of the English forces. They had been together ever since. Together they worked at many a famous siege, and fought in many a battle; together they mourned the death of their brother Robert; together they entered Cadiz as victors, when Horace was knighted; together they won the battle of Nieuport; and together they gallantly defended Ostend, where both were severely wounded. On the retirement of Sir Francis, his brother Horace took his place, though not with the same rank and powers. At first he was only the senior of the four colonels of the English companies, the others being Sir John Ogle, Sir Edward Cecil, and Sir Edward Harwood.

Sir Horace was in his fortieth year, with fifteen years of military experience acquired under his brother, and like him an able and resolute commander. Brave, self-controlled, and judicious, he was alike valorous in the field and wise in council. These qualities he shared with Sir Francis. The difference between the characters of the two brothers was, that while Sir Francis was more self-asserting and stern, Horace was extremely modest, and ruled those under him by kindness rather than by severity, though both were strict disciplinarians. It was said that the soldiers stood in awe of Sir Francis, while they loved Sir Horace. (*Biog. Brit*).

The elder brother lived to see Horace obtain great distinction in

HORACE LORD VERE.

two important actions before the armistice commenced; the first being the recapture of Sluys, and the second the saving of the States' army at Mulheim.

A new general had just appeared at the head of the army of the Archdukes, whose military genius probably saved the Spanish cause in the Netherlands from total overthrow. Spinola was not educated as a soldier. Like Oliver Cromwell, he was a born general. Immensely rich, and belonging to one of the oldest families of Genoa, Ambrosio Spinola took a corps of 9,000 veterans under his own pay, and led them from Italy to the theatre of war. Like his countryman Columbus, Spinola had fair hair and beard, and, like Columbus, he was prematurely gray. He was thirty-four when, he arrived and took charge of the siege of Ostend; and when it fell, on September 24, 1604, he was created Duke of San Severino, and received the Golden Fleece. He was a man of a noble and generous disposition, with gentle and kindly manners, but prompt and vigorous in action, a thoughtful organizer and a consummate general. No one can look upon the expression of his countenance as, in the picture of *"Las lanzas,"* by Velasquez, he gently puts his hand on the shoulder of the defeated governor of Breda, without almost loving Spinola for the noble pity that beams in his face. His whole heart seems to be absorbed in the desire to soften the humiliation of his foe. (Velasquez was present, and he himself appears in the group of officers round Spinola).

Such was the commander against whom Maurice and his officers were now to be matched. The States General had resolved to find compensation for the loss of Ostend by recovering the important fortified town of Sluys. Francis Vere had won his first laurels in its defence. Horace was to win his first success, after his brother's retirement, in its recovery. In April, 1604, Prince Maurice had assembled an army of 14,000 men at Dordrecht, which was finally embarked at Arnemuiden and Flushing. The army included the whole English contingent under Horace Vere, Ogle, and Cecil. Under Maurice, who was accompanied by his young brother Frederick Henry, the Dutch troops were commanded by his cousins, Counts Ernest Casimir, Louis Gunther, and William of Nassau.

A vast number of vessels, (three thousand five hundred, according to Grimeston), had been collected, and they made sail in excellent order, successfully landing the army on the opposite shore, between Vulpen and Cadzand, on the 24th of April. In the two following days, Hofstede and all the other forts on Cadzand Island surrendered to

Prince Maurice; and on the 30th he crossed the channel to Coxie, and captured the forts on that side. Isendike also submitted, the town of Ardenburg opened its gates, and the Dutch cavalry scoured the country to the very walls of Ghent and Bruges. The object of Maurice was to get possession of all the military posts in the vicinity before laying regular siege to the town of Sluys. His movements had been bold and judicious, and were crowned with success. But before a close siege could be formed it was necessary to outmanoeuvre the efforts to relieve the garrison, not only of Don Luis de Velasco, the Spanish general of horse, but of Spinola himself.

Velasco had entrenched his force of 2,000 men in a narrow pass, in front of Damme, the town between Sluys and Bruges, which, with Sluys, long formed one of the two ports of the great Flemish emporium of trade. Leaving garrisons in Isendike and Ardenburg, Maurice advanced against the Spaniards. Count Ernest led the vanguard, with cavalry under Marcellus Bacx, but they were taken at a disadvantage and were observed to be falling back. Sir Horace Vere, seeing that the enemy was gaining ground, entreated the Prince to allow him to charge at the head of the English companies. The request was at once granted. He selected 100 pikes and 200 shotmen from his brother's old regiment, and placed them under the command of Sir Charles Fairfax. A second detachment of 400 men, under Sir John Ogle, was to follow. The way was narrow, and on either side there were swamps and stagnant waters, where the sea had been let in over the polder lands. Fairfax led his men to the attack with great resolution.

After a sharp engagement, he forced the enemy to retire behind their entrenchments, and followed them so closely that they were routed. Velasco himself was one of the first to fly. Many plunged into the swamps and flooded polders. The slain numbered 423, and 400 prisoners were taken. The States General gave the honour of this gallant action to the English companies. (Letter from Sir John Ogle, May 9, 1604. Hatfield MSS). On the same night Colonel Van der Node, who had been governor of Ostend, crossed the Zwin at low water with thirty companies, of which ten were English, and fortified a spot selected by Prince Maurice, opposite to Sluys. The approach from Bruges and Damme was thus commanded, and the investment of the town was completed. In the end of May the Archduke sent a large force with a convoy of provisions for the beleaguered garrison, but it was routed, and all the wagons were captured.

The siege-works were fortified with trenches and square sconces, both against sorties from the town and attacks from outside. Prince Maurice himself was encamped on the north side, Count Ernest on the other side of the Zwin, Count William on the east, and Colonel Van der Node occupied the flooded lands with a large flotilla of armed vessels drawing little water.

In July Spinola himself made an attempt to relieve Sluys. On the 28th he encamped between Bruges and Damme, with 10,000 men and 600 wagons laden with meal. He thence advanced by Ardenburg towards the quarters of Van der Node. His object was to reach the town by a wide causeway which was still open. But Maurice set a large force to work, and in forty-eight hours he had dug a trench across, which effectually stopped the passage. He then mounted several guns between the quarters of Van der Node and Count William, and opened a heavy and continuous fire on the camp of Spinola. On the evening of the 6th of August the Genoese general made an attack on Count William's quarters, and there was a desperate conflict in the trenches which was long doubtful. But at length the assailants were forced to retreat, and on the 18th Spinola gave up hope and marched away.

The garrison was now reduced to great straits by famine, and on the 20th of August, 1604, Sluys surrendered, 4,200 half-starved men presenting a melancholy spectacle as they marched out, some of them scarcely able to walk. A large store of munitions, eighty-four brass and twenty-four iron guns, were captured, and the place was ordered to be well strengthened for the States General. During the siege Count Louis of Nassau died of fever, and Colonel Van der Aa, who had so gallantly seconded Sir Francis Vere at the battle of Turnhout, was mortally wounded.

The army of Prince Maurice had to overcome much greater difficulties in this second siege of Sluys than were encountered by the Duke of Parma in 1586. The place was stronger and better provided, the garrison was more numerous, there were a number of outposts to capture, and there was an active army in the field, operating against the besiegers. On the whole, this was the most difficult and the most ably conducted military operation in which Prince Maurice was ever engaged. (See Meteren, Grimeston, Bentivoglio, etc. Letters from Sir William Browne at Flushing, from Sir Horace Vere, Sir John Ogle, and Sir Edward Cecil. "*Journal de l'expedition en Flandre par Junius, Secretaire de Comte Guillaume de Nassau.* Sluys, May 21, 1604:" in Prinsterer, No. ccxv. Also ccxvi. Ernest Casimir to Count John. "Sluys, June 7, 1604.")

In May, 1604, while the siege of Sluys was proceeding, the veteran Count Peter Ernest de Mansfelt died, at the age of eighty-seven. He had served with Charles V. at Tunis, and behaved with great gallantry at the battle of St. Quentin, where he was wounded. He married Marguerite de Brederode, and had three sons, who were all slain; but his natural son was the famous Count Mansfelt of the Thirty Years' War. (Charles de Mansfelt was slain in Hungary, the second son fell in a duel, and the third met a soldier's death before Knodsenburg Sconce).

The strategic skill of Spinola was displayed to great advantage in the campaign of 1605. This was the least fortunate year, from a military point of view, in the whole career of Prince Maurice. He not only gained no ground, but barely held his own. At one time his active enemy had advanced almost to the borders of Friesland, and for a moment the fortress of Coevorden was in imminent danger. Towards the end of September, Prince Maurice with his army was at Wesel watching the movements of Spinola, who was causing a fort to be constructed on the Rhine, near the mouth of the Ruhr. His headquarters were at Ruhrort, at the junction of the two rivers, and he had detachments stationed several miles up the Ruhr valley. Ruhrort is fifteen miles above Wesel.

The Ruhr, flowing from the Waldeck country, has a course of about eighty miles, with here and there a stretch of fertile plain bordering its banks, while in other places the hills rise almost directly to plateaux, which in those days were covered with forest. Close to Ruhrort is the ancient town of Duisburg, where the great geographer, Gerard Mercator (or Cremer), dwelt for upwards of forty years, and where he constructed the famous map of the world on the projection which bears his name. Ten years before Spinola encamped at Ruhrort, Mercator breathed his last in the neighbouring town, at a good old age. He was buried in the church of St. Saviour at Duisburg, and his statue now graces the Burg-platz. The quaint old tower of St. Saviour is visible from Ruhrort and for miles along the lower course of the Ruhr.

Seven miles up the river stands the town of Mulheim, which was then a small village, consisting of one street on a steep slope, at right angles with the stream. On the opposite or southern bank of the Ruhr the hills rise abruptly, and the old castle of Broick stood on their slope. There it still stands, while all around is changed. The steep hill has been partly faced with terraced walls, and on one of the terraces there is a very ancient elm which may have afforded shade to the soldiers of Spinola. The castle was a quadrilateral work, with round bastions at the angles. Part of the old walls and one bastion remain, and there is a garden with tall shady trees on the rampart overlooking the river. The chief building, pierced by an archway, is on the east side of the courtyard, and over the arch there is a shield of arms with the year 1648, the date of the Peace of Westphalia. This indicates that the castle was restored at the close of the Thirty Years' War. There are also two richly decorated coats-of-arms of the Neuberg branch of the Palatine family, with crown and supporters, on a gable of another block of buildings. Enough remains to enable us to build up the castle of Broick in imagination, as it appeared in the days of Spinola and Maurice of Orange.

Spinola had stationed Count Teodoro Trivulcio, a Milanese nobleman, with a large body of cavalry, at Mulheim; and a detachment under Don Francisco Arirazabal, a Spaniard from the Basque province of Guipuzcoa, occupied the castle of Broick. Maurice was watching his enemy's movements with close attention, from Wesel. Finding that detachments were scattered along the Ruhr valley, and that Trivulcio was several miles from the main body, he made a plan for attacking him simultaneously at Mulheim and Broick, and annihilating his forces before succour could arrive from Ruhrort. With this object, Maurice set out from Wesel as soon as it was dark, on the night of the 8th of October, 1605, with all his cavalry and twenty-four companies of foot, including the English contingent under Sir Horace Vere.

Young Prince Frederick Henry, who had already distinguished himself at the recovery of Sluys, and was now only in his twenty-first year, commanded the cavalry. With him was the veteran Marcellus Bacx. It is said that the infantry were carried in wagons. Maurice also had four fieldpieces. His plan was for Bacx to cross the river above Mulheim and occupy Broick, while Prince Frederick Henry attacked Mulheim and drove the enemy across the river, to be received by Bacx on the other side. Maurice was then to come up with the infantry and complete the victory. It was a well-conceived idea, but it failed through the misconduct of some of the cavalry.

Marcellus Bacx succeeded in crossing the Ruhr out of sight of the enemy, and, riding over a hill called the Cassenberg, he came suddenly upon the detachment of Spanish cavalry commanded by Don Francisco Arirazabal. After a very brief encounter the Spaniards were routed, and Bacx took the castle of Broick without further opposition. Meanwhile, Prince Frederick Henry led his cavalry direct to the head of the street of Mulheim village, which descends to the river bank, and in the upper part is steep and narrow. He first came to the Old Market (Alt Markt) at the entrance to the village, where there was a small fortified house in those days. Thence a narrow lane, called the "Bogen-strasse" (Bow Street), leads down to the main thoroughfare of the village, a steep street called "Delle." On the right of the Bogen-strasse there is a high wall supporting the churchyard and old church, approached from below by many steps. Three arches span the Bogen-strasse, over which the churchyard is reached from the second stories of the houses on the other side.

The prince halted in the Alt Markt at the head of the Bogen-strasse, waiting for his brother with the main body. No enemy had encountered him, for Trivulcio, seeing that Broick had been attacked and occupied by Bacx, had evacuated Mulheim, and began to cross the river. Hearing that this movement was in process of execution, Prince Frederick Henry rode down the Bogen-strasse into the "Delle," formed his men in line, and led them down that thoroughfare to the river bank. Here he halted. Trivulcio was in the act of crossing with his cavalry; but seeing Prince Frederick Henry's troops on the bank he had just left, he wheeled and charged them. An unaccountable panic seized the prince's men, and they fled in complete rout. Two companies, under Sir John Selby of Twizell, alone stood firm. With these the young prince rode up the valley, forded the river higher up, and joined Marcellus Bacx at Broick. That veteran was already hard pressed by reinforcements from Ruhrort, as, well as by Trivulcio with his victorious troops. (Meteren; Grimeston).

On the same morning Spinola was riding up the valley from Ruhrort to visit the camp at Mulheim, accompanied by Don Luis de Velasco, his general of cavalry. What a change have the succeeding centuries effected in that German valley, where the Italian and the Spanish commanders were then so intent on the subjugation of alien peoples, who were to them as mere pawns on a chessboard! Spinola and Velasco saw only forest-covered slopes on either side of them, as they rode through swampy meadows to the secluded little village on the Ruhr. Now these uncultivated tracts are covered with waving crops. From among the trees on the hillsides rise the lofty chimneys of Oberhausen, with its iron-works and weaving and spinning factories. In the Duisburger Wald to the south, which was the haunt of wild boars and deer in Spinola's day, there are now gardens and pleasure-houses, frequented by crowds of children and other holiday folk from the neighbouring towns.

The little village of Mulheim is now, (1878), a handsome and flourishing manufacturing town, with two bridges connecting it with Broick, and a river made navigable by locks. No speculation as regards the future of the country through which they were riding occupied the minds of the southern generals. Yet all the prosperity, in the distant future, was due to the total overthrow of the cause for which they fought, and to the vindication of those rights of nationalities which they sought to trample under foot.

As they rode along the river banks, Spinola and Velasco were met by a messenger from Trivulcio, galloping in hot haste, with news of the attack and a request for help. Spinola went back with the messenger to organize reinforcements, sending Velasco on towards Mulheim. Directly afterwards that officer encountered three companies of cavalry under a Neapolitan captain named Fabricio Santomago. (Bentivoglio).

He placed himself at their head and hurried to the scene of action, which now centred round the castle of Broick. Some of the allied cavalry had been again put to disgraceful rout. Bacx and the young prince were seriously outnumbered. Spinola himself came from Ruhrort with some companies of foot; 2,000 more were on the road, and he adopted the stratagem of sending mounted drummers ahead to sound marches, and make the enemy believe that still further reinforcements were on the road.

This was the state of affairs when Prince Maurice arrived at Mulheim, marched down the Delle Strasse, and obtained a full view of the action raging round Broick castle, from the river bank: most of his cavalry flying in all directions, a small remnant led by his brother and Bacx fighting desperately, but almost surrounded by the enemy, and his own force far too small to encounter the army of Spinola with any hope of success. He got his guns into position and opened fire, and he made desperate efforts to rally the panic-stricken fugitives. There was nothing left but retreat, with every prospect of the movement being converted into a complete rout, unless Spinola gave him time to rally his men and form again, which was not likely.

At this critical moment Sir Horace Vere proposed to Maurice that he should quit his post in the main body, with the English companies, cross the river, and by keeping the enemy at bay, gain time for Bacx and the young prince to fall back, and for Maurice to reorganise his forces preparatory to a retreat. The suggestion was cordially accepted. The place for fording, which was selected by Vere, was at the end of the Delle Strasse. The river is here of considerable width, but the men were only up to their middles in one place, and there are two grassy islets in the channel. The English pikemen marched steadily across, and advanced up the hill shoulder to shoulder, with calm resolution.

Bacx and the prince had routed the first attack of Spanish horse on the plateau of Speldorf, above the castle; but the fugitives rallied behind their infantry, were reinforced by Trivulcio and Velasco, and once more charged the heroic Dutchmen. Again they were forced back. Then reinforcements began to arrive from Ruhrort, accompanied by Spinola in person. Many of the Dutch fled in panic, leaving their two leaders with only 400 men opposed to a thousand. The prince was twice in imminent personal danger. Almost surrounded, and in close hand-to-hand fight, these gallant heroes long held their own, hoping for succour. Then came the diversion organized by Sir Horace Vere, and the remnant of cavalry, nearly worn out, effected a retreat. They had been fighting for seven hours.

The whole Spanish force then turned upon Vere. He had with him four English companies and one Scotch company under the Earl of Buccleuch. They firmly stood their ground for an hour, in a disadvantageous position on the Broick hill-slope, repulsing the enemy with their pikes, and never faltering, notwithstanding the furious charges of the Spaniards. At length a French company came to their help, its leader, the gallant Dommerville, falling while at the head of his men in the river. Vere's object had been attained, and he gave orders for a retreat. As soon as the Spaniards saw his intention they again charged down the hillside in great numbers. Vere selected sixty veterans as a forlorn hope, to cover the retreat of their comrades across the Ruhr. He himself was in the post of danger, disputing the passage with the enemy on the brink of the river. Nearly all the sixty British heroes were killed, and Vere's horse was mortally wounded. It was just able to carry its master across, and fell dead on the opposite bank.

Spinola declared that Sir Horace Vere had saved the army of the States. His brilliant movement and the dogged valour of his men gave time for Maurice to rally the fugitives, and he retreated to Wesel without further molestation. Count Trivulcio was killed by a shot from one of Maurice's fieldpieces, and his body was conveyed to Milan for interment. Santomago was also killed. Young Nicolas Doria, a cousin of Spinola, was wounded and taken prisoner. On the other side 200 fell, including several officers of distinction. Sir Henry Gary was captured, and, being a volunteer, was obliged to pay a very heavy ransom. Captains Pigott and Ratcliffe were also taken prisoners. Shortly after this memorable action the two armies went into winter-quarters.

Prince Maurice fully recognised the importance of the service rendered by Sir Horace Vere at the battle of Mulheim. From that time the English commander became one of the most trusted and valued officers upon whom the Prince of Orange relied. Sir Francis was always on good terms with Maurice, was invariably consulted, and his advice was generally taken. But while Sir Horace succeeded to his brother in these respects, there was a still closer tie of friendship between him and the prince, which continued unchanged until the death of the latter. The armistice of twelve years followed shortly after the battle of Mulheim. Sir Horace Vere thus had leisure to return to his relations in England for a season, and to be with his beloved elder brother during the last years of his life.

CHAPTER 2

Death of Barneveldt

The long years of service in the wars, separated for many months at a time from relations and friends at home, and constantly exposed to dangers and hardships, never seem to have deprived the warrior brothers of the hope that one day they might be able to enjoy the pleasures of courtship and love. At length the truce of twelve years with the Spaniards announced that their labours were over, and that their work was done, and done most nobly. Sir Francis won the heart of a young lady in her seventeenth year. Sir Horace chose for his bride a youthful widow with two little boys. The brothers were married in the same month of the same year.

Mary Tracey was the youngest child of Sir John Tracey of Todington, in Gloucestershire, a knight of most ancient lineage, descended in the male line from the Saxon kings. Her mother, Anne, daughter of Sir Thomas Throckmorton, died on the 21st of May, 1581, three days after the birth of her daughter 1 Mary. Her father, Sir John, followed his wife to the grave in 1591. There were four children. Sir John, the eldest, who succeeded at Todington, married Mary, daughter of Sir Thomas Shirley, of Isfield, and was created Viscount Tracey in 1642. William, the other brother, married Mary, daughter of Sir John Conway, of Arrow, whose brother, Sir Edward Conway, was for several years lieutenant-governor of the Brill for Sir Francis Vere. Sir Edward himself married Dorothy, the elder sister of Mary Tracey.

✶✶✶✶✶✶

The male line came to an end with Henry, eighth Viscount Tracey, who died in 1797. His daughter Henrietta married Charles Hanbury, who took the name of Tracey, and was created Baron Sudeley of Todington in 1838. His grandson is the present, (1878), Baron Sudeley.

Sir Edward Conway was Secretary of State in 1623, and created Baron Conway of Ragley in 1624, and Viscount Conway in 1626. He died in 1630.

******

Mary was in her twentieth year when she was married to her first husband, William Hoby, son of Sir William Hoby, a privy councillor to Henry VIII. She was left a widow with two children about three years after her marriage, and she was twenty-six when she won the heart of Sir Horace Vere, on his return from the Low Countries. It is probable that they first became acquainted through Sir Edward Conway's friendship with the Veres. The marriage took place in October, 1607, (This appears from a letter in the Shrewsbury Correspondence), and Mary Tracey proved to be a fitting helpmate to her gallant husband. She was a woman imbued with strong religious feelings, and endowed with a firm will and clear intellect. She followed her husband to the Low Countries, and devoted herself to his interests. Her residence in Holland strengthened her early convictions, and during a long and useful life she was ever a stanch advocate of civil and religious liberty.

A great sorrow overtook Sir Horace Vere less than two years after his marriage, in the death of his renowned brother, whose remains he followed to their last resting-place in Westminster Abbey. He succeeded Sir Francis as governor of the Brill, the appointment being dated October 18, 1609. Although James I. had abandoned England's ally, and had made a disgraceful peace with Spain, the cautionary towns were to be retained until the States General had cleared off their debt. This important charge and the command of the English troops in the pay of the States made it necessary for Sir Horace Vere to reside in Holland, and between 1610 and 1614 his four eldest daughters, Elizabeth, Mary, Katherine, and Anne, were born there.

******

An Act of Parliament was passed in 1624 for the naturalisation of Elizabeth and Mary Vere. (Rushworth, i.) Elizabeth was Countess of Clare; Mary became Lady Townshend, afterwards Countess of Westmoreland; Katherine married, first, Oliver St. John, and second, Lord Poulett; Anne was Lady Fairfax.

******

During their visits to England Sir Horace and Lady Vere had a house or lodging near the Exchange, in the parish of St. Bartholomew the Great. Their fifth daughter, Dorothy, (afterwards Mrs. Wolstenholme), was born there, and baptized in the church of St. Bartholomew on the 15th of January, 1616. She came to them at a time of sorrow, for the aged mother of Sir Horace died in December, 1615, and his young stepson, Philip Hoby, was buried at Isleworth in January, 1616.

******

> January 13, 1616. Isleworth Parish Register. Holman, in his MS. history of the Veres, says that the two sons of Lady Vere by W. Hoby died aged nineteen and twenty-three respectively. But the Isleworth Register shows that this must be a mistake.

******

The other child of Lady Vere, by her first husband, had died previously.

In 1616 more stirring times began to loom on the horizon, though the truce with Spain did not terminate until 1621. Young nephews and cousins were beginning to reach years of discretion, who were anxious to serve under their famous relative, the greatest living English general. Among these, the youth in whom Sir Horace naturally took the deepest interest was his cousin and the head of his house, Henry, the eighteenth Earl of Oxford.

Edward, the seventeenth Earl, who was a boy at Hedingham in the childhood of Francis and Horace, had led a life of reckless extravagance, and had ended in totally destroying the noble inheritance to which he had succeeded. One by one the numerous manors and estates in Essex and Suffolk were mortgaged and sold. His first wife, the daughter of Lord Burleigh, had died in 1588, leaving three daughters, whose nests were carefully feathered by their grandfather, the Lord Treasurer, with all the remnants of the Vere estates that the law could be made to give them.

******

> The Earl of Oxford, we are told by Dugdale, entreated Burleigh for the life of his friend and cousin, the Duke of Norfolk. The refusal so incensed him that he swore he would do all he could to ruin Burleigh's daughter (who was his wife) by consuming his estate. But Collins denies the truth of this story.

******

There was no son. So in 1590 the spendthrift earl was married again to one of Queen Elizabeth's maids of honour. This was Elizabeth, daughter of Thomas Trentham of Rocester, in Staffordshire, by whom he had an only son, Henry, born in 1593. (Henry, known as Lord Bolebee during the lifetime of his father, was born on February 24, 1593, and baptised at Newington on March 31st; Newington Register.)

In the last years of his life Earl Edward lived in a house at Newington, where he died on the 24th of June, 1604. He was buried in the church at Hackney.

The Dowager Countess of Oxford and her little son, now become Henry, the eighteenth Earl of Oxford, went to live in a house in Canon Row, Westminster, with very small means. As the boy grew up he got into undesirable company, and his poor mother found that she was quite unable to manage him. At last she was driven to the extreme measure of drawing up articles against one John Hunt for corrupting the earl, her son, and preying on his estate.

******

Aubrey Vere, second son of the sixteenth Earl of Oxford, and uncle of Sir Francis and Sir Horace Vere, married Margaret daughter of John Spring of Lavenham, and secondly, Bridget, daughter of Sir Anthony Gibbon of Lynn, in Norfolk. His son Hugh, by his first wife, married a daughter of William Walsh, and was father of Robert, nineteenth Earl of Oxford. His daughter Jane married Henry Hunt of Gosfield in Essex, and was the mother of this disreputable John Hunt, who was thus a second cousin of the young earl whom he led astray. John Hunt had a son, Vere Hunt, who settled in Ireland in 1657, and whose great-grandson was Vere Hunt of Currah, in Limerick. His son, Sir Vere Hunt, was created a baronet in 1784, and married Elinor, daughter of Dr. W. Cecil, Dean of Limerick. Their son assumed the name of De Vere only in 1832, and became Sir Aubrey De Vere. He was the author of *Julian the Apostate* and other poems. Dying in 1846, he left, by his wife Mary Spring Rice, sister of Lord Monteagle, Sir Vere De, Vere, who died in 1880; Aubrey, author of the *Waldenses* and other poems; Sir Stephen, the present baronet, unmarried; William Cecil, a commander R.N., who died child less in 1869; and Francis, in the artillery, who died leaving three daughters.

******

In this document the countess made the following statement:

Under pretence of kindred Hunt insinuated himself into my son's acquaintance, drawing him from his lessons to course with greyhounds; taking him to taverns plays and bad company; and teaching him swearing, and filthy and ribald talk. He withdrew him from my house in Canon Row to a disorderly life in Essex, hunting in deer parks, and other like disorderly actions. He hath impudently presumed to be his bed fellow, and otherwise used him most disrespectfully, has borrowed money in my son's name to his dishonour, and lives wholly on my son's purse, draws him from my house, and causes him to spend all his time in play at an ordinary in Milford Lane, not coming home until 1 or 2 in the morning.—State Papers, Elizabeth, Domestic.

The earl was very young when he thus got into bad company, not more than seventeen, and his poor mother was in despair. She appears, however, to have placed him under the care of trustees, and a few years afterwards he went abroad, remaining in Italy until October, 1618. He came home much improved, and worthy to serve with his great relative, Sir Horace Vere, under whose command he met a soldier's death. Sir Francis took a deep interest in this young head of his house; and when the States General granted him a pension he made an earnest request, which was complied with, that it might be continued, after his death, to his relative, Henry, the eighteenth Earl of Oxford.

Another young follower of Sir Horace Vere was John, a natural son of his eldest brother, John Vere of Kirby Hall. This youth caused his father much embarrassment, and for many years he is said to have lain under dreadful apprehensions of God's wrath on account of the boy's irregular entrance into the world. But his uncles befriended him, and opened for him an honourable career. He was sergeant-major in the regiment of his uncle Horace, and received the honour of knighthood in 1607. There was also a kinsman named Edward Vere, whose precise relationship is not clearly made out, but who served with great distinction under Sir Horace, and was slain at Bois le Duc.

★★★★★★

The above Sir John Vere had a son Edward, but he would have been too young to be identified with the Edward Vere referred to in the text, and moreover he died young. He is probably the Lieut. Edward Vere who was slain at the siege of Maastricht.

★★★★★★

Another young volunteer for service under Sir Horace Vere was his nephew Simon Harcourt. Frances Vere had been married, in 1598, to Sir Robert Harcourt of Stanton Harcourt, in Oxfordshire, an adventurous knight who obtained letters patent from James I. to plant the region between the Amazons and Essequibo in South America. He sailed in the *Rose*, of eighty tons, with his brother Michael, and returned after an absence of three years, leaving Michael behind. (Michael's fate was never ascertained). He published an account of his voyage, (*Relation of a Voyage to Guiana* (1613), 2nd ed. (1626), a very scarce work), and died in 1631, aged fifty-seven. He left two sons by Frances Vere: Simon, the eldest, who became a distinguished officer under his uncle Sir Horace Vere; and Vere Harcourt, to whom his uncle John Vere left an annuity of £40 a year, and who became a clergyman.

These aspirants to military fame had either commenced their careers, or were soon about to seek appointments under their kinsman, when Sir Horace Vere returned to Holland, commissioned to restore the Brill to the States General, after it had been garrisoned by the English for upwards of thirty years. The States General, having repaid the loans from England, received back the cautionary towns in May, 1616. (The treaty by which the cautionary towns were restored to the States General will be found in *Rymer*, xvi.). Vere received a life pension of £800 a year as compensation for the loss of his governorship. (The widow of Lord Burgh, the former governor of Brill, had a pension of £200 a year, which was to be added to Sir Horace Vere's pension on her death).

Sir Horace found his good friend Sir Dudley Carleton at the Hague, as envoy from England, a post which he continued to hold from 1616 to 1628. He was the last English minister who had the privilege of sitting in the Council of the States General, a privilege gained by Queen Elizabeth, and annexed to the occupation of the cautionary towns. The privilege was continued to Carleton as a matter of courtesy after the towns had been restored. There was cordial friendship between Sir Dudley Carleton and Sir Horace Vere, who was at the Hague during the summer of 1616, inspecting the troops. He then went to drink the waters at Spa, and at first found himself rather weakened by them, but after completing the course his friend Carleton reported that he had become a *"novus homo."* (Sir Dudley Carleton to Sir Ralph Winwood, August, 1616; *Carleton Letters*. The Duke of Parma used to take a course of the Spa waters for his gout, in the intervals of campaigning).

★★★★★★

Dudley Carleton was the son of Anthony Carleton of Baldwin Brightwell, in Oxfordshire, and was born on March 10, 1573. He was educated at Westminster School and Christ Church, Oxford, and travelled until 1600, when he became secretary to the embassy at Paris. In 1605 he went to Spain with Lord Norris. In May, 1610, he was appointed to succeed Sir Thomas Edmondes as ambassador to the archdukes at Brussels, but a reason of state intervened and stopped his journey. In September of the same year he was knighted and nominated to the embassy at Venice, and was there engaged in an important negotiation as mediator between the Dukes of Savoy and Mantua. Returning to England in 1615, he was appointed envoy to the States General.

★★★★★★

The truce enabled Sir Horace to visit Spa, which was in the territory of the archdukes, and in September he returned to England. He was with his family at his house in the city during the rest of the year, and in November we find him sending a present of four venison pasties to his friend Carleton. (State Papers, Domestic, James I., vol. xc. No. 11).

During Sir Horace Vere's long residence in Holland, while the truce continued, he resided at the Hague and at Leyden, with periodical visits to the Brill, and latterly at Utrecht. Like his brother, he did not fail to derive inspiration from the principle for which he fought, and to sympathize with the cause of civil and religious freedom. The same sentiment was very prevalent among those who took service under the Veres. Their feelings were enlisted against persecution and tyranny. When the hunted congregation of John Robinson arrived in Holland, and was permitted to establish itself in Leyden during the month of May, 1609, it met with friendly treatment at the hands of warrior country, men, from the general downwards.

★★★★★★

A congregation of separatists was formed by inhabitants of Yorkshire, Nottinghamshire, and Lincolnshire, near the trijunction of the boundaries of those counties, in 1606. They met in the house of William Brewster, the postmaster of Scrooby, near Bawtry, their pastor being John Robinson, a Cambridge graduate who had been ordained, but threw up his cure to join the Separatists. William Bradford, a native of the neighbouring village of Austerfield, in Yorkshire, was another leading member. When a sharp persecution began, they resolved to go to Holland, where they heard that there was freedom of religion for all men. They attempted to embark at Boston, but were seized, thrown into prison, and their goods confiscated. Another attempt to escape was also prevented, but at length the magistrates became ashamed of persisting in the persecution of these helpless people, and they were allowed to go. They reached Amsterdam in August, 1608.

******

Some of those who had served under the Veres even joined its ranks. The period during which the pilgrims of Robinson's congregation abode at Leyden coincides with the truce of twelve years—1609 to 1620. William Bradford, the second governor of the Plymouth colony, belonged to the original Scrooby congregation. But other leading pilgrims were of those who joined in Holland, attracted to the Leyden church by that love of civil and religious liberty which they had imbibed under the Veres, and which was so sturdily represented by those fugitives for conscience' sake.

Miles Standish had been educated in the school of the Veres. A trained soldier of freedom, he settled at Leyden when the truce was proclaimed, and formed friendly relations with the pilgrims. He was the military adviser of the infant colony.

******

He came of an old Lancashire family, and was born in 1584. After serving the colony faithfully for many years, both as a soldier and a councillor, he died at Duxbury, in Massachusetts, in 1656.

******

Young Edward Winslow, scion of an old Worcestershire family, was in Holland during the truce, but he had not actually served against the Spaniards. He also joined the Leyden congregation, and eventually became, next to Bradford, the chief leader of the colony. So that when the pilgrim fathers sailed from Delftshaven in July, 1620, to lay the first foundation of the great republic across the Atlantic, they had amongst them at least one, if not more companions who were pupils of the Veres.

******

William Bradford was a Yorkshireman, a native of Austerfield, of humble birth. He was born in 1588, and formed one of the Scrooby congregation. He went to America in the *Mayflower*, and was governor of the Plymouth colony for many years. He wrote a *History of the Plymouth Colony and People*, 1609-46. He died in May, 1657, and his descendants still flourish, (1878), in the United States, Edward Winslow was the scion of a good family at Kempsey, in Worcestershire. The Winslows were long established on a small estate in that parish, called Clerkenleap. Edward was born at Droitwich, on Oct. 19, 1595. He joined himself to the Leyden church when only twenty-two, and went out in the *Mayflower*. He conducted the negotiations with the native chief Massasoit, went on missions to England as agent for the colony, and was twice governor. He wrote *Good News from New England*, an account of the colony which is abridged in Purchas. The Protector appointed him chief commissioner in the Jamaica expedition, and he died at sea, near the Jamaica coast, on May 8, 1655. His descendants still, (1878), form a distinguished New England family.

★★★★★★

There were other warriors of that school who took a leading part in founding the American settlements: such as Sir Ferdinando Gorges in Maine, Lion Gardiner in Connecticut, and Edward Maria Wingfield in Virginia. (Wingfield was the first president of the colony of Virginia, He wrote a *Discourse of Virginia*, first printed in *Archaeologia Americana*, iv. from the manuscript in the Lambeth Library, and edited by Mr. Charles Deane).

The deplorable events in Holland which preceded the termination of the truce were not connected with the English contingent further than that Sir Horace Vere served, in the ordinary course of duty, under the orders of the Prince of Orange. Throughout the war Maurice and Olden Barneveldt had acted together with cordiality, both actuated by the one great object of securing the independence of their common country. Barneveldt was the ablest and most patriotic statesman of the age in which he lived. Maurice was one of the greatest military commanders; but in civil affairs he was guided by the old friend and councillor of his father.

The truce was, however, most distasteful to Maurice, who cared for nothing but the movements of armies, the strategic plans for a campaign, and the game of chess. Barneveldt felt that the country required breathing time, and that the truce was practically an acknowledgment of Dutch independence, and as such a great and important triumph. From that time the feelings of Maurice towards the old statesman were embittered, and he came to look upon Barneveldt as his enemy, and as one that must be cleared from his path, although he concealed his feelings, which continued to grow in intensity for several years.

Yet it is difficult to reconcile the crime which the prince committed, and which has tarnished his fame beyond recall, with the tenor of his life history. As a military commander, he was surrounded by steadfast personal friends, and he acquired the respect and faithful service of officers and men. In his family relations he was generous and affectionate to a remarkable degree. He treated his stepmother, Louise de Coligny, not only with kindness and respect, but as a trusted friend and adviser. He adopted his half-brother Frederick Henry, looked upon him as a son, and never married, in order that he might succeed as his heir.

He forgave his sister for marrying the Portuguese Pretender, and liberally supported her and her children. He received the fugitive King and Queen of Bohemia and their large family, made them a home at the Hague, and treated them with untiring kindness. It is hard to understand how this man can have been guilty of such an atrocious crime as was involved in the execution of his father's old friend, the patriot statesman who had guided his country safely through many dangers, the virtuous Olden Barneveldt. The only explanation is that Maurice was embittered by the opposition to his wishes involved in the truce, that he nursed his anger until it turned to unreasoning hatred, and that, in this frame of mind, he really believed the absurd calumnies that were whispered into his ear.

Under the mask of outward calm and formal friendliness he watched an opportunity for vengeance. It came in the heated religious controversy of the time. The Calvinistic followers of Gomer commenced a violent persecution of the disciples of Arminius. Neither Barneveldt nor Maurice were partisans of either side in their hearts. The dogmatic hair-splittings were distasteful alike to the statesman and the soldier. But Barneveldt desired to stop persecution and to maintain religious liberty. For that reason alone Maurice adopted the other side. Barneveldt had promoted the raising of local levies in the different States, to preserve order and prevent persecution. Consequently Maurice determined to put down the new levies with his army, and to seize this excuse for bringing about the destruction of Barneveldt and his friends.

Sir Dudley Carleton was instructed to take the side of Maurice against Barneveldt, because the French envoy had been told to adopt the opposite course. Sir Horace Vere, as a military commander, simply obeyed his orders. But his brother's old friend, Sir John Ogle, could not be equally indifferent. He was in command at Utrecht when the fanatical tumults were at their height. Barneveldt had ever been the admirer and warm supporter of his great chief, Sir Francis Vere. Ogle did not conceal his feelings in the matter, and he was removed from his command. The Prince of Orange proceeded to disarm the new levies, and first he marched to Utrecht with Sir Horace Vere, and met with no opposition. He then made a progress through Holland, accompanied by Sir Horace, who received the governorship of Utrecht in July, 1618. (*Carleton Letters*). He was there joined by Lady Vere.

The execution of Barneveldt took place at the Hague on the 13th of May, 1619. There is no indication that Prince Maurice ever felt contrition or regret for having committed this crime. Years afterwards, when the sons of Barneveldt were condemned to death for conspiring against him, their mother petitioned for mercy. The prince asked her why she prayed for the life of her sons, when she had never done so for her husband. She replied that her husband was innocent, her sons were guilty. If Maurice had felt any regret for his past conduct, he would surely have seized this opportunity of showing mercy. But he showed none. If he was a good friend, he was certainly a bitter and relentless foe.

It is to be regretted that Sir Horace Vere should have had any concern in this business, however slight. But he simply obeyed orders as a soldier, and he was absent at Utrecht when Barneveldt was arrested and put to death at the Hague.

The affairs of the Palatinate, and the interest taken in them by the English people, not only because they represented the cause of Protestantism, but also because they involved the welfare of an English princess, led to the employment of Sir Horace Vere on a distant and most difficult military expedition. Early in 1620 he was busily engaged in preparations; his youngest child Susan having been born in the previous year, and baptized on March 20, 1619, in the church of St. Bartholomew the Great. She was his Palatinate child, having been born just before he set out, and dying a few months after his return.

For various reasons there had been differences between Sir Horace Vere, Sir Edward Cecil, and Sir John Ogle. Cecil never lost anything for want of asking, and was not easily satisfied. Ogle saw the conduct of Maurice with regard to the religious troubles in a different light from Vere. There had been estrangements. But through the mediation of Sir Dudley Carleton, the three commanders were reconciled and became good friends before Sir Horace Vere departed for the Palatinate.

CHAPTER 3

The War in the Palatinate

The expedition to the Palatinate was undertaken for a cause which was very dear to the people of England. The defence of a Protestant country and of the rights of an English princess went to the very hearts of Englishmen. But these reasons for undertaking a chivalrous enterprise did not recommend themselves to James I. and his son. They cared nothing for the wishes of the people, less if possible for the cause of Protestantism, and were heartlessly indifferent to the dangers and distress of a daughter and sister.

By the Peace of Augsburg, in 1555, the German princes who favoured the Reformation were allowed to introduce Protestantism into their dominions; but there was a strong Catholic reaction towards the end of the century, and the Protestant cause was threatened. This led to the formation, by German princes of the reformed religions, of the Protestant Union in defence of their creed, in 1608. The head of the Union was Frederick IV., the Elector Palatine, whose wife was Louisa Juliana, sister of Prince Maurice. On the Elector's death he was succeeded by his son, Frederick V., and soon afterwards proposals were made for a marriage between this young prince and Elizabeth, daughter of James I. It is not easy to make out what induced James to consent to this union.

Possibly he wished to spite his wife who detested it, for the reasons which actuated him were generally as base as they were foolish. (Anne of Denmark was a Roman Catholic, had no influence with her husband, and lived apart from him). His consent was given. Elizabeth was married to the Elector Frederick on February 14, 1613, and she proceeded to Heidelberg, the capital of her husband's dominions, attended by a gay train of English courtiers. The Palatinate was then one of the most flourishing states in Germany, and Frederick was made chief of the Protestant Union, which included the Elector of

Brandenburg, the Duke of Würtemberg, the Margraves of Anspach and Baden Durlach, and the Duke of Neuburg.

For the first five years of their married life Frederick and Elizabeth passed a time of happy prosperity at Heidelberg. Frederick made a garden for his wife, by cutting terraces in the steep cliffs below the castle, planting orange and mulberry trees, and leading cascades to fall over the cliffs. (Benger's *Life of the Queen of Bohemia*, i.). He strove to convert the castle of Heidelberg and its grounds into a place of all earthly delights, and for a time he succeeded. But unwisdom and ambition shattered all this happiness for ever. The Bohemians, dissatisfied with their Hapsburg rulers, declared their monarchy to be elective, deposed their king, Ferdinand II., and offered the crown to the Elector Palatine. The decree of deposition was dated August 16, and Ferdinand was chosen Emperor of Germany on August 18, 1619. Frederick hesitated for a time, but at last he accepted the offer. He and his wife set out from Heidelberg, and in October they reached Prague, and were crowned King and Queen of Bohemia.

By this fatal act the whole of Catholic Germany, led by the Duke of Bavaria, was roused against Frederick. The Elector of Saxony and the Landgrave of Hesse maintained an unfriendly neutrality; and the princes of the Protestant Union, although they declared that they were willing to defend the hereditary dominions of the Elector Palatine, refused altogether to meddle in the affairs of Bohemia. (By the treaty of Ulm, on June 23. 1620, the Protestant princes agreed with the Duke of Bavaria and the Catholic League not to interfere in the Bohemian question).

Frederick only had an inefficient force under the Prince of Anhalt, and a mercenary army raised and commanded by Count Ernest Mansfelt. From the first his cause in Bohemia was hopeless.

But this was not the worst. The emperor resolved that Frederick's hereditary dominions should be taken from him. As all the Catholic forces of Germany were engaged in the destruction of Frederick's hopes in Bohemia, it was arranged between the emperor and the archdukes, that a Spanish Army under Spinola should march from Brussels and overrun the Palatinate.

All eyes were turned to England, but, alas! the great queen was dead. James would send embassies, would give advice, but would not help. The States General ordered their envoy, Noel Caron, to press the King of England to comply with the wishes of his people, and to take up arms in defence of his son-in-law and of religion. Frederick himself sent Count Dohna as an envoy to James, to entreat him to interfere on his behalf. The English people were indignant at the contemptible conduct of their rulers. James was daily urged to take action, but he cared as little for the great cause as he did for his unfortunate daughter. In fact, he was at that very time coquetting with Spain, and hoping to get a large dowry through a Spanish marriage. He had the meanness to ask the Dutch to defend his own daughter's rights. At last he consented to allow Count Dohna to raise a body of volunteers in England for the defence of the Palatinate.

The enthusiasm was great throughout the country when the news of even this small concession spread abroad. There could be no doubt to whom Count Dohna would offer the command of this forlorn hope. Sir Horace Vere was, since his brother's death, the ablest English military officer then living. He was too modest to seek the appointment, but he accepted it without hesitation when it was offered to him. (On October 1 1619, he wrote to Sir Dudley Carleton "that there is much seeking for the command of such troops as his Majesty shall employ for Bohemia.")

Sir Edward Cecil had used all the interest he possessed to get the command for himself, and was very angry at being disappointed.

******

The Duke of Buckingham, to whom Cecil paid humble court intended that his flatterer should have the command; and if it had been in the gift of James, Buckingham's wish would have been law. As it was, Cecil was furious, abusing and insulting Count Dohna. As for Buckingham, he treated Cecil's rejection as a personal insult to himself.

******

Never was service more popular. The flower of the young nobility pressed forward for the honour of serving under Sir Horace Vere, and volunteers crowded to the standard in the city of London by beat of drum. (Camden's *Annals*). James had only sanctioned the raising of one regiment, but it was a large one, consisting of 2,200 men complete. The historian of the expedition says:

> This regiment was the gallantest for the persons and outward presence of men that in many ages (I think) hath appeared either at home or abroad.

The Earls of Oxford and Essex raised 250 men apiece, and Arthur Wilson, the historian, accompanied Essex. The gallant John Burrough was sergeant-major general.

******

The family of Burgh, or Burrough, descended from Hubert de Burgh, Earl of Kent, who died in 1243. Sir Thomas de Burg fought for Edward IV. at Barnet, and married Elizabeth, daughter of Sir Henry Percy, the heiress of Gainsborough. Sir Thomas, his son, was created Baron Burgh of Gainsborough, in 1487, by Henry VII. The sixth Lord Burgh was governor of the Brill, and died in 1594. There were two Sir John Burroughs who distinguished themselves in the Low Countries. One was a brother of the sixth Lord Burgh. He was knighted by Leicester, and also by Henry IV. in France, and was killed in a duel on March 7, 1594, aged thirty-two. The Sir John Burrough who served in the Palatinate was of course much younger, and of a different family, although, no doubt, descended from the same ancestors. He was a son of Richard Burrough of Stow, near Lincoln, who died in 1616, and to whose memory there is a brass monument in Stow church. His mother was Amy, daughter of A. Dillington, Esq., of the Isle of Wight, who died in 1631.

******

Among the other officers were Sir Gerard Herbert, Sir Robert Knolles, Sir Edward Sackville, Sir Charles Rich, Sir John Wentworth; Captains William and John Fairfax, Greatorex, Pointer, Buck, Stafford, Wilmot, Knightley, and Robert Markham. The chaplain was Dr. Burgess. On the 9th of July, 1620, Sir Horace Vere went to Theobalds to take leave of the King, and on the 22nd the well-equipped little expedition sailed from Gravesend.

The service on which Vere was now engaged appeared to those acquainted with the state of affairs to be one of great risk. Sir Dudley Carleton, in August, 1620, wrote:

> We cannot yet conceive with what safety they can make into the Palatinate; Spinola being before them with one army, Don Luis de Velasco in the way with another. Spinola has 30,000 men, and departed from Brussels towards Maastricht. The Prince of Orange has left the Hague for Arnhem.—Carleton to Naunton, Aug. 8, 1620. *Carleton Letters.*

In fact, Spinola had already marched to the Rhine with upwards of 24,000 men, (he left Brussels on August 9th), leaving Velasco in the Netherlands with an army 18,000 strong to watch Prince Maurice. Spinola crossed the Rhine below Coblentz, feigning a march to Bohemia, but suddenly wheeled, recrossed the river, and entered the city of Mayence on the 19th of August. The Princes of the Union had assembled a force under the Margrave of Anspach, in compliance with their engagement to defend the Palatinate, and were encamped at Oppenheim, on the left bank of the Rhine, between Mayence and Worms. The English envoys, Sir Edward Conway and Sir Richard Weston hurried to Oppenheim to confer with the princes, and found that the Margrave had with him a force of 22,550 men. (Consisting of 13,600 foot and 8,950 horse, under the Margraves of Anspach and Baden, the Duke of Würtemberg, the Landgrave of Hesse, and Count of Solms).

✶✶✶✶✶✶

Son of Sir Jerome Weston of Roxwell, co. Essex. Sir Richard was born in 1577, was ambassador to Bohemia and Brussels, and Chancellor of the Exchequer. In 1628 he was created Baron Weston of Neyland, became Lord Treasurer and K. G., and in 1633 Earl of Portland. He died in 1634, and the peerage became extinct on the death of his son, the fourth Earl, in 1688.

✶✶✶✶✶✶

But the leaders were lukewarm and apathetic. They were no match for Spinola, who was watching them from Mayence, where he had established his base of operations. On the 30th of August the active Genoese made a rapid march up the valley of the Nahe, and captured Kreuznach. The princes of the Union then retreated, in some confusion, to Worms, and Spinola entered Oppenheim on the 4th of September. The Duke of Deux Fonts was conducting the civil administration of the Palatinate, in the absence of the Elector.

The object of Sir Horace Vere was to form a junction with the army of the Margrave of Anspach, but the distance was very great, and the long march had to be made with a watchful enemy of vastly superior force ever on the alert. It was indeed a forlorn hope. It was arranged that the little English force should be accompanied by a body of Dutch cavalry under Count Henry of Nassau, until they were within touch of their German allies. Vere marched from Arnhem to Wesel, where preparations were made to cross the Rhine. The expedition reached Wesel on the 25th of August, 1620.

The progress of this truly national enterprise was watched in England with the deepest interest and anxiety. Many a family, through the length and breadth of the land, had a dear one in the regiment of Sir Horace. Letters doubtless passed to and fro, full of fond hopes and cheering news. Few have been preserved. But we have the correspondence of the two gallant young sons of Sir Thomas Fairfax, the old friend and comrade of Sir Francis Vere in years gone by.

******

Sir Thomas Fairfax of Denton, Nunappleton, and Bilbrough, in Yorkshire, was born at Bilbrough in 1560. He served with Sir Francis Vere, with whom he formed a close friendship, and was knighted before Rouen in 1594. He was created Baron Fairfax of Cameron on May 4, 1627, and died on May 2, 1640. He lies buried under an altar tomb in Otley church. He married Ellen, daughter of Robert Aske of Aughton, and had twelve children. The eldest, Ferdinando, second Lord Fairfax, was father of Sir Thomas (third Lord) Fairfax, the Parliament general. Henry was in holy orders, Rector of Bolton Percy, ancestor of the present, (1878), Lord Fairfax. Charles was an accomplished writer and lawyer as well as a soldier. William was born in 1593, John in 1597, at Nunappleton. There were also Thomas and Peregrine.

******

He was now settled quietly down as a country gentleman at Denton, in Yorkshire, writing political pamphlets and breeding horses. But the departure of his boys aroused in him all the feelings of youth. They were no sooner gone than he longed to gladden his eyes with the sight of them once more, before they were face to face with Spinola and the horrors of war. William Fairfax wrote to one of his brothers:

> The report of Spinola's intention to oppose the march has brought my gray-headed old father into the Low Countries.

Old Sir Thomas marched with his boys as far as Wesel, whence William wrote:

> My father lodges with his sons in the field before Wesel. (*Fairfax Corr.*, i.).

Here he bade them a last farewell. He was destined never to see them again.

Sir Horace Vere crossed the Rhine by a bridge of boats provided by Prince Maurice, a little below Wesel, and marched through the territory of Jülich, Count Henry of Nassau, with 2,000 horse, clearing the road before him and acting as a guide. When they approached

Coblentz they intended to cross the Rhine again into the Nassau territory. But knowing that Spinola would have spies out in all directions to bring him news, Count Henry made a feint towards the Moselle in sight of the walls of Coblentz. They were so near that a bullet from the town passed between Sir Horace Vere and Lord Essex, striking a gentleman named Flood on the elbow. That night there was a skirmish between some English and the country people, for Captain Fairfax being sent to ask for provisions, he was fired upon, and some of his men were hurt. But he continued to advance, and the people took to their boats and hurried down to Coblentz. The town of Bacherach, higher up the Rhine, was still held for the Elector. Sir Horace, therefore, sent Captains Row and Baxter, with ninety-four sick and wounded, to that town by water. A few days afterwards Bacherach was summoned by Spinola, and yielded without any resistance. The English were treated civilly and allowed to return home.

After remaining a day before Coblentz, Sir Horace and Count Henry drew back about two miles, and crossed the whole force over the Rhine, in punts that had been collected for the purpose, on the 16th of September. They advanced three miles on the other side, to the village of Hembach, the same night. They then made long marches over the hilly country of the Taunus towards Frankfort. Spinola was apprised of their movements. He passed over the Main with all his cavalry and 4,000 foot, to intercept the English; but the stream was full and strong, and he lost some of his wagons and fieldpieces, which induced him to retreat.

Meanwhile Sir Horace Vere and Count Henry led their troops across the Main by a ford near Frankfort, on the 24th of September. The infantry were up to their middles, and that night the men were sorely in need of rest. But they had to stand to their arms, there being two alarms of Spinola's approach. Next day there was a long march to Darmstadt. As Sir Horace Vere was now close to the forces of the Union, Count Henry of Nassau took his leave, and returned to Holland with his cavalry. Next day Vere was joined by 1,500 German horse, sent by the Margrave of Anspach, and on the 27th of September he reached the town of Bensheim.

Sir Horace Vere was leading an enterprise of knight-errantry, and he had penetrated into the very heart of the German Fatherland. The Rhine flows through the centre of this famed region, with flourishing cities along its course. On its left bank are Speyer, Frankenthal, Worms, Oppenheim, and Mayence; and on its right bank is the important

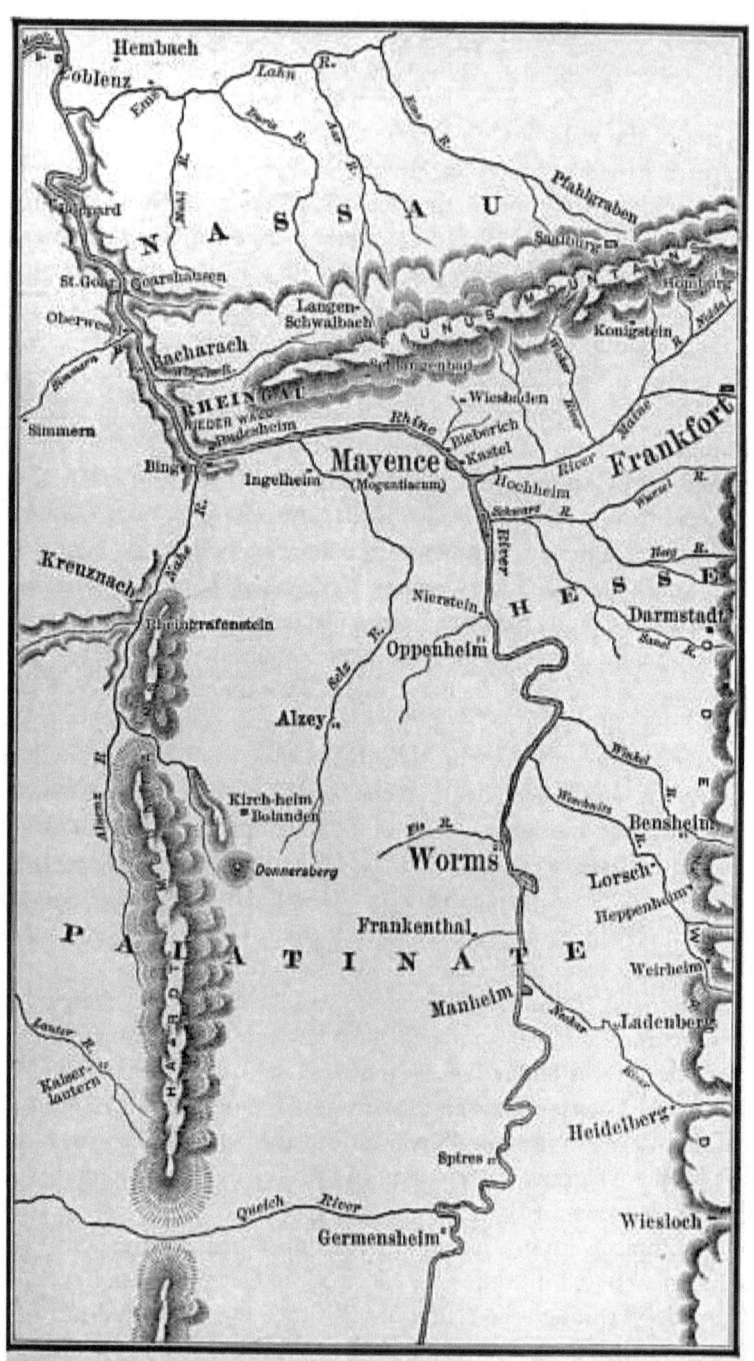

THE FIELD OF THE PALATINATE.

city of Manheim. The Lower Palatinate extended over the country on both banks. To the west a flat plain borders the river, and further inland there are bare undulating hills and dales, backed by the Donnerberg and other peaks of the Hardt range, which, on the banks of the Nahe, near Kreuznach, forms grand porphyritic cliffs.

Here is the famous Rheingrafenberg precipice. To the east of the Rhine there is also a plain near the river, but a few miles inland the forest-clad hills of the Odenwald rise to nearly 2,000 feet. To the south is the beautiful gorge of the Neckar, with the city of Heidelberg lining the riverside, and its famous castle crowning the hill. To the north is the line of the River Main, with the imperial town of Frankfort seated on its banks. This region is the centre of the romantic legends of the *Nibelungen-lied;* but they are equalled in interest by the exploit undertaken by the Puritans of England in defence of their religion and their princess. For it was the people, and especially the Puritan party, not the royalist courtiers, who displayed this true spirit of chivalry.

Bensheim was then a little walled town, nestling at the foot of the Odenwald, with vine-clad slopes backed by wooded uplands. Here the English rested; the troops exercising by divisions every day, in motions and postures. (*Fairfax Corr.*, i.). Sir Horace divided his little force into four divisions of 500 men each. The Earls of Oxford and Essex led the first. The former had sown his wild oats, and was serving steadily under his illustrious kinsman. The latter had gone through agonies of sorrow and mortification, due to the infamy and profligacy of the Stuart court. (The careers of Carr and his mistress, Lady Essex, form a loathsome story, which occupies the foulest page in English history).

After long retirement he had adopted the profession of arms. The second division was under Sir Charles Rich and Sir John Wentworth. The third was commanded by Colonel Pointer, with Captains Greatorex and Fairfax; and the fourth by Sir Gerard Herbert, Sir Stafford Wilmot, who died soon afterwards, and Captain Buck. The English were to have the van of all the field, and Vere was to be general of the whole force for the King of Bohemia.

On leaving Bensheim Sir Horace Vere marched over the plain of the Rhine, and by Lorsch and the adjacent forests, to the island of Rosengarten, on the banks of the river. This was the scene of one of the most famous achievements in the *Nibelungen-lied*, where Siegfried slew the dragon, or *worm*, whence the city took its name, which was visible on the opposite shore. About a quarter of a mile from the river bank the eastern wall of Worms could be seen,—built of sandstone of a warm red colour, with high square towers at intervals. Behind rose the beautiful cathedral, with its exquisite arcaded domes and minaret-like towers. At Worms the English were to join the army of the Protestant Union, and they crossed the Rhine by a bridge of boats on the 1st of October, 1620. The Margrave of Anspach and the other princes received them on the opposite bank, and accompanied Sir Horace Vere into the city. They expressed admiration at the equipment and bearing of the English infantry; "wondering at the gallantry of such foot, who were with them the meanest of the people." (Wilson).

In those days the Episcopal palace to the northwest of the cathedral, where the famous Diet assembled to hear Luther's defence, was still standing, and was doubtless occupied by the princes and the English general. But there was also an inn in the Andreas Strasse, with the sign of the "*Römische Kaiser*" which was opened in 1604. It is still flourishing as the "*Alter Kaiser*" hotel.

Spinola had recrossed the Rhine at Mayence, and had taken the field on the left bank, but his exact position was unknown to the allies. It was, however, resolved that the Protestant army should march with the object of bringing him to battle. The princes had only reinforced Vere with 4,000 horse and 6,000 foot. Marching westward over a succession of bare undulating hills, Vere's army reached the town of Alzey, in a deep hollow, on the banks of the little River Selz, which falls into the Rhine between Mayence and Bingen. Here there was an important castle belonging to the Palatinate, of which there are still extensive ruins.

Two days after his arrival at Alzey, Vere heard that Spinola with his whole army was in his rear and approaching the town. He at once sounded to arms, marching out in the direction of Worms, and in three hours the scouts were skirmishing. The cavalry of the princes advanced, but were repulsed by Spinola's cannon. The fieldpieces of the allies were then got into position on a hill flanking the enemy's right; a wide bottom and vineyard-clad slopes being between the two armies. Vere resolved to make an attack with a picked body of English infantry. He selected 80 men from each division to lead, and while the chaplain, Dr. Burgess, was encouraging them with a short discourse, he went to reconnoitre, accompanied by Oxford and Essex. To his great disappointment he found that Spinola was in full retreat, with the foot guarding a train of wagons, and the cavalry bringing up the rear. The Earl of Essex galloped off to the Margrave, and urged him to follow with his horse. Anspach replied that there was a fort a little further on, and that he would be obliged to pass within range of it. When he heard this excuse, Vere exclaimed, with some scorn, "When shall we fight, then, if we shun the cannon!"

This was the only time when Spinola showed any inclination to give battle. He began a succession of marches and counter-marches, with the apparent object of wearing out his antagonist. Wilson says that "he led them a dance, like children at hide-and-seek." Meanwhile, winter was approaching, and the nights passed on the bare and desolate hills were cold and miserable. One night the cold was so great and fuel so scarce that the commanders sacrificed several wagons wherewith to make fires and warm themselves and the men. Eventually, towards the middle of November, it became necessary to go into winter-quarters; and Vere resolved to hold the three most important strongholds of the Palatinate, dividing his English among them. He occupied Manheim himself, Sir Gerard Herbert became governor of Heidelberg Castle, and the Sergeant-Major General John Burrough undertook to defend Frankenthal, an important place near the Rhine, between Worms and Speyer.

But the hope of success appeared more forlorn than ever. News arrived that on the 29th October a battle was fought outside Prague, in which the army of the Elector Palatine was totally defeated, while Count Mansfelt was sulking at Pilsen. Frederick and Elizabeth became homeless fugitives, and they took refuge at the Hague. This event would liberate the army of the Catholic League, which would be able to join the Spaniards in the conquest of the Palatinate. The news of the battle of Prague reached London on the 24th of November. The agitation was great; the people laid the blame on the king, who made promises of help which he had no intention of keeping. He betrayed his true feeling by his refusal to allow his daughter to come to England. She and her husband were hospitably received by Prince Maurice at the Hague, and the States General granted them an allowance. Vere sent the Earls of Essex and Oxford home, to urge upon the English government the necessity for granting help if he were to hold his position, and to explain the state of affairs.

But their representations were useless. James was busy making court to Count Gondomar, and all his courtiers were expected to show their loyalty by following his example. The Spanish ambassador used to live at Ely House in Holborn, and went to court in a litter by way of Drury Lane and the Strand. He gave the courtiers many presents, and his daily journeys to court resembled triumphal processions, the royalist ladies saluting him from the balconies. Away, then, with England's interests and English honour! What cared James and his court whether Vere and his forlorn hope were annihilated in the Palatinate, or whether an English princess became a homeless fugitive!

Public affairs looked gloomy enough, but the English troops in the Palatinate were also saddened by a melancholy event of a private nature, before they went into garrison. A young man named Duncombe, who was a soldier in the division of the Earl of Oxford, left a young lady in England to whom he had vowed his love; but his father refused his consent, and sent him to the Palatinate. During the campaign he wrote a loving letter to the girl, and another to his father, in which he promised to renounce her. But unfortunately the directions of the letters were interchanged, so that the young lady received the one intended for his father; and that for the young lady fell into the father's hands. In course of time he received furious answers from both, which were incomprehensible to him. The grief at last overcame his reason, and he killed himself, to the great sorrow and regret of all his comrades. Wilson remarked on this sad event that:

> By Duncombe's example parents who are too rigid with their children may see what murderers they are; for it was not the young man's hand, but the old man's hard heart that killed him.

Wilson went home with Lord Essex. Referring to this first year, he said:

> I have the more particularly described this expedition because I was an eye-witness of what passed.

The Spaniards and Imperialists held the open country, while the English protected the three last strongholds of the unfortunate Frederick; and in the spring of 1621 the gallant followers of Sir Horace Vere were entirely deserted by their allies. The princes dissolved the Protestant Union on the 2nd of April, and they signed a treaty at Mayence on the 4th of May, by which they agreed to abandon the Palatinate and its English defenders to their fate. Vere received his commission to command in the Lower Palatinate from Frederick, but his men were now ill paid and badly provided, for the fund with which he left England had been exhausted. There came some prospect of help as the year rolled on. Ernest Mansfelt was one of the most remarkable military commanders of that age.

It was indeed only in a very exceptional state of society that such a commander could have existed. He was at the head of a freebooting army of about 15,000 men, recruited by himself, and he served whom he chose. He, however, continued faithful to the unhappy Elector, and though he received large bribes from the other side, he merely took them without in the least altering his course of action. Another friend in need was young Christian of Brunswick, who for love of his cousin Elizabeth, (his mother was a sister of Anne of Denmark, Elizabeth's mother), raised a small army in the north of Germany.

Spinola left the Palatinate in 1621, for in that year the truce of twelve years with the States General came to an end, and it was necessary that he should take command of the army which was to oppose the Prince of Orange. (The Archduke Albert died in 1621, aged sixty-two; from which time, until her death in 1632, his widow, the Archduchess Isabella, ruled the Spanish Netherlands alone). He had, in fact, arranged his plans for the siege of Bergen-op-Zoom. But he left a Spanish force under Gonzales de Cordova and Verdugo to cooperate with the Imperialist general, Count Tilly, against Sir Horace Vere. Mansfelt and Christian of Brunswick, judging that they could do little good in the field against Tilly and Cordova, resolved to fight their way to the seat of war in the Netherlands.

In an encounter with Cordova's army near Namur, young Christian lost his bridle arm, and many English officers had the opportunity of fighting gallantly for their princess, who was so shamefully deserted by her kindred in England, but who was called "the Queen of Hearts" by all true Englishmen, and "who in those days carried a great stream of affection towards her." (Wilson). Maurice was thus strongly reinforced, and Spinola was obliged to raise the siege of Bergen-op-Zoom. During the winter Mansfelt went to Hagenau and his recruiting ground in Alsace, while Christian raised a new army in the north; both intending to return to the Palatinate in the ensuing year.

Meanwhile, Cordova had been pressing Sir Horace very closely by cutting off supplies, and in September, 1620, he laid siege to Frankenthal. This town is in the flat plain of the Rhine, about a mile from the left bank of the river. It must have been an ancient place, for it contains the ruins of a Romanesque cloister, but it first became commercially prosperous after the arrival of many skilled Dutch artisans in about 1550, fugitives from the cruelties of Alva. The Romanesque church, with its richly ornamented portal, was given to these people, and was known as the "old Dutch church." It stood in the marketplace near the centre of the town, and its style of architecture is indicated by the façade of the cloister which survives. The town was within a parallelogram, 600 yards from north to south by 460; but the defences were antiquated, and not suited to resist siege operations in the seventeenth century. Cordova, however, was unprovided with a regular siege train.

The old walls were built of the same warm red stone which so heightens the beauty of Worms cathedral. There were earth ramparts behind the walls, and circular bastions at the angles, perforated by slits for shooting arrows. (The southeast bastion is still standing, 1878, and some bits of the walls). A running stream entered the town near the centre of the south wall, and left it, flowing to the Rhine, on the east side, and the means were thus supplied of filling a moat. There were four gates, one in the centre of each side. The main street led from north to south through the market-place, called the *Wurmser Strasse* on the north and the *Speyerer Strasse* on the south side; and in the southwest angle of the town there was a large house, surrounded by a garden, called the *Schafforet*. It belonged to the Elector, and was originally intended as the dower house for Elizabeth.

Stout John Burrough did what was possible to strengthen the defences. Outside each gate he constructed a ravelin, surrounded by water from the moat; and where the stream flowed in, by the Speyer Gate, he added an additional outwork. The east ravelin, facing the Rhine, was entrusted to the English, and was known as the English ravelin. In July, 1621, Dr. Burgess, the chaplain, left Frankenthal to go home, much regretted by the little garrison. ("Whom we greatly miss." (*Fairfax Correspondence*, i.). By September Frankenthal was closely besieged by Cordova, who pressed forward his approaches vigorously. Burrough had with him those gallant and accomplished brothers William and John Fairfax, and young Robert Markham, a nephew of Francis and Gervase Markham, who served under Sir Francis Vere, and wrote works on military subjects.

✶✶✶✶✶✶

William had especially distinguished himself at Cambridge. Though so young, he was a good scholar and an antiquary. He corresponded with Selden. In one of his last letters he expressed a wish that his old manuscripts and Roman coins should be presented to Selden.

✶✶✶✶✶✶

Early in September there was a sortie, in which John Fairfax was wounded in the arm. On Friday night, the 5th of October, John Fairfax was stationed in the Speyer outwork with eighty men. Just after dusk he was furiously assaulted, the work was carried by the enemy, and every soul in it was put to the sword. William Fairfax, then acting as sergeant-major, hurried to the rescue, but was too late. His gallant attempt to enter the work was fiercely met at push of pike and repulsed. He himself was wounded, but was rescued and carried into the adjoining ravelin by Foxcroft, his clerk, and a soldier named Carr. His wound was in the leg, but a week afterwards he could walk with the help of a stick, and went down into the English ravelin. There he was struck on the thigh by one of the enemy's shot, the bone being broken. John Burrough says in the letter announcing the news to the broken-hearted old father:

> He died towards morning. . . . . They both died with the general fame of honest men and valiant gentlemen.—*Fairfax Correspondence*, i.

Lord Clifford also wrote a letter of condolence to Sir Thomas Fairfax. The gallant brothers were buried with military honours, and a monument was erected to their memory in the old church at Frankenthal.

******

The inscription was copied by their nephew, Brian Fairfax. The church was destroyed by the French in 1689, and the monument has disappeared. About eighteen old monuments have recently been collected and placed in the public garden at Frankenthal, but that to the brothers Fairfax does not appear to be among them. Some of the inscriptions are, however, quite obliterated.

******

Two or three days after the death of William Fairfax, Sir Horace Vere marched from Manheim, and Cordova was forced to raise the siege of Frankenthal.

******

There is a letter at Dropmore (Mr. Fortescue's) from Sir Horace Vere to the favourite Buckingham, dated December 15, 1621, in which he describes the condition to which his troops had been reduced.

******

Early in 1622 Mansfelt had collected a considerable force at Germersheim on the Rhine, above Speyer; and the Margrave of Baden Durlach was prepared to cooperate with a small army, while Christian of Brunswick was advancing from the north. Mansfelt invited the Elector Palatine to join him, and after some hesitation the unlucky Frederick left the Hague, and travelling through France *incognito*, he arrived at Germersheim on the 2nd of April. He was received with some enthusiasm, and Mansfelt took the field against the Imperialist army under Count Tilly. At first there was a gleam of success. Tilly was defeated at Wiesloch, south of Heidelberg. Frederick and Mansfelt then captured the town of Ladenburg, and the Elector once more visited his towns of Manheim and Heidelberg, with their trusty English garrisons. But this was his last glimpse of good-fortune.

Cordova hastened to reinforce Tilly. The Margrave of Baden Durlach declined to unite his troops with those of Mansfelt. He preferred to act on his own account, and entrenched himself at Wimpfen, in the upper valley of the Neckar. There, on the 26th of April, he was attacked by Tilly and Cordova, who practically annihilated his force, capturing all his artillery. This left the road open to Alsace, and as all Mansfelt's plunder was stored at Hagenau he hurried off for its protection, leaving the Elector to his fate. Soon afterwards Christian of Brunswick was surprised in his camp at Höchst, on the Main, a few miles below Frankfort, and entirely defeated. (There are two large pictures at Brussels of the battles of Wimpfen and Höchst, by P. Snayers. They are well worthy of examination, as they show the arms, accoutrements, and system of formation. The latter also shows the way in which a field camp was formed in those days.)

James now sent Lord Chichester as an envoy to negotiate an armistice between the Elector and Tilly. But it was too late. Chichester found Frederick at Manheim when he arrived, and he attempted to open negotiations.

******

Arthur Chichester was the second son of Sir John Chichester of Raleigh, in Devonshire, by Gertrude, daughter of Sir William Courtenay of Powderham Castle. He was at Exeter College, Oxford, but early embraced a military career. first going to Ireland with a young Fortescue as his companion. He was in Lord Sheffield's ship at the repulse of the Spanish Armada, was in the Ostend garrison under Edward Morris, served in France, and was at the Cadiz action under the Earl of Essex. He received knighthood in France from Henry IV. Going to Ireland with Lord Mountjoy, he was made sergeant-major general of the army there. In 1604 he became Lord Deputy of Ireland, holding the post for twelve years. In 1614 he was created Baron Chichester of Belfast. He died childless in 1624. His life was written by Sir Faithful Fortescue, and an elegy by A. Spicer. The Marquis of Donegal is descended from his brother Edward.

******

Tilly, however, refused to treat, telling Chichester that he did not consider him as an ambassador. Sir Arthur replied that if his master had sent him with brave men instead of useless messages he would soon show Tilly that he was a soldier as well as an ambassador. He went to Frankenthal to help Burrough with his advice, and remained there from July until the beginning of September. Frederick, in despair, on the 13th of June, 1622, departed from Manheim, never to return.

The little English band of heroes was now indeed left to its fate. It was divided between the three strongholds of Manheim, Heidelberg, and Frankenthal, under three glorious leaders, Sir Horace Vere, Sir Gerard Herbert, and Sergeant-major General Burrough. They were surrounded by an overwhelming force of Imperialists and Spaniards, under such generals as Tilly, Cordova, and Verdugo. Vere knew that his military position was hopeless, but the three faithful governors resolved to hold out to the last.

******

There are eight important letters from Lord Chichester to Lord Cranfield, written from the Palatinate in 1622, in the possession of Earl De la Warr. One, dated June 2nd, describes the state of army. Another, of June 24th, alludes to the want of money. Three are from Frankenthal, dated July 9th and 22nd, and August 13th. They describe the bad condition of the troops and the movements of Tilly. On September 14th Chichester reports that he left Frankenthal on the 4th, and came to the Frankfort. He also gives an account of the fall of Heidelberg, On November 12th he reports the fall of Manheim.

******

Cordova ravaged the open country and burnt the villages. Tilly occupied the Heiligenberg, a height on the right bank of the Neckar, and threatened Heidelberg on the 20th of June; and on the 15th of August he began the siege in earnest.

The position of Heidelberg in the deep ravine of the Neckar, just at the point where the river issues from the mountains and enters the flat plain of the Rhine, has prevented any great change by an increase in the size of the town. All the positions can be clearly traced out. The beautiful castle still stands on its terrace, commanding the town, and in turn commanded by surrounding wooded heights. There are still the exquisite façades of Otto Heinrich and Friedrich IV., the terrace of the *Altane*, from which one looks down into the streets of the town, and the grand old octagon tower. In the town the tall tower of the "*Heilig-Geis*" still marks the position of the market-place and of the richly carved front of Belier's house; the *Marstall* survives with its old walls and angle bastions, and there is even a tower of the old wall; but the covered wooden bridge, with its towers of defence, has long since been replaced by the present stone bridge.

Sir Horace Vere had entrusted the defence of the town of Heidelberg to a Dutch officer named Van der Merven, while Herbert had command of the castle. The town was divided into the *Altstadt*, between the castle-hill and the Neckar, and the *Vorstadt*, extending westward to the plain of the Rhine. Both were surrounded by a strong wall with towers, and the bridge was well fortified. On the south side of the *Vorstadt* there was an outwork on the slope of the hill called the *Trotz Kaiser*, and two smaller forts. But the works were of great extent, while the garrison was weak and insufficiently provided with supplies. The castle was still more difficult to defend. It is true that it was impregnable on the side of the Neckar, where the cliffs rise almost sheer from the town. But on the south the steep mountains continue to rise abruptly, and completely command the castle.

Towering above the others is the *Königstuhl*, and to the west of it there is another height called the *Geisberg*, at the foot of which is the *Trotz Kaiser* fort. A road led from the castle terraces eastward between the hills and the cliffs overhanging the Neckar, to the pretty valley of the *Wolfsbrunnen*, a favourite resort of Frederick and Elizabeth in their happy days. Herbert did his best to put the castle in a posture of defence. Ravelins and half-moons were thrown up in the lovely terraced gardens, where Solomon de Caus had exhausted all his art to combine the wealth of exotic vegetation with the beauties of nature. He also constructed forts on the road from the Wolfsbrunnen, with entrenched outworks across the space now occupied by the Schloss Hotel.

✶✶✶✶✶✶

Solomon de Caus was the artist employed by the Elector Palatine to design the gardens of Heidelberg Castle. He published a description of them, entitled *Hortus Palatinus*.

✶✶✶✶✶✶

On the 15th of August Count Tilly began the siege in earnest, investing both the castle and the town. He planted batteries on the *Königstuhl* and the *Geisberg*, as well as along the right bank of the Neckar, and began approaches on the Wolfsbrunnen road, in front of the *Trotz Kaiser*, and against the western wall of the town. A heavy cannonade was commenced on the 22nd, and continued for twenty days. An attempt to storm the town on the 5th of September was repulsed, but the *Trotz Kaiser* and other outworks were captured. A heavy fire of artillery was then kept up for several days, the gates were blown in, and on the 16th the town was taken by storm. Van der Merven and the soldiers retreated into the castle, but Tilly gave Heidelberg up to sack and pillage, and appalling atrocities were committed on the hapless people for three days. Forty houses were burnt to the ground.

Sir Gerard Herbert defended the castle for some days longer. With heroic resolution he held the outwork in the garden, repulsing all the assaults of the enemy, until this gallant hero fell, mortally wounded. Van der Merven then surrendered the castle on the 19th, the troops being allowed to march out with all the honours of war.

★★★★★★

Little injury was done to Heidelberg Castle during Tilly's siege. After the Elector Charles Louis was restored to his dominions by the Peace of Munster, he kept his court there for thirty years, until his death in 1680. The destruction of the castle took place during the atrocious devastation of the Palatinate by the French in 1693 and 1694. Then it was that the "Shattered Tower" (*Gesprengte Thurm*) was blown up, and the palace was gutted by order of the French General Melac. There are two plans of Heidelberg, showing the defences and Tilly's siege works of 1622, in the museum at the castle—

1. *Vahre contrafactur der Churfurstlichen Statt Heidelberg und wie dieselbige von General Tilly belagert und eingenomen worden, anno* 1622. (Matthaeus Merianus.)

2. *Vera effigies urbis Heidelbergae quo eadem modo, anno 1622 tempore obsessionis fortificata et extracta erat.*

★★★★★★

Sir Horace Vere was now besieged in Manheim, with a garrison of 1,400 men, to defend very extensive fortifications. He had no money and no supplies. When he was reduced to extremities he retired into the citadel, and capitulated on honourable terms in the end of September. He and his brave garrison marched out with all the honours of war. Sir Horace went first to Frankfort, and thence to the Hague. The gallant Burrough still held out at Frankenthal. The defences were antiquated and feeble, his supplies exhausted. Yet he maintained the place against Tilly, and afterwards against Verdugo and the Spaniards all through the winter. He did not surrender until the 14th of April, 1623, and then he did so only by reason of orders from home. Moreover, the surrender was not made to the Imperialists, but to the Archduchess Isabella, with a promise that the place should be restored to the Queen of Bohemia as her dowry. The promise was broken. Burrough was knighted for his defence of Frankenthal.

******

Sir John Burrough was second in command in the expedition to the Isle of Rhé. Robert Markham remained with him at Frankenthal to the last, and accompanied him to Rhé, where both were slain. Markham, however, lived long enough to write a poetical elegy on his beloved commander Sir John Burrough, which was afterwards published. Sir John was buried in Westminster Abbey.

******

Sir Horace Vere returned to England in January, 1624, and was received by King James so gratefully and thankfully, that, forgetting himself, His Majesty stood bare-headed before his illustrious subject.

The Palatinate was the most prosperous country in Germany before the Elector accepted the crown of Bohemia. From that time until the end of the Thirty Years' War it was devastated most ruthlessly by successive armies. Villages were burnt, crops destroyed, the inhabitants killed or hunted into the woods like wild beasts. At length, when Charles Louis, the son of the ill-fated Frederick, was restored to part of his dominions by the Peace of Westphalia, he returned to a scene of heart-rending desolation. For thirty years he devoted all his energies to the good of his people and to the restoration of their prosperity. His memory was justly revered. In England he took the side of the parliamentary party, which always advocated his mother's cause, against the brother who treated her with cold neglect. In Germany he was the father of his people.

Chapter 4

Death of John Vere

The conduct of the Palatinate enterprise by Sir Horace Vere added to his fame as a resolute and able general. The insurmountable difficulties of the undertaking, with the forces at his command, and the way in which he faced them and held his own against tremendous odds for upwards of two years, were fully recognized by his countrymen. On February 16, 1623, he was appointed Master-General of the Ordnance for life, and on July 20, 1624, he became a member of the Council of War.

Domestic sorrows, occurring at this time, cast a passing shadow over his public success. Little Susan, his youngest child, born just before he set out for the Palatinate, was taken from him soon after his return, at the age of four years. She was buried on May 24, 1623. John Vere died a year afterwards, on April 12, 1624. This eldest brother had always been very dear to the three soldiers, Francis, Horace, and Robert. His house at Kirby was their home whenever they came on brief visits to England. Here the aged mother lived in peaceful comfort with her eldest boy, while the others were exposed to the dangers and hardships of a soldier's life. John acted as an agent for his brothers, transacting their business and looking after their interests in England. After his mother's death in 1617, he and his wife continued to live quietly at Kirby, but they had no children who survived infancy.

John had one illegitimate son. He became a distinguished soldier, yet he caused his father much remorse and anxiety. John Vere was for several years in dreadful apprehension of God's wrath, "but at last, by God's goodness and blessing on the ministry, he received comfort and died triumphant." He made his will in 1612, but added no less than seven codicils between that year and his death. Tilbury and the other lands of Sir Francis Vere had reverted to his elder brother on the death of his widow. (She died in 1623).

John left Stone Lodge, near Greenhithe, in Kent, and a house in Aldgate, to his wife absolutely, as they were her property before marriage; and he left Tilbury and Kirby Hall to his wife for her life, and then to his brother Horace. He left an annuity to his sister Frances, Lady Harcourt; and another annuity of £40 a year to his nephew Vere Harcourt. He also left a house in Hedingham, and a small endowment in trust for the use of poor people of the parish. By a codicil in 1623, he cancelled the reversion of his estates to his brother Horace, and left them all to his illegitimate son John. But three weeks afterwards he again cancelled this codicil, and gave the reversion to his brother. His mind seems to have vacillated with regard to his duty to this son.

******

John Vere's illegitimate son became Sir John Vere, and sergeant-major in the regiment of his Uncle Horace. He was knighted in 1607. He died in the Low Countries in 1631, and his will, dated Dec. 13, 1630, was administered by Robert, nineteenth Earl of Oxford, on Nov. 14, 1631. Sir John had a son Edward, who was probably the same Edward Vere that became a lieutenant, and was slain at the siege of Maestricht in 1632. He appears to have been illegitimate; for by his wife Mercy, daughter of Sir James Pytts of Kyre Wyre, in Worcestershire, Sir John had an only daughter, Mary, who died intestate and unmarried, administration being granted to her uncle James Pytts, on August 15, 1631. Sir John Vere is mentioned, in legal documents, as of Netherwood.

******

John Vere had reached the age of sixty-six. He was buried in the church at Castle Hedingham, the funeral sermon being preached by Mr. Brewer, on the 15th of April, 1624. A monument was erected to his memory, with an inscription which has now disappeared. (Holman, writing a century ago, says that the reason why the inscription on John Vere's monument was so worn out, was because a school was formerly kept in the chancel of Hedingham church). As John Vere's widow survived Sir Horace, the reversion of Tilbury and Kirby was never enjoyed by the latter.

In 1624 Spinola made great preparations for the siege of Breda, and Sir Horace Vere proceeded to the Hague, to join the army of Prince Maurice, and concert such measures as were practicable for its defence. His young kinsman, the Earl of Oxford, had got into trouble after his return from the Palatinate. He was accused of having "spoken some words to the dishonour of the king and disparagement of his government," for which he was sent to the Tower, (*Rapin*, ii.) and detained there over two years. (He returned from the Palatinate in January, 1621, was committed to the Tower, examined July 13, and enlarged Dec. 30).

He had simply said what everybody else thought. He was, however, fortunate in his matrimonial affairs, for although he had little to offer but his ancient title, he won the heart of Lady Diana Cecil. This was a love match, but the married life of the lovers, which commenced in 1623, was destined to endure for a few months only.

✶✶✶✶✶✶

In a letter from Lord Conway to Buckingham, dated from Whitehall, April 12, 1623, the story of the love of Lord Oxford and Lady Diana is related, and his lordship's poverty is alluded to. Chamberlain, in a letter to Sir Dudley Carleton, dated April 19, 1623, says that Lord Oxford is to have with Lady Diana, £4,000 in money and £5,000 in land.

✶✶✶✶✶✶

In 1624 the Earls of Oxford, Southampton, and Essex, and Lord Willoughby, raised four regiments for service in the Netherlands; and a great dispute arose between the Earls of Oxford and Southampton on a question of precedence. The quarrel gave rise to much correspondence and to official arbitration, but it was closed very summarily. Southampton and his son died of fever at Rosendaal, and not many months had passed before Oxford was also in his grave.

✶✶✶✶✶✶

The Council of War made a report on this question to the king, on July 21, 1624. Oxford was to have precedence at court and in all civil entertainments, Southampton as colonel. The report is signed by Lord Grandison, Lord Chichester, Lord Conway, and Sir John Ogle.

✶✶✶✶✶✶

In the brief remainder of his life, however, he again served under his great kinsman with distinguished gallantry, in attempting the relief of Breda.

The siege of Breda was commenced by Spinola in August, 1624. The occasion was one of great importance, both as regards the strength of the place and the value attached to it, and with reference to the vast preparations that had been made for its reduction. The eyes of all Europe were turned to the historical old Brabant city. In 1404 the heiress of Breda had married Count Engelbert of Nassau, whose splendid tomb still adorns the church, and whose descendants made Breda their chief residence. Henry of Nassau built the castle, which was fortified with walls, bulwarks, and double ditches, and beautified with terraces and pleasant gardens. The turf ramparts were set thick with a continuous row of old oak-trees. Above all rose the spire of the church-tower from the centre of the town, 262 feet high. When William the Taciturn fled to Germany in 1567, Breda was seized for the King of Spain by the Duke of Alva. In 1577 it was retaken by Count Hohenlohe. It was surprised by the Sieour de Hautepenne in 1581, and remained in the power of the Spaniards until, by his famous stratagem of the peat boat, Prince Maurice recovered it in 1590.

The historian of the siege described the country round Breda as:

> Pleasant, rich of corn and pasture, the meadows beset round with young sprouts of trees and separated by small brooks. Rows of trees shaded all the walks and houses round the town; and not far from the walls there were four woods, one of fir and the other three of oak.

The rivers Marke and Aa unite before the walls, and separate to fill the moat, both again joining to form the famous harbour into which the patriot-laden peat boat was piloted thirty-four years before. The walls round the town included fifteen bulwarks, with artillery, numerous ravelins, and five formidable horn works. Justin of Nassau, the half-brother of the Prince of Orange, was governor of Breda, with sixteen companies of infantry and five troops of horse, in all 1,600 men. In addition to the garrison, 1,800 townsmen bore arms under the command of Aertsen, Lord of Wermont, as town colonel. Supplies were sent into the town, consisting of 8,200 measures of wheat, oats, cheese, and dried haberdine.

On the 21st of July, 1624, Spinola set out from Brussels with one division. Two others followed under Don Louis de Velasco, Conde de Salazar, the general of horse, and Juan Bravo, the governor of Antwerp. There were fifteen regiments, consisting of 198 companies of infantry and thirty-nine troops of horse, making a total force of 18,000 men. In five days Spinola reached the village near Breda, called Gilsen. A reconnaissance was made, and Spinola's council pronounced the place impregnable, and dissuaded him from undertaking the siege. A month was wasted in discussion; but on the 26th of August Francisco Medina was sent to occupy Ginehen, the nearest village to Breda, while an Italian regiment was stationed at Terheyde, on the side opposite to Ginehen. Spinola also sent soldiers to the villages of Teteringen and Hage, and made a bridge over the Marke. Juan Niño de Tabara, afterwards Viceroy of the Philippine Islands, and Diego Luis de Olmeyra commanded in the lines which were drawn round the town, with redoubts of earth, ditches, counterscarps, and palisades.

Justin of Nassau had dismissed his cavalry. He entrusted the defence of the Ginehen Gate to the French Colonel Hauterine and his Walloons. Colonel Morgan held the Bois-le-Duc Gate, and Loquerane, with the Scots and Dutch, were at the Antwerp Gate. The Prince of Orange advanced with an army from the Hague, and Spinola waited in battle array for two days to receive him. But this was the great warrior's last appearance in the field. Maurice was taken seriously ill, and returned to the Hague. He died on April 23, 1625, his last words being an inquiry whether Breda was succoured or lost. He had done hard and good service for his country during forty years. His patriotism and heroic fortitude may be placed in the balance against his want of magnanimity. His half-brother, Frederick Henry, whom he had adopted as his son, quietly succeeded as *stadtholder* and general of the army, as well as to the family honours as Prince of Orange.

Meanwhile, Spinola pushed forward his approaches. Having made a double line of circumvallation, with strong forts at intervals, he drowned all the lower lands by cutting the dikes at Terheyde, and he made a stockade over the drowned meadows to hinder relief by boats. The only ways to approach the siege works from outside were by the causeways of Gertruydenburg and Sevenburg. But one was palisaded and cut through; the other was also cut, and fortified with a redoubt and breastwork. Notwithstanding these obstacles, the Prince of Orange resolved to send Sir Horace Vere to make a desperate attempt to force the causeways.

The dikes were twenty or thirty feet wide. Vere had with him about 6,000 men, including 300 pikemen led on by his young kinsman the Earl of Oxford. An hour before dawn the English marched along the dikes with dauntless resolution, threw in fire-balls, and, after a sharp engagement, captured the redoubt and a half-moon. Then Spinola sent strong reinforcements, and, after a long and most gallant struggle, the English were forced to retreat, many being killed and wounded. The Earl of Oxford was wounded and received a sunstroke, dying at the Hague a few months afterwards, aged thirty-six.

******

In a letter to his countess, dated May 15, 1625, at Gertruydenburg, he wrote: "This letter is to show I am well lest reports might err. The vanguard attacked Terheyde under the Lord General Vere and myself. Our nation lost no honour, but many brave gentlemen their lives. My ensign T. Stanhope was killed upon the place. Captain J. Cromwell is dangerously hurt. We fought as long as our ammunition lasted, and I was shot in my left arm." (Letter in possession of Miss Conway Griffith, Carreglwyd, Anglesea. *Fifth Report of Comm'rs App.*)

******

The gallant young English officer who strove to plant his colours on the Spanish fort was slain by push of pike. Sir Thomas Winne, Captain Dacres, and Lieutenant Cheyney were also killed. Their generous enemy who wrote the history of the siege said:

"They ended their days with wounds as honourable and fair as their gallant behaviour could deserve, and they were worthy to have had the victory."

The brave Captain Skippon, Lieutenant Corbett, and others were wounded. Sir Horace Vere conducted the retreat in perfect order, under the eye of the Prince of Orange.

From that time all hope of raising the siege was abandoned. The capitulation, on favourable conditions, was signed on the 2nd of June, 1625. Justin of Nassau, a venerable old gentleman, with his wife and children, was received by Spinola in the space between the town and an inner ditch. The scene has been immortalised by Velasquez in his magnificent picture of *Las Lanzas* at Madrid. The siege of Breda was also fortunate in its historians. (*The Siege of Breda*: Written in Latin by R. F. Herman Hugo, of the Society of Jesus, translated into English by C. H. G., and dedicated to the soldiers of our nation in general. A. D.1627; with maps and plans), The narrative of Herman Hugo is admirably told, and he bestows praise impartially on friend and foe, although the work was intended as a eulogy on Spinola.

The story, as told by honest Henry Hexham, who began his military career as page to Sir Francis Vere at the siege of Ostend, is also clear, graphic, and impartial.

******

A true and brief relation of the famous siege of Breda: Besieged and taken by the able and victorious Prince of Orange. Composed by Henry Hexham, Quartermaster to the Regiment of Colonel Goring (Delft, 1637). Sold by Hendricus Hondius, near the Gevangen Port in the Hague. It opens with a narrative of the former siege by Spinola.

******

After the surrender of Breda, Ambrosio Spinola took his leave of the Netherlands. There was no more noble-minded and magnanimous commander engaged in the war from its commencement. Breda did not long remain in the hands of the Spaniards after his departure. It was recaptured in 1637.

******

In 1628 Spinola went to Spain, and on his way through France he visited Louis XIII. at the siege of Rochelle. He was sent by the King of Spain to conduct an attack on the Duke of Mantua, and died in the castle of Castelanovo di Scrivia, on Sept. 25, 1630, aged sixty-one. By his wife, Juana Bacciadonna, he had two sons. One was a cardinal; the other was a statesman, and president of the Council of Flanders at Madrid.

This siege, directed by Frederick Henry, Prince of Orange, lasted from July 23 to October 10, 1637. Sir Jacob Astley was sergeant-major of the English *tercio*. The Elector Palatine, Princes Rupert and Maurice, the Earls of Warwick and Northampton, Lord Grandison, Colonel Goring, Sergeant-major Skippon, and many other English officers, were at this siege.

******

Sir Horace Vere felt the death of his kinsman, the head of his house, very deeply. He and his brother Francis had taken a warm interest in the welfare of their cousin from his early youth. He had now fallen gallantly and on the field of honour, but he was childless. (His widow (Lady Diana Cecil) married secondly Thomas, Earl of Elgin. He erected a mausoleum of octagonal form, adjoining Manden Church in Bedfordshire, to her memory, in 1656). His remains were conveyed to England, and Henry, eighteenth Earl of Oxford, found his last resting-place in Westminster Abbey. The title passed to his second cousin, Robert Vere, who succeeded as nineteenth Earl of Oxford. He was a grandson of Aubrey, the uncle of Sir Francis and Sir Horace Vere. His father was Hugh Vere, who had served in the first campaign under Leicester.

A famous question arose on the accession of the nineteenth Earl. Hitherto the hereditary Lord Chamberlainship of England had gone with the title. But now Lord Willoughby claimed it by right of his mother, Lady Mary Vere, heiress of the sixteenth Earl of Oxford. It was a complicated and difficult case, and the judgment is a most learned and exhaustive discussion of the question, and contains a valuable history of the Oxford peerage. Finally, in 1627, the title of Earl of Oxford was adjudged to Robert Vere, the office of Lord Great Chamberlain to Lord Willoughby and his heirs, while the baronies of Bolebec, Sandford, Badlesmere, and Plaiz fell into abeyance.

Robert had served for some years under his kinsman Sir Horace Vere before he succeeded to the earldom, and was looked upon as a brave and efficient officer. He had married in the country to Beatrix Hemmema, of a noble Frisian family. (See note later on).

On his return from Holland, after the gallant action before Breda, Sir Horace Vere found that Charles I. had succeeded his father, and that a new reign had commenced. The great general was at the summit of his fame, and was without question the most distinguished military officer among living Englishmen. When a peerage was suggested for his brother Francis, Queen Elizabeth replied: "I consider that he is above it already." Times were changed. Sir Horace was created Baron Vere of Tilbury on the 25th of July, 1625.

******

Besides the Vere mullet, Lord Vere of Tilbury bore a mullet to indicate a third son. His arms are recorded with twenty-one quarterings (Vere, Bolebec, Sandford, Badlesmere, Fitz Barnard, St. Hilary, Lisle, Fitz Hamon, Mareschal, Clare, Delafield, Serjeaux, Archdeacon, Causton, Kilvington, Milburne, Kentbury, Trussel, etc.), and his wife bore Tracy and Baldington quarterly. The supporters granted to the peerage were dexter, a boar azure, with a shield of the arms of Holland round its neck, and sinister, a harpy with a shield of the arms of Zeeland. (Record in the Herald's College.)

******

No doubt he chose the title of Tilbury from affectionate remembrance of his brother Francis, whose estate it was, and who lived there during the last years of his life. Horace had a reversionary interest only in the Tilbury estate; for the widow of his brother John, who enjoyed it for her life, outlived him. Not only did Sir Horace's great services entitle him to a peerage, but his official position as Master General of Ordnance for life and Councillor of War made it desirable that he should receive that rank. A further reason for the creation was that Sir Horace was heir presumptive of the most ancient earldom in England,

and consequently a personage of the first distinction.

★★★★★★

Lord Vere of Tilbury was heir presumptive to the earldom of Oxford until the birth of the nineteenth Earl's son in 1627; and again from the death of the nineteenth Earl to his own death.

★★★★★★

If a consciousness of never having himself preferred a claim, and of having steadfastly and earnestly sought to perform his duty to his country without self-seeking, could give satisfaction to Lord Vere in assuming the title that had been conferred on him, then, most assuredly, that nobleman had the right to indulge in such reflections to the fullest extent. His undoubted capacity as a general was not more remarkable than his modesty and the absence of selfish motives throughout his career.

Chapter 5

The Sieges of Bois-le-Duc and Maestricht

Lord and Lady Vere removed from their lodgings in the city to a pleasant house at Clapton, near Hackney, where they lived with their five young daughters, in the intervals during which the general was able to be absent from his duties in Holland. He was, however, obliged to be with his troops for the greater part of the years 1627 and 1628.

A year after the creation of the peerage, a marriage was arranged between Elizabeth, the eldest daughter of Lord Vere, and Lord Haughton, the son and heir of the Earl of Clare. The brothers of the Holles family were cousins of the Veres, and had been companions in arms for many years.

✶✶✶✶✶✶

They were sons of Denzil Holles, by Eleanor, daughter of Edmund Lord Sheffield and of Lady Anne Vere, sister of Geoffrey and aunt of Sir Francis and Sir Horace Vere. So that the Holles brothers were first cousins once removed of Sir Francis and Sir Horace.

✶✶✶✶✶✶

John Holles, the eldest, served as a volunteer under Sir Francis Vere, and was with him in the "Island Voyage." In 1616 he purchased the barony of Haughton from James I. for ,10,000, and was created Earl of Clare in 1624. His son, born in 1595, was also a gallant soldier, and was thirty when he became engaged to Elizabeth Vere. Sir George Holles, the next brother to the Earl of Clare, was sergeant-major general at the Battle of Nieuport and siege of Ostend, and lost his left eye in action. Dying unmarried in 1626, he was buried with great military pomp in Westminster Abbey on the 23rd of May, the Earl of Clare and Lord Vere of Tilbury being the chief mourners. (The statue of Sir George Holles, attired as a Roman soldier, overlooks the tomb of Sir Francis Vere).

The youngest brother, Thomas Holles, was lieutenant-colonel of Lord Vere's regiment. The marriage of Lord Haughton with Elizabeth Vere was solemnised in Hackney church on the 24th of September, 1626.

******

Hackney Parish Register. They had six daughters and one son, Gilbert Holles, third Earl of Clare, who, dying in 1689, left by his wife, Lady Grace Pierpont, a son John, fourth Earl of Clare, created Duke of Newcastle. By his wife, Lady Margaret Cavendish, the
 had a daughter and heiress, Lady Henrietta Cavendish Holles, who married Lord Harley. Their only child, Lady Margaret Cavendish Harley, became Duchess of Portland. Through her a large number of families are directly descended from Sir Horace Vere. Elizabeth (Vere), Countess of Clare, was buried at St. Mary's, Nottingham, on January 11, 1684. Her husband, the second Earl of Clare, had died in 1665.

******

The second daughter, Mary, soon followed her sister to the altar. On May 17, 1627, she was married, at Hackney church, to Sir Roger Townshend, Baronet, of Raynham in Norfolk, who had been so created in 1617.

******

Sir Roger Townshend died on the 1st of January, 1638, aged forty-one. Their children were Roger, who died in 1640; Horace, who was created Viscount Townshend, and was the father of the second Viscount Townshend, Secretary of State; and four daughters. Mary (Vere), the widowed Lady Townshend, was married secondly to Mildmay Fane, Earl of Westmoreland, on June 21st, 1638, at Hackney, only five months after the death of her first husband. By him she had Vere Fane, fourth Earl of Westmoreland, and four daughters. Her second husband died in 1665. She herself died on October 18, 1669, and was buried at Raynham.

Through the Townshends the name of Horace passed to the Walpoles.

******

In 1628 the Dutch achieved a famous triumph at sea. Piet Heyne captured the Spanish plate fleet, and brought to Holland the vast treasure which was to have furnished the sinews of war for the Spaniards. Frederick Henry, on the strength of this great success, determined to undertake some important action. Lord Vere proceeded to the Hague to assist at the consultations which took place, and it was resolved that the next campaign should be signalized by the siege and capture of the city of Bois-le-Duc (or Hertzogenbosch). The place was usually called 's *Bosch* by the Dutch, which Englishmen turned into *Busse*. Lord Vere missed his old and tried friend Sir Dudley Carleton at the Hague. He had been superseded as British envoy by Sir Harry Vane.

★★★★★★

In December, 1625, Carleton was recalled to take part in an embassy to France, jointly with the Earl of Holland, to press Louis XIII. to return ships which had been lent to him, and which he was employing against the Rochellers, a proceeding which raised a great clamour in England. The representations of the ambassadors met with partial success, and on Carleton's return he was elected M. P. for Hastings. In 1626 he was made Vice-Chamberlain of the Household, and was created Baron Carleton of Imbercourt. He returned to the Hague from June, 1627, to April, 1628. He died in 1632, aged fifty-nine, and was buried in Westminster Abbey. The volumes of his letters are valuable depositories of information. His constant correspondent was Mr. John Chamberlain, of the Court of Wards.

★★★★★★

The Prince of Orange, having resolved to take the field, appointed the rendezvous at Schenken Schanz, on the 26th of April, 1629. On Tuesday, the 24th of April, General Lord Vere set out from the Hague, lodging that night at Utrecht, and next day he joined the Prince at Arnhem. Crowds of young gentlemen came over to serve in this campaign. With Lord Vere's own regiment were his nephew Simon Harcourt, his son-in-law Lord Haughton, his cousin the Earl of Oxford, young Thomas Fairfax,—the future general for the Parliament,—gallant Philip Skippon; and with them occur the names of Luttrell, Byron, Hotham, Cave. A second English regiment was commanded by Edward Cecil, who, by paying assiduous court to the favourite Buckingham, had obtained a peerage, and was now Viscount Wimbledon. With him were thirty-nine volunteers, including Lords Doncaster, Fielding, and Craven; Sir Thomas Glemham and Sir John Suckling.

There were twenty-six volunteers attached to General Morgan's regiment, thirty-six to that of Colonel Harwood, and eight to that of Sir Edward Vere. Sir Harry Vane, the English ambassador, and many other persons of distinction, followed the army.

The Prince of Orange and his staff, accompanied by the English forces, marched from Arnhem across the Betuwe to Nymegen, and effected the passage of the Maas by a bridge of boats about a musket-shot from Grave. There were fifty-six troops of horse and 286 companies of foot. Three brigades of the army encamped on a heath on the left bank of the Maas. All that night the men were on the alert, with the butt ends of their pikes sticking in the ground. Thence the army advanced along the line of the Maas towards Bois-le-Duc, until, on the 30th, the prince lodged in a house at the village of Vucht, with the Lord General Vere in a house next him; Count William of Nassau, the Lord of Brederode, and Count Solms being stationed in a line between Vucht and the Maas. Solms guarded the Dutch shipping at Engelen.

The city of Bois-le-Duc was one of the most important military positions in Brabant, and had for years served as a base of operations whence the Spanish armies could invade the Bommel-waart and threaten the Betuwe. It was strongly fortified, and its moat was supplied with water from the rivers Aa and Dommel, which flow from the great Peel morass to the Maas. The Sieur de Grubbendonck was governor of the town, and Count Henry de Berghe was in the field with a force of 30,000 men. But there was no longer a Spinola to direct operations.

The Prince of Orange gave orders that each company should entrench with spades and pickaxes, the line of circumvallation, thirty English miles in circuit, being strengthened with horn-works, sconces, half-moons, redoubts, and traverses, on the most improved principles of military art. This line was designed to resist any attack from the army of Count de Berghe, as well as sorties of the garrison. The count kept the besiegers awake for three weeks with constant alarms, and then marched away. In August the besiegers began to push forward the approaches, and service in the trenches was severe and dangerous. Sir Edward Vere was mortally wounded on the night of Saturday the 18th of August. His regiment was given to the Earl of Oxford. Sir Jacob Astley, Sir Simon Harcourt, and Sir Edward Harwood relieved each other in the trenches until the breach was ready for assault.

Then, on the 17th of September, Bois-le-Duc was surrendered

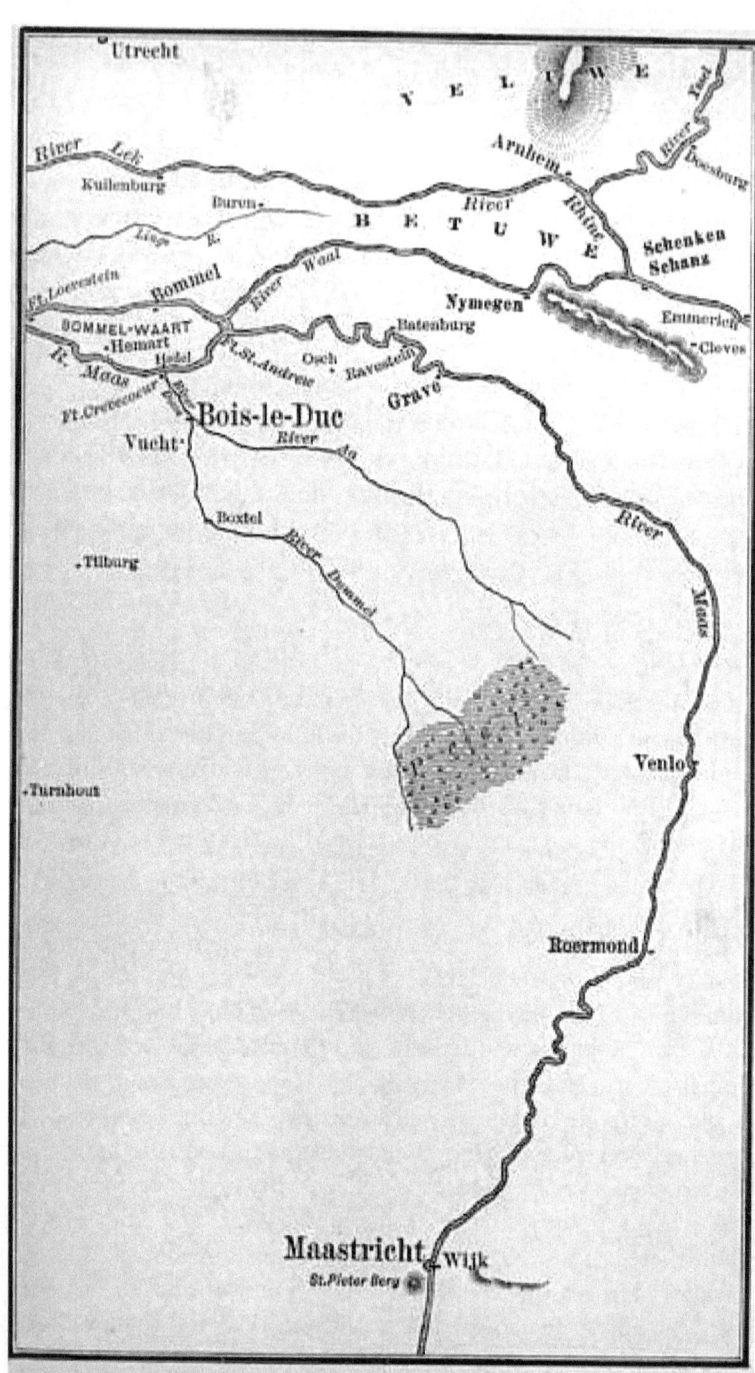

BOIS-LE-DUC AND MAASTRICHT.

to the Prince of Orange, and the garrison marched out. That day the prince dined with the King and Queen of Bohemia, who had come to see the end of the siege. Afterwards the priests and Jesuits came out of the town in wagons, and the friars on foot. Next followed Governor Grobbendonk's wife in her coach, with her daughter and child on a nurse's lap in the forepart. The prince came down to the coach and held some courteous discourse with the lady, who then went on; and in the evening came the governor, marching out with the rest of his troops.

The death of Sir Edward Vere was the most serious loss sustained by the besieged. Lord Vere and the Earl of Oxford attended his funeral at Bommel. He was a kinsman, but it is not clear to what branch of the family he belonged. Edward Vere had joined the army as a page when he was very young. It is said that Sir John Holles, afterwards Earl of Clare, was the first to put a pike into the hands of young Edward, and that Sir Francis Vere said, "You will make that scurvy boy but over-proud." He persevered in his profession, and rose to be not only a brave soldier, but an accomplished scholar. A manuscript folio is still preserved, containing Polybius translated into English by Sir Edward Vere.

******

Thick folio, 1010 pages, MS. iii., in the possession of Lord Leconfield.

In a letter from John Hampden to Sir John Eliot, this passage occurs: "Sir Edward Vere had this character:—all summer in the field, all winter in his study; in whose fall fame makes this kingdom a great loser."

******

He rose to the command of a regiment under his kinsman, and met a glorious death in the trenches before Bois-le-Duc.

This siege is remarkable for the number of officers present who were afterwards distinguished in the civil war in England. There were Thomas Fairfax and Philip Skippon, the future organizers of the new model army, on one side; Jacob Astley and Thomas Glemham, on the other. Henry Hexham, the diligent recorder of the events; n which he took an active and honourable part, is again our interesting and trustworthy guide at the siege of Bois-le-Duc.

******

A historical relation of the famous siege of Busse, together with the articles and points of composition granted by H. E. the Prince of Orange to those of the town: written by H. H., Quartermaster to my Lord General Vere his regiment. (Delft, 1630.) 12mo. Dedicated to the company of merchant adventurers residing in Delft.

******

Lord Vere returned to the Hague with the rest of the illustrious company which had surrounded Prince Frederick Henry during the enactment of this great military achievement. He continued to divide his time, as duty required his presence, between London and Holland, until, in the year 1632, he was called by the Prince of Orange to join in another victorious campaign. This time he took the field with power to confer knighthood. The point of attack was the city of Maastricht on the Maas, and a rendezvous was appointed at Nymegen for the 22nd of May, 1632.

The Maastricht campaign was a fitting close to the services of the Veres in the Netherlands. When young Francis first trailed a pike under the Earl of Leicester, nearly fifty years before, the line of the Maas was lost to the patriots. Maastricht, Venlo, Roermond, and Grave fell before the victorious arms of the Duke of Parma. The recovery of Grave was the last military service on which Sir Francis Vere was engaged. The capture of the other strong places on the Maas was destined to be the closing service of his brother.

The army of Prince Frederick Henry consisted of a Dutch, an English, and a French brigade, comprising 28 regiments of foot in 381 companies; 28 troops of horse, 83 pieces of ordnance; 12 boats for bridges, carried on wagons; and 1,500 provision wagons with 100,000 pounds of biscuit. Lord Vere's regiment was divided into 23 companies, Howard's into 12, Morgan's and Packenham's into 11 each, Count Brederode's into 12, Count Solms's into 11. On the 1st of June the army came before Venlo, the town surrendering on the 4th. Roermond followed the example next day, and on the 7th the Prince of Orange left that place for Maastricht.

The city of Maastricht, a name which means the passage of the Maas, is situated on that river just below the lofty height of Pietersburg. It is the capital of the province of Limburg. The strongly fortified city itself is on the left, its suburb of Wijk on the right bank. When the troubles began it was garrisoned by Spaniards, but in 1579 it was captured by the patriots. The Duke of Parma, after a siege of eight months, took the place by assault on the 20th of June, 1579, and there was a dreadful massacre. In 1632 it was well provided for a siege, with a strong garrison commanded by the Comte La Motterie. The enemy also had forces in the field on both banks of the river. The Marquis of Santa Cruz was advancing with an army from Brussels, and Count Pappenheim was at the head of another force on the right bank of the Maas.

The Prince of Orange sent Mr. Percival, the quartermaster-general, to reconnoitre the ground, and a quartermaster and sergeant of each company accompanied him, to have their stations in the camp allotted. A line of circumvallation, with suitable defensive works, was carefully planned, and Colonel Harwood began to break ground on the 14th of June. But the garrison was not disposed to offer a passive resistance only. Many workmen were slain by the fire of heavy guns from the town, and at midnight of the 11th a large force sallied out to interrupt the labours of the besiegers. They were encountered by Sergeant-major Skippon with eighty men in the open field, and driven back. On the 25th the Spanish Army arrived at the village of Tongeren. The troops were encamped in the villages of Neerhaeren and Lanaekar, with the wood of Petersheim on their right flank, and the Marquis of Santa Cruz took up his quarters at a monastery called the Hoogt Kloster, (the ruins of this cloister may still be seen in the garden of the *château* of Petersheim, which belongs to the Comte de Merode), only a mile or two from the works of the besiegers. But he made no serious attempt to molest them.

The Prince of Orange, with Lord Vere, fixed his headquarters near the centre of the line to the west of Maastricht, facing the Brussels Gate. On each side of him the regiments of Brederode, Henry of Nassau, and the English extended to the river. On the right bank, surrounding the suburb of Wijk, the lines were occupied by Dutch troops and by the regiment of the Duc de Bouillon. Count de Sturm was on the river bank at Borghaven, Count William of Nassau at the village of Ambrij, the Duc de Bouillon at Heer, and the Prisons on the river at Heugen. The approaches were pushed rapidly forward towards the western walls of the town in two zigzag lines, called respectively the English and French approaches.

One day, in the early part of August, the breach was so enlarged that an assault seemed likely to succeed. The Earl of Oxford, who was commanding in the trenches, gave the order, and a gallant rush was made. There was fierce resistance. Sir Simon Harcourt was shot through the cheeks and badly torn in the thigh by a grenade. Lieutenant Garth was slain. While the contest was at its height the sky had become overcast. A heavy fall of rain had the effect of slackening the fury of the combatants, and a retreat was sounded. That night the enemy sprung a mine under the English approaches, and in the following days the garrison made many desperate sorties. Every night Lord Vere himself took command of the line which protected the English advanced parties.

The most desperate fighting was on the 17th of August. On that day the enemy came out in force and attacked the English trenches. The combatants were at fierce push of pike for some minutes round the *corps du garde*. Sergeant-major Williamson, who led on the defenders, fell mortally wounded. At this critical moment the chivalrous Lord Craven and brave Philip Skippon hurried up to the rescue, giving fresh vigour to the defence. The assailants were driven back, but they still kept up a galling fire from their works. Later in the evening the Earl of Oxford was bringing up fresh troops to relieve the wearied men in the trenches, when he received a mortal wound in the head.

★★★★★★

Robert, nineteenth Earl of Oxford, married a Frisian lady of the Hemmema family. Hetto Hemmema, living in 1438, had a fortified house at Berlikum, in Friesland, between Leeuwarden and the sea. His great-grandson Hetto (Hector) Hemmema did homage to Charles V. in 1515, and was buried at Berlikum in 1572, aged eighty-two. The son of Hetto, by his wife Barbara Grietma, was Sicco Hemmema, a learned mathematician and refuter of judicial astrology. His curious work, *Astrologia refutata*, was published at Antwerp in 1583, the year of his death. It is dedicated to Bernard, Baron de Merode, then governor of Friesland.

The son of Sicco was Sjierck Hemmema, who died at Dordrecht in 1603, leaving several children. The eldest son, Doco Hemmema, was a captain in Prince Maurice's guard, and was buried at Berlikum, aged ninety-six, in 1698. His son Erasmus, a distinguished officer who was slain in a battle with the Swedes in Funen in 1659, died childless. The daughters were both married to Englishmen. Barbara was the wife of Captain John Spencer, and Banck (or Beatrice) married the nineteenth Earl of Oxford, and was mother of the twentieth and last Earl. She died at Bertelhal in 1657. The last of the Hemmemas married Du Tour of Bellinckhaven, and there is only one representative of the Du Tour family now living.

The church of Berlikum was founded in 1324, and in 1375 the towers were built. In 1432 a tiled roof replaced the old thatched one. It was the burial-place of the Hemmema family from time immemorial, and also of the Boomstras, Grietmas, Roordas, and Andringas. In 1779 the old church was pulled down and replaced by an octagonal edifice with a dome. The old "slot" of the Hemmemas was at the end of the village farthest from the church, and was surrounded by a wide moat. There are still some vestiges of it,—a great archway and two smaller arched doorways, now parts of a modern house. On the gable of the same building there is a shield of arms and a helmet carved in stone. The arms are those of Hemmema (*rubrum cum cane venatico assiliente argentcum*).

In the neighbouring church of St. Anna in Bilt there is a richly carved pulpit, and oaken pew with the arms of Van Haren impaling Hemmema. A niece of the Countess of Oxford married William van Haren, who died in 1708.

The above details were kindly obtained for me by Mr. Arnold van Tets, from two manuscript genealogical works respecting the Frisian nobility, by the Baron van Spaen, and Heemstra, and from a printed handbook of noble families of Friesland by Haan Hettema and van Halmael. I visited Berlikum and St. Anna in Bilt in 1879.

******

Hexham says:

> What a sudden impression of grief it was to my Lord General the symptoms of his face did discover. Nevertheless, his Lordship, suppressing it as well as he could, gave further instructions that the men should continue to fire on the enemy, and that the guard should be relieved.
>
> It was midnight before everything was restored to order, and the general could retire to indulge his grief.

******

Robert, nineteenth Earl of Oxford, left an only son Aubrey, by his Frisian wife Beatrice Hemmema. Aubrey was born in 1627, and was brought up in Friesland with his mother's family. In 1632 he succeeded his father as twentieth Earl of Oxford. He was, in fact, the last of the Veres. Entering the service of the States General, he served in a regiment of English foot until the Peace of Westphalia in 1648. His mother having died in 1657, he came to England after the Restoration, and was made a Knight of the Garter and Lord Lieutenant of Essex. He signed a petition to James II. to call a Parliament, and, heartily approving of the revolution, he joined the Prince of Orange, and was made a lieutenant-general in February, 1689. He carried the sword of state at the coronation of William and Mary, was colonel of the horse guards, and served at the battle of the Boyne. He died at his house in Downing Street, in his seventy-eighth year, on March 12, 1703, and with him the ancient earldom of Oxford became extinct.

He had no children by his first wife Anne, daughter of Paul Viscount Bayning. She died in 1659, and by his second wife Diana, daughter of George Kirk (groom of the bedchamber to Charles II.), he had a daughter Diana, married on April 10, 1694, to Charles Beauclerc, first Duke of St. Albans. Earl Aubrey was buried in Westminster Abbey. The Duke of St. Albans, who quarters the Vere arms, is now the representative of that ancient family. His Grace bears the title of Baron Vere of Hanworth. All his children have De Vere for their second name.

******

Another kinsman, young Lieutenant Edward Vere, also fell on that night.

The noble house of Vere had not spared its blood in the cause of freedom. Lord Vere's own brother Robert heads the list of slain; next, the eighteenth Earl of Oxford fell at Breda, Sir Edward Vere at Bois-le-Duc, the nineteenth Earl and young Edward at Maastricht, while Francis and Horace were riddled with wounds.

The siege proceeded, hitherto with little molestation from the enemy outside the lines of circumvallation. But one day, while Lord Vere and other officers were dining with Lord Craven in the trenches, they heard a sudden cannonade from the hill beyond Wijk, whence Count Pappenheim had been threatening the lines on the other side of the river. That officer was firing on the Dutch quarters, and he followed up his cannonade by making a dash with 6,000 men through trees and orchards at a point where the line was not yet completed. In the little churchyard of Ambrij an Italian regiment came to push of pike with the Dutch.

******

At Ambrij the ground begins to rise, and further back there is an amphitheatre of hills 1,600 feet surrounded high, round the suburb of Wijk. Ambrij is a pretty little village, by orchards.

★★★★★★

But the guns of the besiegers raked through and through the ranks of Pappenheim. At first he charged his own men in rear with cavalry, to force them to advance, but at length he allowed them to retreat. Santa Cruz remained inactive, and never attempted any diversion to further Pappenheim's plan of attack.

By the 20th the trenches and gallery were well advanced. The mine being ready, Colonel Holles, with Lord Vere's regiment, had command in the trenches when the order was given for the assault. Lieutenants Kettleby and Holmes led the forlorn hope, with Quartermaster Watkins as engineer. Next came the companies of Manley, Sydenham, and Stanton, followed by Colonel Sir Thomas Holles, Lord Craven, and Sergeant-major Huncks. At nine o'clock in the forenoon the mine was sprung. A huge mass of the wall fell into the moat, and the gallant Englishmen climbed to the top of the breach, a height of eighty feet. Here they met the enemy at push of pike, while at the same time a heavy flanking fire was opened upon them.

Then Captain Dudley, Lieutenant Wrangham, and young Garrett, who was Lord Vere's ensign for his Dort company, sallied along the moat, crossed the counterscarp, and carried the half-moon by the Brussels Gate. Lord Vere himself stood on the battery, where the bullets flew thick, to see the breach assaulted. Perceiving that the loss was becoming serious, he ordered a retreat into the works. Next day Maastricht was surrendered to the Prince of Orange, articles of composition having been drawn up and signed on the 21st of August. The garrison was allowed to join the army of Santa Cruz. That noble Spaniard was upbraided both by La Motterie and Pappenheim for never having lifted his little finger to help them during the whole siege. At the time of Pappenheim's assault Santa Cruz was playing at cards with some friends.

The losses were heavy. Count Ernest of Nassau, Robert Earl of Oxford, Lieutenant Edward Vere, and Sergeant-Major Williamson were slain. Sir Thomas Holles, Sir Simon Harcourt, Captains Edmund Manley, Dudley, Wentworth, Martin, and many others were wounded. The total number of slain, of all nations, was 909.

★★★★★★

Simon Harcourt was Lord Vere's nephew, son of his sister Frances, Lady Harcourt. He was slain in Ireland in 1642, and buried at Dublin. He married Anne, daughter of William Lord Paget, and had a son, Sir Philip Harcourt. His widow married Sir William Waller, of Osterly, the parliamentary general. Many of her letters, written when Lady Waller, are preserved at Nuneham, and have been privately printed. Her son Sir Philip married her stepdaughter Anne, daughter of Sir W. Waller, and was father of Simon Viscount Harcourt, the Lord Chancellor, whose great-grandson was Dr. William Vernon Harcourt, Archbishop of York. Sir William Vernon Harcourt, grandson of the archbishop, married Elizabeth, daughter of John L. Motley, the historian. (See note on Motley's criticism of Vere.)

✶✶✶✶✶✶

The historian of the siege of Maastricht was again Henry Hexham, Lord Vere's diligent quartermaster.

✶✶✶✶✶✶

A Journal of the taking of Venlo, Roermont, the memorable siege of Maastricht, the town and castle of Limburg, under the able and wise conduct of H. E. the Prince of Orange, anno 1632: with an exact card drawn by Charles Floyd (now Ensign) and since lessened cut by cut, by Henricus and Willhelminus Hondius dwelling by the Gevangen Port in the Hagh: compiled together by Henry Hexham, Quarter Master to the Regiment of the Lord General Vere. (Delft, 1633) Dedicated to his honourable kinsman Master Francis Morrice Clarke of His Majesty's Ordnance.

Hexham says he was incited to write in praise of the Prince of Orange because Herman Hugo had written so well in praise of the Marquis Spinola.

✶✶✶✶✶✶

This military author deserves more than a passing notice. He entered the army as a boy, and early obtained the appointment of page to Sir Francis Vere, serving in that capacity during the siege of Ostend. There is some reason to think that he was a relation of Sir Christopher Heyden, an officer who was a companion in arms of Sir Francis Vere during many years, and this would account for the boy having secured a post so near the great general's person.

✶✶✶✶✶✶

Master Francis Clarke, to whom Hexham dedicated his *Siege of Maastricht*, married the widow of his deceased uncle, Mr. Jerome Heydon, a merchant of London.

Sir Christopher Heyden, knighted at Cadiz, was of Baconsthorpe, in Norfolk. His daughter Frances married Dr. Philip Vincent of Firsby, who wrote a copy of verses in praise of H. Hexham.

★★★★★★

The lad's first attempt as an author was in the form of a narrative of his personal experiences during the siege of Ostend. It is by the unimpeachable and undesigned evidence of Hexham that one of Mr. Motley's most damaging attacks on the fair fame of Sir Francis Vere is entirely refuted; so that the boy was the means of doing useful service to the memory of his beloved master centuries after both had ceased to exist. Hexham continued to serve in the army with credit and diligence, and eventually attained to the responsible post of quartermaster in Lord Vere's own regiment. He appears to have made his home in Holland, and there he published his narratives of the sieges of Breda, Bois-le-Duc, and Maastricht. He also wrote a curious dialogue, in which the causes of the war are fairly argued both from a Spanish and a Dutch point of view, which was published in London in 1623, and dedicated to Sir George Holles.

★★★★★★

A tongue combat lately happening between two English souldiers in the tilt boat of Gravesend, the one going to serve the King of Spain, the other to serve the States General of the United Provinces, wherein the cause, course, and continuance of those warres is debated and declared. (London, 1623). To the Honourable Sir George Holles, Knight, Sergeant-Major to General Vere, by Henry Hexham. The interlocutors are the *Red Scarfe*, the author, and *Tawny Scarfe*, the answerer, of the tongue combat.

★★★★★★

Hexham's *Principles of the Art Military practised in the Warres of the United Netherlands* is a folio volume, with numerous plates, which was long a standard work on the subject of which it treats. It describes the duties of officers in their several grades, the pike and musket drill of that period, the evolutions of companies, and has an appendix giving the draconic articles of war ordained by the States General.

★★★★★★

The principles of the art militarie practised in the warres of the United Netherlands, represented by figure, the words of command, and demonstration: Composed by Henry Hexham, quartermaster to the regiment of the Honourable Colonel

Goring. (London, 1637, folio.) Dedication to the Earl of Holland.

******

But his writings were not entirely confined to military subjects. The great work which entitles Hexham to be remembered as a geographer as well as the recorder of the deeds of soldiers was his splendid English edition of the *Atlas of Mercator and Hondius*, in two folio volumes. This was not a mere translation. In his preface Hexham describes it as presenting:

> The laborious work of those two cosmographers, Gerard Mercator and Judocus Hondius, with lively descriptions clad in new robes, by Mr. Henry Hondius, son to Judocus.
> At the request of Henry Hondius, and according to my weak ability, I have undertaken the translation of their Atlas Major into English, and have enlarged and augmented it out of many authors of my own nation.

He sets forth the importance of geography as a science, especially to a soldier or a student of history, and he gives elaborate descriptions of the different countries to which the maps refer, their people and government. Before the preface there is a copy of verses addressed to Hexham by his friend Dr. Philip Vincent, of Firsby, a Yorkshireman.

******

> Gerardi Mercatoris et J. Hondii: Atlas or a geographick description of the regions, countries, and kingdomes of the world, through Europe, Asia, Africa, and America, represented by new and exact maps. Translated by Henry Hexham, quartermaster to the regiment of Colonel Goring, (Amsterdam, 2 vols. folio, 1636.)
> He calls himself "Philippus Vincentius Firsbaeus, Anglobritannus, Eboracensis, Theologiae et Medicinae Doctor." Addressing Hexham, he says:

> —*Ostend and many a siege beside*
> *Have been thy school. Thou art a soldier tried.*

Dr. Philip Vincent married Frances, daughter of Sir Christopher Heyden

******

Hexham's last work was a Dutch and English dictionary, the first, it seems, that ever was compiled. It was published at Rotterdam in 1648.

******

A copious English and Nether Duytch Dictionarie, composed out of our best English authours, with an appendix of the names of all kind of beasts, fowles, birds, fishes, hunting and hawking, as also a compendium for the instruction of the learner: by Henry Hexham. (Rotterdam, 1648.) He dedicated this work to his honoured friend Sir Bartholomew van Waren, counseller at law. The dedication is dated September 21, 1647, and in it he says that "never was any such dictionary extant before;" and he submits it to his friend as "a token of that love and respect an old soldier bears you."

✶✶✶✶✶✶

Many gallant soldiers, many able statesmen and earnest patriots, were reared in the school of the Veres. It was not alone the example of the generals, but the cause for which they fought, the atmosphere of freedom in which they lived, that tended to nourish noble thoughts, and to foster enlightened and liberal views. It was a nursery of good and useful men; and not the least faithful soldier, not the least accomplished scholar among them, was he who began life as page to Sir Francis, and closed it as quartermaster to Horace Lord Vere, brave old Henry Hexham.

The siege of Maastricht was the last important military operation in which Lord Vere was engaged. He still continued to give the aid of his knowledge and long experience to the States, but his active service in the field had come to an end. He was approaching the close of a long and well-spent life.

Chapter 6

Death of Lord Vere—Conclusion

The last year of Lord Vere's life was passed at home, where he was engaged in performing the duties of his command and in transacting the business of the ordnance office; while he enjoyed the society of a wife who sympathized in his pursuits and opinions, and of amiable and intelligent daughters. On the 30th of January, 1634, his third child, Katherine, was married, at Hackney church, to Oliver St. John, son and heir of Sir John St. John, Bart.

******

The famous Henry St. John, Lord Bolingbroke, was her great grandson. Katherine Vere married, secondly, John Lord Poulett of Hinton St. George. Lord Poulett was a royalist, but he obtained an easy composition from the Parliament through the intervention of his brother-in-law, Lord Fairfax. He died in 1665. By him she had John Lord Poulett, whose son was created Earl Poulett in 1706; Horace, and Vere, who died unmarried. At Hinton St. George, the seat of Earl Poulett, there were portraits of Mary, wife of Sir Horace (Lord) Vere, by Gibson; of Lord Vere himself; of their daughters, Lady Mary Townshend and Katherine Lady Poulett; of Lady Mary Vere, the wife of Lord Willoughby; and of John, sixteenth Earl of Oxford.

******

Another marriage had been proposed, previous to the death of Lord Vere, between his fourth daughter Anne and young Thomas Fairfax, who had served under him at the siege of Bois-le-Duc. The alliance had his cordial approval, although the marriage did not take place until after his death. The family of Fairfax, like that of Holles, was allied to the Veres through the Sheffields; and several of its members had been companions in arms of Sir Francis and Sir Horace Vere.

★★★★★★

Lady Anne Vere, daughter of the fifteenth Earl of Oxford, married Lord Sheffield. Her grandson, Edmund Lord Sheffield, was created Earl of Mulgrave. His daughter Frances married Sir Philip Fairfax of Steeton, and his daughter Mary was the wife of Ferdinando, second Lord Fairfax, and mother of Thomas (afterwards third Lord Fairfax), who married Anne Vere.

★★★★★★

Sir Thomas Fairfax of Denton, who was created Baron Fairfax of Cameron, the grandfather of the intended bridegroom, was an old and intimate friend of Sir Francis Vere, and served with him in several of his earlier campaigns. His brother, Sir Charles Fairfax, was at the battle of Nieuport, the siege of Ostend, and the recovery of Sluys. His two gallant sons, William and John, were slain at Frankenthal. His grandson, Thomas, the future parliamentary general, was in Lord Vere's regiment at Bois-le-Duc. Thomas Fairfax was married to Anne Vere, in Hackney church, on the 20th of June, 1637, (Hackney Parish Register). The youngest daughter, Dorothy, was the wife of John Wolstenholme, Esq., of Stanmore, in Middlesex.

★★★★★★

Her husband died childless on September 12, 1669, and was buried at Stanmore. She died on May 15, 1688. In the chancel at Stanmore there is a monument with a canopy of white marble, decorated in front with the arms of Wolstenholme of Nostell impaling Vere. Under the canopy is the figure of a lady resting on her right arm, and weeping over the remains of her husband.

★★★★★★

Lord Vere lived to see his three elder daughters happily married, and his fourth daughter Anne engaged to a kinsman of whom he heartily approved. He saw much of his old companions in arms, and had collected a series of portraits of his principal officers, which were afterwards at Raynham. His death was sudden, but, as old Fuller observed, (Worthies):

> No doubt but he was well prepared for death, seeing such was his vigilancy that never any enemy surprised him in his quarters.

On the 2nd of May, 1635, he was dining with Sir Harry Vane at Whitehall. He called for fresh salmon, and reaching out his plate to take it from one that carved, he could not draw his arm back again, but sank down in a fit of apoplexy, dying two hours afterwards. (*Strafford Letters,* i.). Lord Vere was in his seventieth year. He was buried in Westminster Abbey, by the side of his brother Francis, with much military pomp, on the 8th of May, and the same tomb serves for both. Minute-guns were fired from the tower during the funeral. His title became extinct, and by his will (proved May 6, 1635) his widow, Lady Vere, succeeded to all his personal and landed estates, and was made sole executrix. His daughters are not mentioned in the will, so that Lady Vere was left with power to bequeath portions to them according to her discretion. There appears to have been perfect trust and confidence between Lord and Lady Vere, who had lived happily together for more than a quarter of a century.

There is a portrait of Lord Vere, half length, painted by Cornelius Jansen when the great general was advanced in years. It is now the property of the Marquis Townshend. It was engraved by Vertue, and is given in Collins's "House of Vere." There is a copy of this picture at Wentworth. Another portrait, full length, attributed to Jansen, is the property of Sir H. St. John Mildmay.

Lady Vere continued to live at Clapton until the death of the widow of her brother-in-law, John Vere, in 1639, when she succeeded to Kirby, Tilbury, and other estates in Essex.

******

The will of Thomasine, widow of John Vere of Kirby Hall, was dated April 1, 1639, and proved on November 14th following. The record of her burial is in the Castle Hedingham parish register, May 6, 1639.

After the death of Lady Vere, Kirby Hall was sold, in 1675, to Richard Sheffield, who again sold it in 1702 to Richard Springer. In 1762 it became the property of Mr. Peter Muilman, an antiquary and collector of materials for county history. On Lady Vere's death Tilbury went to her grandson, Sir Roger Townshend. Horace, Lord Townshend, sold it to Andrew Hackett, a son of the bishop.

******

From that time she resided chiefly at Kirby Hall, where she was often visited by her daughters and their young families. Her noble husband and his brother had devoted their lives to the defence of those rights and liberties which all free people hold dear. She was not likely to fall away from the principles of the Veres in her long widowhood. She was a firm friend of the Parliament, and was so trusted by the leading statesmen of the popular side that the king's children were entrusted to her care for some time.

******

Clarendon says of Lady Vere: An old lady much in their (the Parliament's) favour, but not at all ambitious of that charge, though there was a competent allowance assigned for their support. She received the children on the death of the Countess of Dorset, and shortly afterwards gave up the charge to the Earl of Northumberland.

******

Her correspondence was extensive, and she was a clear-headed and judicious adviser. She was strongly opposed to the trial and execution of the King; and her courageous daughter, Lady Fairfax, not only shared her views, but went so far as publicly to interrupt the trial. "A Vere of the fighting Veres," Carlyle called her.

******

Letters and Speeches of Cromwell, ii.
Having been bred in Holland, she had not that reverence for the Town Church of England as she ought to have had. (Clarendon.)

******

Lady Vere lived to extreme old age. She died at Kirby Hall, on Christmas Eve of 1670, aged ninety years. Her funeral sermon was preached in Castle Hedingham Church, on February 10, 1671, by Mr. Gurnall, the Vicar of Lavenham.

The history of the lives of the two Vere warriors is the military history of England during half a century. It extends from the time when Queen Elizabeth undertook the defence of the rights of her neighbours, to within a few years of the time when the Parliament of England entered upon armed resistance to the unconstitutional tyranny of Charles I. It connects these two momentous events, and thus makes their history continuous. From a purely military point of view the period was one of great importance. When the war began Spain was in the height of her power. The Spanish infantry had no equal. The soldiers of Holland and England were unable to face their enemies in the open field.

They had, by slow and painful experience, to learn from those enemies. The Veres were at first diligent pupils. But in the course of time they became great masters in the art of war, and did for Englishmen what the Princes of Orange did for their Dutch compatriots. They created a school, and at last they habitually led their troops to assured victory. They and their companions in arms attended closely to drill and to constant practice in manoeuvring, their men were trained in all the work of entrenching and in siege operations, and their discipline was strictly maintained.

The Veres were alive to every new improvement, and studied the progress of invention and adaptation in every branch of their profession. They watched over and defended the rights and interests of all who served under them, whether officers or men, and thus created a feeling of loyalty and of *esprit de corps*, which can be traced through the whole history of the English troops in the Low Countries. It did not signify whether they were volunteers, or soldiers of Queen Elizabeth, or companies in the pay of the States. They maintained the feeling and tradition of one corps throughout; they were soldiers of a free country, serving in the cause of freedom,—soldiers of the school of the fighting Veres.

It was from the school of the Veres that the best commanders came, who were afterwards distinguished in the civil war, whether on the side of the King or of the Parliament. Among the royalists was Sir Jacob Astley, the best officer on that side; and Sir Thomas Glemham, who defended York, Carlisle, and Oxford. Lord Grandison, Sir Richard Grenville, Lord Byron, Sir Ralph Hopton, and Lord Goring, also served under Lord Vere.

But by far the greatest amount of military talent which had been brought out and fostered by the Veres was enlisted on the side of the Parliament. The Earls of Warwick and Peterborough, of Bedford and Essex, had served campaigns in the Low Countries. The Earl of Essex, who was one of Sir Horace Vere's diligent lieutenants in the expedition to the Palatinate, and had also served in the attempt on Cadiz, accepted the appointment of general of the troops raised by the Parliament. Sir Thomas Fairfax, Lord Vere's son-in-law, who received his first lesson in war at the siege of Bois-le-Duc, did still greater credit to the teachings of their master.

After his skilful work in Yorkshire, Fairfax was selected as commander-in-chief of the new model army, by the unanimous vote of Parliament. By general consent this pupil of Lord Vere was judged to be the ablest officer in England; and he soon ended the war, and restored the blessings of peace to his country. As a regimental and staff officer, Sergeant-major Skippon was the best and most experienced organiser who had been brought up in the school of the Veres, and had survived the risks of war. His merits were so well known that great efforts were made by the royalists to secure his services. But honest Philip Skippon had fought too long in the good old cause to become a partisan of the feeble Stuart tyranny in his mature years. He was a stanch Parliament man. To him is due, under the general superintendence of Sir Thomas Fairfax, the credit of the organization of the new model army. He was the chief of the staff under Fairfax, and arranged every detail with careful exactness.

******

Popular histories of England will probably continue to make the erroneous statement that Oliver Cromwell created and organised the "new model" army. The facts remain that he had nothing whatever to do with its military organisation, that he was not even present during the process, and that he did not succeed in evading the self-denying ordinance until after it had taken the field under Fairfax and Skippon.

******

One more pupil of Lord Vere, who rose to distinction in the civil war, must be mentioned. George Monk gained his first knowledge and grounding in the military art in Lord Vere's regiment. (Clarendon, xvi.). In later times he was Cromwell's ablest general. Fairfax and Monk restored the monarchy.

The captains who gave their help in founding the American colonies were not less indebted to the training supplied by campaigns in the Low Countries. Miles Standish had served under the Veres. Lion Gardner was another disciple of those great generals. Edward Winslow, though too young to have actually taken part in the war, came over to the Low Countries, where Sir Horace Vere was commanding, as soon as he was old enough to travel. Sir Ferdinando Gorges, whose name is so well known in connection with American colonization, fought side by side with Sir Francis Vere at the siege of Sluys. Edward Maria Wingfield, of Virginian fame, was a companion in arms of the Veres. In the opening page of American history the name of Vere should have an honourable place.

The indirect influence which the Veres had on the opinions of three generations of their countrymen was probably more important than the direct teaching of those masters in the art of war. As the ablest English military commanders of their day, they trained the men who settled the question between King and Parliament, and the men who founded the colonies of New England. But as the upholders of a great cause, their examples made a far deeper and more enduring impression on their contemporaries. When Queen Elizabeth's noble declaration sent crowds of enthusiastic volunteers into Holland, it was felt that a great principle was at stake. The queen announced that oppressed people had a right to defend their institutions and ancient privileges against the illegal encroachments of their rulers. It was to uphold this principle that Englishmen entered upon the war. Their feelings are expressed in the letters of Lord North and many others.

It was seen that those constitutional rights, those parliamentary privileges, which Englishmen held so dear, would be endangered by the destruction of liberty in a neighbouring country. In fact, the parliamentary cause which was fought out in England, until it triumphed, by Essex and Fairfax, had been contended for in the Low Countries by the previous generation under Francis and Horace Vere. This was the justification for calling it "the good old cause." The Veres had fought for it during nearly half a century in the Netherlands, until the triumph of their arms was complete. Their pupils fought for it in England, until the system of Charles and Laud was destroyed for ever on the battlefield of Naseby.

Sir Francis Vere was sincerely attached to the cause of civil and religious liberty for which it was his duty to fight. His opinions were so well known, that, on more than one occasion, he was officially censured. It was suspected that he might be more anxious to further that cause than to obey orders which seemed to endanger it. As a diplomatist, as well as in his capacity as general of the English forces, Sir Francis was first and before all things the faithful and loyal servant of England and of the great queen, but he was almost equally the champion of freedom. His brother fully shared his feelings in all respects, and Lady Vere, in her loyal adherence to the Parliament, indicated the form that those feelings would have taken, in the great constitutional question which arose after the Veres had passed away.

It was the fashion for young Englishmen to serve a campaign under the Veres, even if they had no intention of embracing the military career. It was natural that a great number of them should catch some of the enthusiastic feeling which animated their chiefs and the veterans with whom they came in contact. There can be no doubt that in this way the upper and middle classes of Englishmen were leavened with a more jealous attachment to the constitutional liberties inherited from their ancestors than would have been the case if they had merely lived at home at ease.

The lives of Sir Francis and Sir Horace Vere thus had an important indirect influence on the generation which succeeded them. For that reason their careers are worthy of attentive study. They displayed no extraordinary genius. They were simply officers of talent, energy, and perseverance, who with single-minded zeal devoted their lives to the duty they had undertaken, never turning aside until the work was done. They lived to see the triumph of the cause to which their whole lives had been devoted. This gives a completeness and a finish to their career, which increases the interest attaching to it as a prominent episode in the history of the English-speaking race. The cause for which they fought in the Netherlands had soon afterwards to be maintained nearer home. The Veres were the military godfathers of the great Lord Fairfax.

Appendix

NOTE RESPECTING THE STORY TOLD TO THE DISPARAGEMENT OF AN EARL OF OXFORD, IN FROISSART.

Some traditions and tales met with in history are based on facts, though incorrectly told. Others are baseless and without foundation in fact. It can be shown that the following story, reflecting upon a Vere, Earl of Oxford, which occurs in Froissart, belongs to the latter class.

When the Dukes of York and Gloucester and other discontented nobles confederated against Richard II. and his favourite Robert de Vere, ninth Earl of Oxford and Duke of Ireland, Froissart, (II vol. 4), tells us that they disparaged the favourite, among other ways, by abusing his father. They said:

> We are not ignorant who the Earl of Oxford was, and that in this country he had not one good quality, either of sense, honour, or gentility, allowed him. Sir John Chandos, added a knight, made him feel this very sharply once, at the palace of the Prince of Wales at St. Andrews, in Bordeaux. 'How so?' demanded another, who wished to know the particulars. 'I will tell you,' replied the knight, 'for I was present. Wine was serving round to the Prince of Wales and a large party of English lords, in an apartment of his palace; and when the Prince had drunk, the cup was carried to Sir John Chandos, as Constable of Aquitaine, who took it and drank, without paying any attention to the Earl of Oxford, father of this Duke of Ireland, or desiring him to drink first. After Sir John Chandos had drunk, one of the squires presented the wine to the Earl of Oxford; but, indignant that Chandos had drunk before him, he refused it, and said, by way of mockery, to the squire who was holding the cup, "Go, carry it to thy master Chandos; let him drink."

"Why should I go to him? for he has drunk. Drink yourself, since it is offered you; for, by St. George, if you do not, I will throw it in your face."

'The earl, afraid lest the squire should execute what he had said, for he was bold enough to do so, took the cup, and put it to his mouth and drank, or at least pretended to drink. Sir John Chandos was not far off, and heard and saw the whole; and the squire, while the prince was in conversation with others, came and told him what had passed. Sir John Chandos took no notice of it until the prince had retired, when, stepping up to the Earl of Oxford, he said, "What, Sir Aubrey, are you displeased that I drink first, who am the Constable of this country? I may well drink and take precedence before you, since my most renowned sovereign the King of England and my lords the princes assent to it. True it is that you were at the Battle of Poitiers, but all now present do not know the cause of it as well as I do. I will declare it, that they may remember it. When my lord the prince had finished his journey to Languedoc, Carcassonne, and Narbonne, and was returned to this city of Bordeaux, you took it in your head that you would return to England. But what did the King say to you? I know it well, though I was not present. He asked if you had accomplished your service; and afterward, what you had done with his son. You replied, 'Sir, I left him in good health at Bordeaux.'

'What!' said the king, 'and have you been bold enough to return hither without him? Did I not strictly enjoin you, and the others who accompanied you, never to return without him, under the forfeiture of your lands? And yet you have dared to disobey my commands. I now positively order you to quit my kingdom within four days, and return to the prince; for, if you be found on the fifth day, you shall lose your life and estates.' You were afraid to hazard disobedience, as was natural, and left England. You were so fortunate that you joined the prince four days before the Battle of Poitiers, and had, that day, the command of forty lances, while I had sixty. Now, consider if I, who am Constable of Aquitaine, have not the right to take precedence and drink before you do." The Earl of Oxford was much ashamed, and would willingly have been anywhere but there. He was forced, however, to bear with what Sir John Chandos said, who spoke aloud, that all might hear him.'

Assuredly this story is circumstantial enough. It is told of Sir Aubrey Vere, Earl of Oxford, who is alleged to have been father of the Duke of Ireland. But the name of the father of the Duke of Ireland was Thomas, not Aubrey.

There were four Veres who were, or became, Earls of Oxford, contemporaries of Sir John Chandos, namely: John, the seventh earl, grandfather of the Duke of Ireland; Thomas, the eighth earl, his father; and Aubrey, the tenth earl, his uncle. Robert, the ninth earl, afterwards Duke of Ireland, was a child of seven when Sir John Chandos died, in 1370.

The points of the story require that the earl to whom it applies should have been Earl of Oxford at the same time that Sir John Chandos was Constable of Aquitaine; that he should have gone to Bordeaux with the Prince of Wales in August, 1355; and that he should have been at the Battle of Poitiers on September 1, 1357. This is not true of any Earl of Oxford.

As regards John, the seventh Earl of Oxford, he was certainly at the battle of Poitiers. But he died in 1359, and Sir John Chandos was not made Constable of Aquitaine until 1363. The story, therefore, cannot be true as regards him.

Thomas, eighth Earl of Oxford, father of the Duke of Ireland, and of whom the story is actually told, was not at the battle of Poitiers. He first bore arms with his father, at the early age of 18, in 1359, three years afterwards; when three sons of Edward III.—Lionel, aged 21; John, aged 19; and Edmund, aged 18—also first bore arms. He was only 15 at the time of the Battle of Poitiers, and 13 when the Prince of Wales went to Bordeaux, in 1355. The prince was 25, and it is too much to believe that Edward III. ordered a boy of 13 to go out in charge of his grownup son and not to come home without him. The eighth earl died in 1370, aged 28. So that the story cannot be true as regards the Duke of Ireland's father.

Aubrey, tenth Earl of Oxford, did not succeed to the earldom until 1393, and Sir John Chandos was killed in 1370. Aubrey was 10 when the Prince of Wales went to Bordeaux, in 1355, and he certainly was not at Poitiers. He was then a lad of 12. The story is not true as regards him.

The above facts prove that the story in Froissart, told to the disparagement of an Earl of Oxford, is without any foundation in fact, that Sir John Chandos never made the speech attributed to him, and that the statements it contains are false.

ALSO FROM LEONAUR
AVAILABLE IN SOFTCOVER OR HARDCOVER WITH DUST JACKET

THE FALL OF THE MOGHUL EMPIRE OF HINDUSTAN by H. G. Keene—By the beginning of the nineteenth century, as British and Indian armies under Lake and Wellesley dominated the scene, a little over half a century of conflict brought the Moghul Empire to its knees.

LADY SALE'S AFGHANISTAN by Florentia Sale—An Indomitable Victorian Lady's Account of the Retreat from Kabul During the First Afghan War.

THE CAMPAIGN OF MAGENTA AND SOLFERINO 1859 by Harold Carmichael Wylly—The Decisive Conflict for the Unification of Italy.

FRENCH'S CAVALRY CAMPAIGN by J. G. Maydon—A Special Correspondent's View of British Army Mounted Troops During the Boer War.

CAVALRY AT WATERLOO by Sir Evelyn Wood—British Mounted Troops During the Campaign of 1815.

THE SUBALTERN by George Robert Gleig—The Experiences of an Officer of the 85th Light Infantry During the Peninsular War.

NAPOLEON AT BAY, 1814 by F. Loraine Petre—The Campaigns to the Fall of the First Empire.

NAPOLEON AND THE CAMPAIGN OF 1806 by Colonel Vachée—The Napoleonic Method of Organisation and Command to the Battles of Jena & Auerstädt.

THE COMPLETE ADVENTURES IN THE CONNAUGHT RANGERS by William Grattan—The 88th Regiment during the Napoleonic Wars by a Serving Officer.

BUGLER AND OFFICER OF THE RIFLES by William Green & Harry Smith—With the 95th (Rifles) during the Peninsular & Waterloo Campaigns of the Napoleonic Wars.

NAPOLEONIC WAR STORIES by Sir Arthur Quiller-Couch—Tales of soldiers, spies, battles & sieges from the Peninsular & Waterloo campaigns.

CAPTAIN OF THE 95TH (RIFLES) by Jonathan Leach—An officer of Wellington's sharpshooters during the Peninsular, South of France and Waterloo campaigns of the Napoleonic wars.

RIFLEMAN COSTELLO by Edward Costello—The adventures of a soldier of the 95th (Rifles) in the Peninsular & Waterloo Campaigns of the Napoleonic wars.

AVAILABLE ONLINE AT **www.leonaur.com**
AND FROM ALL GOOD BOOK STORES

ALSO FROM LEONAUR
AVAILABLE IN SOFTCOVER OR HARDCOVER WITH DUST JACKET

OFFICERS & GENTLEMEN *by Peter Hawker & William Graham*—Two Accounts of British Officers During the Peninsula War: Officer of Light Dragoons by Peter Hawker & Campaign in Portugal and Spain by William Graham.

THE WALCHEREN EXPEDITION *by Anonymous*—The Experiences of a British Officer of the 81st Regt. During the Campaign in the Low Countries of 1809.

LADIES OF WATERLOO *by Charlotte A. Eaton, Magdalene de Lancey & Juana Smith*—The Experiences of Three Women During the Campaign of 1815: Waterloo Days by Charlotte A. Eaton, A Week at Waterloo by Magdalene de Lancey & Juana's Story by Juana Smith.

JOURNAL OF AN OFFICER IN THE KING'S GERMAN LEGION *by John Frederick Hering*—Recollections of Campaigning During the Napoleonic Wars.

JOURNAL OF AN ARMY SURGEON IN THE PENINSULAR WAR *by Charles Boutflower*—The Recollections of a British Army Medical Man on Campaign During the Napoleonic Wars.

ON CAMPAIGN WITH MOORE AND WELLINGTON *by Anthony Hamilton*—The Experiences of a Soldier of the 43rd Regiment During the Peninsular War.

THE ROAD TO AUSTERLITZ *by R. G. Burton*—Napoleon's Campaign of 1805.

SOLDIERS OF NAPOLEON *by A. J. Doisy De Villargennes & Arthur Chuquet*—The Experiences of the Men of the French First Empire: Under the Eagles by A. J. Doisy De Villargennes & Voices of 1812 by Arthur Chuquet.

INVASION OF FRANCE, 1814 *by F. W. O. Maycock*—The Final Battles of the Napoleonic First Empire.

LEIPZIG—A CONFLICT OF TITANS *by Frederic Shoberl*—A Personal Experience of the 'Battle of the Nations' During the Napoleonic Wars, October 14th-19th, 1813.

SLASHERS *by Charles Cadell*—The Campaigns of the 28th Regiment of Foot During the Napoleonic Wars by a Serving Officer.

BATTLE IMPERIAL *by Charles William Vane*—The Campaigns in Germany & France for the Defeat of Napoleon 1813-1814.

SWIFT & BOLD *by Gibbes Rigaud*—The 60th Rifles During the Peninsula War.

AVAILABLE ONLINE AT **www.leonaur.com**
AND FROM ALL GOOD BOOK STORES

www.ingramcontent.com/pod-product-compliance
Lightning Source LLC
Chambersburg PA
CBHW030218170426
43201CB00006B/122